THE ĀGAMAŚĀSTRA OF GAUḌAPĀDA

THE ĀGAMAŚĀSTRA OF GAUḌAPĀDA

EDITED, TRANSLATED AND ANNOTATED
BY

Vidhushekhara Bhattacharya
Asutosh Professor of Sanskrit,
University of Calcutta

FOREWORD BY :

Christian Lindtner

MOTILAL BANARSIDASS PUBLISHERS
PRIVATE LIMITED
DELHI

First Edition.: 1943
Reprinted: Delhi, 1989

Also available at :
MOTILAL BANARSIDASS
Bungalow Road, Jawahar Nagar, Delhi 110 007
Chowk, Varanasi 221 001
Ashok Rajpath, Patna 800 004
24 Race Course Road, Bangalore 560 001
120 Royapettah High Road, Mylapore, Madras 600 004

ISBN: 81-208-0652-2

PRINTED IN INDIA
BY JAINENDRA PRAKASH JAIN AT SHRI JAINENDRA PRESS, A-45 NARAINA INDUSTRIAL AREA, PHASE I, NEW DELHI 110028 AND PUBLISHED BY NARENDRA PRAKASH JAIN FOR MOTILAL BANARSIDASS PUBLISHERS PVT. LTD., BUNGALOW ROAD, JAWAHAR NAGAR, DELHI 110007.

TO

THE REVERED MEMORY

OF

GURUDEVA

RABINDRANATH TAGORE

bhedo yasya na vastuto'sti bhuvane prācī pratīcīti vā
mitratvaṃ prakaṭīkṛtaṃ ca satataṃ yenātmanaḥ karmaṇā |
viśvaṃ yasya padaṃ prasiddham aniśaṃ satye ca yasya sthitir
bhūyāt tasya jayo raver anudinaṃ tenāstu tṛptaṃ jagat ||

CONTENTS

FOREWORD

About the general position of the *Āgamaśāstra* (also known as *Gauḍapādīya-Kārikā(s)* or *Māṇḍūkya-Kārikā(s)*) within the history of Indian philosophy, there can be little doubt. It is the earliest extant fairly systematic exposition of Vedāntavāda that shows a deep, decisive and palpable influence of Buddhism in its Mahāyāna form. Traces of Mahāyāna influence can also be detected in earlier Vedānta texts such as Bhartṛhari's *Vākyapadīya* and the *Brahmasūtra*—not to speak of later texts such as *Paramārthasāra, Yogavāsiṣṭha* and many others—but by no means to the same extent. The author of the GK, to be sure, does not want to be considered a *bauddha* himself, but the numerous echoes of, or even quotations from Mahāyāna *sūtras* and *śāstras* (some of the works of Nāgārjuna, Maitreya, Asaṅga and Vasubandhu above all) render this part of his background very clear. In the GK we find a *māyāvāda*, an *ajātisamatāvāda*, an *advaitavāda* which is as Buddhist as can be. On of the key-terms, *ajātisamatā*, can, just as the celebrated *ghaṭākāśadṛṣṭānta*, be traced back to the *Āryasatyadvayāvatārasūtra* (see O.Quarnström, *Hindu Philosophy in Buddhist Perspective*, Lund 1989, p. 109). When, nevertheless, the author himself, as well as his ancient and modern followers staunchly deny such influence the reason for this untenable position has a sociological rather than a doctrinal basis. There is a good deal of *odium theologicum*, perhaps more than we can easily imagine, to be found in the ancient texts influenced by Buddhism.

Bhaṭṭācārya Vidhuśekhara's edition of the *Āgamaśāstra* deserves to be reprinted not just because it is the work that has done most to further the understanding of the GK in a historical and philological fashion, but also because it is still the only edition that comes close to what by modern standards can be considered a critical one. It cannot be said to have been superseded by Raghunath Damodar Karmakar's *Gauḍapāda-Kārikā*, Poona 1953 (reprinted 1973) which was published, as the editor says, because "Prof. Bhattacharya had allowed himself to be carried a little too far by his leanings towards Buddhism, and hence some of his interpretations appeared clearly to be biased and forced". Karmakar collated a few additional manuscripts, but none of them, he reported, "show any marked variations of reading".

Nevertheless, there are still many obscure points connected with the study of the GK. Is it the work of one author, or is it rather the work of a group of authors, a "school-work" of the Gauḍas and the Drāviḍas as Max Walleser suggested in 1910? And what about the text as we have it transmitted in 215 verses comprising four chapters? Are these chapters, as some Indian scholars contend, to be regarded as a unit? Or should we look upon them as four more or less independent essays, but by the same author, as Bhaṭṭācārya Vidhuśekhara opined? Or should we rather follow Vetter who, in a very important paper published 1978 in *Wiener Zeitschrift für die Kunde Südasiens*, raises the question of the original order of the chapters, and concludes, accepting one author, that for a proper understanding of the GK we must read the four chapters in the reverse order, i.e. IV, III, II, I? But who, then, changed the original order, and why? It goes without saying, that an opinion about these matters is essential for understanding the philosophy of our text as we have it today.

The question of the *date* of the GK is intimately related to the question of the relationship to Buddhism. The GK must, of course, have been composed later than Nāgārjuna, Asaṅga and Vasubandhu to some of whose works it explicitly refers. Here, then, we have the *terminus post quem*. The *terminus ante quem* is provided by the quotations, or so it seems, in Bhavya's *Vadānta-tattvaviniścaya* (edited by Quarnström, ref. to above), and in Śāntarakṣita's *Madhyamakālaṃkāra*. This would give us the date ca. 500 A.D. for GK. And yet the relationship between GK and Bhavya may be rather more complex than we would at first assume. Can we exclude the possibility of interpolations and revisions?

Related to these problems is also the question about the authenticity of the *Āgamaśāstravivaraṇa*, traditionally ascribed to the famous Śaṅkara. This attribution was accepted and supported by various arguments by scholars such as Vetter and Hacker. But, on the other hand, as I have pointed out (in *Indo-Iranian Journal* 1985), Śaṅkara more than once displays gross misunderstanding of GK. This fact may not affect the validity of the traditional attribution, but how is it compatible with the traditional account that Gauḍapāda was the *paramaguru*, or preceptor's preceptor, of Śaṅkara? In other words, Śaṅkara may well be separated from Gauḍapāda by more than one generation. That, again, has some bearing not only on the date of the GK but also on that of Śaṅkara. In any case, Śaṅkara's *floruit* must be later than Dharmakīrti (ca. 530-600, see *Acta Orientalia* 1980), who is quoted in the *Upadeśasāhasrī*, but also earlier than Maṇḍana-miśra (*floruit* ca. 700) who, in his *Brahmasiddhi*, almost certainly refers to Śaṅkara.

With regard to the date of the GK a good deal of confusion has been created by some curious pieces of information found in the *Jagadgururatnamālāstava* of Sadāśivabrahmendra. It claims (verse 10) that some foreign philosophers, viz. Apalūnya, Dāmīśa and others, were among the students of Gauḍapāda. No doubt this is intended to refer to Apollonius of Tyana, the Neopythagorean sage, born about the beginning of the Christian era, and

Damis of Nineveh, both figures so well known from Philostratus' *Life of Apollonius*. But of the Sanskrit text of the *Jagadguru-ratnamālāstava* there is only a printed edition (no date, no place), no manuscripts, and, as my esteemed friend Dr. Kunjunni K. Raja informs me, not even the most credulous modern adherents of Śaṅkarācārya regard it as anything else than a modern forgery. So we can safely say that this tradition, which, if true, would upset our chronology totally, is simply apocryphal and without any value as a piece of historical evidence.

It is to be hoped that this reprint of a classical text on Indian philosophy will inspire scholars to take up further work in this most interesting and important field of human research. Once again the firm of Motilal Banarsidass deserves our credit for making a rare out-of-print work readily available to a wider audience.

CHRISTIAN LINDTNER

PREFACE

Introductory

It was in July, 1919, that, in order to prepare some lectures for my pupils in the Visvabharati, Santiniketan, I had to read the Upaniṣads anew; and in doing so when I, now with a little acquaintance with Buddhism, began to study the *Āgamaśāstra* of Gauḍapāda, popularly known as the *Gauḍapādakārikā* on the *Māṇḍūkya Upaniṣad*, I was struck with its contents which were known to me before this quite in a different light. I found there something new. In 1922, in the Second All-India Oriental Conference held in this University, which was presided over by my esteemed friend, Prof. Sylvain Lévi, then the first Visiting Professor of the Visvabharati, I read a paper on the subject, in which I said that a book under the title of *The Āgamaśāstra of Gauḍapāda*, embodying the result of my studies in it, would shortly be ready for the press. But, unfortunately, it could not be done earlier than now. However, I wrote some stray articles in English and Bengali on the subject. While they arrested the attention of certain scholars trained on modern lines, they gave rise to adverse criticism mainly from the orthodox section of my friends strictly following the indigenous interpretation of the Upaniṣad, given by Śaṅkara, the commentator of the present work.

Not being satisfied with the interpretation offered by Śaṅkara and his followers, or some other teachers I have attempted in the following pages to present to the readers my own interpretation of the work as I have understood. But in no way do I claim that my interpretation is *the* interpretation, *i.e.*, the interpretation intended by Gauḍapāda himself. Gauḍapāda has not appeared to me and said that mine is the true interpretation, nor has God told me anything to the effect, nor am I an omniscient being. It is quite natural and well-known to all that the same thing sometimes appears differently to different persons owing to a variety of circumstances. It would be sheer foolishness on my part, I am perfectly conscious, if I pretend to claim by writing the following pages any superiority to the commentator, whether he is or is not identical with the great author of the commentary on the *Brahmasūtras*, who is known by the same name, Śaṅkara. I have simply put down my views here and I request my readers only to see if the text can be explained also in the way I have followed here.

I may say here in the following words of Yaśomitra (AKV[1], p. 2):

yuktā ced grāhyeyaṃ na ced ato 'nyathā vidhātavyā |
na hi viṣame'rthe skhalituṃ na sambhaven mādṛśāṃ buddhiḥ ||

On points related to Buddhism, which are frequently raised in the course of my explanation, I have in many cases quoted in support of my views more passages than one, though a single passage could serve the purpose, having meant them specially for those of my readers who are not adequately acquainted with Buddhist thoughts or have no easy access to Buddhist works.

In the present volume I have given a new edition of the text of the *Āgamaśāstra* based on a number of MSS and different editions as described below, followed by an English translation. After this comes my annotation.

At the end there are Appendixes including the text and English translation of the *Māṇḍūkya Upaniṣad*, Variants of the MSS used for the edition of the text of the *Āgamaśāstra*, and different Indexes as the Contents will show.

Manuscripts

Let us give here a description of the MSS. referred to above :

1. A[1]. Adyar Library. No. IX. G. 52. It is in folios 20-28 of the codex. Written in Devanāgarī on paper in black ink, punctuated with red marks, and bounded on either side by double lines. Size 12.3″×4.8″. Eleven lines on each page. No date, nor the name of the scribe. In this MS we have the MāU and the GK.

2. A[2]. Adyar Library. No. IX. F. 99. Fols. 30-39 of this codex contain the MāU and GK. Size 10″×6″. Number of lines on each page 12 or 13. Written neatly in Devanāgarī on paper, punctuated and bounded on each side by a double line. No date, nor the name of the scribe.

3. A[3]. Adyar Library. No. IX. F. 130. Fols. 38-53 of this codex, too, contain MāU together with the GK. Written in modern Devanāgarī on paper, bounded on each side by a triple line. Size 10.1″ × 5″. There are 8 or 9 lines on each page. No date, nor the name of the scribe.

4. A[4]. Adyar Library. No. IX. B. 181. It is written on hand-made paper in Śāradā script. There are 30 folios. Size 9″ × 6″. Each page has 18-25 lines. The borders of the MS are completely worn out, and last 12 folios are torn and destroyed in the middle. It is written in black ink, but the numbers of the folios are given in English figures in red one. No date is to be found, but from the worn out condition of the codex it seems to be not less than two hundred years old. The name of the scribe is also not given.

This codex contains different Upaniṣads, 19 in all, the *Vedāntasāra* (*Śaivadarśana*), and the *Taittirīya Brāhmaṇa*, III. 10. 9-11. Here we have also the MāU and only the first *prakaraṇa* of GK.

5. B[1]. Bhandarkar Oriental Research Institute, Poona. No. 272 of 1879-80. It is written on paper in Devanāgarī. Size 10.5″×4.7″. Originally it had 67 fols., but the first 15 fols. are missing, and so we have now only 52 fols. Each page contains 10 to 14 lines. It is dated as 1765 (*bāṇa-aṅga-aśva-avanī*), but it is not known whether it is Saṃvat or Śaka era.

This MS contains only the last three Books of the GK beginning with the first kārikā of Book II.

6. B². Bhandarkar Oriental Research Institute, Poona. No. 778 of 1891-96. It is written on paper in Devanāgarī. Fols. 45. Size 9″ × 5″. Like the preceding one it, too, has only the last three Books of GK together with Śaṅkara's commentary.

The kārikās, specially those in the last Book are numbered very carelessly; thus the last kārikā of the last Book is numbered as 93 instead of 100. No date, nor the name of the scribe.

7. D¹. Dayananda Anglo-Vedic College, Lahore. No. nil. Written neatly in Devanāgarī on paper. Size 11.4″ × 6″. There is no date, nor the name of the scribe. It contains MāU and the GK together with the commentary of Śaṅkara on both of them. Originally there were 42 fols., but fols. 18, 19, 30-35 containing kārikās 10-53 of the fourth *prakaraṇa* are missing. In three or four cases some letters are lost, the paper being torn or damaged. In this MS *b* is written for both *b* and *v*.

8. D². Dayananda Anglo-Vedic College, Lahore. No. nil. Written neatly on paper measuring 11.2″ × 5.6″ and bounded on both sides by thick lines. There are 69 fols. It contains the MāU and the GK with Śaṅkara's commentary on both of them. No date, nor the name of the scribe.

9. D³. Dayananda Anglo-Vedic College, Lahore. No. nil. Fols. 2-35. Size 12.2″ × 5.5″. Written neatly on paper in Devanāgarī. It contains the first 7 passages of the MāU, first 14 kārikās of the first *prakaraṇa* of the GK and parts of Śaṅkara's commentary with Ānandagiri's ṭīkā.

10. IO. India office. No. 2783. In this codex there are three MSS, *viz.*, (1) *Prapañcasāravivaraṇa*, (2) *Laghukaumudī*, and (3) MāU together with the GK only up to the Book I. The ślokas of *maṅgalācaraṇa* of Śaṅkara's commentary are given with GK. The script is Devanāgarī. No date, but it seems to be old. Almost correct.

11. K[1]. Govt. Sanskrit College, Kāśī (Benares). No. 290 (Cover No. 9). Written in Bengali character on paper. Size 9.2″ × 4.2″. Fols. 24. Lines in each page 7. There is no date, yet it appears to be very modern. Writer's name is not given. There are mistakes and omissions. The MS contains both MāU and GK.

12. K[2]. Govt. Sanskrit College, Kāśī (Benares). No. 163. This is a part of a bigger MS of which we have only 24 fols. (29-52). Size 12″ × 5″. Each page has 9 lines. There is no date, nor the name of the scribe. This MS contains only the third Book of the GK with Śaṅkara's commentary. It is not quite correct. Some of the kārikās are here misplaced.

13. K[3]. Govt. Sanskrit College, Kāśī (Benares). No. 13 (Cover No. 4). Size 14.3″ × 6.2″. Script Devanāgarī. Fols. 10. Average number of lines in each page 13. Saṃvat 1907. Written at Vṛndāvana. The scribe is not mentioned.

It contains the original text of the MāU together with the commentary called *Māṇḍūkyopaniṣadarthaprakāśa*. Though the name of its author is not mentioned here he is no other than Kūranārāyaṇa, a follower of the Rāmānuja school. This commentary is published in the Anandashram Series, No. 62.

14. K^{3}. Govt. Sanskrit College, Kāśī (Benares). No. 304 (Cover No. 9). It is the first 12 fols. of a bigger codex. Size 10.3″ × 5.4″. Number of lines in each page 8. Written on paper in Bengali script. It extends up to the kārikā 12 of Book I together with Śaṅkara's commentary. No date. Appearance modern. No name of the scribe.

15. PU^{1}. The Panjab University Library, Lahore. No. 948. Script Devanāgarī. Fols. 9. Size 12″ × 6″. Lines on each page 13-18. Date about 1850 V.S., as says one Bhojlal, a manuscript dealer and book-seller from whom it seems to have been secured.

It contains MāU up to prabhavāpyayau hi bhūtānām. atraite ślokā bhavanti, and the GK of Book I.

16. PU^{2}. The Panjab University Library, Lahore. No. 746. Script Devanāgarī. Fols. 142. Size 14″ × 7″. Number of lines on each page varies from 13 to 18. No date, but said to be of about 1850 V.S. Obtained at Amritsar, and said to be of Kashmir recension. It contains the MāU and the GK together with the commentary of Śaṅkara followed by Ānandagiri's ṭīkā.

17. V^{g}. Visvabharati. No. 1317. It is written in Grantha character on palm-leaf. Fols. 58. Size 15.7″ × 1.3″. Lines 7-8 on each page. It contains the following works: (1) *Śrīmad Bhagavadgītā* (fols. 1-29), (2) *Īśopaniṣad* (fols. 30^{a}), (3) *Kenopaniṣad* (fols. 30^{b}-32^{a}), (4) *Kaṭhopaniṣad* (fols. 32^{b}-37^{a}), (5) *Praśnopaniṣad*

(fols. 37^a-41^a), (6) *Muṇḍakopaniṣad* (fols. 41^a-44^a), (7) *Māṇḍūkyopaniṣad* with GK (fols. 44^a-52^a), and (8) *Taittirīyopaniṣad* (fols. 52^a-58). This MS seems to be about 150 years old, but there is no date nor the name of the scribe.

18. V^n. Visvabharati. No. 1632. Written on palm-leaf in Devanāgarī. Fols. 13. Size 11.5″×4″. Lines on each page 7-8. The scribe was one Vāsudeva Bhide, the son of one Nārāyaṇa. It was written at Śrīpañcavaṭī in the presence of (god) Śrīrāma on the 7th day of the black fortnight of the month of Caitra in the Śaka era 1733 (*Prajāpati saṃvatsara*) = 1811 A.D. It contains the MāU with the GK beginning with the benedictory Vedic ślokas, bhadraṃ karṇebhiḥ° (ṚV, I. 89. 8), and svasti na indra° (RV, I. 89. 6) to which are added the first two ślokas, *viz.*, prajñānāṃśu° and yo viśvātmā° of Śaṅkara with which he is said to have begun his commentary on the MāU.

As regards the relationship of the MSS described above it may briefly be observed that A^1 and A^2 are from the same family and have close connexion with A^3, IO, PU^1 and PU^2. B^1 and B^2 are closely related and so are D^1 and D^2. V^g and V^n agree in many cases with A^1, A^2, D^1 and D^2.

Among the MSS mentioned above A^1 and A^2 are the worst giving very wrong readings. Yet, at least in one case (IV. 56^a) A^1 with IO gives the right reading. See Introduction, § 5. The Readings of the Text.

In addition to the MSS described above the readings collected from the thirteen MSS, utilized for the preparation of the second edition of the MāU and GK together with Śaṅkara's commentary and Ānandagiri's sub-commentary in the Anandashram Series, No. 10, have also been consulted. The MSS collected for that edition are mentioned here, where necessary, according to the abbreviations used there, *viz.*, K, Kh, G, Gh, etc. Besides, such editions as of Maheśacandra Pāla, Calcutta, 1806 Śaka era; of MM. Durgācaraṇa Sāṅkhya-Vedānta-tīrtha, Calcutta, 1331 Bengali era; and of Gita Press, Gorakhpur, 1993 V.S., have been consulted.

The most important readings are discussed in their respective places in the main work, while variants will be found in the Appendix II, pp. 229 ff. See Introduction, § 4.

Acknowledgment

I am deeply indebted to the authorities of the following Institutions, who have kindly given me on loan the MSS described above: Adyar Library, Madras; Bhandarkar Oriental Research Institute, Poona; Dayananda Anglo-Vedic College, Lahore; Government Sanskrit College, Benares; India Office, London; Panjab University Library, Lahore; and Visvabharati Library, Santiniketan.

I am thankful to my pupils Śrī P. Anujan Achan, Government Archæologist, the State

Museum, Trichur; Śrī A. Chalamayya, Superintendent, the Orphanage, Pithapuram; Śrī Anukul Chandra Banerjee, M.A., B.L., Assistant Lecturer in Pali, and Śrī Ajit Ranjan Bhattacharyya, M.A., Ex-Puranchand Nahar Fellow, both of the University of Calcutta; the first two kindly collated for me some of the MSS used in the present edition of the book, and the last two helped me in preparing two of the Indexes appended hereto. I am thankful also to Śrī Dinabandhu Ganguli, B.A., the able Superintendent, Calcutta University Press, for the kind care he has taken in carrying the book through the press, and to Śrī Ramakrishna Chakravarti, M.A., of the same press for his very careful assistance in reading the proofs.

I am grateful to my friends Prof. Umeshchandra Bhattacharyya, M.A., and Pandit Narendrachandra Bhattacharyya, Sāṃkhya-Mīmāṃsā-Vedāntatīrtha, M.A. of our University, for their kindly reading some of the proof-sheets. I also offer my sincere thanks to my esteemed friend, Professor Vanamali Chakravarti, Vedāntatīrtha, M.A., who has given me immense and invaluable help in various ways in my work. He has given me the benefit of discussing with him almost all the difficult points of the book, of reading proofs, and of giving various suggestions.

In conclusion I must express the deep sense of my gratitude to the authorities of the University of Calcutta, and specially to Dr. Syamaprasad Mookerjee, M.A., B.L., D.Litt., LL.D., Barrister-at-Law, M.L.A., President, Councils of Post-Graduate Teaching in Arts and Science, under whose benign and sympathetic patronage the book is included in the publications of the University.

Brahmavihāra,
CALCUTTA.
May, 1943.

VIDHUSHEKHARA BHATTACHARYA.

ABBREVIATIONS

Ā	Ānandagiri.
AAA	Abhisamayālaṅkārāloka (Prajñāpāramitās, Vol. I), Gaekwad's Oriental Series, No. LXVII.
AAS	Abhidhammatthasaṃgaha with Vibhāvanı ṭīkā, ed. Fernando and Silva, Colombo, 1898.
AK	L'Abhidharmakośa de Vasubandhu traduit et ennoté per Louis de la Vallée Poussin, Paris, 1923-31.
AKB	Abhidharmakośabhāṣya (Tibetan Text), BB.
AKV[1]	Abhidharmakośavyākhyā of Yaśomitra, Fasc. I-II, BB.
AKV[2]	Abhidharmakośavyākhyā of Yaśomitra, ed. U. Wogihara, Tokio, 1932-1936.
AmK	Amarakośa.
AN	Aṅguttara Nikāya, PTS.
AO	Acta Orientalia.
AP	Abhidhānappadīpikā, Colombo, 1900.
ĀŚ	Āgamaśāstra of Gauḍapāda.
AS	Aṭṭhasālinī, PTS.
ĀS	Ācārāṅga Sūtra, PTS.
ASP	Aṣṭasāhasrikā Prajñāpāramitā, BI.
ASU	Aṣṭottaraśatopaniṣad, ed. W. Laxman Shastri Pansikar, Nirnayasagar, 1917.

AU Ātmopaniṣad.
AV Atharvaveda.
BA Bodhicaryāvatāra, BI.
BAP Bodhicaryāvatārapañjikā, BI.
BB Bibliotheca Buddhica.
Bbh Bodhisattvabhūmi, ed. U. Wogihara, Tokio, 1930. See BSB.
BBU Brahmabindu Upaniṣad.
BBV Bṛhadāraṇyakabhāṣyavārttika, Anandashram, 1892-94.
BCK Buddhacarita Kāvya, ed. Johnston, 1936.
BG Bhagavadgītā.
BI Bibliotheca Indica.
BJS Brahmajāla Sutta in DN, PTO.
BP Bhāgavata Purāṇa.
BS Brahmasūtras of Bādarāyaṇa.
BSB Bodhisattvabhūmi, ed. U. Wogihara, Tokio, 1930. See Bbh.
BU Bṛhadāraṇyaka Upaniṣad.
ChU Chāndogya Upaniṣad.
CN Chullaniddesa, PTS.
CŚ Catuḥśataka, Sanskrit and Tibetan Texts, ed. Vidhushekhara Bhattacharya, Visvabharati, Part II, 1931.
CŚ' Catuḥśatikā, ed. Haraprasad Shastri in the Memories of the Asiatic Society of Bengal, Vol. III, No. 8, pp. 449-514.
CVP Cittaviśuddhiprakaraṇa, ed. Prabhubhai Paṭel, Visvabharati (not yet published). See JASB, 1898.

DA Divyāvadāna, ed. C o w e l l and N a i l, Cambridge, 1886.

DäV Der älter Vedānta von M a x W a l l e s e r, Heidelberg, 1911.

DB Daśabhūmikasūtra, ed. R a h d e r, Paris, 1926.

D· The edition of the MāU by D u r g ā c a r a ṇ a. S ā ṅ k h y a - V e d ā n t a - t ī r t h a, Calcutta, 1331, Bengali Era.

DN Dīgha Nikāya, PTS.

DP Dhammapada.

DPA Dhammapada Aṭṭhakatha, PTS.

DPP Doctrine of Prajñāpāramita, by E. O b e r m i l l e r, Acta Orientalia, Vol. IX.

DS Dharmasaṃgraha, ed. K a s w a r a, M a x M ü l l e r, and W e n z e l, Anecdota Oxoniensia, Aryan Series, Oxford, 1885.

DSn Dhammasaṃgani, PTS.

DV Daśavaikālika Sūtra, Devchand Lalbhai Pustakoddhārasamiti, No. 47.

ERE Encyclopædia of Religion and Ethics, ed. H a s t i n g s.

Ex Expositor, PTS (Translation Series).

G[e] The edition of the MāU from the Gītā Press, Gorakhpur, 1893.

GK Gauḍapādakārikā.

GM Gaṇaratnamahodadhi, ed. B h ī m a s e n a Ś a r m a n, Prayāga (Allahabad), 1894.

HU Hitopadeśa, ed. P. P e t e r s o n, Bombay, 1887.

HV Harivaṃśa.

IU Īśā Upaniṣad.

JM Jagadgururatnamālāstava of Sadāśivabrahmendra with the com. of Ātmabodhendra Sarasvatī included in Vedāntapañcaprakaraṇī, Śrīvidyā Press, Kumbhakonam.

JS Jñānasārasamuccaya (Yes.śes.sñiṅ.po.kun.las-btus.pa), now only in Tibetan. Cordier, III. p. 298.

JU Jābāla Upaniṣad.

KlU Kaivalya Upaniṣad.

KN Kūranārāyaṇa.

KnU Kena Upaniṣad.

KP Kāśyapaparivarta, ed. Baron A. Von Staël-Holstein, Sanghai, 1926.

KtU Kauṣītaki Upaniṣad.

KU Kaṭha Upaniṣad.

KV Kathāvatthu, PTS.

LA Laṅkāvatāra Sūtra, ed. Bunyiu Nanjio, Kyto, 1923.

LC Laghucandrikā, Śrīvidyā Press, Kumbhakonam, 1893.

LV Lalitavistara, ed. Lefmann, Halle, 1902 and 1908.

MA Madhyamakāvatāra (Tibetan Text), BB, IX. French translation by Poussin, *Le Muséon*, 1907

MAc Madhvācārya.

MAK Madhyamakālaṅkārakārikā of Śāntirakṣita, Tibetan Text, Sde.dge, Sa, 53a^1-56b^8.

MāU Māṇḍūkya Upaniṣad.

MB Mahābhārata, The South Indian Text, ed. T. R. Krishnamacharya and T. R. Vyasacharya, Kumbhakonam, 1906-1914.

MBU Maṇḍalabrāhmaṇopaniṣad.

MD Mīmāṃsādarśana.

M° The edition of the MāU by Maheśacandra Pāla, Calcutta, 1806 Śaka Era.

MHK Madhyamakahṛdayakārikā of Bhavya, Tibetan Text, Sde.dge, Dza, $1b^1$-$40b^7$.

MHKV Madhyamakahṛdayakārikāvṛtti Tarkajvālā of Bhavya, Tibetan, Sde.dge, Dza, $40b^7$-$329b^4$.

MK Mūlamadhyamakakārikā of Nāgārjuna, BB, IV.

MKU Muktikā Upaniṣad.

MM Mahārthamañjarī with commentary, Parimala, TSS.

MN Majjhima Nikāya, PTS.

MNs Mahāniddesa, PTS.

MnU Mahānāradīya Upaniṣad (Minor Upaniṣads, Adyar).

MnU Mānasollāsa of Sureśvara, Nirnayasagar Press, Bombay, 1959, V.E., 1825 Ś. E.

MP Manorathapūraṇī, Mahāmukuṭarājavidyālaya, Siam, 2463 Buddha Era.

MPñ Milindapañha, ed. V. Trenckner, London, 1928.

MS or MSA — Mahāyānasūtrālaṅkāra, ed. Sylvain Lévi, Paris, 1907; French Tr, 1911.

MSBT, MVBT, or MVST, q.v.

MSt — Mahāsaddanīti, ed. A. Seelananda Thera, Colombo, 1909.

MSV — Mīmāṁsāślokavārttika, Chaukhamba Sanskrit Series, 1896.

MT — Madhyāntavibhāgaṭikā, ed. S. Yamguchi, Nagao, 1934.

MU — Maitrī Upaniṣad.

MuU — Muṇḍaka Upaniṣad.

MV — Madhyamakavṛtti, ed. Louis de La Vallée Poussin, BB. IV.

MVBT — Madhyāntavibhāgasūtrabhāṣyaṭikā, ed. V. Bhattacharya and G. Tucci, Part I, Calcutta Oriental Series, 1932.

MVD — Madhyāntavibhaṅga Discourse, translated from Sanskrit by Th. Stcherbatsky, BB, XXX, 1936.

MVT — Madhyāntavibhāga ṭikā of Sthiramati, édition per Susumu Yamaguchi Nagoya, 1934.

MVg — Mahāvagga of Vinaya, ed. H. Oldenberg, London, 1879.

MVt[1] — Mahāvyutpatti, ed. Sakaki, Japan.

MVt[2] — Mahāvyutpatti, ed. Minaeff, BB.

MVu — Mahāvastu, ed. E. Senart, Paris, 1882-97.

N — Nāgārjuna.

NAT Nyāyāmṛtataraṅgiṇī of Rāmācārya, ed. T. R. Krishnacharya, Nirnayasāgar.

NK Nyāyakandalī on Praśastapādabhāṣya, Vizianagram Sanskrit Series, No. 6, 1895.

NPTU Nṛsiṃhapūrvatāpanī Upaniṣad.

NPU Nāradaparivrājaka Upaniṣad.

NS Nyāyasūtra.

NSi Naiṣkarmyasiddhi with Candrikā, ed. G. A. Jacob, Bombay, 1891.

NSt Nirupamastotra in *Two Hymns of Catuḥstava of Nāgārjuna*, ed. G. Tucci, JRAS, 1932, pp. 309 ff.

Nt Nirukta of Yāska.

NUTU Nṛsiṃhottaratāpanī Upaniṣad.

P Puruṣottama.

Pāṇ Pāṇini.

PAS Prajñāpāramitārthasaṃgraha of Diṅnāga as quoted by Obermiller in his paper *The Doctrine of Prajñāpāramitā*, Reprint from *Acta Orientalia*, Vol. XI.

PB Praśastapādabhāṣya, ed. V. Dvivedin, Vizianagram Sanskrit Series, No. 6, Benares, 1895.

PD Pañcadaśī of Vidyāraṇya.

PO Poona Orientalist.

PP Padma Purāṇa.

PS[1] Paramārthasāra, of Ādiśeṣa, Trivandrum Sanskrit Series, No. XII, 1911.

PS[2] —of Abhinavagupta, ed. L. D. Barnett, JRAS, 1910, pp. 707 ff.

PS[3] —of Ādiśeṣa, Transliterated Text, English Translation and Notes, ed. S. S. Suryanarayana Sastri, Karnatak Publishing House, 1941.

PŚP Pañcaviṃśatisāhasrikā Prajñāpāramitā, ed. Nalinaksha Dutt, Calcutta Oriental Series, No. 28, 1934.

PU Praśna Upaniṣad.

PV Pramāṇaviniścaya of Dharmakīrtti, Tibetan Text. Cordier, III, p. 298.

PVk[1] Pramāṇavārttika of Dharmakīrtti, ed. Rahula Sāṅkṛtyāyana, Patna, 1938.

PVk[2] Pramāṇavārttika of Dharmakīrtti with Manoratha Nandin's Commentary, ed. Rahula Sāṅkṛtyāyana, Patna.

RPR Review of Philosophy and Religion.

RUTU Rāmottaratāpanī Upaniṣad.

RV Ṛgveda

Ś Śaṅkarācārya.

SāS Sāṅkhyasūtra.

ŚB Śatapatha Brāhmaṇa.

SDS Sarvadarśanasaṃgraha, BI, 1858.

SK Sāṅkhyakārikā of Īśvarakṛṣṇa.

SKr Sūtrakṛtāṅga Sūtra, Āgamodaya Samiti, 1917.

SMV Śārīrakamīmāṃsābhāṣyavārttika, ed. Anantakrishna Sastri and Ashokanath Bhattacharya, Asutosh Sanskrit Series, No. 1, Calcutta, 1941.

SN	Saṃyutta Nikāya, PTS.
SNS	Sandhinirmocanasūtra, Texte Tibétain, édité et tradiut per Etienne Lamotte, Louvain et Paris, 1935.
SNt	Suttanipāta, PTS.
SP^1	Saddharmapuṇḍarīka, BB, 1912.
SP^2	Saddharmapuṇḍarīka, ed. U. Wogihara, 1934.
SR or SRS	Samādhirājasūtra, ed. Rai Sarat Chandra Das Bahadur and Pandit Sarat Chandra Sastri, Fasc. 1, Buddhist Text Society, Calcutta, 1898.
SS	Subhāṣitasaṃgraha, ed. C. Bendall, *Le Muséon*, N.S. IV. 1903; V. 1904.
ŚS	Śikṣāsamuccaya, ed. C. Bendall, BB, 1902.
ṢS	Ṣaḍdarśanasamuccaya with Guṇaratna's Com., ed. L. Suali, BI, 1905 ff.
SŚP	Saptaśatikā Prajñāpāramitā, ed. G. Tucci, Roma, 1923.
SSS	Sarvasiddhāntasaṅgraha, ed. Premsundar Bose, Calcutta, 1919.
St. LA	Studies in Laṅkāvatāra Sūtra by D. T. Suzuki, London, 1930.
ŚU	Śvetāśvatara Upaniṣad, Anandashram, 1905
ŚV	Śivasūtravimarśinī of Kṣemarāja, ed. J. C. Chatterjee, The Kashmir Series of Texts and Studies, Vol. I, 1911.
TA	Taittirīya Āraṇyaka, Anandashram, 1898.

TAl	Tattvaratnāvalī of Advayavajra in *Advayavajrasaṃgraha* ed. Haraprasad Shastri, Gaekwad's Oriental Series, No. LX, 1927.
TAk	Tantrāloka of Abhinavagupta, Kashmir Series of Texts and Studies, No. XXX.
TG	Theragāthā, PTS.
TJ	Tarkajvālā, See MHKV.
Tk	Triṃśikā of Vasubandhu, ed. Sylvain Lévi in the *Vijñaptimātrasiddhi*, Paris, 1925.
TM	Tattvamuktākalāpa and Sarvārthasiddhi of Veṅkaṭanātha Deśika with the *Ānandadāyinī* and the *Bhāvaprakāśa*, Bibliotheca Sanskritica, Mysore, 1933, 1940.
TP	Tattvaprakāśa, Trivandrum Sanskrit Series, 1926.
TS	Tattvasaṃgraha of Śāntirakṣita, Gaekwad's Oriental Series, Nos. XXX and XXXI, 1926.
TSN	Trisvabhāvanirdeśa of Vasubandhu, ed. Sujitkumar Mukhopadhyaya, Visvabharati, 1939.
TSP	Tattvasaṃgrahapañjikā of Kamalaśīla, See TS.
TTU	Tripurātāpanī Upaniṣad.
TU	Taittirīya Upaniṣad.

TV	Tantravārttika of Kumārila as printed with the Śābarabhāṣya on the MD, Anandashram Series.
U or UP	Upaniṣad.
UC	Uttaracarita of Bhavabhūti.
US	Upadeśasāhasrī.
VāP	Vāyu Purāṇa.
Vbh	Vibhaṅga, PTS.
Vc or Vch	Vajracchedikā Prajñāpāramitā, ed. Max Müller, Anecdota Oxoniensia, 1881.
VeS	Vedāntasāra, ed. G. A. Jacob, Nirnayassgar Press, Bombay, 1894.
ViP	Viṣṇu Purāṇa.
ViS	Vijñaptimātratāsiddhi, La Siddhi de Hiuan-Tsang traduite et annotée par Louis de La Vallée Poussin, Paris, 1928-29.
ViV	Vigrahavyāvartanī, ed. K. P. Jayswal and Rāhula Sāṅkṛtyāyana, JBORS, XXIII.
Vk	Viṃśatikā of Vasubandhu. See Tk.
VM	Visuddhimagga, PTS.
VP	Vinayapiṭaka, ed. H. Oldenberg, London, 1879-1883.
VS	Vājasaneyi-saṃhitā.
VSN	Viṣṇusahasranāma, Bibliotheca Sanskritica, Mysore, No. 19.
VSt	Vaiśeṣika Sūtra.

VV Śrīvātulasūtravṛtti, Kashmir Series of Texts and Studies, No. 39.

YB Yogācārabhūmi of A s a ṅ g a , MS with the present author.

YŚ Yogaśāstra of Hemacandra, Bibliotheca Indica, 1907.

YS Yogasūtra.

YV Yogavāsiṣṭha Rāmāyaṇa, Nirṇayasāgar Press, 1918.

INTRODUCTION

§ 1. *The Māṇḍūkya Upaniṣad and its Extent*

What work or works are we to understand by the name of MāU? And what is its real extent?

It is generally believed that the MāU comprises only the twelve prose passages beginning with "om ity etad akṣaram°" and ending with "ātmānaṃ ya evaṃ veda" (see pp. 223-25).[1] It is also assumed that the kārikās of Gauḍapāda are mere explanation of these passages. These two works are thus separate, though related to each other very closely as text and commentary.

But this is not admitted on all hands. Some hold that the Upaniṣad is composed not only of the twelve prose passages referred to above, but also of the kārikās, twenty-nine in all, attributed to Gauḍapāda, as contained in Book I. Thus according to them those prose passages and the kārikās in Book I are regarded as *Upaniṣad* or *śruti*.[2] This view seems to have partly

[1] Of these passages the first seven are found with slight variations in some cases also in NPTU, IV. 1-2; NUTU, II; and RUTU, 5.

[2] In 1925 I had an occasion to write (IHQ, Vol. I, pp. 119ff.) with regard to the present subject that this view was at least as old as Madhvācārya (1199-1274 A.D.), the great champion of the Dvaita school of the Vedānta philosophy. For, according to him and his followers, such as Vyāsatīrtha and Śrīnivāsa, both the prose passages and the kārikās referred to are handed down by Varuṇa in the form of a *maṇḍūka* 'frog' (see the commentary on the MāU by Madhvācārya with Śrī-

been subscribed to by Śaṅkara, the commentator of MāU, who says in the introduction to his commentary

nivāsīya, Kumbhakonam, pp. 2-3). In support of it Madhvācārya quotes the following two passages from the PP and HV respectively:

(*i*) dhyāyan nārāyaṇaṃ devaṃ praṇavena samāhitaḥ |
maṇḍūkarūpi varuṇas tuṣṭāva harim avyayam ||

(*ii*) iti maṇḍūkarūpī san dadarśa varuṇaḥ śrutim |

These lines are not found, so far as I know, in printed editions of the works.

Here Madhvācārya writes (*ibid.*, p. 2): maṇḍūkarūpiṇā varuṇena catūrūpo nārāyaṇo 'tra stūyate. He regards the kārikās as *mantras* which are said to have been visioned by Brahman, the creator. On this he quotes the following couplet not yet traced in the same work (p. 8):

brahmadṛṣṭān ato mantrān pramāṇaṃ salileśvaraḥ |
atra ślokā bhavantīti cakāraivaṃ pṛthak pṛthak ||

Vyāsatīrtha's ṭīkā, too, introduces the kārikās under *mantras*.

The commentator of NPTU, who is known by the name of Śaṅkarācārya and identical with the author of the *Prapañcasāra*, a Tantric work (see my paper, *Śaṅkara's Commentaries on the Upaniṣads*, in *Sir Asutosh Mookerjee Silver Jubilee Volumes, Orientalia*, 2, pp. 101 ff. and against it Raghuvara Miṭṭhulāl Shastri: *Proceedings and Transactions, Fifth Indian Oriental Conference*, 1928, Vol. I, pp. 691 ff., as well as T. R. Chintamani: *Proceedings and Transactions, Third Oriental Conference, Madras*, 1924, pp. 419 ff.) is also of the same opinion, though he does not give particulars as to whether the *ṛṣi* 'seer' of the Upaniṣad is Varuṇa or whether the kārikās are seen by Brahman, the creator. Kūranārāyaṇa, another commentator of MāU belonging to the Rāmānuja school of the Vedānta maintains the same view taking the kārikās in Book I as *mantras*, which, in his opinion, too, together with the prose passages form the original Upaniṣad. Appayya Dīkṣita (a person different from the celebrated author of the *Siddhāntaleśa*) who is a commentator of the one hundred and eight Upaniṣads, seems to subscribe to the same views, for his commentary on the Upaniṣad extends only up to the prose passages and the kārikās of Book I. See the Catalogue of *Sanskrit Manuscripts* in the *Adyar Library*, Vol. I, Upaniṣads, pp. 116, 287-8.

After what I wrote as above in 1925, so far as my information goes, it was B. N. Krishnamurti Sarma who in 1931 took up the case in right earnest and advocated it very strongly. His first paper (*New Light on the Gauḍapādakārikā*) appeared in RPR, Vol. II, No. 1, pp. 35 ff. He wanted on it that the first of the four sections (*prakaraṇa-catuṣṭaya*) of the *Āgamaśāstra* begins with "om ity etad akṣaram°" (MāU, 1), though the question as to whether that particular section or all the sections are regarded as *śruti* or not is not raised by him. Leaving aside what is said by this Śaṅkara whose identity with the great author of the commentary on the *Brahmasūtras* is doubtful,[3] it appears plausible that the view under discussion dates back at least from the time of Rāmānuja (1055-1137 A.D.), as he seems to quote in his commentary on BS, I. 1. 1, a kārikā of Gauḍapāda (I. 16) as *śruti*.

mainly to show that Madhvācārya cannot rightly be accused of holding the view that the kārikās in Book I are regarded as *śruti*, and form a part of the original MāU. In doing so he tried to demonstrate that teachers "of the three schools of Vedānta, such as Śaṅkara, Ānandagiri, Madhusūdana, Brahmānanda, Rāmānuja, Kūra-nārāyaṇa, Mahācārya, Madhva, Jayatīrtha, Vyāsācārya svāmin, Rāmācārya, etc.," are of the same opinion. In the same journal (RFR, 1932, Vol. III, No. 1; 1933, Vol. IV. No. 2) he wrote two papers more on the same subject. His writings gave rise to an interesting and long controversy in which took part some scholars, such as Y. Subrahmanya Sharma (RPR, 1933, Vol. IV, No. 3), and A. Venkata Subbiah (PO, 1936, Vol. I. Nos. 1-2), B. N. Krishnamurti's rejoinder being given in PO, 1936, Vol. I, No. 2, and 1937, Vol. II, No. 1. Besides, A. Venkata Subbiah wrote in IA, 1933, pp. 181 ff. an independent paper entitled *The Māṇḍūkyopaniṣad and Gauḍapāda* which deserves to be mentioned in this connection.

[3] Those who think that the two Śaṅkaras, the author of the *Śārīrakabhāṣya* on BS and the author of the commentary on ĀŚ, are one and the same should consider in the latter not only the question of *maṅgalācaraṇa*, the inferior quality of composition of the ślokas, the defect of metre (Ānandagiri's explanation can hardly be accepted), and the grammatical mistakes, but also the explanation offered of such kārikās as I. 10, II. 37, III. 25, and IV. 83 as to whether it is possible for the former. *Cf.* here his explanation of the words *bhūta* and *abhūta* in III. 23 with that in IV. 3; of *sambhūti* in III. 25 with that of IU, 12. See note 2.

He writes : jīvasyaiva hi nirodhaḥ *śrūyate*° anādimāyayā supto yadā jīvaḥ prabudhyata (I. 16) iti ca. By the word *śrūyate* evidently he regards the line as *śruti*.

B. N. Krishnamurti Sarma thinks that the above date is to be pushed back to the time of Sureśvara, the author of the BBV or even that of Śaṅkara, the author of the *Śārīrakabhāṣya* on BS. But in spite of what he has said in support of the view one can hardly accept it when the statements made by the above two teachers themselves are taken into consideration. Sureśvara quotes ĀŚ, I. 11 (kāryakāraṇa°) in his NSi, IV. 41, and tells us (*Op. cit.*, IV. 44) that it is said by the revered Gauḍas. The word *Gauḍa* here refers to Gauḍapāda. As regards Śaṅkara, he, too, quotes in his commentary on BS, II. 1. 9, a kārikā of Gauḍapāda (anādimāyayā°, I. 16), and says it is a saying of those teachers who know the tradition of the Vedānta,[5] just as said by him in another case (BS, I. 4. 14) with regard to another kārikā of Gauḍapāda (mṛlloha°, III. 15).[6] Here Sureśvara and Śaṅkara say in the clearest possible language that the kārikās referred to above are by revered teachers. Hence, according to them, they are not *śruti*.

4 evaṃ gauḍair drāviḍair naḥ pūjyair ayam arthaḥ prabhāṣitaḥ. This line, as in the printed text is metrically defective. The word *ayam* seems to be omitted here.

5 atroktaṃ vedāntasampradāyavidbhir ācāryaiḥ.

6 tathā ca sampradāyavido vadanti.

7 For detailed discussion of this question readers are referred to the scholars and their papers mentioned in note 2 of this section

In the face of this clear statement, the passages from some works attributed to Śaṅkara, and as such of doubtful authority, which are quoted by B. N. Krishnamurti Sarma in order to support his view that the kārikās of the Book I are *śruti*, do not, as it appears to me, carry any particular weight.

Sureśvara's words, *viz.*, *vedāntokti* with regard to GK, I. 14, and *āgamaśāsana* with regard to GK, I. 3, which are quoted by him for the same purpose from BBV, I. 4. 615 and 744 respectively, do not necessarily imply that the kārikas are *śruti* in the primary sense of the word, for the same author, Sureśvara, takes elsewhere, as we have already seen, one (I. 11) of the GK kārikās of Book I in which the above two kārikās are included, as a statement of Gauḍapāda. We should remember here that the above phrases are applicable also to works of human origin dealing with the Vedānta or Āgama.

That this controversy is not new, but an old one is known from the words of Rāmācārya, the author of the NAT, p. 223, where with regard to the two kārikās of Gauḍapāda, I. 17 and 18, he raises the question as to whether they are *śruti*, and arrives at the conclusion that they are really so.[8]

Thus we reach the conclusion that at least from the time of Rāmānuja, the author of the *Śrībhāṣya* of

[8] See RPR, 1933, Vol. IV, No. 2. It is interesting to note here that sometimes the kārikās of Book I of GK is referred to as *Gauḍapādīyoktaśruti* (LC, p. 580), and *Māṇḍūkyopaniṣadvivaraṇa-Gauḍapādīyavārttika* (NAT, p. 123b). The reader may think over here as to how these two words are used here loosely.

BS, there were some authoritative teachers according to whom the kārikās of Book I of the GK were regarded as *śruti* and as such they formed a part of the MāU.

Speaking generally our old teachers were *śraddhādeva*, 'trustful,' to use the word of the *Śatapatha Brāhmaṇa* (I. 1. 4. 15), with regard to the authenticity of our sacred or Sanskrit texts. Any work dealing with Upaniṣadic matter would readily be accepted by them as Upaniṣad.[9] Remember the number of Upaniṣads and their language, subject matter and the way of treatment therein. Are they all Upaniṣads, though they are called so? The *Bhagavadgītā* is not an Upaniṣad in fact, yet, it bears the name. We all know its colophon in which occurs the following: *iti śrīmadbhagavadgītāsu upaniṣatsu*. And it is so only owing to the fact that it is *like* an Upaniṣad. The practice of taking what is actually not an Upaniṣad as an Upaniṣad appears to have been in existence from the time of Pāṇini, as says Satyavrata Sāmaśramin in his *Trayīparicaya*, Calcutta, 1893, p. 69. From his work (I. 4. 79)[10] we may gather a word, *upaniṣatkṛtya*, which means 'having made *like* an Upaniṣad.' Does it not lead us to conclude as above? But grammarians differ here on the meaning of the word *Upaniṣad*, according to some it being *tattvajñāna*, the 'knowledge of reality,' while to others, *rahasya*, a 'secret' or 'secret doctrine'. Let us take here the case of Purāṇas. A Purāṇa is said to have 'five characteristics' (*purāṇaṃ pañcalakṣaṇam*). But there are Purāṇas which are, in

[9] See Śaṅkara on BG, II. 19 and 20 where he uses the words *ṛc* and *mantra* referring to the above two stanzas.

[10] jīvikopaniṣadāv aupamye.

fact, not so, though they are known to us under the same name. Similar is the case with regard to Upaniṣads and other works. It may be noted here in this connexion that it is not only the Book I of GK but also the remaining three Books of it which are sometimes held to be Upaniṣads, as *Advaitaprakaraṇa Up.*, *Alataśāntiprakaraṇa Up.*, etc.[11]

We have seen above that according to some authorities including specially Madhvācārya only Book I of GK is *śruti*, and the last three books are not so, and as such they do not form any part of MāU, as does Book I. In other words, they form a separate work or works with which the former has no connexion. If it is not so, it will be very difficult to explain as to why the last three Books are not commented upon by those teachers. Why have they explained only the Book I? It cannot be said that these last three Books were not known to them or in their time, as their existence before them can very satisfactorily be proved by the very simple fact that the great Śaṅkara who flourished long before them has quoted in his commentary on BS, I. 4. 14, a kārikā (III. 15) from one of those three Books.

The fact that they did not comment upon the last three Books can be explained in two ways. First, it might have been their honest belief that those three Books had no connexion whatsoever with the MāU which, according to them, comprised only the twelve prose passages

11 See MSS labelled ZZE of BBRAS. Similarly each of the five chapters of the NPTU is regarded as a separate Upaniṣad. The case is the same with the TU, the three chapters (*Sikṣāvallī*, *Brahma*°, and *Bhṛgu*°) of which are held to be three Upaniṣads.

and the twenty-nine kārikās of Book I of GK. Secondly, it might be said that they could not explain them, for the dominant thoughts therein, *viz.*, *Advaitavāda* 'absolute monism' and *Vijñānavāda* 'idealism' would go against their own views, *viz.*, *Dvaitavāda* 'dualism' or *Viśiṣṭādvaitavāda* 'qualified monism.' The first answer seems to be more reasonable than the second, for had they known that the last three Books, too, were really included in or connected with the original Upaniṣad they would have undoubtedly explained them, as is done[12] by Puruṣottama, the grandson of Vallabhācārya, the great teacher of the *Śuddhādvaita* 'pure monism' school of the Vedānta.[13]

§ 2. *The Relationship between the Prose Passages and the Kārikās in Book I*

As Madhvācārya says,[1] the twelve prose passages of the Upaniṣad are divided into four parts.[2]

[12] I have seen the commentary only on the first two Books as edited by Bhaṭṭa Ramānātha Śāstrin and published from Puṣṭimārga-Kāryālaya, Bombay, Vikrama 1980. That Puruṣottama wrote or intended to write his commentary also on Book III (*Advaita Prakaraṇa*) is known from his own words (*advaitākhye vicārayiṣye*), p. 55. It seems that he commented or intended to do so also on the last Book.

[13] It is known from the Tibetan sources that in about the first half of the eighth century A.D. the GK was regarded as an *Upaniṣat śāstra* (gsaṅ.baḥi.bstan. bcos). For Kamalaśīla, a disciple of Śāntirakṣita (705-763 A.D.) and the author of the *Pañjikā* of his MAK quotes some kārikās from Books II and III of our work which he calls *Upaniṣat śāstra*. It is to be noted that Kamalaśīla's remark cannot be considered with reference only to the above two Books.

[1] MāU with *Śrīnivāsīyavṛtti*, p. 8.

[2] Part I, passages 1-6; Part II, passages 7; Part III, passages 8-11; and Part IV, passage 12.

Just after each of them there is a line : atraite ślokā bhavanti 'here are these ślokas.' These introductory lines when compared with similar sentences in different Upaniṣads[3] will show that the ślokas are quoted there only to support what has been stated before. And we have already seen that M a d h v ā c ā r y a and others, specially the former, say the very thing quite clearly. Thus it follows from it that the ślokas or kārikās were already in existence and the prose passages came into being afterwards.

This will be confirmed if we compare the contents of the prose passages with those of the corresponding kārikās. The comparison will further show that it is the kārikās on which the prose passages are based and not *vice versa*.

Supposing that the kārikās are explanations of the Upaniṣad, *i.e.*, of the twelve prose passages which are generally held to be so, one may naturally expect to see the difficult points in the latter explained in the former. And it also goes without saying that an exposition may add something new to what is said in the original, but it does not or should not omit the most important and difficult words or points in it. If these facts are borne in mind, it will be evident that it is the kārikās that should be regarded as the earlier work, and not the prose passages.

3 See BU, IV. 3. 11, 4. 8: tad ete ślokā bhavanti; *Op. cit.*, II. 2. 3, IV. 4. 6, 7: tad eṣa śloko bhavati; ChU, II. 21. 3, III. 11. 1, etc.: tad eṣa ślokaḥ; TU, II. 1. 1, 2. 1, etc.: tad apy eṣa śloko bhavati; ChU, III. 12. 5: tad etad ṛcābhyuktam.

According to the general view, kārikās 1-5 are to be taken as the exposition of the prose passages 3-5.[4] Now the words *saptāṅga* 'with seven limbs,' and *ekonaviṃśatimukha* 'with nineteen mouths' in the passages 3 and 4 are the most difficult and they are explained differently by different commentators[5]; but not even the slightest mention of them is made in the kārikās. Why should the kārikās which are supposed to have been written in order to explain the text, *i.e.*, the prose passages, omit these two important words?

Again, in the prose passages 3 and 9 we have the word *vaiśvānara* and not *viśva*, while in the kārikās (I. 1-4, 19, 23) there is only *viśva* and never *vaiśvānara*. Why is this discrepancy? A commentator is to explain what is actually found in the text, he is not allowed to take the liberty of changing it. Nor are the two words *vaiśvānara* and *viśva* identical or synonymous. It is difficult to account for this alteration. That it is owing to the exigency of metre is an absurd hypothesis.[6]

In this connexion, there are three words more, *viz.*, *jāgaritasthāna*, *svapna*°, and *suṣupta*° in the prose passages 3, 4 and 5 respectively. But they are entirely omitted in the kārikās. But why? It cannot be explained away by simply saying that they are not so important or difficult as to require any explanation; for, in order to

4 It is to be noted that the first two passages have nothing in the kārikās as we have them before us.

5 See Ś here and on NPTU, IV; Madhva, KN, and P on the passages; Vidyāraṇya on NUTU, I; and Nārāyaṇa on RUTU, 3.

6 Note there is *prajñānaghana* in the prose passage 5, for which we have *ghanaprajña* in kārikā 1.

understand the main thought of the passages the importance of these three stages, *viz.*, wakefulness, dream, and deep sleep, can in no way be ignored.

The fact is that the kārikās are older, and from them, as well as from some older Upaniṣads, the MāU, *i.e.*, the prose passages to which that name is usually given is compiled or made,[7] and in doing so some of the thoughts of these kārikās and of some older Upaniṣads are here in the prose passages simplified, modified or explained adding something new. Thus, it appears, in the present case, the author of the prose passages having found the word *viśva* in its special sense nowhere in the Upaniṣads[8] seems to have substituted for it *vaiśvānara* which is used in such old Upaniṣads as ChU (V. 11. 12) and BU (V. 9. 1).[9] Now the author of NUTU, I where the entire MāU is quoted with some slight variants,[10] seeing both the words *viśva* in the kārikās and *vaiśvānara*[11] in the older Upaniṣads, has adopted both of them[12] and simplified the text to some extent.[13] As to why these two terms are taken together in NUTU and what is

[7] See pp. 223 ff., and D e u s s e n : *Upaniṣads des Veda*, p. 574.

[8] Excepting perhaps MU, VI. 7 which is not so old.

[9] On the greatness of Vaiśvānara see RV, I. 59. 6; 98. 1; Nt, VII. 21-23; BS, I. 2. 32.

[10] The MāU is almost entirely found also in NPTU, I.

[11] For a different view of Viśva-Vaiśvānara, Taijasa and Prājña *cf.* Īśvara and Prājña, Hiraṇyagarbha and Taijasa, and Vaiśvānara and Taijasa in PD, I. 16-29.

[12] Sthūlabhuk caturātmā viśvo vaiśvānaraḥ prathamaḥ pādaḥ.

[13] This is also with NPTU, I. For example, *sūkṣma* is substituted here for *pravivikta* in the kārikās. Here *sūkṣma* is undoubtedly simpler than *pravivikta*. For details the reader is referred to that Up.

their special significance is clearly shown by V i d y ā - r a ṇ y a in his ṭikā on it and in PD I. 28-29. See also VeS, § 17.

Similarly the three states, *jāgarita*, *svapna*, and *suṣupta* in the prose passages (3-4) are later additions from BU, or ChU, or both for a clear exposition of the terms *bahiṣprajña*, *antaḥprajña*, and *ghanaprajña* in kārikā 1.

That the MāU (*i.e.*, the prose passages) has drawn upon the kārikās and some other Upaniṣads can be gathered from the comparison of both the texts. In the kārikās we have simply *ghanaprajña* (1) and *ānandabhuj* (3) or *ānanda* (4), while the prose passage (5) reads as follows (see p. 224):

yatra supto na kañcana kāmaṃ kāmayate na kañcana svapnaṃ paśyati (BU, IV. 3. 9) tat suṣuptam. suṣuptasthāna ekībhūtaḥ[14] *prajñānaghana* (BU, IV. 5. 13) *evānandamayo* (TU, II. 5. 1) hy ānandabhuk cetomukhaḥ prājñas tṛtīyaḥ pādaḥ.

Which of these two, the kārikā and the prose passage, is the original, and which is the exposition, may now easily be ascertained.

The word *ghanaprajña* in the kārika is no doubt, identical with *prajñānaghana* in a somewhat different form, and to explain it the prose passage has introduced the word *ekībhūta* found, in fact, in the form of *ekībhavati* in different Upaniṣads.[15]

[14] *Cf. ekībhavati*, BU, 6. IV. 4. 2 (seven times). See PU IV. 2 (twice); NPTU. IV. 1; NUTU, I.

[15] See note 14.

The kārikā I. 19 runs thus:

viśvasyātvavivakṣāyām ādisāmānyam utkaṭam |
mātrāsampratipattau syād āptisāmānyam eva ca ||

And the corresponding prose passage (9) is this:

jāgaritasthāno vaiśvānaro 'kāraḥ prathamā mātrāpter ādimattvād vā. āpnoti ha vai sarvān kāmān ādiś ca bhavati ya evaṃ veda.

It means that Vaiśvānara whose sphere is the waking state is the first *mātrā* 'measure,' the letter *a*, on account of obtaining (or pervasiveness) or on account of its being the first (*āpter ādimattvād vā*). One who knows thus obtains one's all desires and becomes first of all.

Now, if these two texts are compared it will at once be clear that the second is merely the exposition of the first with a tinge of the language used in the Brāhmaṇas.

Here is one point more. In the first text the reason is advanced as to why Viśva (=Vaiśvānara of the second text) is to be regarded as the letter *a*. And the reason is *sāmānya* 'similarity'—similarity between Viśva and the letter *a*. And this similarity is 'beginning' (*ādi*) or 'obtaining' or 'pervasiveness' (*āpti*). Now, according to the order of Viśva, Taijasa and Prājña, Viśva is at the beginning or first (*ādi*); just so is at the beginning or first the letter *a* of *a*, *u* and *m* of which Om is composed. Owing to this similarity Viśva is said to be identical with the letter *a*. The second similarity is *āpti* which by Śaṅkara is thus explained: As Viśva pervades all the visible world, so does the letter *a* all the speech. On account of this similarity, too, Viśva is to be regarded as the letter *a*. The second text, however, gives a somewhat different explanation of this identity of Viśva and *a*. For, while the first text says that owing to *both* the similarities of *ādi* and *āpti* they are identical, the second text clearly says that it is owing to *either* of them (āpter ādimattvād vä).[16] All these seem to be later developments.

The case is exactly the same with kārikās 1. 20, 21 and the corresponding prose passages 10 and 11 of the Upaniṣad, to which the reader is referred.

There is one thing more to be noted with regard to the kārikā I. 21 and the corresponding prose passage 11 of the Upaniṣad. In the former one of the two similarities is *māna* 'measure' from √*mā* 'to measure' while in the latter the word is not *māna*, but *miti* 'measure' from √*mi*. Similarly, while in the former we have *apīti* 'disappearance' from *api-*√*i*, in the latter there is *laya* 'disappearance.' There is, however, no difference of meaning, as shown, in the two cases. Yet, how far such divergency between an original text and its explanation in Sanskrit can be accounted for is to be considered seriously.

The conception of *ātman* as having four fourths or quarters (*catuṣpād*) is not so explicit in the words of kārikās[17] as in those of the Upaniṣad, 2. This idea

16 One may, however, say that the word *vā* in the text may be taken in the sense of *ca* or *api*. But Śaṅkara or Śaṅkarānanda does not say so.

17 See I. 10-15 (where the fourth state is described), 24, and 29 (where Oṅkāra is described with or without *mātrā*).

is, however, fully developed in the Upaniṣad 2 from the very beginning. This fact also goes to show the priority of the kārikās.

The distinction between Turya or Turīya 'fourth' and the other three, *viz.*, Viśva, Taijasa and Prājña, as made in the kārikās (I. 10-15), has nothing corresponding in the Upaniṣad, but the nature of Turya, which is expressed in a kārikā (I. 29) simply by two words, *śiva* 'blissful' and *dvaita-upaśama* 'cessation of duality' is thus elaborated in two passages, 7 and 12, of the Upaniṣad:

(*i*) nāntaḥprajñaṃ na bahiṣprajñaṃ nobhayataḥprajñaṃ na prajñānaghanaṃ na prajñaṃ nāprajñam adṛṣṭam avyavahāryam agrāhyam alakṣaṇam acintyam avyapadeśyam ekātmapratyayasāraṃ prapañcopaśamaṃ śāntaṃ śivam advaitaṃ caturthaṃ manyante. sa ātmā sa vijñeyaḥ.

(*ii*) amātraś caturtho 'vyavahāryaḥ prapañcopaśamaḥ śivo 'dvaita evam oṅkāra ātmaiva. saṃviśaty ātmanātmānaṃ[18] ya evaṃ veda.

These two passages are mere amplification or exposition of what is briefly said in the kārikā, I. 29, and consequently appear to be later developments, as shows also the language used here.

Again, it is to be noted that though in the Upaniṣad (1) Brahman or Ātman is said to have four quarters (*catuṣpād*) which are explained there later on (3-6), there is no express mention of them in the kārikās which are supposed to be an explanatory work.

18 See VS, XXXII. 11 : ātmanātmānam abhisaṃviveśa.

Compare the kārikā I. 24 with the prose passage 8 of the Upaniṣad and it will be found that the former is explained in the latter in some detail and not *vice versa*.

The kārikā (I. 6) opening the discussion about the origin (*prabhava*) of all things may be connected with the last part of the passage 6 of the Upaniṣad: prabhavāpyayau hi bhūtānām.[19] Here *prabhava* is described in the kārikās I. 6-9 at some length, but *apyaya* 'disappearance' is not even touched in the kārikās. This would hardly be possible if the kārikās were meant to explain the Upaniṣad.

All these considerations lead me to conclude as follows:

(*i*) The kārikās in Book I are not the exposition (*vyākhyāna*) of the MāU.

(*ii*) The MāU is mainly based on the kārikās,[20] and not *vice versa*.

(*iii*) And as such the MāU is later than the kārikās.[21]

Here we must remember what Madhvācārya has said on the point. Serious charges may be and have been brought against him saying "that he is addicted to the fabrication of evidence and that he very frequently cites passages from books which do not and

19 It is taken from KU, II. 2.

20 It has drawn much also upon some older Upaniṣads as will be seen from the text printed herewith, pp. 223 ff.

21 See Max Walleser: *Der älter Vedānta*, p. 5. He says that the kārikās do not show that the Upaniṣad was before them.

did not at any time exist."[22] Or Appayya Dīkṣita in his *Madhvamatavidhvaṃsana* may give a list of such books, or may say of him :

tathāpy ānandatīrthīyaṃ matam agrāhyam eva naḥ |
yatra vaidikamaryādā bhūyasy ākulatāṃ gatā ||[23]

Or, again, most of the authorities cited by him in his commentary on the MāU may not be traced ; or one may or may not attach any value to the myth he has given us that Varuṇa having assumed the form of a frog received the *mantras*, *i.e.*, the kārikās originally visioned by Brahman, the creator ; yet, in the present case, we have to accept, as we have shown above, his view that the *mantras* or kārikās are older and on them is based our MāU.[24]

§ 3. *The Inter-relationship of the Four Books of the Āgamaśāstra*

It is generally held that the *Āgamaśāstra* has four *prakaraṇas* or Books, *viz.*, *Āgamaprakaraṇa*, *Vaitathya*°, *Advaita*°, and *Alātaśānti.*° Here arise the following questions : Are these Books, in fact, four parts of the same work, or are they four independent treatises compiled in one volume? Again, is it that

[22] A. Venkatasubbiah: IA, 1933, p. 189.

[23] See RPR, Vol. II, p. 51.

[24] This view was originally expressed by me long ago in IHQ, 1925, Vol. I, pp. 119-125, 295-302. Against this see S. K. Belvalkar's observation in his *Vedanta Philosophy* (Sreegopal Basu Mallik Lectures), Part I, pp. 192-193. But I do not think that the modification of my opinion is necessary.

while one or more of the Books form a work, the remaining one or ones constitute another work?

Śaṅkara, the commentator, with his followers, holds that the four Books are the different parts of the same work entitled *Āgamaśāstra*. And so, in order to show their mutual connexion first with reference to Books I and II, he writes just at the beginning of his commentary on Book II: "'When (the Reality) is known there is no duality'—This is already said (I. 18*d*),[1] and it is supported by such *śrutis* as 'There is only one without a second (ChāU, VI. 2. 1).' This is, however, only a statement of scripture (*āgamamātra*). With a view to showing that the unreality of duality can be established also by reasoning (*upapatti*) Book II is begun with the words '*vaitathyam*,' etc."

Now, as regards the relationship between Books II and III Ś observes (III. 1): "The determination of

[1] Ś could easily refer here also to I. 16, 17 and 29. Moreover, in the manner which he has adopted in showing the relationship between the first two Books the following might also be added in his favour, as in his opinion the *Āgamaprakaraṇa* begins with "Om ity etad akṣaram ity ādi," in other words, it includes the MāU. We read in the concluding kārikā (29) of Book I: dvaitasyopaśamaḥ śivaḥ, which is in fact the same as prapañcopaśamaṃ śāntaṃ śivaṃ and prapañcopaśamo 'dvaitaḥ of the MāU, 7 and 12 respectively. This very thing is re-assured in Book II. 35 by a phrase which is exactly the same in sense as the above, *i.e.*, prapañcopaśamo 'dvaitaḥ. Again, in I. 10 we have advaitaḥ sarvabhāvānām, and the same thing in one or other form is seen in many places in Book II: tasmād advayatā śivā (II. 33); advaite yojayet smṛtim (II. 36), advaitaṃ samanuprāpya (II. 36). *Cf.* here also advaitaṃ paramārtho hi (III. 18) And this truth is established there (II. 1 ff.) by strong reasons showing the unreality (*vaitathya*) of all things as in dream. Thus does it not show that these two Books are closely connected with each other?

Om is made only by a proposition (*pratijñāmātra*): 'The Ātman is the cessation of expression, blissful and without a second, (MāU, 12).' It is also said that 'When (the Reality) is known there is no duality' (I. 29). There in the Book called Non-reality (*vaitathya*), *i.e.*, II, the absence of duality is set forth by the illustrations of dream, magic, castle-in-air, etc. (II. 31), by reasons such as the 'capability of being seen' (*dṛśyatva*)[2] and 'the state of having the beginning and the end' (*ādyantavattva*),[3] and also by reasoning (*tarka*). Now, it is asked: Is it that non-duality can be understood only by scripture or also by reasoning?[4] The reply is: It can be done also by reasoning. How is it? For this Book III is begun."

Finally with reference to Book IV, Ś says in introducing it: "Through the determination of Om non-duality is proposed (*pratijñāta*). It is then established (*siddha*) by showing the non-reality of the different external objects (in Book II). Again, in Book III it is directly ascertained by scripture (*āgama*) and reasoning concluding that it is the highest truth (III. 48). At the end[5] it is hinted that the Dvaitins 'Dualists' and Vaināśikas 'Nihilists' are opposed to this view of non-duality which is the meaning of the scripture (*āgama*), and their views are wrong views as they cause such evil passions as attachment and aversion, on

2 Where is it in Book II?

3 II. 7.

4 advaitaṃ kim āgamamātreṇa pratipattavyam āhosvit tarkeṇāpi.

5 In fact, it is not 'at the end' (*ante*), nor is it in any of the original kārikās. It is the commentator's *own* observation. See the commentary on II. 7.

account of their mutual contradiction. As there is no place of evil passions in it, the view of non-duality is the right view, and as such it is praised. Now, here (in Book IV) having shown in details that their views are not right being mutually contradictory they are to be thrown away, and by doing so the establishment of the view of non-duality is to be concluded by the method of inference called *avīta*[6] 'negative.' For this, (the Book called) 'The Cessasion of the Fire-brand' is begun."

Let us now examine the above statement of Ś. By his observation regarding the connexion between Books I and II, he wants to mean that though it is said in Book I that there is no duality, yet, it is merely an expression of *āgama*, no reason being offered there in its favour. And so in order to support it by reasons Book II is written. But is it really so? Is it that there is no reasoning at all in Book I? None can give the answer in the affirmative. Certainly various reasons are advanced in Book II, but it cannot be said that Book I is altogether conspicuous by their absence. For, they are to be clearly found in kārikās 16-18, though not to that extent as in Book II. Here arises a question: If the connexion between Books I and II is really as it is shown by Ś to be, then why is it that the author of Book II himself does not say so just at its beginning, though he could do so easily? But instead of doing this he begins it without any reference to Book I, only alluding to the

6 Ānandagiri unnecessarily takes it as *āvīta* saying that *āvīta* is nothing but *avīta*.

opinion of the wise that all things in dream are unreal. He could also write here that the determination of Om is through the realization of non-duality which depends on the unreality of external things, which is dealt with in Book II. But he has not done so.

Let us consider here another point. We have already seen that in accordance with some teachers such as Madhvācārya, the MāU is composed of the twelve prose passages and the twenty-nine kārikās in Book I. It is quite clear from it that, in their opinion, the work is a complete one having no connexion with any of the remaining three Books of the ĀŚ. This view seems to be confirmed by the fact that its subject matter, *i.e.*, the determination of Om, is here dealt with completely, as one can easily understand from the last two kārikās of Book I, after reading which one does not feel that anything more remains to be further discussed and elucidated; and, in fact, we see nothing directly of Om in the following Book or Books. Thus it follows that the treatise consisting of the kārikās of Book I has no relationship to any of the Books that follow. It is also to be noted here that the views of the teachers referred to above cannot be ignored altogether.

Further, if Book II is a continuation of Book I, it could be expected that the former should somehow or other presuppose the latter. But does it do so? If so, where? Moreover, what does one lose if one takes Book II as an independent work on the *advaita* Vedānta? Does one find in reading this Book in that light anything improper, non-sensical or unintelligible without assuming its connexion with Book I? Or does one really feel that without Book I it appears to be incomplete?[7] That it is complete in itself will be clear if we attentively read at least the concluding portion of it, *i.e.*, kārikās 35-38.

Now with regard to the connexion between Books II and III let us remember what Ś says. His words, put briefly, would amount to this that non-duality can be understood not only by *āgama*, but by reasoning (*tarka*) as well. Consequently to exhibit the reasoning Book III is required. If that is so, we shall have to accept that according to Ś the object of both the Books II and III is one and the same, *i.e.*, giving the arguments for non-duality. In that case, why should there be two separate Books instead of one in which all could be included? This leads one to think of a different object for which Book III must have been written. And what this object was will be clear if one examines the contents with some amount of care. Here at the beginning (III. 1-2) the author tells us about 'non-origination' (*ajāti*) and having established it concludes in the end(III. 48) that it is the highest truth (*uttama satya*). In doing so he discusses the Vedānta, and in that connexion the absence of difference between Jīva and Brahman. He treats also of a *samādhi* 'intense abstract concentration' called *asparśayoga* meant for the realization of the Truth.

It is not that there is no mention of non-duality in this

[7] These questions with necessary modifications here and there should be put in discussing the relationship also of the following Books.

Book. It is there (III. 18),[8] but only incidentally, and as such is not discussed. But can one say rightly that because of the mention of non-duality in this Book, Books II and III must have some direct connexion between them? If so, is it not that there will be no difficulty whatsoever in finding out a relationship between any two works on the same subject? But that relationship will certainly not be as that between the different chapters of the same work. It is to be noted that Ś himself has not suggested such relationship. Thus it appears to me that there is nothing against one's thinking that Book III, too, is an independent work on *advaita* Vedānta.

We now come to Book IV. It has already been seen how Ś wants to connect it with the preceding Books. He assumes that the views of Dvaitins and Vaināśikas[9] are to be shown in details[10] in this Book as wrong, and by doing so the conclusion is to be established that the theory of non-duality is right. First, we are to examine here as to how far this assertion can be accepted. Let us take for granted that, as he says, owing to their mutual contradiction the views of the Dvaitins and the Vaināśikas are wrong and this is to be shown *in detail* in this Book. But where and how much is it done? Dvaitins are referred to by the word *vādins* 'disputants' only in two places (IV. 3 and 6); but even there in

8 Book III. 18 : advaitaṃ paramārtho hi. See Book I. 17 : advaitaṃ paramārthataḥ.

9 See III. 17.

10 Com. on IV. 1 : tad iha vistareṇa anyonyaviruddhatayā asamyagdarśanatvaṃ pradarśya, tatpratiṣedhenādvaitadarśanasiddhir upasaṃhartavyā.

the first place, though only their mutual contradiction is simply referred to, no detail of it is to be found. There is no allusion to Vaināśikas in this Book. But if by that word the Buddhists are meant, no mutual contradiction with the Dvaitins, (or among themselves,) is to be found of their views. On the contrary, the author of the ĀŚ has accepted or approved of them throughout the Book as the present writer has attempted to show. How is it then that in accordance with Ś, one can expect to understand from this Book that the views of the Dvaitins and the Vaināśikas are wrong and the view of non-duality is right? Thus one can hardly connect in this way the present Book with the preceding one or ones. We should also remember here the questions that have already been put in discussing the relationship between Books I and II. See p. lii.

Is there then no relationship of any kind between Books IV and others? How can it be so? Certainly there is a relationship and it is rather a close one, as the following lines will show. A careful reader will see that a large number of expressions in various forms in the first three Books are literally quoted or alluded to in Book IV. And it will be noticed that some matters dealt with in the former are done so again in the latter. For instance, I. 16[c] = III. 36[a] = IV. 81[a]; II. 6-7 = IV. 31-32[11]; (*cf.* II. 1, 4 with IV. 33, and II. 2 with IV. 34[12]); III. 20-22 = IV. 6-8[13]; III. 29-30

11 See III. 2, 48; IV. 4, 5.

12 The second half is, however, identical.

13 Here is a slight variation, and it is that for the word *bhāva* in the former there is *dharma* in the latter with regard to the first and the last kārikās.

=IV. 61-62[14]; III. 48=IV. 71. Besides, such expressions or topics as the following are to be found in more than one Book: *jñeyābhinna jñāna* 'the knowledge is not different from the knowable' is in III. 33 and IV. 1; *ajātivāda* 'the theory of non-origination' in III. 2 ff and IV. 3 ff. Such being the case it must be accepted that Book IV is rather closely related to other Books.

But this relationship is not such as between a work and its different chapters on the following grounds:

With reference to later Sanskrit works it is a well-known practice that their commencement is with a *maṅgalācaraṇa* 'prayer for success' which includes a *namaskāra* 'paying homage' to one for whom the authors have regard. Now, as we have at the very beginning of Book IV a kārikā embodying *maṅgalācaraṇa*, it naturally induces one to think that it is not a chapter of any work, but itself an independent work.

It is, however, true that *maṅgalācaraṇa* is found not only at the commencement of a work, but also in other places of it, as in the case of the *Nyāyakandalī* of Śrīdhara on the *Praśastapādabhāṣya*, or of the *Sañjīvanī* of Mallinātha on the *Raghuvaṃśa*. But it is to be noted here that in such cases it is done in each of the chapters, and not in any particular one, whereas in the present case, here in ĀŚ we have it

[14] With the following variations: For spandate māyayā manaḥ in III there is cittaṃ calati māyayā in IV, and for *manaḥ* in III there is *cittam* in IV.

only in Book IV, so far as the extant editions and the MSS that are examined can show.[15] Here we may remember a Buddhist work, *viz.*, the *Pañjikā* of Prajñākaramati on the *Bodhicaryāvatāra*. It consists of nine chapters. Here the *maṅgalācaraṇa* is *only* in the first[16] and the last chapters, and not in others. Evidently the *maṅgalācaraṇa* at the beginning of its chapter IX does not mean to say that it is an independent work. Considering the contents of this chapter of both the *Bodhicaryāvatāra* and its *Pañjikā*, which deal with *prajñāpāramitā*, it appears to me that the only thing that can be said is this that the *maṅgalācaraṇa* of the *Pañjikā* simply suggests a special importance of both the works, the *Pañjikā* and the BA. Thus the *maṅgalācaraṇa* of Book IV cannot conclusively show that it is an independent work and not the continuation of the preceding ones. But here is a thing which should not be left unnoticed. Both at the beginning and at the end of Book IV there is a *maṅgalācaraṇa* in the form of *namaskāra* 'paying homage.' Does it not imply that the Book is an independent work and complete in itself?

Let us discuss here another point. We have already seen that a number of kārikās in Books II and III

15 We have some ground to think that at the beginning of Book I a few kārikās are now missing. It is not improbable that there was a *maṅgalācaraṇa* in those kārikās.

16 As the first folio of the MS, the basis of the present edition (Bibliotheca Indica) of BAP is lost, and the second one, in some parts illegible, is broken down, the beginning lines of BAP could not be printed. Hence it could not be ascertained from the edition as to whether there is any *maṅgalācaraṇa* at the beginning. Yet, from its Tibetan version we know that it actually exists.

are repeated in Book IV. Why is this repetition? Moreover, certain things treated of before are discussed again in Book IV; *e.g.*, *ajātivāda* 'theory of non-origination' discussed in III is discussed again in IV. But why? A point discussed and settled once in a chapter may, if necessary, be alluded to in a subsequent chapter, but why should it be discussed and settled again? Is it not useless? Why should the author of Book IV indulge in such a useless action? This leads one to think that Book IV is an independent work in which the author has incorporated certain things that are already dealt with by him elsewhere, while others are discussed again more elaborately or in a different way. The discussion of the *ajātivāda* is an instance on the point.

Thus we arrive at the conclusion that these four Books are four independent treatises and are put together in a volume under the title of the *Āgamaśāstra*.

§ 4. *The Text of the Āgamaśāstra*

We are now to discuss a few points regarding the text of the ĀŚ, as we have now in the extant editions and the MSS examined for them. Here arises a question: Is it that the text is a complete one? It seems to me that the answer cannot be given in the affirmative. It will at once occur to the mind of a reader that the first kārikā of Book I has found its place there quite abruptly. Without any reference to the three states, waking, dreaming and deep sleep as described in the prose passages of the MāU this kārikā is not intelligible.[1] It appears therefore that one or more kārikās here are missing.[2]

It may be said that as in Book IV,[3] so here, too, at the beginning of Book I, a *maṅgalācaraṇa* is expected, but it is not found. Hence it appears that originally at least one kārikā was composed here for it, but subsequently somehow or other it was lost. This point of *maṅgalācaraṇa* cannot, however, be much insisted upon. For, in the time of the author of the ĀŚ this practice of *maṅgalācaraṇa* was not so much persisted in as in later days. The great Ś a ṅ k a r a , the author of the *Śārīraka-bhāṣya*, does not follow it, so far as his undisputed works are concerned.[4] So it may be that the author did not like it at the beginning of Book I, though he actually followed it in Book IV. Thus this point is not of much importance.

Let one read kārikās 5 and 6 and say if there is any connexion between them. Kārikā 6 seems to have come here all of a sudden. The commentator Ś is silent here on their mutual connexion. Does this not lead one

1 This fact should not, however, be taken as a reason for supposing the priority of the MāU to the kārikās refuted elsewhere on strong grounds.

2 According to also those who hold that the kārikās of G a u ḍ a p ā d a are written as an explanation (*vyākhyāna*) of the MāU, one might naturally expect at the beginning some words to that effect, but they are not found. In accordance with this theory also at least one kārikā is lost here.

3 The commentary on the *Sāṅkhyakārikā* may also be added here, but it is not quite certain that its author and the author of ĀŚ, though both of them are known by the same name, G a u ḍ a p ā d a , are identical.

4 It is disputed that the beginning ślokas of the commentary on the TU, which go by his name are actually written by him

to think that a kārikā or kārikās are missing here? They might have been in existence in the time of the commentator, and possibly they were commented upon by him, but all this was lost afterwards.

Undoubtedly Om is one of the subject matters of Book I which consists of 29 kārikās, but until kārikā 19 there is no mention whatsoever of the word. This does not seem to be quite proper. And here is one thing more to be borne in mind; it is this that without a knowledge of the fact that Om can be analysed into *a*, *u*, and *m* this kārikā (19) can hardly be understood, so one expects here something like the prose passage 8 of the MāU.

With reference to some of the karikās it appears to me that their original order has been somehow or other changed, so that their proper elucidation has been difficult. Let us take kārikā II. 33. I am afraid, it does not fit well here after kārikā II. 32. Its right place seems to be after II. 30. Similarly in Book IV kārikās 38, 39, 40 and 41 appear to be 40, 38, 41 and 39 respectively, as is discussed in a foot-note on p. 146.

As regards IV. 77, it seems to me that between its two lines at least two more lines are lost, as will be seen from the discussion on p. 184, to which the reader is referred.

This consideration coupled with that of the variants that are supported by Ś in his commentary, as I have discussed in their places, shows that the original text of the ĀŚ of G a u ḍ a p ā d a underwent some serious changes at least by the time of Ś, if not ealier.

§ 5. *Readings of the Text*

We may now speak here a few words with regard to the readings of the ĀŚ. The collation[1] of the MSS referred to above as well as of the different editions of the work has resulted in showing or suggesting true or better readings in many cases, which have mainly been discussed under the kārikās concerned, giving the grounds for the readings adopted. There are, however, other cases where I have not offered my reasons for selecting a particular reading, as they can easily be understood by the reader himself. Below will be found, for example, some notable readings that are chosen or suggested :

1. *dve tu* (I. 11^{d}) for *dvau tu*.

2. *saṃvṛtatvaṃ* na (II. 4^{d}) for *saṃvṛtatvena*.

3. *'pi pratipadyate* (II. 7^{d}) for *vipratipadyate*. See IV. 32^{b}.

4. *'vyavasthitān* (II. 13^{b}) for *vyavasthitān*.

5. *nānyabhāvena* (II. 34^{a}) for *nātmabhāvena*.

6. *sa-yathā* (III. 11^{d}) for *kham yathā*.

7. *yad a*° (IV. 12^{a}) for *yady a*°. As we have *yadi* in ^{b}, it cannot again be expected in *a*; nor can it, in that case, be construed properly. Besides, the reading *yad a*° is actually found in V^{g}.

8. *'nādiḥ* (IV. 23^{a}) for *'nādeḥ*, and *jātir*$^{(d)}$ supported by PU^{1} for *hy ādir*.

9. *saṃsāro nopalabhyate* (IV. 56^{d}) supported by A^{1} and IO for *saṃsāraṃ na prapadyate*.

[1] For a detailed account see Appendix II, Variants, pp. 229-244.

10. *svabhāvena* (IV. 57[a]) for *sadbhāvena*.

11. *saṃvṛtyā* (IV. 58[b]) supported by V[u] and Ś for *jāyante*.

12. *paratantro 'bhi°* (IV. 73[c]) for *paratantrābhi°*.

13. *paratantro 'bhi°* (IV. 74[c]) for *paratantrābhi°*.

14. *dharmadhātūḥ svabhāvataḥ* (IV. 81[d]) for *dharmo dhātusva°*.

§ 6. *The Name of the Work*

The present work popularly known as *Māṇḍūkya-kārikā* (or *°kārikās*) or *Gauḍapādakārikā* (or *°kārikās*) is traditionally called *Āgamaśāstra*. It is owing to this fact that the commentary on it by Ś is called *Āgamaśāstra-vivaraṇa*.[1] Sometimes it is named also *Āgamagrantha* or *Upadeśagrantha* as some of the colophons show (p. 244), occasionally both of these names are used together (*loc. cit*). It is also called or described as *Māṇḍūkyavārttika*,[2] or *Māṇḍūkyopaniṣad-gauḍapāda-vyākhyāna*, or *Gauḍapādīyakārikā*, or simply *Gauḍa-pādīya* after its author, as is shown by some MSS. Again, sometimes it is referred to as *Māṇḍūkyaśākhā*.[3]

[1] See the Colophons, pp. 231, 234, 236, 244.

[2] The word *vārttika* is not properly used here, as the present work has not the characteristics of a *vārttika*, for a *vārttika* is said to be a work which criticizes what is said, what is not said, and what is said wrongly in the original work, as says R ā j a ś e k h a r a in his *Kāvyamīmāṃsā*, GOS, No. I, 1916, II. p. 5: uktānuktaduruktacintā vārttikam.

[3] S ā y a ṇ a on TA, VII. 1 (p. 483); VII. 2 (p. 570):

māyāmātram idaṃ dvaitam advaitaṃ paramārthataḥ |
iti māṇḍūkyaśākhāyāṃ śrutivākyam udāhṛtam ||

Here I. 17 of our text is referred to. For other two namas see § 1, note 8, p. xxxv.

It may be noticed here that two MSS, D[1] and D[2], describe the work as *Vedāntamūla* 'origin of the Vedānta' which is very significant.

Now let us discuss as to why this book is called *Āgamaśāstra*. The word *āgama* among other things means 'a traditional doctrine' or 'anything handed down and fixed by tradition'; and *śāstra* gives the sense in such cases as the present one, of 'a religious or authoritative treatise.'[4] Thus the compound word, *Āgamaśāstra*, means a *śāstra* pertaining to *āgama*, *i.e.*, authoritative treatise which deals with or is based on a traditional doctrine or doctrines. That the *Āgamaśāstra* is in fact of such character is fully borne out throughout the book itself, as the following few lines will show.

Besides the general meaning 'to remember' the root √*smṛ* figuratively means also 'to hand down *memoriter*, declare,' and so its past participial form *smṛta* is used in the sense of 'handed down *memoriter*, or declared, mentioned,' etc. Thus the sentence *śāstre smṛtam* means 'it is handed down *memoriter* or declared in a scripture.' And though the subject of the sentence is not expressed in this or similar cases, it is easily understood, it being a teacher or teachers or a similar person or

For *āgama* see MV, pp. 268-9. For the Buddhist interpretation of the word *śāstra* one may be referred to MVST, p. 4 from which the following is quoted here :

yac chāsti ca kleśaripūn aśeṣān santrāyate durgatito bhayāc ca |
tac chāsanāt trāṇaguṇāc ca śāstram° ||

It is quoted also in MV, p. 3. For a description of *śāstras* see Rājaśekhara, *Op. cit.*, II. For the significance and importance of the word *śāstra* (Tibetan *bstan.bcos*, Chinese *lun*) mark its use in Nāgārjuna's fundamental work, *Madhyamakaśāstra*.

persons who may or may not have been mentioned before. Now with regard to our case the word *smṛta* is employed by our author not less than eleven times.[5] This fact clearly shows that our author refers to or deals with some doctrine or doctrines handed down traditionally. This is clear also from his employment of the following phrases in the work :

1. satām iti viniścayaḥ (I. 6); 2. svapna āhur manīṣiṇaḥ (II. 2); 3. svapna āhuḥ prakāśitam (II. 3); 4. evam āhur manīṣiṇaḥ (II. 5); 5. dṛṣṭaṃ vedānteṣu vicakṣaṇaiḥ (II. 31); 6. iti tattvavido viduḥ (II. 34); 7. °munibhir vedapāragaiḥ | nirvikalpo hy ayaṃ dṛṣṭaḥ prapañcopaśamo 'dvayaḥ || (II. 35); 8. vādinaḥ kecid (II. 3); 9. vivadanto 'dvayā hy evam ajātiṃ khyāpayanti te (IV. 4); 10. khyāpyamānām ajātiṃ taiḥ (IV. 5); 11. jātim icchanti vādinaḥ (IV. 6).[6]

§ 7. *The Author*

We have already seen,[1] as the great Śaṅkara says in his commentary on the BS, I. 4. 14 and II. 1. 9, that the work was by an Ācārya 'teacher' to whom the tradition of the Vedānta was known. But the question

[5] I. 1, 20, 26; II. 4. 7; III. 1; IV. 32, 46, 88, 90, 94.

[6] Besides, the following words may be referred to here: 1. *anya* (I. 7); 2. *apara* (II. 26); 3. *āśramavid* (II. 27); 4. *kālacintaka* (I. 8); 5. *kālavid* (II. 24); 6 *guṇavid* (II. 20); 7. *cittavid* (II. 25); 8. *(dig-) vid* (II. 24); 9. *pādavid* (II. 21); 10. *prāṇavid* (II. 20); 11. *buddhivid* (II. 25); 12. *(bhuvana-)vid* (II. 24); 13. *(bhūta-)vid* (II. 20); 14. *bhoktṛvid* (II. 22); *(bhojya-)vid* (II. 22); 15. *manovid* (II. 25); 16. *mūrtavid* (II. 23); 17. *(laya-) vid* (II. 28); 18. *lokavid* (II. 21); 19. *sūkṣmavid* (II. 23); 20. *sṛṣṭivid* (II. 28); 20. *sthitivid* (II 28

[1] See *supra*, § I, notes 5 and 6, p. xxxiv

is: who is that Ācārya? That he is Gauḍapāda[2] is well-known traditionally and found in the colophons of each of the four Books in MSS of the original and its commentary. He is sometimes called Gauḍapādācārya,[3] Gauḍācārya,[4] or simply Gauḍa.[5] From this we may think that his real name is Gauḍa, the words *-pāda*, *-pada*, *-caraṇa*, or *-ācārya* being added to it simply as honorific.[6] That his actual name is Gauḍa is stated very clearly by Bālakṛṣṇānanda Sarasvatī (middle of the 17th century A.D.) in his SMV, p. 6, ll. 9-12.

Now the question arises: Is the word Gauḍa his personal name or does it simply signify that he belongs to a country called Gauḍa?[7] In Sureśvara's NSi, IV. 44, there are two words, *Gauḍas* and *Drāviḍas*, which refer to Gauḍapādācārya, the author of the present work and the great Śaṅkarācārya, the author of the *Upadeśasāhasrī*, respectively, according

[2] Sometimes we have Gauḍapada (JM, 10) and Gauḍacaraṇa (SMV, p. 5, l. 23), most probably for metrical exigency.

[3] Ś on ŚU, I. 8 (p. 30).

[4] PD, II. 23; Sāyaṇa on TA, VII. 2 (p. 565).

[5] NSi, IV. 44.

[6] A Venkatasubbiah (IA, 1933, p. 193) is of the same opinion.

[7] There is evidence to show that the country called *Gauḍadeśa* was once regarded as the land between 82° and 88° longitude and 25° and 28° latitude along with the adjacent districts of North Bengal (*Matsya P.*, XII. 30; *Kūrma P.*, Part I, 20-9; *Liṅga P.*, Part I, l. 65, 34; JASB, 1908, pp. 273 ff.) Recent researches show that the country is identical with North Bengal. See Haranchandra Chakladar: *Annals of the Bhandarkar Oriental Research Institute*, Vol. III, Part I, pp. 43 ff.

to the commentator, J ñ ā n o t t a m a .[8] It may be said that as Ś a ṅ k a r a is referred to by a name related to his native country, Draviḍa (*i.e.*, Kerala, the modern Malabar), and not by a personal name, so the case must have been the same with G a u ḍ a p ā d a ; in other words, he, too, must have been alluded to by a name connected with his country which is Gauḍa. Otherwise, why should S u r e ś v a r a mention him in a different way?

W a l l e s e r (*op. cit.*, p. 3) is of opinion that by the two words of S u r e ś v a r a , *Gauḍas* and *Drāviḍas*, we are to understand two Vedantic schools. If we are to know by the word *Drāviḍas* a school founded by Ś a ṅ k a r a in Malabar (the representative work of which is here said to be the *Upadeśasāhasrī*), we must take also the *Gauḍas* as a native school established in North India in the land of Gauḍas,[9] which might have already been much advanced in culture. It is, however, immaterial, to my mind, to discuss as to whether the words actually refer to the two

[8] It may be noticed here that in the second edition (*Bombay Sanskrit Series*, No. XXXVIII, 1906) of the NSi occurs the following line in J ñ ā n o t t a m a ' s commentary on IV. 44: kevalānām api drāviḍatva-prasiddheḥ. Seeing this the editor, C o l o n e l G . A . J a c o b writes in his notes (p. 247): "Who are the *kevalas* referred to in the commentary?" The fact is that the word *kevala* is wrongly written, or read, or printed for *Kerala*, the ancient name of the country. The same mistake occurs also in the revised edition (1926) of the book, p. 193.

[9] W a l l e s e r thinks that the country might have been so named owing to much cultivation of sugar-cane (*guḍa*). *Cf.* the word *puṇḍra* for North Bengal, which also means 'sugar-cane' (of red variety).

representative teachers or to the two schools represented by them, both the interpretations being equally possible.

It may be pointed out here that merely the word *Gauḍa* cannot invariably refer to one who is an inhabitant of the Gauḍadeśa. One may not actually be an inhabitant of it, yet, may be regarded as a Gauḍa. A b h i n a n d a , the author of the *Yogavāsiṣṭhasāra* or *Laghuyogavāsiṣṭha*, though a Kashmirian, is called Gauḍa. Similarly B r a h m ā n a n d a , the well-known author of the *Laghucandrikā*, though not born in Gauḍadeśa, has the epithet *Gauḍa*, probably as he was educated in Gauḍadeśa, Bengal, being, as is said, a fellow student of G a d ā d h a r a B h a ṭ ṭ ā c ā r y a . One who has any connexion, past, present, or future, in respect of oneself or one's ancestors, with the Gauḍadeśa may be a Gauḍa. On this one may be referred to MD, I. 3. 23 with Ś a b a r a s v ā m i n ' s commentary in which it is said that a man who has set out for the city of Mathurā is regarded as a Māthura; similarly one who lives in the city of Mathurā, or one who has come out from the city of Mathurā is also called a Māthura.[10]

With regard to our author we should remember here the views of B ā l a k ṛ ṣ ṇ ā n a n d a S a r a s v a t i already once referred to. He writes (SMB, p. 6, ll. 9-12): There was in the country of Kurukṣetra a river

[10] mathurāyām abhiprasthito māthura iti mathurāyām vasan mathurāyā nirgataś ca.

called Hirarāvatī.[11] On its banks there were some Gauḍa people, the pre-eminent of whom was our author, and as he was absorbed in deep meditation beginning from the *Dvāpara* age, his special name is not known to modern people and so he is celebrated by the general one.[12]

Let us notice here the observations made by Walleser (*op. cit.*, pp. 6 ff.). He thinks there was none named Gauḍapāda who is believed to have been the author of the present work. By the word *Gauḍa-pādas* we are to understand the four Books (*prakaraṇas*) of the work and *Gauḍapādīyakārikā* is the name for the whole work, as found in MSS. This last title seems to be somewhat artificial and it can be guessed that the work was commonly known as *Gauḍapādī* in the same way as the provincial expression *Bhadracarī* for *Bhadracaryā*. In fact both the titles *Gauḍapādī* and *Āgamaśāstravivaraṇa* have been shown by C. F. Hall in one of his contributions.[13] Walleser says further that the quotations from later works correspond to his opinion that no teacher known as Gauḍapāda was the author of the book, but it

[11] It remains to be identified. It is doubtful if the name is correctly written by the scribe of the MS or read or edited accurately by the editors.

[12] gauḍacaraṇāḥ kurukṣetradeśagata-hirarāvatī-nadītīrabhavagauḍajātiśreṣṭhaḥ deśaviśeṣabhavajātināmnaiva prasiddhāḥ. dvāparayugam ārabhyaiva samādhiniṣṭhatvenādhunikajanair aparijñātaviśeṣābhidhānāḥ sāmānyanāmnaiva lokavikhyātāḥ.

[13] Such practice is still very common in the country; *e.g.*, *Vidyāsagarī*, a ṭīkā by Ānandapūrṇa Vidyāsāgara on the *Khaṇḍanakhaṇḍakhādya*; *Rāmabhadrī*, a ṭīkā on the *Nyāyakusumāñjali* by Rāmabhadra; so are *Dinakarī*, *Rāmarudrī*, etc. etc.

existed among the contemporary people as a fundamental work of a school and not as a production of a definite author. He shows from the Tibetan sources[14] that though the work was known to the Buddhist authors as a *Vedāntaśāstra* in which the doctrines of the school are explained, nothing is known there of Gauḍapāda who is supposed to have composed it. Śaṅkara in his *Śārīrakabhāṣya* quotes twice, as shown above, from the work referring to our author (or authors) as those to whom was known the tradition of the Vedānta (*vedāntārthasampradāyavid* or simply *sampradāyavid*). The commentator, Govindānanda in his *Ratnaprabhā* and Ānandagiri in his *Nyāyanirṇaya* introduce the above opinion of Śaṅkara as the 'approval of the old' (*vṛddhasammati*, BS, I. 4. 14 and II. 1. 9). Sureśvara has quoted two kārikās (NSi, IV. 41, 42; our text I. 11 and 15 respectively) mentioning their author as Gauḍas (*gauḍaiḥ*),[15] while he takes Śaṅkara as the representative of the Drāviḍa tradition. In the commentary on the NSi Jñānottara describes the quoted passages as *gauḍapādīya-vākya*. We have already seen in the PD (II. 28) the *Gauḍa* teaching, but the commentator, Rāmakṛṣṇa, does not know

14 That is, the Tibetan translations of Śāntirakṣita's *Madhyamakalaṅkārakārikā* together with its commentary by Kamalaśīla, as well as of Bhāvaviveka's *Madhyamakahṛdayakārikā* and its commentary *Tarkajvālā* by himself *Vide infra*.

15 It is, however, not true that Sureśvara never mentions the name *Gauḍapāda*, for he uses it at least for once in his BBV, IV. 4. 886 (p. 1866). In the same work he has also used the words *gauḍapādīya vacas* (I. 4. 389, p. 510) and *gauḍācārya* (II. 1. 386, p. 951).

the author, he describes the passage quoted as *ācārya-*[16] *sammati*. Sadānanda quotes in his VeS, § 33, two kārikās, III. 44, 45, referring as *tad uktam*, and Nṛsiṃha Sarasvatī, the commentator, does not name their author simply alluding to them as *vṛddhasammati* 'the opinion of the old.' Rāmatīrtha, another commentator, says that it is a contemporary opinion. Again, if we examine Kāśmīraka Yati, the author of the *Advaitabrahmasiddhi* (p. 277) we find no evidence that the *Gauḍapādakarika* was known to him as a work of a single author. Vijñānabhikṣu has quoted kārikās (II. 32, III. 5, 26) from the work in his *Sāṅkhyapravacanabhāṣya*, (I. 45, 47; 153; VI. 50). But there is nothing to show that Gauḍapāda was taken to be their author. Walleser thus says that not a single passage[17] can be quoted from all these texts which can make us believe that *Gauḍapādī* had Gauḍapāda as its author. We are told that Śaṅkara received instruction from Govinda who was a disciple of Gauḍapāda with whom the former had a conversation and he had another conversation with Vyāsa himself. The same sort of contradiction is found also with regard to the residence of Govinda; one source gives it as the banks of the Narmadā and the other the Himālayas. This sort of things does not give us a historical clue.

[16] Not *vṛddha-*, as writes Walleser.

[17] Excepting, as he himself has pointed out, one passage from Ś's commentary on the ŚU, I. 8, where the following line occurs: tathā ca śukaśiṣyo gauḍapādācāryaḥ. But that the commentary is not by the great Ś is the view not only of Walleser but also of others including the present author.

W a l l e s e r thus finally observes that the whole tradition is fabulous, and with this the last of the arguments in favour of the authorship of *Gauḍapādī* by a certain G a u ḍ a p ā d a vanishes. And as one could not explain the word *Gauḍapādī* one imagined a fictitious G a u ḍ a p ā d a . Now he adds that for the history of Vedānta we can gather from the preceding discussion that in a time considerably before the activities of Ś a ṅ k a r a there existed a philosophical school in the country of Gauḍa and in the same district in which Buddhism flourished till the eighth century. This school for the first time put the traditions of the Vedas and Upaniṣads in the form of a *śāstra, i.e.*, a school doctrine and embodied it in a collection of sayings (*Spruchsummlung*) consisting of the four *pādas* of the *Gauḍapādakārikā*. Already in the time of Ś a ṅ k a r a this text, the only older Vedānta text which has been preserved and perhaps the only one which was ever produced, enjoys high consideration quite independently of legendary traditions which connect Ś a ṅ k a r a with G o v i n d a and Ś u k a with G a u ḍ a p ā d a . The existence of the North Indian school at the beginning of the century preceding Ś a ṅ k a r a seems well-established.

We are, however, to consider here the following without entering into a hair-splitting discussion. There is a text before us known as the *Āgamaśāstra* or *Gauḍapādakārikā*, or passing under any other similar name; and of this text there must be an author. There may, however, be more than one author. The work may represent the view of the predominant school of a particular people. But can we only for this reason think that it is the production of the whole people of the land? When a very prominent man of a country pronounces something in public, it may be regarded as the opinion of the country itself, and not as his personal view, though he may not consult the people of the country before doing so. In the same way, it appears to me, that the present work is by one person and yet, it represents the views of the entire country to which he belonged. But who is that person? He is one Gauḍa. When there is no contradiction nor any incongruity, why should we not accept the tradition, as far as possible? Thus, as we have already seen, the actual name of the author is Gauḍa, or with the honorific word *-pāda* or *ācārya* added to it Gauḍapāda, or Gauḍācārya.

Much could be known of any author from the old records on which naturally one inclines to depend for ascertaining the truth. But they are so fantastic and self contradictory in the present case that it is almost impossible to find out the truth from them.[18] These

[18] On their unreliability observes S. K. Belvalkar in his *Vedānta Philosophy*, Poona, 1929, pp. 231-232: "while all the other so-called Prācīna, Bṛhat, or Keralīya Śaṅkaravijayas are prejudiced in favour of one or the other Pontifical See, and so contain almost shameless tampering of traditions and documents which is provable to the hilt even by the accusations on the score of falsification of records which each party finds it possible to bring against the other. When such is the case of the avowed followers of the School, it need hardly be wondered at if the pronounced opponents belonging to the Mādhva and the Rāmānujīya Schools have gone one better, and indulged in a merciless throwing of mud in the hope that some of it might stick."

records are the accounts of the life of the great Śaṅkara and those who were connected with him in some way or other.[19] Readers desirous of knowing these legendary accounts of Gauḍapāda are referred to those works themselves which are to be used very cautiously.

§ 8. *The Date of Gauḍapāda*

Now let us discuss the date of our author, and in doing so we shall begin from one of the old accounts of the school already referred to, *viz.*, JM, in which Gauḍapāda is mentioned as having some connexion with a few Greeks. It is said there (10)[1] that the feet of Gauḍapāda were adored by Ayārcya, and he was the preceptor of such Niṣāka mystics as Apalūnya. Here Ātmabodhendra, the commentator, adds something on the authority of such works as *Gauḍapādollāsa* of Harimiśra, and *Patañjalivijaya* (=°*carita*? of Rāmabhadra Dīkṣita). He writes that when Gauḍapāda on a peak of the Himālayas was seeking after the truth of the self under the guidance

[19] Gopinath Kavirāj singles out the following books in his learned Introduction (in Hindī) to the *Brahmasūtras* published from the Acyuta Press, Benares, 1936, pp. 26 ff: (1) *Śaṅkaradigvijaya* of Mādhavācārya (not of Vidyāraṇya), (2) *Śaṅkaravijaya* of Ānandagiri, (3) *Śaṅkarābhyudaya* of Rājacūḍāmaṇi, (4) *Śaṅkaravijaya* of Cidvilāsa, (5) *Śaṅkaravijaya* of Sadānanda, (6) *Puṇyaślokamañjarī* of Sarvajña Sadāśivabodha, (7) *Puṇyaślokamañjarī-pariśiṣṭa* of Ātmabodha, (8) *Gururatnamālā* of Sadāśivabrahmendra. Its ṭīkā, *Suṣumā*, by Ātmabodhendra is a good one.

[1] abhiyuñjad-ayārcya-pūjyapādān apalūnyādiniṣākasiddhanetṛn |
atha gauḍapadān phaṇīśabhāṣya-prathamācāryakapaṇḍitān prapadye ||

of Śuka,[2] it was through his influence that the wrong Buddhistic views (*śauddhodani-kadadhvanām*) of the persons headed by Ayārcya who was being attended by such Yogins belonging to the Western border of the country as Apalūnya and Damīśa (*apalūnya-damīśādyaparāntyayogibhiś ca*), as well as by Prāvṛti, the Śākya chief of Taxila (*takśaśilādhīśa-śākyaprāvṛti-pramukhaiḥ*), were made to disappear.

If here one turns over the pages of *The Indian Travels of Apollonius of Tyana* by Osmond de Beauvoir Priaulx, JRAS, 1860, pp. 70 ff., one will easily see that Apalūnya in the Sanskrit text is no other than the Pythagorian philosopher Apollonius of Tyana, who flourished in the first century A.D. He travelled to India and came to the court of Phraotes who was the same as Prāvṛti in the Sanskrit text, the king of Taxila. And Damīśa of our text is indentical with Damis,

[2] In connection with Gaudapāda's *tapasyā* in the Himālayas the following story may be related here from Nārāyaṇa's ṭikā on MāU: The four parts of the MāU of the recension of the RV (yet, note that the Upaniṣad is said to belong to the AV) were explained by Gauḍapāda by his four Books (*prakaraṇas*). He was a disciple of Śuka and the grand preceptor of Ś. He flourished at the end of the age called *Dvāpara*. At the hermitage of Badarikā by his devotion he propitiated Nārāyaṇa and having obtained a boon from him he entered into a cave of a mountain, so that he would not look at the face of any one born in the age of *Kali*. In this state he was approached by Ś and requested to come out from the cave, but he did not comply with the request. Yet, having written the four Books of his work on the leaves of a Banyan tree with red chalk he gave them to Ś. *Report of Sanskrit Manuscripts in Southern India* by E. Hultzsch, No. III, p. 133. But there is no end of such legends on which one can hardly rely.

the fellow traveller and friend of Apollonius. The last person in our text, Ayārcya, is the same and one with Iarchas (probably a corruption from Rac'hyaś, *op. cit.*, p. 83, note), a Greek king.[3]

All this looks well, but do you gain anything from it about the date in question? The Greek account simply relates the travel of Apollonius,[4] being completely silent about Gauḍapāda. There is no doubt that some names of both the accounts are identical, but it does not follow from it that the persons having the same names are also identical. Supposing that the account is true it will be for a further creation of confusion in settling the date even of the great Ś, into which we do not enter here as useless.

Hence without having recourse to such legendary records for the determination of the date of our teacher

[3] Perhaps it is M. Hiriyanna (IHQ, 1926, pp. 415-416) who has first made the identification. See also Gopinath Kaviraj, *op. cit.*, pp. 22-23.

[4] How far this account is true it is not easy to say, Priaulx, the author of the paper observes (*Op. cit.*, p. 104): "of Damis's geography, I can only say that it reminds me of a fairy tale. ... Who shall explain these discrepancies, account for these mistakes and fix localities thus vaguely described?" "Reviewing the whole work of Philostratus (*i.e.*, the original author of the life of Apollonius) it seems to me that Apollonius certainly pretended to have travelled through and made some stay in India, but that very possibly he did not visit it, our Damis never accompanied him; but if we may judge from cinnamon and pepper-trees .. fabricated this journal perhaps from books written upon India, and tales current about India, which he easily collected at the great mart for Indian commodities, and resort for Indian merchants—Alexandria."

we should take a safer course by which at least the upper and lower limits of his time can be ascertained.

I think we have no reason for discarding what Walleser has said in this respect. So far three Buddhist writers are known to us, who have actually quoted Gauḍapāda, *viz.*, Bhāvaviveka (*cir.* 500-550 A.D.),[5] Śāntirakṣita (705-762 A.D.), and his disciple Kamalaśīla. Bhāvaviveka is the author of the *Madhyamakahṛdayakārikā* as well as of its commentary *Tarkajvālā*, the full title being *Madhyamakahṛdayavṛtti Tarkajvālā*. In chapter VIII of his work Bhāvaviveka reviews the system of the Vedāntins as he does in other chapters the systems of Sāṅkhya, Vaiśeṣika and Mīmāṃsā. In doing so Bhāvaviveka in his TJ, VIII has quoted passages from such texts as ChU, ŚU and MuU. Besides, there are some other passages quoted, four of them (10-13) being very important in the present connexion. While the first three have the closest relationship with three kārikās of our text the last (*i.e.*, TJ, VIII. 13) is entirely identical with III. 5 of our

5 Or Bhavya, as he is sometimes called, or Bhavyaviveka as suggested from the Tibetan sources (legs.ldan.ḥbyed). Bhāvaviveka was the founder of the *Prāsaṅgika* school of Nāgārjuna's Mādhyamika system. He is much criticised by Candrakīrtti in his MV, I. Bhāvaviveka's *Prajñāpradīpaśāstra* (Nanjio, No. 1185) was translated into Chinese by Prabhākara Mitra in 630-632 A.D. He was a junior contemporary of Dharmapāla (Th. Watterr: *On Yuan Chuang's Travels in India*, II. p. 222) who lived in the 5th century A.D. (Winternitz: *History of Indian Literature*, Eng. Tr., 1933, Vol. II, p. 362). Thus it can be said that the date of Bhāvaviveka is 500 A.D., or a few years after it.

text. There is, therefore, not an iota of doubt here that the GK was known to Bhāvaviveka. With reference to the other three kārikās cited by Bhāvaviveka, which are not identified in the GK, but have the closest relationship, we have to seek after another source.

As regards Śāntirakṣita he is the author among others of the *Madhyamakālaṅkarakārikā* as well as of its commentary called *Madhyamakālaṅkāravṛtti*. Besides, his disciple Kamalaśīla has written a *Pañjikā* on the former work just as on the *Tattvasaṃgraha*. Śāntarakṣita in his MAK, 93, discusses the views of the Aupaniṣadas (lit. Aupaniṣadānusārins, Tib. gsaṅ.ba.paḥi. rjes.su.ḥbraṅ.ba.dag),[6] and in doing so he cites there not less than ten kārikās from our text which is referred to by Kamalaśīla in his *Pañjikā* as an *Upaniṣat śāstra*.[7]

Now as we have seen above we cannot reasonably deny the existence of the GK before Bhāvaviveka who has actually quoted it. Thus one may ascertain that the time of Gauḍapāda is *cir*. 500 A.D.

The following consideration, too, leads us to the same decision. Gauḍapāda has quoted almost fully, partially or substantially from works of some

[6] Generally in Buddhist texts we come across similar words, as *Aupaniṣadika* (TSP, Śl. 328), and *Upaniṣad-vādin* (BAP, pp. 455, 465), and not *Vedāntavādin* or *Vaidāntika*.

[7] It may be noted that though Śāntirakṣita has quoted here so many kārikās from GK he has not done so at all in TS (Śls. 328-335) either from this or any other work. For the kārikās quoted in Tibetan works see our text II. 3, 4, 5, 6, 18, 19, 20; III. 4, 5, 6, 8.

celebrated Buddhist teachers who flourished between 200 A.D. and 400 A.D. For instance, see our text, IV. 22^{a-b} :

svato vā parato vāpi na kiñcid vastu jāyate |

And read here Nāgārjuna's (200 A.D.) MK, XXI. 13^{a-b} :

na svato jāyate bhāvaḥ parato naiva jāyate |

See our text, pp. 105 ff. and 127 ff. Again, we read in our ĀŚ, 7^{c-d} and 29^{c-d} :

prakṛter anyathābhāvo na kathañcid bhaviṣyati ||

And in MK, XV. 8^{c-d} we have :

prakṛter anyathābhāvo nahi jātūpapadyate ||

The following line occurs in ĀŚ, IV. 4^{b} :

abhūtaṃ naiva jāyate |

And let us cite here the following from the CŚ, 373^{a} of Nāgārjuna's disciple Āryadeva who probably lived, in the words of Winternitz (*A History of Indian Literature,* Eng. Tr., 1933, Vol. II, p. 350), "at about the turning point of the second and third century A.D." :

nābhūto nāma jāyate ||

See our text III. 44 (pp. 77-78) :

laye sambodhayec cittaṃ vikṣiptaṃ śamayet punaḥ |
sakaṣāyaṃ vijānīyāc chamaprāptaṃ na cālayet ||

With this read the following from MAS, XIV. 9^{c-d}—10^{a-b} of Maitreyanātha or Asaṅga (400 A.D.):

līnaṃ cittasya gṛhṇīyād uddhataṃ śamayet punaḥ |
śamaprāptam upekṣeta tasminn ālambane punaḥ ||

Thus Gauḍapāda quoting the above teachers can in no way be placed before them, in other words he cannot be assigned a date before 400 A.D.

Here we are to consider another kārikā of our author, *i.e.*, IV. 13 which runs thus (see pp. 114-115):

jātāc ca jāyamānasya na-vyavasthā prasajyate |

Compare this with the following line quoted in MV, p. 13 from the AKV:

utpannasya punar utpattau kalpyamānāyām anavasthāprasaṅgaḥ.

Now this work, AKV, is by Yaśomitra. Before he wrote his own commentary on the AK of Vasubandhu (400 A.D.) there were at least three commentaries, two of them being written by Guṇamati (425 A.D.) and Vasumitra, as he himself says in the introductory ślokas of his work. This shows that Yaśomitra lived in the 5th century A.D. And so, if Gauḍapāda's kārikā (*i.e.*, IV. 13) is in fact based on the above line of the AKV his date naturally falls in the 5th century A.D.

Certainly this will militate against the traditional time of Śaṅkara or the succession of teachers and disciples of his school. But how far the accounts of this succession can be relied upon is a question which has not yet been settled finally or satisfactorily. Are not the traditional succession lists kept in different Maṭhas unscrupulously manipulated? Under these circumstances we have no course left to us other than the evidences of quotations and cross-references in early and reliable texts.[8]

§ 9. *Alleged Borrowing by Gauḍapāda*

Let us discuss the question from a different point of view. There is a work *Paramārthasāra*[9] attributed to Śeṣa who is apparently the mythical Śeṣa, as he his referred to in the work itself as *ādhāra* (8), *i.e.*, *jagad-ādhāra* (87). From this some take him as Patañjali, the less mythical Śeṣa, the author of the *Mahābhāṣya* on Pāṇini.

It is also called *Āryāpañcāśiti* owing to the fact that it is composed in eighty-five stanzas in the *Āryā* metre, though in fact there are eighty-seven stanzas.[10]

8 Our old traditions are so divergent that according to them as well as the modern researches we shall have to place Śaṅkara some time between the 6th century B.C. and the 9th century A.D., *viz.*, 6th century B.C., 4th century B.C., 1st century B.C., 4th century A.D., 6th century A.D., and the 9th century (788-820) A.D. The last date is now accepted by many a scholar. See Gopinath Kaviraj, *op. cit.*, pp. 23 ff; Belvalkar, *op. cit.*, pp. 209 ff.

9 There are so far at least five editions of this book, the latest and critical one being by S. S. Suryanarayana Sastri (Transliterated Text, English Translation and Notes), Karnataka Publishing House, Bombay, 1941.

10 It may be that the first two stanzas which are not in *Āryā*, but *Upajāti*, were added later on. But, if it is so, as regards the first of them, it was added long before Abhinavagupta who has adopted it just at the beginning of his PS², 1. The last stanza (87 : vedānta°) does not also appear to constitute the original, being added by a second hand, as is suggested by Suryanarayana Sastri, *op. cit.*, p. 40, note. Mark here the employment of the perfect tense, in the word *babandha*. The original number, 85, can however, be obtained by reckoning an additional stanza between 18 and 19 given from a MS in a foot-note in the Trivandrum edition (PŚ) being fully supported by PS², 9 (and not 6 as in PS¹).

It is a Vedāntic work.[11] Its excellence and importance can be understood by the simple fact that Abhinavagupta (in the end of the tenth and the beginning of the eleventh century A.D.), the great teacher of the *Pratyabhijñā* school and Poetics, adapted it,[12] though retaining the original title, for writing a manual of the *Pratyabhijñā* school, by some omissions, additions, alterations and improvements.[13] That it is an adaptation of the first work is known from the statement of Abhinavagupta himself.[14]

In this work of Śeṣa there are some passages, or words, or thoughts that supply certain points of resemblance to those of our ĀŚ. In order to see if this fact can throw any light on the question of the time of Gauḍapāda we should like to discuss it in the following few lines.

S. S. Suryanarayana Sastri (*op. cit.*, p. viii) has noticed some of these points of resemblance[15]

[11] The last stanza (87) of it says that it was composed by its author having looked through the entire *Vedānta-śāstra*.

[12] V. V. Sovani: JRAS, 1912, pp. 257 ff; K. C. Pandey: *Abhinavagupta*, 1935, pp. 57 ff; S. S. Suryanarayana Sastri: NIA, Vol. I, pp. 37 ff.

[13] For instance compare PS¹, 35 and 36 with PS², 36 and 37 respectively. Abhinavagupta's work contains 105 kārikās, though he himself states that it has 100 kārikās. On this see K. C. Pandey, *op. cit.*, p. 56.

[14] See PS², 1 and 2. Iyengar's observation (JRAS, 1910, p. 1338) does not appear to be reasonable.

[15] For easy reference I write below the kārikās of PS¹ mentioning the numbers of the corresponding kārikās of the GK:

(*a*) prāṇādyanantabhedair ātmānaṃ saṃvitatya jālam iva |
saṃharati vāsudevaḥ svavibhūtyākrīḍamāna iva || PS¹, 30.
cf. GK, II. 19.

and writes (p. ix) after discussing them as follows: "It seems plausible that Gauḍapāda was drawing on some earlier sources, agreeing in part, while rejecting in part, and that the rejection was not consistent or thorough. Such a hypothesis may well consider the *Paramārthasāra* the original drawn upon." There is not the least doubt that Gauḍapāda has drawn much upon earlier works, as it is perfectly clear throughout his book,[16] but can Śeṣa's PS[1] be included in them, though it may appear to be so?

In order to avoid prolixity I propose to discuss only two points raised by Suryanarayana Sastri

(*b*) tribhir eva viśvataijasaprājñais tair ādimadhyanidhanākhyaiḥ |
jāgratsvapnasuṣuptair bhramabhutaiś chāditaṃ turyam || PS[1], 31.
cf. GK, I. 1-5; MāU, 3-7 (pp. 223-234).

(*c*) mohayatīvātmānaṃ svamāyayā dvaitarūpayā devaḥ |
upalabhate svayam evaṃ guhāgataṃ puruṣam ātmānam || PS[1], 32.
cf. GK, II. 12.

(*d*) jaladharadhūmodgatibhir malinikriyate yathā na gaganatalam |
tadvat prakṛtivikārair aparāmṛṣṭaḥ paraḥ puruṣaḥ || PS[1], 35.
cf. GK, III. 8.

(*e*) ekasminn api ca ghaṭe dhūmādimalāvṛte śeṣāḥ |
na bhavanti malopetā yadvaj jīvo 'pi tadvad iha || PS[1], 36.
cf. GK, III. 5.

(*f*) himaphenabudbudā iva jalasya dhūmo yathā vahneḥ |
tadvat svabhāvabhūtā māyaiṣā kathitā viṣṇoḥ || PS[1], 53.
cf. GK, I. 9.

(*g*) yad yat siddhāntāgamatarkeṣu prabruvanti rāgāndhāḥ |
anumodāmas tat tat teśāṃ sarvātmavādadhiyā || PS[1], 65.
cf. GK, IV. 5.

(*h*) utpattināśavarjitam evaṃ paramārtham upalabhya |
kṛtakṛtyaḥ saphalajanmā sarvagatis tiṣṭhati yatheṣṭam PS[1], 79.
cf. GK, III. 32.

[16] For this the reader is referred to my Annotation of the ĀŚ, and the notes added thereto.

in the hope that this may decide the case He writes: "Both are concerned with the three forms—Viśva, Taijasa and Prājña—as veiling the fourth which is the real."[17] This refers, as he says, to PS[1], 31 and GK, I. 1 and 11.

The most important thing to be pointed out here first is that between the two texts, ĀŚ and PS[1], the latter is certainly a later development, as a perusal of the texts will show. Let us, however, make an attempt to understand PS[1], 31 as it is before us without taking any help either from the commentator or from Abhinavagupta.[18] The word *jāgrat-svapna-suṣupta* is an adjective of *viśva-taijasaprājña*. But what is to be understood from the abrupt statement that Viśva, Taijasa and Prājña are *jāgrat*, *svapna* and *suṣupta* respectively? What are these three, Viśva, Taijasa and Prājña? How can one know them? How is one to understand that there is only one and the same who is regarded as three (*i.e.*, Viśva, etc.) owing to three different stages (*i.e.*, *jāgrat*, etc.)? How is it that *turya* undoubtedly referring to *Vāsudeva* in the preceeding kārikā (30) is put in the neuter gender,

17 Is the last part of this statement exactly so? Do *chādita* in PS[1], 31 (=*āvṛta* in P[3], 34) and *-baddha* in *kāryakāraṇabaddha* and *kāraṇabaddha* in GK, I. 11 convey the same idea? We are to consider here GK, I. 15 and NSi (IV. 41, 42) where these two kārikās of Gauḍapāda are quoted.

18 He has here the following two kārikās (PS[3], 34 and 35):

sṛṣṭisthitisaṃhārā jāgra'svapnau suṣuptam iti tasmin |
bhānti turīye dhāmani tathāpi tair āvṛtaṃ bhāti ||

(In the first half of this kārikā in PS[3] quoted in foot-note 2- *svapnam* is to be read as *-svapnau*.)

jāgrad viśvaṃ bhedāt svapnas tejaḥ prakāśamāhātmyāt |
prājñaḥ suptāvasthā jñānaghanatvāt tataḥ paraṃ turyam ||

while the latter word is in the masculine?[19] Moreover, what is the significance of *taiḥ* in the first half? If it is not superfluous, what is it that it refers to? How far are we justified with the commentator in taking the word with *chādita* in the second half? Again, why is it that *eva* should be used in the first half after *tribhir?* All this taken together shows, as far as I can judge, that Śeṣa's work presupposes that of Gauḍapāda, and not *vice versa.* Śeṣa had before him ĀŚ, I. 1-5 (as well as MāU, 3-7) upon which he has drawn adding something (*ādimadhyanidhana*) more quite independently as he has done throughout his book. While in ĀŚ there are five kārikās, Śeṣa has only one, and even in it he has made some addition. This on one hand and the metrical exigency on the other did not allow him, as seems to me, to express his ideas adequately with the result that there occurred some anomalies. Comparing PS[1] and PS[2] with the GK here it appears to me that as Śeṣa could not express himself adequately and consequently his kārikā became obscure Abhinavagupta added here one kārikā more, as has already been pointed out, explaining all that was absolutely necessary for its proper elucidiation.

Now, what is the source or sources of Abhinava's interpretation here (kārikās 34, 35), without which we cannot understand the kārikā of Śeṣa? Certainly it was not only Gauḍapāda, for such things as

[19] Abhinava is quite justified in putting *turya* in the neuter gender as he has before it (kārikā 34) *dhāman*, neuter, which is referred to by the former word and we can think that he got it from GK, I. 5, 22.

sṛṣṭisthitisaṃhāra cannot be known from his work. One is therefore inclined to say with some amount of certainty that it was partly the work of Śeṣa, and partly the tradition connected with him, though under the present state of our knowledge we do not know if this tradition is recorded anywhere Nevertheless, we have to accept its existence, as we cannot explain the difficulties without it. The question arises here as to how Abhinava came to know that tradition. Does it not persuade one to think that the distance of time between Śeṣa and Abhinava is not as wide as it is supposed to have been? What is there against thinking that PS[1] and PS[2] belonged to the same period, though the former must have evidently been a little earlier? In this case the question of the interpretation of the present kārikā of Śeṣa given by Abhinava can very satisfactorily be explained. What is there that can be offered for pushing back the date of PS[1] to a period before GK?

Again, with reference to the creation of the world Śeṣa in his work which deals with the Vedānta has effected a synthesis of the Sāṅkhya and the Vedānta systems by the introduction of the creation from Upendra (=Viṣṇu = Vāsudeva = Hari = Nārāyaṇa-Paramātman = Brahman) through *prakṛti* with the gradual evolution from it of *buddhi* (=*mahat*), etc. In the process of the creation he has accommodated also the theory of *aṇḍa* 'cosmic germ,' found, as for instance, in the *Manusaṃhitā*, I. 8 ff. and the *Viṣṇu Purāṇa*, I. 2. 58 ff. Here we are to note what Kullūka observes on *Manusaṃhitā*, I. 8 :

abhidhyanapūrvikāṃ sṛṣṭiṃ vadato manoḥ prakṛtir acetanā svatantrā pariṇamata ity ayaṃ pakṣo na sammataḥ. kintu tridaṇḍivedāntasiddhānta evābhimataḥ pratibhāti.

It is further elucidated by him in another place (I. 15):

nanv abhidhyanapūrvakasṛṣṭyabhidhānad vedāntasiddhānta eva manor abhimata iti prāg uktaṃ, tan na saṅgacchate. idānīṃ mahadādikrameṇa sṛṣṭyabhidhanad vedantadarśanena ca paramātmana evākāśādikrameṇa sṛṣṭir uktā.° ucyate. prakṛtito mahadādikrameṇa sṛṣṭir iti bhagavadbhāskarīyadarśane 'py upapadyata iti tadvido vadanti.[20]

Now Bhāskara is one of the post-Śaṅkara commentators of the BS. Undoubtedly he was in the ninth century A.D. being criticised by Vācaspati Miśra (841 A.D.) in his *Bhāmatī* (BS, III. 3. 29). Śeṣa seems therefore to have been well acquainted with the Vedantic system maintained by Bhāskara and has then combined his theory with that of Manu and others according to whom in the process of ceation there intervenes the theory of *aṇḍa*.

I do not therefore think that I can concur with Suryanarayana Sastri in suggesting that "the *Paramārthasāra* is the original drawn upon." (p. ix).

[20] See Bhāskara's commentary on the BS (Chaukhamba Sanskrit Series, 1914), II. 1. 26: tataś ca brahmaṇaḥ pariṇāmānupapatteḥ pradhānam eṣṭavyam iti tātparyārthaḥ. Udayana observes in his *Nyāyakusumāñjali*, p. 332: brahmapariṇater iti bhaskaragotre yujyate.

In passing we are to take up another question in this connexion. B. L. Atreya having noticed "much common between *Kārikās* (*i.e.*, GK) and *Yogavāsiṣṭha* not only in thought, but also in language"[21] concludes that the latter is prior on the following three grounds: (1) The kārikās do not form "an independent treatise on the *Advaita Philosophy*," being "a sort of commentary on the *Māṇḍūkya Upaniṣad.*" (2). "On the other hand, the philosopher Vasiṣṭha claims to have received his doctrines directly from the cosmic mind (Brahmā) and to have realised their truth in his own experience. The philosophy of Vasiṣṭha includes almost all the views held by Gauḍapāda." And (3) "*Gauḍapāda-kārikās* represent a later phase of the *Advaita* philosophy, when it tended to become critical, hostile and polemical towards other contemporary schools of thought, whereas *Yogavāsiṣṭha* represents the earlier phase."

As the space at my disposal does not allow me here to enter into a detailed discussion I desire simply to make a few observations as briefly as I can. I do not see that I can follow the above arguments. For, supposing that the GK is a sort of commentary and Vasiṣṭha received his doctrines directly from Brahmā, are we in any way justified in thinking that the YV is prior to the GK? Does it follow from that? As regards the third argument of Atreya he thinks that the Advaita philosophy as represented in the GK is of a later phase, because it is "critical,

21 *Yogavāsiṣṭha and its Philosophy*, 1932, pp. 14-15.

hostile and polemical towards other" systems. But may one ask here: Is there anything in the GK that may be regarded as "critical, hostile and polemical?" If so, what and where is it so? On the contrary, one may find there (GK, III. 17; IV. 3-6) clear non-hostility (*avirodha*), and there is no instance of anything that is critical and polemical. If, however, the mention of different views in the GK is meant thereby, the case is the same also with the YV.[22]

It is not always safe to conclude the priority or posteriority of one of two works simply seeing the same or similar passage, or thought, occurring in both of them. For instance, we read the following in the GK, II. 6[23] and IV. 31:

ādāv ante ca yan nāsti vartamane'pi tat tathā |

The same line occurs also in the YV, IV. 45. 45 and a similar one in III. 11. 13, as quoted in our text, p. 142, note 3. Now, apart from the question of the date of the GK, can we determine with any amount of certainty the priority or posteriority of one of the two works unless we take into consideration the other factors that are connected herewith? One may be referred here to the present Annotation on GK, IV. 31; and it will be found that the same thought only in slightly different words is expressed in such works as MK and ĀS, which are undisputably far earlier than YV. Now, if we see that Gauḍapāda has abundantly drawn upon

[22] For instance, see III. 62. 10-11; 84. 22-27 vivadante hy asambuddhāḥ svavikalpavijṛmbhitaiḥ

[23] Atreya has noticed it.

such earlier works can we ever think in this or similar cases that he has borrowed from YV, unless there is any strong ground for doing so? When there are two texts containing the same thing, one earlier and the other later, one may quote from either of them; but to decide definitely as to from which one it is actually done one should discuss carefully.

Another instance of what is common to both GK and YV, as noted by Atreya, is the non-difference between the states of wakefulness and dream (*jāgrat* and *suṣupta*), as found in GK, II. 5 and YV, IV. 9. 11 ff. Here, too, when we see that the first half of the GK clearly refers to the BU, IV. 3-14 (see p. 19), upon which, just as upon other Upaniṣads, Gauḍapāda draws so much, as is evident from the work itself,[24] how can we think that YV is here the source of GK? On the contrary, a careful perusal of YV will at once show that in his answer to the question put to him by Rāma about the difference between wakefulness and dream Vasiṣṭha has written a number of ślokas (YV, IV. 19. 9 ff), and attempted thereby only to explain what is very briefly stated in GK. Does this fact point to the priority or posteriority of YV to GK?[25]

[24] See next section.

[25] According to Atreya the date of YV is the sixth century A.D. But his arguments do not appear to me to be strong or convincing. It may be noted here in this connection that there are two things that may specially be mentioned in Svāmī Bhūmānanda's paper entitled *Priority of the Yogavāsiṣṭha to Śaṅkarācārya*: (1) Śaṅkara quotes (BS, III. 4. 50) the *Vasiṣṭhadharmaśāstra* (ed. A. A. Führer, Bombay, 1883), X. 18;

§ 10. *The Works of Gauḍapāda*

With regard to the works ascribed to Gauḍapāda the only one that can be accepted with certainty as written by him is the ĀŚ. The authorship of a few other books is ascribed to him. The most important of them is a *bhāṣya* on the *Sāṅkhyakārikā* of Īśvarakṛṣṇa. There is a *bhāṣya* under his name also on the *Uttaragītā*. But there is no strong ground for holding that they are actually by Gauḍapāda, the author of the ĀŚ, nor is there anything of the nature that can decide the case otherwise, though I incline to subscribe to the view that they are not by Gauḍapāda. A commentary, too, on the NUTU is attributed to him. There are three other works which pass under the name of Gauḍapāda as their author. A commentary on the *Durgāsaptaśatī* is one of them. This is referred to by the great Tantric teacher Bhāskararāya in his commentary on the same

and (2) mentions the name of Vasiṣṭha in his commentary on the BG, XIII. 4. But the question whether these two Vasiṣṭhas, the Vasiṣṭha of YV as well as the Vasiṣṭha in the list of the teachers of the Śaṅkara school are identical, remains to be settled, though according to some of the authors of the ṭīkās on BG, the Vasiṣṭha referred to by Śaṅkara is the author of YV.

[1] There is a manuscript, No. 1405, of this work in the Grantha character in the Visvabharati Library, Santiniketan. The following occurs there on folio 24*a*:

> kavacaṃ bījam ādiṣṭam argalā śaktir iṣyate |
> kīlakaṃ kīlakaṃ prāhuḥ saptaśatyāṃ mahāmanoḥ ||

iti gauḍapādadhṛtavacanāt.

And again: yady api vedāntamūrdhanyair gauḍapādācāryaiḥ sarvam idaṃ nirviśeṣacitpratipādakaśāstraparatvena vyākhyātam.°

work.[1] The other two are Tantric treatises, *viz.*, *Subhagodaya*[2] and *Śrīvidyāratnasūtra*.

Here arises a question: Can we think that there are two G a u ḍ a p ā d a s , one Vedāntic and the other Tantric, being the authors of works on the Vedānta and Tantricism respectively? In the *Śrīvidyārṇava* which is a Tantric work by P r a g a l b h ā - c ā r y a , Ś a ṅ k a r ā c ā r y a is said to have been the founder of a Tantric school. There is in this work also a list of the succession of his teachers and disciples. But it seems impossible to reconcile this list with the traditional one of the Advaita Vedānta school. So the list in the *Śrīvidyārṇava* hardly helps us in this matter. Nevertheless, we may simply note in the list given here that there are two G a u ḍ a p ā d a s , one of them being mentioned as G a u ḍ a (No. 55) and the other G a u ḍ a p ā d a k a (No. 65),[3] who is, in fact, the same as G a u ḍ a p ā d a , the suffix *-ka* being evidently on account of the metrical exigency. On this the reader may form his own judgment.

§ 11. *The Sources*

The sources of the *Āgamaśāstra*, which one naturally desires to know, roughly fall into three classes, *viz.*,

[2] It is said that there is a *bhāṣya* on it by Ś a ṅ k a r a.

[3] In the verse containing the word as quoted by R ā j e n d r a n ā t h a G h o ṣ a in his *Advaitavāda* (in Bengali), p. 227, the actual reading is *Gauḍapādakaḥ*. But G o p i n a t h K a v i r a j (*op. cit.*, p. 53), who has not quoted the verse, reads only *Gauḍapāda* leaving out the suffix *-ka* which seems to be right.

(1) Vedic texts: Vedas and Upaniṣads, (2) Schools or Teachers, and (3) Buddhist works.

With regard to class (1), these are mostly Upaniṣads, Vedas being quoted in not more than two cases (III. 24*b* and *c*). It is, however, to be noted in this connexion that when there is a passage which occurs both in a Veda and in an Upaniṣad it is very difficult to ascertain as to whether the reference is actually to the former or to the latter. For instance, here in III. 24*b* we have indro māyābhir iti. This is found in RV, VI. 47. 18 as well as in BU, II. 5. 19. How can we, in this case, ascertain that the reference is in fact to the one and not to the other? The case is exactly the same with the second instance III. 24 c) of a quotation from a Veda. Similarly with regard to II. 24 we know much of *kāla* 'time' from the AV, XIX. 53, 54 and the ŚU, I. 2, IV. 1. But here it is very difficult to conclude whether the reference is actually to the former or to the latter, or to the both of them. Again, the *Kālavids* 'knowers of time' are, as says Ā n a n d a g i r i, astronomers, and it is not impossible that our author might have alluded to some work of them, or simply to the view held by them or to their school.

In the course of the present Annotation many references to different Upaniṣads have been inserted in support of a point or points in our text, but which of them, if any, is in fact meant by the author in any particular case we cannot say definitely. It may be that in some cases the Upaniṣadic authority, really meant by the author, is different from what the present annotator has quoted. For instance, with regard to *pāda* (II. 21) which is capable of being interpreted differently, various references are given in the Annotation, or still other references may be shown. But it is not easy to ascertain the particular reference or references the author himself intended. Nevertheless, it is certain that the author had in his mind any one or more of these or similar passages when he was writing his book.

Among the references in the Annotation the names of the *Bhagavadgītā* (XIII. 22 in II. 22 of our text) and the *Brahmasūtra* (II. 3. 19-32 in II. 23 of our text) will be found. But we cannot be sure that these two works are actually drawn upon by our author, though they may elucidate the texts to some extent.

Similarly for the explanation of our text there will be found some references in the Annotation to such minor Upaniṣads (for instance, in II. 32) as *Avadhūta* Up., 8; *Āśrama*°, 4; *Ātma*°, 31; *Jābāla*°, 6; *Tripurātāpanī*°, V. 10; *Brahmabindu*°, 10. But whether these minor Upaniṣads are prior to the *Āgamaśāstra* is to be left as an open question, though some of them such as *Brahmabindu*° and *Jābāla*°, are before Śaṅkara as is quite clear from his commentary on BS, III. 2. 18 and 4. 20 respectively.

In five places (III. 12, 24, 25, 26 and 36) passages from Upaniṣads are expressly quoted, while in III. 11 and 23 the words *Taittirīya* and *śruti* are actually mentioned and in II. 3 a passage of the BU, IV. 3. 10 is clearly alluded to with the word *śrūyate*. Similarly in II. 5 another passage from the same Upaniṣad (BU, IV. 3. 14) is clearly referred to though with the word *manīṣins* and not *śruti* as before and usual. In III. 12, 13 and 15 references to Upaniṣads are also very clear. In two or three more places (I. 2, 8, 9) references seem to have been made to Upaniṣads.[2]

It will be seen that no Upaniṣad is quoted or referred to by our author in his last Book, *Alātaśānti*. There is absolutely nothing of the kind.[3]

As regards class (2) of the sources readers are referred to § 6 : *The Name of the Work* of the present Introduction, p. lxiii, where the names of different schools or teachers alluded to in our text, are mentioned.

It appears from these names that some of the schools or teachers mentioned by our author here were undoubtedly prominent at his time, but gradually they have lost their prominence and have fallen almost into a state of oblivion.

With regard to class (3) of our sources, *i.e.*, the Buddhist texts, the reader is referred to the Annotation on II. 31, 32, 35 (*cf* 38), 44, 46, and most of the kārikās in Book IV.

§ *12. The Bṛhadāraṇyaka Upaniṣad as the Main Upaniṣadic Source of the Āgamaśāstra*

In the preceding section we have seen that the BU is one of the sources of the ĀŚ in which there are

[1] As in the Upaniṣad itself (BU, IV. 3. 14) there is atha khalv āhuḥ our author seems to have closen to take the nominative as *manīṣins* and not *śruti*. See II. 1, 5; IV. 54, and Appendix X: Additional Notes, II. 1.

[2] See the Annotation.

[3] With regard to the word *durdarśa* in IV. 100 we cannot say definitely that it refers to KU, II. 12, as it is often found also in Buddhist works.

some quotations from or references to the former. In the present section it is proposed to examine to some extent the inter-relationship of these two works by which we shall see that the main Upaniṣadic source of the ĀŚ is the BU.

From the text of the ĀŚ as it is before us it is quite clear that G a u ḍ a p ā d a has drawn much upon it. In fact, Book I of our text is mainly based on it. Nay, it may be declared that Book I of the ĀŚ is nothing but an epitome or essence of the BU, IV. 2-3 with some clear exposition and an addition of the *upāsanā*[1] 'meditation' of *Praṇava* or *Om*. By writing the first Book of the ĀŚ G a u ḍ a p ā d a has in reality made a key to that portion of the BU, without which it would have been extremely difficult to understand its true significance.

The opening part of the ĀŚ, *i.e.*, the part dealing with the three divisions of the One (*i.e.*, Puruṣa) such as Viśva, etc. (I. 1-4, 10), is to be found only in different words in the BU, IV. 2-3, as says Ś a ṅ k a r a very clearly on BU, IV. 3. 1 (p. 519).[2]

[1] III. 1 and Appendix X on it.

[2] atra ca jāgratsvapnasuṣuptaturīyāṇy upanyastāny anyaprasaṅgena indhaḥ (IV. 2. 2), praviviktāhārataraḥ (IV. 2. 3), sarve prāṇāḥ (IV. 2. 4), sa eṣa neti neti (IV. 2. 4). idānīṃ jāgratsvapnādidvāreṇaiva mahatā tarkeṇa vistarato 'dhigamaḥ kartavyaḥ (p. 519).

See here also Ś a ṅ k a r a 's observation in showing the relationship between BU, IV. 2 and IV. 3 (p. 518):

°vijñānam ānandaṃ brahmety avagatam. tad eva punar indhasaṃjñaḥ praviviktāhāras tato 'ntarhṛdaye liṅgātmā praviviktāhārataras tataḥ pareṇa jagadātmā. See further on IV. 3. 1 (p. 519).

We see in our text (I. 1-4, 10) that the One, *i.e.*, Puruṣa[3] (=Brahman=Ātman of the MāU, 2) owing to different states is called Viśva, Taijasa, Prajña and Turya (or Turīya, I. 15). None of these names excepting Prājña (BU, IV. 3. 21 and 35) is, however, to be found in the BU. For Viśva it reads (IV. 2. 2) *Indha* 'shining' which is the same as *Indra*, the former, as the Upaniṣad would say, being used by people cryptically.[4] As to why the Puruṣa is called *Indha* Sureśvara says (BBV, IV. 2. 37) that 'because he shines day and night' (idhyate 'harniśaṃ yasmād indhanāmā tataḥ pumān). This 'shining' implies, according to Ānandagiri, his enjoyment of gross things in the waking state (sthūlārthabhoktṛtvena sadā jāgare sphūrteḥ). Śaṅkara is found to have employed both the terms in his commentary on the BU, *Indha* (BU, IV. 3. 1, p. 519) and *Vaiśvānara* (BU, IV. 2. 2-4, pp. 513-519), but not *Viśva*, so far as goes my information, with regard to the commentary referred to. From the text of the BU (IV. 2. 3, 3. 11, 35) itself it appears that

[3] As in the original of the text, *i.e.*, BU, IV. 3 we have this word.

[4] It is a well-known saying in Brāhmaṇas that gods are fond of the cryptic, as it were, and dislike the evident 'parokṣapriyā iva hi devāḥ pratyakṣadviṣaḥ —BU, IV. 2. 2). Sureśvara says (in BBV, IV. 2. 37; p. 1365) that even now people do not like to call a superior person directly by his personal name:

pratyakṣanāmagrahaṇam pradviṣanti jagaty api |
śreyāṃso 'mukamiśrās ta ity uktiṃ kāmayanti ca ||

In referring to a superior person the use of *amuka* 'so and so' or *uni* in Bengali, is still found. It is to be noted that in the country, at least in Bengal, a woman does not call her husband by his name, but for it uses such words as *uni*.

if any other term for *Viśva* is to be chosen from that work it is only *śārīra* 'existing in the body,' 'embodied.' But G a u ḍ a p ā d a has not accepted it, but has adopted a new name, *Viśva*, probably thinking the latter to be more expressive of the idea behind it. Finally in the hand of the author of MāU it has undergone a further change in the form of *Vaiśvānara* 'common-to-all' perhaps for the same purpose.

Of these names *Turya* (or *Turīya*) 'fourth' is evidently not a name in fact, but as it is described after the first three *Viśva*, etc., it is so called, being their fourth. In the BU *Indha-Indra* is a name, no doubt, but *Taijasa* and *Prājña* were originally mere adjectives,[5] becoming names afterwards. Sometimes the appellation *Liṅgātman* is found for *Taijasa*, as writes Ś a ṅ k a r a in his commentary on the BU, IV. 2. 3 (p. 515), IV. 3. 1 (p. 518). Similarly *sauṣupta* is used for *Prājña* as says Sureśvara (BBV, IV. 3. 5, p. 1377). Undoubtedly this word clearly expresses the state of the Person.

As regards the wording of our text in the first Book of ĀŚ with which we are now concerned the following comparison may be made:

(*i*) With regard to Viśva our author writes (I. 2): *dakṣiṇākṣimukhe* viśvah.[6] See here BU, IV. 2.2: indho ha nāmaiṣa yo ' yaṃ *dakṣiṇe 'kṣan* puruṣaḥ (=BU, II. 3. 5; IV. 2. 2; V. 5. 2, 4).[7]

5 See BU, II. 5. 8.

6 Mark that the MāU is here silent.

7 The idea that a person is seen in the eye and specially in the right one is often found in Upaniṣadic texts. Besides the BU quoted above see ChU, IV. 15. 1, VII. 7. 4; KtU, IV. 2, 17; MU, VII. 11. It simply signifies that

(*ii*) In I. 2 we have *ākāśe ca hṛdi* prājñaḥ, and we read ya eṣo *'ntar hṛdaya ākāśaḥ* in BU, II. 1. 17, IV. 2. 3, 4. 22. *Cf.* TU, I. 6. 1.

(*iii*) In I. 3 there is *praviviktabhuj*,[8] and in this connexion we read tasmād eṣa *praviviktāhāratara* ivaiva bhavati in the BU, IV. 2. 3.

(*iv*) With regard to the third or *suṣupta* state of the Person in I. 3, 4 there is *ānandabhuj* or *ānanda*, and in BU, IV. 3. 32 we read eṣo'sya parama *ānandaḥ*. See also, *Op. cit.*, IV. 3. 33.[9]

It is to be noted here that the above conception of Puruṣa is found also in ChU, VIII. 7-12 in the course of Prajāpati's instruction to Indra and Virocana. Here, too, the first three names, *Viśva*, etc. are not given, Saṅkara has used different appellations for them; *viz.*, for *Viśva* he writes *Akṣipuruṣa* 'eye-person' (VIII. 7, 4, 7 9), or *Chāyāpuruṣa* 'shadow-person' (VIII. 10.4), or *Chāyātman* 'shadow-self' (VIII. 7. 4, 8. 1, 2);[10]

he is visible to our eyes, and this means that he is the ordinary incorporated soul (*śārīra ātman*). This is quite evident from Gauḍapāda's employment of the word *-mukha* after *dakṣiṇākṣi-* (I. 1: *dakṣiṇākṣimukhe* 'in the front of the right eye'). As to why the *right* eye is specially mentioned Sureśvara says (BBV. V. 2. 37-38, p. 1365) that it may be due to some excellence of the right eye, which might have been known to the *smṛti*, or to the fact that the right limbs of a man is more vigorous than the left ones. Sometimes the left eye is also referred to (BU, IV. 2. 3). See below.

[8] See also I. 4.

[9] That the sentence yatra supto na kiñcana° in the MāU, 5, p. 224, is quoted from the BU, IV. 3. 19 is already shown. Introduction: §2, p. xlii.

[10] He uses this term also in his commentary on BS, I. 2. 13; on I. 3. 43 he has also *śārīra*.

for *Taijasa* he has *Svapnātman* (VIII. 11. 1-2); and for *Prājña* he employs *Suṣuptastha* (VIII, 11. 1-2).[11] For *Turya* we have in the Upaniṣad (VIII. 12. 3)

[11] It is to be noted that Śaṅkara while in his commentary on BU gives all the three names, *Viśva*, etc., he does not do so in the commentary on the ChU. It is further to be noticed that he, though so very fond of quoting *śrutis* does not refer to ChU in his commentary on BU, nor BU in that on ChU.

A few words may be added here as to why *Viśva* is said to be in the eye or in the right eye and consequently is called *Akṣipuruṣa*, *Chāyāpuruṣa* or *Chāyātman*.

To understand the Highest Self (*paramātman*) is very difficult for a man who is not properly trained. It took Indra, as says the ChU, VIII. 7. 3 ff., not less than one hundred and one years to realize him. So he is instructed to do it gradually, following the maxim of the view of the star *Arundhatī* 'Alcor' belonging to the Great Bear (*Arundhatīdarśananyāya*). The star being a very small one cannot be seen at once. So a man in order to show it to another man first points out to the latter somethings other than the actual star one by one and finally succeeds in doing so. Śaṅkara writes (ChU, VIII. 12. 1) the same thing in another way: On the second night of the bright half of a month a man desirous of showing a second man the fine moon first points out a tree before the latter saying: 'See, there is the moon.' In the same way he points out to him a series of trees one by one and then the peak of a mountain, on which the moon is visible, and thus the second man actually sees her. Similarly in our case, the mind of an ordinary man being too much attached to external things cannot at once grasp the Highest Self who is extremely subtle. Therefore, he is first instructed to know his incorporated Self (*śārīra ātman*), other Selves or the different states of the Self being described gradually. Now, how to know the corporated Self? What is the best means for it? The sage of the Upaniṣads says: "Look here. Here is my right eye. Look at it. What do you find in it?" Certainly he would see himself reflected thereon. And pointing out the shadow the sage would tell him 'Here is the Self.' This is elaborately described in the episode of Prajāpati and his two disciples, Indra and Virocana, in the ChU, VIII. 7-12, where it is said that the Self is to be seen not only in the eyes, but also on a looking glass (*ādarśa*), water (*ap*), and an earthen jar filled with water (*udaśarāva*). Śaṅkara rightly adds here (ChU, VIII. 7. 4) also such things as the blade of a sword (*khaḍgādi*). See KtU, IV. 2, 11. 17-18.

quite appropriately *Uttamapuruṣa* 'the Highest Self.'[12]

That this conception of Puruṣa in ChU is a later development of that in the BU goes without saying. Now, though the ChU like the BU is far earlier than our text, there is nothing which can show that it is the former and not the latter which has been drawn upon by our author; yet, we have already seen what can be said in favour of BU.

In support of the view that the main source of the ĀŚ is BU we may discuss here one point more. The idea of Brahman (=Puruṣa=Ātman) as having four fourths or quarters (*catuṣpād*) at the beginning of the MāU is not a new one as it is found long before it even in the RV, X. 90. 3[13] as well as in ChU, III. 18. 2.[14] The difference of these texts lies, however, in the fact that the quarters (*pādas*) are different in them. For instance, in the RV referred to above all the beings (*viśvā bhūtāni*) are regarded as one quarter, and the remaining three quarters (*tripād*) are said to be in the heaven, while in the ChU, IV. 5-8

2 See BG, XV. 17-18:

> uttamaḥ puruṣas tv anyaḥ paramātmety udāhṛtaḥ |
> yo lokatrayam āviśya bibharty advaya īśvaraḥ ||
> yasmāt kṣaram atīto'ham akṣarād api cottamaḥ |
> ato'smi loke vede ca prathitaḥ puruṣottamaḥ ||

Ś has here quoted no *śruti*. Śrīdhara refers to BU, V. 6. 1 (sa vā ayam ātmā), but not appropriately.

13 See ĀŚ, II. 21.

14 For minor Upaniṣads see *Brahmopaniṣad*, 2: tatra catuṣpādaṃ brahma vibhāti; NPTU, V. 1; NUTU, 1; RUTU, 3: so 'yam ātmā catuṣpād.

the four quarters each consisting of four parts (*catuṣkala*) are named as *Prakāśavat* 'shining,' *Anantavat* 'endless,' *Jyotiṣmat* 'luminous,' and *Āyatanavat* 'having an abode.'[15] In another place of the same Upaniṣad (III. 18. 1-6) the quarters of Brahman are described differently with reference to person (*adhyātma*) and with reference to divinities (*adhidaivata*). With reference to person they are speech (*vāc*), breath (*prāṇa*), the eye (*cakṣus*) and the ear (*śrotra*) representing respectively with reference to the divinities fire (*agni*), wind (*vāyu*), the sun (*āditya*) and quarter (*diś*). But in the MāU the quarters are described quite in a new way and it is remarkable. It is said that these four quarters are nothing but the same Self with its four states. The first three of them are waking (*jāgrat*), dreaming (*svapna*), and deep sleep (*suṣupta*). And the Self with them is called *Vaiśvānara*. 'common-to-all,' *Taijasa* 'brilliant,' and *Prājña* 'intelligent' respectively. The fourth state is the true or absolute essence of the Self having no connexion whatsoever with anything else. In this state the Self is regarded as *śānta* 'quiescent,' *śiva* 'blissful' and *advaita* 'without a second.'

It is to be noted here that while in RV and ChU the Puruṣa or Brahman is represented as the Universal or World Self, in the MāU it is represented as the individual Self though ultimately in fact it is identical with the Universal Self.

Now, it is remarkable that though in the MāU, as

15 For details see the Upaniṣad.

we have seen above, there is a clear mention and description of the four quarters of the Self (*catuṣpād*), in the ĀŚ it is not so. Even the particular word *catuṣpād* or any of its possible equivalents is not to be found here. Up to kārikā 5 we come across the threefold division of the Self, *viz.*, *Viśva* (instead of *Vaiśvānara* as in the MāU, 3), *Taijasa* and *Prājña* (I. 1-4). It is clearly said in our text (I. 1-2) that the One exists in three ways in the body, and this idea is further expressed in I. 3-5. Yet, it cannot be said from this that the idea of four quarters is altogether unknown to the author of the ĀŚ, as it is implied in I. 10-15 in which the word *turya* or *turīya*, which is the same in meaning 'fourth,' as *caturtha* in the MāU, 7, is used. It is further implied by the author's employment of the word *pāda* in I. 25.[16] This difference between the ĀŚ and the MāU with regard to the idea of four *pādas*, implied in the former and expressed in the latter, is significant. It shows that the origin of the ĀŚ is not the MāU, but the BU in which the idea of *pādas* in this connexion did not then so develop.[17]

En passant we should like to discuss one thing more. There is a very striking difference at the very

16 See BU, IV. I. 2-7 where each of the following six things, *vāc* 'speech,' *prāṇa* 'breath,' *cakṣus* 'eye,' *śrotra* 'ear,' *manas* 'mind,' and *hṛdaya* 'heart' is regarded as a *pāda*. Consult Śaṅkara and Sureśvara (BBV, IV. I. 16 ff) according to whom each of the above six is explained as *catuṣpāda* 'having four quarters.'

17 This fact will also show that the ĀŚ is prior to the MāU in which the obscure points of the former are made clear.

beginning between the two texts, MāU and ĀŚ. It is this that while the MāU begins (1-2) highly extolling Om symbolically identifying it with Brahman-Ātman, the ĀŚ has here nothing of the kind. It simply proceeds gradually to describe the One with its first three states, *Viśva*, *Taijasa* and *Prājña* (I. 1-5) the fourth having come afterwards (I. 10). Here in the ĀŚ till kārikā 19 there is no mention of, or reference to Om. So it is to be found that here in our text mention is made first of the One and then of Om. This order is quite right and logical. For, here there are two things, the object which is to be approached or realized (*upeya*) and its means (*upāya*). And it is reasonable that the object is stated first and then the means. Here the object is the realization of the Puruṣa or Self in its absolute state and the means is the meditation of Om. This is done in the ĀŚ, but it is quite reverse in the MāU, for here the means Om is stated first and then gradually the object (3-7) which is repeated later on (12). The author of the MāU seems to have been much influenced by earlier Upaniṣads, (such as ChU, I. 1. 1; TU, I. 8. 1) and too much bent on the glorification of Om, and this is why he has changed the reasonable order found in the ĀŚ. There is no *upāsanā* of *Praṇava* in the BU and this is why our author of the ĀŚ did not include it in the main thesis of his work. Then independently of the BU in which no means for the realization of the object is shown G a u ḍ a p ā d a has added the remaining portion of the first Book of his ĀŚ setting forth *Praṇava* and its *upāsanā*.

So far with regard to Book I. Let us now take up Book II and see the connexion it has with the BU. This Book is rightly called *Vaitathya* 'unreality' as it shows the unreality of the world in the waking state just like that of the experience in dream. This is the subject discussed herein by G a u ḍ a p ā d a with various arguments. And here, too, he has taken his stand on the BU, IV. 3, where it is clearly declared that the two states, waking and dream, are in fact one. Not only are passages quoted from the BU, or referred to by him (II. 3, 5), but they are supported by his own arguments. This will be quite clear if one takes pains to read BU, IV. 3 and the second Book of the ĀŚ. And it should be noted that here in the latter we find the oldest interpretation of that portion of the BU, though in a concise, yet, very substantial form.

In Book III we are referred to BU not less than six times (12, 13, 15, 24, 25 and 26).

Thus we may safely conclude that the main Upaniṣadic source of the ĀŚ is the BU.

§ 13. *Pre-Śaṅkara Teachers of the Vedānta and their Works*

Setting apart what we know of the Vedānta from the *Śruti-prasthāna* 'the Course of Revelation' or the Vedic literature, *i. e.*, the Mantras and Brāhmaṇas including the Āraṇyakas and Upaniṣads, as well as from the *Smṛti-prasthāna* 'the Course of Tradition or Remembered Texts', such as the *Mahābhārata* with the

Bhagavadgītā, it may conveniently be divided into two, pre-Śaṅkara and post-Śaṅkara.

Among the teachers of the pre-Śaṅkara Vedānta the most distinguished is Bādarāyaṇa, the celebrated author of the *Brahmasūtras*, the source of which is the Upaniṣads. It is the *Brahmasūtras* that constitute the *Sūtra-prasthāna* 'the Course of *Sūtras*.'

We all know that the difference of opinions is but natural. Owing to various factors the same thing is viewed differently by different persons. So it is found in the Brāhmaṇas that there are both the offering of oblation before sun-rise (*anudita-homa*) and the offering of oblation after sun-rise (*udita-homa*), there being a regular discussion thereof establishing that the latter is preferable and not the former (*Aitareya Brāhmaṇa*, XXV. 5-6; *Taittirīya Brāhmaṇa*, II. 1. 2-8 ; *cf.* however, II. 1. 2. 12). There are also functions in these Brāhmaṇas, which are discarded saying that these are not to be preferred (*ādṛtya*) or performed (*kārya*), though they are actually enjoined by others. There are many such contradicting, obscure or dubious cases, and an attempt has also been made in later works to find out a solution of these problems.[1]

Now as with regard to *karman* the teachers had their different views, so they differed also on points of *jñāna*. In some cases they entertained even quite opposite views. For instance, with regard to creation while a sage of a certain Upaniṣad (*i.e.*, TU, II. 7. 1 ;

1 For instance, see MD. X. 8. 6 with reference to *Ṣoḍaśigrahaṇa*.

see ChU, III. 19. 1) tells us: 'In the beginning, verily, this was non-existent (asad vā idam agra āsīd),' but from another text (i.e., *Aitareya Āraṇyaka*, II. 4. 1) we know: 'Verily, in the beginning this was only Self (ātmā vā idam eka evāgra āsīd).' And the following is found in the ChU, VI. 2. 1-2, evidently refuting TU, II. 7. 1 quoted above: "Verily, in the beginning this was, my dear, existent only one without a second. On this some say that verily in the beginning this was non-existent only one without a second; from that non-existent the existent was produced. But, my dear, whence could it be? How from non-existent could the existent be produced? On the contrary, my dear, verily, in the beginning this was existent, only one without a second."

From the above it is quite clear that all the *śrutis* do not always tell us the same thing, clearly there is difference among them.[2] Such being the case the question arises as to which of them is to be accepted as valid and which is to be rejected as not valid. How can one say that this is valid, and that is not valid? For, as *śruti* there is no difference whatsoever.[3] Therefore if you accept one, you will have to accept all of them. And in that case you cannot arrive at any definite

[2] See with the *Prakāśa* of Puṇyarāja the *Vākyapadīya* of Bhartṛhari, I. 8:

> tasyārthavādarūpāṇi niścitya svavikalpajāḥ |
> ekatvināṃ dvaitināṃ ca pravādā bahudhā smṛtāḥ ||

[3] Śaṅkara has rightly observed (BS, III. 2. 15): nahi vedavākyānāṃ kasyacid arthavattvaṃ kasyacid anarthavattvam iti yuktaṃ pratipattuṃ pramāṇatvāviśeṣāt.

conclusion. And if there is no conclusion of any kind the teaching of the Vedānta has no value to a person as it does not or cannot lead him to his final goal. The Vedānta is not a science for mere speculation, for one is to adjust one's life according to it. For only in this way one can fulfil the mission of one's life. It was therefore felt absolutely necessary by the teachers to bring into a harmony, a compromise or a connected sequence, all conflicting, obscure or dubious statements of the sages of the Upaniṣads. This was the origin on one hand of the *Mīmāṃsāsūtras* with regard to the question of *karman*, and on the other of the *Brahmasūtras* in respect of *jñāna*.[4]

[4] Let us however put here a question: Are we right in thinking that even through the methods or maxims (*nyāyas*) shown in the *Brahmasūtras* in connexion with the explanation of the Upaniṣadic texts, we can in all cases get their *true* significance? By 'true significance' we mean the significance intended by their respective sages. It is true that the word *asat* may imply in some cases 'unfolded' or 'that of which the name and form are unfolded' (*avyākṛta* or *avyākṛtanāmarūpa*). For instance, see asac ca sac ca parame vyoman (RV, X. 5. 7); or nāsad āsīn na sac āsīt tadānīm, (*Op. cit.*, X. 129. 1). In such cases *asat* does not mean 'false, non-existent' (*nirupākhya asat*), as the son of a barren woman, though in other cases it may actually mean so. Now considering the above passage of the ChU it is clear that the word *asat* in the TU quoted above is used in its literal sense, *i.e.*, the sense of unreal non-existent (*nirupākhya asat*), though an attempt is made in explaining it away figuratively to mean 'unfolded' (*avyākṛta*) according to the subsequently established maxims of the Vedānta. But a question arises: Well, in the TU the word *asat* may imply *avyākṛta* as you maintain (see here BU, I. 4. 7: tad dhedaṃ tarhy avyākṛtam āsīt), but how do you ascertain that this meaning is in fact intended by the sage himself? How do you know that he does not want here to mean thereby absolutely non-existent (*nirupākhya asat*)? We can only accept that the meaning *avyākṛta* is *your* explanation. But this may or may not be intended by the sage himself. There is this doubt that can hardly be removed.

It is well-known that Jaimini and Bādarāyaṇa are the authors of the *Mīmāṃsāsūtras* and the *Brahmasūtras* respectively. But there are reasons to think that there were also other authors of the *Mīmāṃsa-* and the *Brahma-sūtras* which are different from the extant ones.[5] For instance, Bādari, a teacher, is quoted not less than four times both in the present *Mīmāṃsā-* (III. 1. 3; VI. 1. 27; VIII. 3. 6; IX. 2. 33) and *Brahma-sūtras* (I. 2. 30; III. 1. 11; IV. 3. 7; IV. 4. 10). From this it may appear that Bādari was an author of both the *sūtras*. But we cannot ascertain only from this that he was actually so. It may be that he had some views on some particular points of *karman* and Brahman and these are alluded to in those two works by their authors. Jaimini, as the author of the *Mīmāṃsāsūtras* is known to us all. He is referred to eleven times in the *Brahmasūtras* on different topics (I. 2. 28, 31, 3. 31, 4. 18; III. 2. 40, 4. 2, 18, 40; IV. 3. 12, 4. 5, 11). Here, too, we may think that Jaimini wrote also *Brahmasūtras*. But though from only this it is not safe to decide that he really did so, Sureśvara's Nsi (2nd ed. by Hiriyanna), p. 52, shows that it is a fact. Kāśakṛtsna, a teacher, is quoted in BS, I. 4. 22, and his *Mīmāṃsā* is mentioned not less than three times by Patañjali in his *Mahābhāṣya*.[7] This *Mīmāṃsā* may be both *Karmamīmāṃsā* and *Brahmamīmāṃsā*[6] (*i.e.*, the *Mīmāṃsāsūtras* and the *Brahmasūtras*),

5 See Belvalkar, *Op. cit.*, p. 140.

6 See *Jaimini's Śārīrakasūtra* in the *Garbe-Festgabe*, 1927.

7 Kielhorn, Vol. II, pp. 206, 249, 325.

or either of them, and in this case probably the latter. B ā d a r ā y a ṇ a in his BS refers also to Ā t r e y a (III. 4. 44), Ā ś m a r a t h y a (I. 2. 29, 4. 20), K ā r ṣ ṇ ā j i n i (III. 1. 9)[8], and A u ḍ u l o m i[9] (I. 4. 21, III. 4. 45, IV. 4. 6).[10]

Then comes a number of teachers, some of whom flourished before and some after the great Ś a ṅ k a r a. Some of them explained the BS of B ā d a r ā y a ṇ a, some the *Bhagavadgītā*, and some an Upaniṣad or Upaniṣads. There were also some who interpreted more than one kind of the above works. This was done either by writing a gloss (*vṛtti*) or a commentary (*bhāṣya*). As we are concerned here with the pre-Ś a ṅ k a r a Vedānta the following teachers who are connected with it may be mentioned in this connexion.

So far as we know the first of all these teachers is B o d h ā y a n a (about the first or second century A.D.). He wrote a lengthy gloss or commentary (*vistīrṇa vṛtti*) on the BS of B ā d a r ā y a ṇ a on which is based the Viśiṣṭādvaita system of R ā m ā n u j a, the *Mīmāṃsā-sūtras* of J a i m i n i, and the *Devatākāṇḍa*, in other words, on the whole of the *Mīmāṃsāśāstra*. This

8 He is mentioned also in MD, IV. 3. 17, VI. 7. 35.

9 The *Bhedābheda* doctrine of the N i m b ā r k a school owes its existence to him.

10 To them may be added the names of K ā ś y a p a alluded to by Ś ā ṇ ḍ i l y a in his *Bhaktisūtras*, 29, and of such sages as A s i t a, D e v a l a, B h ṛ g u, and P a r ā ś a r a referred to in different works. But we do not know if they were the authors of different *Brahmasūtras* or if any one of them wrote also *Mīmāṃsāsūtras*, though we know something of their views from the fragmentary accounts available from certain books, some of which are referred to above.

vṛtti is called *Kṛtakoṭi* (*Prapañcahṛdaya*, TSS, p. 39; *Journal of the American Oriental Society*, 1911, p. 17).

Next comes U p a v a r ṣ a. He is credited with the authorship of a *vṛtti* on both the *Mīmāṃsāsūtras* and *Brahmasūtras*. This *vṛtti* was, however, in fact a *bhāṣya* or *Mahābhāṣya* and consequently he was regarded as a *Mahābhāṣyakāra* as well as a *Vṛttikāra*, being the author of the *vṛtti*.

According to R ā m ā n u j a (*Vedārthasaṃgraha*, p. 154) and Ś r ī n i v ā s a d ā s a (*Yatīndramatadīpikā*, Poona ed., p. 2) G u h a d e v a, K a p a r d i k a (or K a p a r d i n) and B h ā r u c i are three ancient Vedānta teachers and authors. The former two, being referred to by R ā m ā n u j a among the *śiṣṭas* 'wise men', seem to have been in favour of the Viśiṣṭādvaita-vāda. One B h ā r u c i as an author of a *Dharmaśāstra* is mentioned in such works as V i j ñ ā n e ś v a r a 's *Mitākṣarā* on the *Yājñavalkya-smṛti* (I. 18, II. 124), and M ā d h a v ā c ā r y a 's ṭikā on the *Parāśarasaṃhitā* (II. 2. 3, Bombay Sanskrit series ed., p. 510). It is not known if the Vedāntic B h ā r u c i is identical with B h ā r u c i, the writer on the *Dharmaśāstra*. If it is so, he may be held to have belonged to the first half of the ninth century A. D.

B h a r t ṛ h a r i 's name is found among a host of writers on the Vedānta (*Siddhitraya*, p. 5). He may be identified with the celebrated author of the *Vākyapadīya* (600-650 A.D.), the very first kārikā of which points to the Vedāntic doctrine.

With him is mentioned in the same work Bhartṛmitra. According to the *Nyāyaratnākara* on the *Ślokavārttika* (I. 10) he wrote a commentary on the *Mīmāṃsāsūtras* and made the *Mīmāṃsāśāstra* atheistic. Whether this Mīmāṃsist Bhartṛmitra and the Vedāntic Bhartṛmitra are one and the same is not known, nor do we know anything of any Vedāntic work that might have been written by the latter.

Brahmanandin (or Brahmānandin) is another teacher. He is known as the *Vākyakāra* or *Chāndogyavākyakāra* quoted or referred to by Rāmānuja in his commentary on BS and Madhusūdana Sarasvatī in his ṭikā on the *Saṃkṣepaśārīraka* (III.218-220). According to Bhāskara on BS, I. 4. 25, Brahmanandin approved the *Parināma-vāda*, but Madhusūdana Sarasvatī (*Op. cit.*) is of opinion that it was in fact gradually to lead one to *Śuddhādvaita-vāda* 'Pure monism' through the *Vivarta-vāda* or the doctrine maintaining that the appearance of the universe is imposed on Brahman which is the only reality, the phenomenal world being held to be a mere illusion.

After him is Draviḍācārya or Dramiḍācārya (*cir.* 750 A.D.). He was in favour of the *Viśiṣṭādvaita-vāda* 'Qualified monism' and as such is mentioned and quoted by Rāmānuja in his commentary on BS. As Madhusūdana Sarasvatī says (*Saṃkṣepaśārīraka*, III. 218-220), he wrote a *bhāṣya* on Brahmanandin's *vākyas* owing to which the latter was called *Vākyakāra* (Brahmanandi-viracitānāṃ vākyānāṃ sūtrarūpāṇāṃ bhāṣyakartā draviḍācāryo'pi). It is known from Ānandagiri's ṭīkā on Śaṅkara's *bhāṣya* on the ChU that Draviḍācārya wrote a vast commentary on the ChU compared with which Śaṅkara's commentary was a smaller one (*alpagrantha*). He is said to have written a *bhāṣya* also on the BS.

Brahmadatta was a renowned teacher of the Vedānta. In the *Prapañcahṛdaya* he is said to have composed a commentary on the BS. Some of his views are alluded to in such works as the *Sarvārthasiddhi* (II.16), a ṭīkā by Veṅkaṭanāthadeśika on his *Tattvamuktākalāpa*; Nsi, I. 67-68; and Śaṅkara's commentary on the BU, I. 4. 7. One of them may be mentioned here and it is this that it is the long *bhāvanā* 'meditation' of the knowledge arising from the *Vedānta-vākya* and not the knowledge itself, as holds Śaṅkara, that removes one's illusion. Some informations of him as collected by Hiriyanna will be found in Nsi (2nd ed.), p. xxiii, and the *Journal of Oriental Research*, Madras, Vol. II, Part I, p. 1 ff. See also Gopinath Kaviraj, *Op. cit.*, p. 13 ff.

Bhartṛprapañca was also a great Vedāntic teacher before Śaṅkara. It is known from the words of Madhusūdana Sarasvatī (*Saṃkṣepaśārīraka*, I. 7) that Bhartṛprapañca explained the *Sūtras* of Vyāsa, *i.e.*, Bādarāyaṇa (kaiścit tatsūtraṃ vyācakṣāṇair bhartṛprapañcādibhiḥ). Yāmunācārya (*Op. cit.*, p. 5) says that he was one of the writers on the Vedānta, and we know from the introductory lines of Ā n a n d a g i r i ' s ṭīkā on Ś a ṅ k a r a ' s *bhāṣya* of BU (p. 2) that while Ś a ṅ k a r a commented on the Upaniṣad belonging to the Kāṇva recension B h a r t ṛ - p r a p a ñ c a wrote his commentary on the text of the Mādhyandina recension, and the former's commentary was bigger than that of the latter. In many cases Ā n a n d a g i r i in explaining S u r e ś v a r a ' s *vārttika* on the BU, refers to or quotes from B h a r t ṛ p r a p a ñ c a. Of all the commentators before Ś a ṅ k a r a, the works of whom could not yet been discovered it is B h a r t ṛ p r a p a ñ c a whose quotations are now mostly available. For the fragments gleaned together from his writings by H i r i y a n n a see *The Indian Antiquary*, 1924, pp. 76-86 ; and *Proceedings and Transactions of the Third Oriental Conference*, Madras, 1925, pp. 439.

I should like to mention here one teacher more of the pre-Ś a ṅ k a r a Vedānta. He is S u n d a r a - p ā ṇ ḍ y a. He was a great Mīmāṃsist and Vedāntin of South India (8th century A.D.). His three kārikās (gauṇamithyātva°) are quoted by Ś a ṅ k a r a in the last portion of his commentary on BS, I. 1. 4. A m a l ā n a n d a in his *Kalpataru* (BS, III. 25) quotes his other three kārikās (nihśreṇyārohaṇa-prāpya°). These last three kārikās together with two more are cited by K u m ā r i l a in his *Tantravārttika* (Benares ed.), pp. 852-853. It seems that these kārikās are from a *vārttika* of S u n d a r a p ā ṇ ḍ y a that he wrote on some *vṛtti* or *bhāṣya* of some unknown author.[11]

There were also some teachers who wrote independent works on the Vedānta and of these authors the most distinguished is Gauḍapāda, the author of our *Āgamaśāstra* which is the most important work, still extant, representing one of the most remarkable phases of the Vedānta. Here we find the first interpretation of some of the most important *śrutis* as we shall see later on.

§ 14. *The Conspectus of the Contents of the Āgamaśāstra*

Now we may give here a conspectus of the contents of our text, and in doing so Book I may conveniently be divided into two parts; part (*i*) containing kārikās I. 1-18, and part (*ii*) the remaining kārikās, *i.e.*, I. 19-29. While part (*i*) discusses what is to be realized, part (*ii*) is devoted to show its means.

It is well-known that in the Upaniṣads all thoughts centre round the Puruṣa (Ātman = Brahman), 'Self' who is 'all that has been and that will be' (RV,X.90.2: puruṣa evedaṃ sarvaṃ yad bhūtaṃ yac ca bhavyam). He must be known, according to the sages of Upaniṣads, for the fulfilment of the mission of one's life.

[11] S. Kuppuswāmī Śāstrī: *Journal of Oriental Research*, 1927, p. 1 ff.

On the main topic of this section see Gopinath Kaviraj, *Op. cit.*, and P. V. Kane: *Proceedings and Transactions of the Fifth Indian Oriental Conference*, pp. 937 ff.

But how can he be known properly ? As he is extremely subtle, G a u ḍ a p ā d a leads us gradually from the gross to the subtle, following our common and every-day experience. And in doing so he takes his stand on such Upaniṣads as the BU and ChU, and shows (I. 1-5) that the self, though in reality, only one (eka eva) remains in the body in three forms (tridhā dehe vyavasthitaḥ), in accordance with his three states, *jāgrat* 'waking', *svapna* 'dream' and *suṣupta* 'deep sleep.' When the self is in the waking state he is called Viśva 'all' (because as an embodied one (*śārīra*) he is known to every man). In the state of dream he is named Taijasa 'brilliant' (because he himself is his light (*svayaṃjyotis*) in that condition ; *i.e.*, he does not depend for his light on others for seeing things there, as he does in the waking state in which he is to take light from such things as the sun, the moon, and fire).[1] In the state of deep sleep he is called Prājña 'intelligent' (because he is never dissociated from his intelligence).[2]

Viśva is the embodied self (*śārīra ātman*), hence it is metaphorically said that he remains in the front of one's right eye,[3] meaning thereby that he may be seen reflected in one's right[4] eye (or in such things as

1 See BU, IV. 3. 1-9 : svena bhāsā svena jyotiṣā prasvapity atrāyaṃ puruṣaḥ svayaṃjyotir bhavati.

2 BU, IV. 3. 23 ff. : yad vai tan na paśyati paśyan vai tan na paśyati. nahi draṣṭur dṛṣṭer viparilopo vidyate 'vināśitvāt. na tu tad dvitīyam asti tato 'nyad vibhaktaṃ yat paśyet.

3 See p. lxxxxviii

4 As the right portion of the body of a male person is said to be more powerful than the left the reflection therein is brighter. See p. lxxxxvii, note 7.

water or a looking-glass). Taijasa is in the mind, as it is here that a man dreams. Prājña's seat is in the space of one's heart. Again, Viśva has the consciousness of outside, Taijasa of inside, while Prājña has his consciousness compact. These three enjoy or experience the gross, the subtle and bliss [5] respectively.

In passing the author refers (I. 6-9) to the opinion of the sages that all things have their origin and mentions different theories or purposes of creation. The first theory is this that one creates all as the rays of one's mind (*ceto'ṃśu*). This simply means that it is the mind that appears in the form of the external world which has, in fact, no reality. This is the author's own view.

Then he reverts to his main subject, the Self, and says (I-10) that besides his three forms or quarters (*pādas*) in accordance with the three states, waking, etc., referred to above, there is one form more ; it is his real, natural or innate form. It has no particular appellation as he is beyond all expressions and is designated by the simple word Turya (or Turīya) 'fourth' as occupying the fourth place in order with the above three. This Turya is above all changes and duality, all-pervading, and when realized removes all miseries

Gauḍapāda then shows (I I-18) some points of mutual agreement and disagreement of these four forms or quarters (*pādas*) of the Self, and says that one, if awakened from one's sleep due to illusion

[5] BU. IV. 3 32 ff.

(*māyā*), can realize the state of Turya in which there is no duality at all. Duality, *i.e.*, the expansion of the visible world, or the expressions, is mere illusion, and as such it has absolutely no reality. (Here it may be said that as there is no duality, in fact, it does not cease to exist. It is just a knot made and loosened by dint of illusion (māyayaiva kṛto granthir māyayaiva vimocitaḥ).[6] Nevertheless, we have our common practice with duality, but it is only for our instruction, *i.e.*, it is only by that practice that we can understand and attain to the state of non-duality which is the highest (advaitaṃ paramārthataḥ). Here ends the first part of Book I.

The second part (19-29) demonstrates the means for the realization of that non-duality or Turya. It is nothing but the *upāsanā* 'meditation' (*dhyāna*) of the Puruṣa (= Ātman = Brahman), 'Self' through the symbol of *Praṇava* or Om.

In Book II Gauḍapāda discusses and establishes the unreality (*vaitathya*) of the external world. For this purpose he begins this Book as Book I basing it on the BU, specially on its IV. 3. 8 ff. He says referring to the sages[7] of that Upaniṣad that all things in dream are unreal on the following three grounds:

6 See the following saying of the Bhagavat (*i.e.*, Buddha), as quoted in MV, p. 540: ākāśena kṛto granthir ākāśenaiva mocitaḥ.

7 Gauḍapāda does not employ here or elsewhere (*i.e.*, II.5, *cf.* IV. 54) such words as *ṛṣi* or *muni* (II. 35) as is generally done in similar cases, but he has here the word *manīṣin*. This word, which is a Vedic one forming a phrase with *āhuḥ*, is used twice in our work (II. 1, 5) as in KU, I. 3. 4 and BG, XVIII. 3 (with a variation that *pra-* is prefixed to *āhuḥ*).

(*i*) becuase the things (such as a mountain, or an elephant) seen therein are inside the body ; (*ii*) because the time being short one does not see the things having gone to those far places where one dreams them ; and (*iii*) because one on waking is not found in the place where one dreams oneself to be. Having supported this proposition (II. 3) by a reference to the BU, IV. 3. 10, he asserts (II. 4) that the things in the waking state, too, are as unreal as those in dream, because in this state also the things are similarly inside the body, for the mind which appears in the form of different things around us is inside the body. Proceeding the teacher says (II. 5) on the authority of a scripture (BU, IV. 3. 14), supported by reasons, that the two states, dream and waking, are the same on account of the fact that the things experienced in them are of the same kind, there being no difference at all. Here, having offered one reason more in his favour and met an objection of his opponent, he says (II.9-10) that the experiences in waking and dream are equally unreal, both of them being the creation of the mind. Here arises a question (II. 11) : If in both the states the things are unreal, then who is it that cognizes them? Who is it that imagines them? The answer is given (II. 12-15) according to the decision of the Vedānta that it is the Self that imagines himself as the Self through his own illusion, and it is he who cognizes the things. He creates some things in the mind which are not fixed and as such they vanish at once ; and he creates also some other things in the mind which are outside and fixed. There is, however, no difference between these two sorts of creation—the creation of those inside which exists as long as exists the thought (*citta*), and the creation of those outside, which exists as long as exists the (notion of) the two, *i.e.*, the perceptible (*grāhya*) and the percipient (*grāhaka*); both of these two creations are only imagined and there is nothing for their difference. Again, the things which are within and not-manifest, and the things which are without and manifest are all imagined, indeed, the only difference there being that the latter are cognized by different organs of sense. As to the creation of the internal and external things he tells us (II. 16) that first one imagines oneself as a personal Self and then various things, internal and external, following the recollection of one's experience. Of this he says further (II.17-18) that as in the dark a piece of rope, or a continuous line of water, etc., not determinately known, is imagined to be a snake, so is imagined the Self. Now when the piece of rope is known determinately the things that are imagined there disappear at once,[8] so is to be known about the ascertainment of the Self (Ātman). It is an illusion of the Self owing to which he is imagined differently by differnt persons, such as the Breath (*prāṇa*) by those who know it, or Elements (*bhūtas*) by those who know them (II. 19-30). But the reality is, concludes (II. 31-34) the teacher, that according to those

[8] The illustration of *rajju-sarpa* which is so widely known in Vedāntic works is found perhaps for the first time here in the ĀŚ. It is not in any of the Upaniṣads used for his *Concordance* by J a c o b.

who are well-versed in the Vedānta, the universe is just like a dream (*svapna*), or an illusion (*māyā*), or an imaginary town in the sky (*gandharvanagara*). The highest truth is that there is neither disappearance nor origination; neither bondage, nor one desirous of emancipation. The universe is not manifold, either through its own nature or through that of others; it is neither different nor non-different. The sages (II. 35-38) who have fully mastered the Vedas have seen the truth that it is the cessation of the universe (*prapañcopaśama*), which is free from duality. Having known this, therefore, one should meditate on non-duality, and having realized it, one should behave as a fool among the people becoming an ascetic, and realizing the truth inward and outward, should remain unmoved from it.

Book III is devoted to show the non-origination of the universe. The author proposes (III. 2) that nothing originates, and concludes (III. 48) that this is the highest truth. In the course of the discussion he says (III. 5ff) that as the space (*ākāśa* or *mahākāśa*), owing to jars (*ghaṭas*), assumes the forms of the spaces occupied by the jars (*ghaṭākāśas*), and these forms, when the jars are destroyed, merge into the space, even so springs up the Ātman in the form of Jīvas 'individual persons' owing to the conglomerations of the different limbs, etc., and when these conglomerations are destroyed the Jīvas merge into the Ātman. If the space occupied by one jar is soiled with dust or smoke, not all the spaces occupied by other jars are soiled therewith, even so (*i.e.*, not affected) are the Jīvas with reference to happiness, etc. The forms, functions and names of the jars may be different, but the space is the same. This is the case also with Jīvas. As the space of a jar is neither a transformation, nor a part of the space, so is a Jīva neither a transformation nor a part of the Ātman. As the space is never soiled with a dirty thing such as dust and smoke, yet it appears to be so to the ignorant, so appears the Ātman with impurities to those who are not enlightened. In death or birth, in moving forward or backward, he exists in all bodies just like the space. All the conglomerations of limbs, etc., as in dream, are created by the illusion of the Ātman.

Now having shown what the Jīva is according to the Upaniṣads (TA, II. 1-6 and BU, II. 5) G a u ḍ a - p ā d a says (III. 13) that the praise of the identity of the Jīva and the Ātman as well as the censure of their difference in the Upaniṣads is reasonable. And so, though their difference is found in some Upaniṣadic texts it is merely attributable with reference to the future state, and certainly it is not in the primary sense (III. 14-16). Indeed in the scriptures the creation is described with various illustrations showing a distinction between the Jīva and the Ātman. But in fact there is no distinction. It is only to lead one to the truth. For, there are three kinds of people, *viz.*, of the lower, the middle, and the higher visions and in order to help them an *upāṣanā* is meant here (by the description of the creation involving some distinction which is mere atiributive). Here (III. 17-18) with regard to the view of non-duality which he holds, our author says that it does not conflict with that of the dualists and shows how it does not do so.

G a u ḍ a p ā d a reverts now (III. 19-32) to his main proposition, *i.e.*, non-origination and offers some arguments in favour of it, refuting the views of his opponents. He says that though it is said that it is the unborn that is born, it cannot be maintained. It is true that in the scriptures creation or origination is found both from the existent (*bhūta*) and the non-existent (*abhūta*), yet, that which is reasonable is to be accepted. In scriptures origination is said to be through illusion, it is denied there and its cause is negatived. Now, origination may be either of the existent (*sat*) or of the non-existent (*asat*), but neither of them is possible. That which exists may originate only through illusion and not in reality; because, if it originates in fact, it is to be accepted that the thing which had already been originated originates again. The origination of the non-existent is not reasonable either in reality or through illusion, as in the case of the son of a barren woman.

As in dream so in waking there is only the mind, yet it appears in the form of the duality of the percipient and the perceptible. The duality is perceived by the mind, but when it becomes non-mind, *i.e.*, when its function of thinking (*manana*) ceases, there is no duality. The author says here (III. 33-36) that the mind which becomes non-mind, and as such is free from the states of dream and deep sleep and has no determination (*nirvikalpa*), is identical with Brahman.

This state of the suppressed (*nigṛhīta* = *niruddha*) mind is different from that in the deep sleep, because while in the latter it falls into a condition of stupidity (*mūḍha avasthā*), it is not so in the former. This is attainable (III. 37-47) through an intense abstract concentration, called *Asparśayoga* 'contactless concentration,' which, though very difficult, can be realized gradually by the means suggested by the author. When by that process the mind is completely suppressed being free from the states at stupefaction and distraction, not moving at all and having no sense-image whatsoever, it becomes Brahman. And it is said that in this state it rests on itself (*svastha*), it does not originate and is identical with the knowable which also does not originate. Here the author concludes (III. 48) that there is nothing that originates, and this is the highest truth.

Gauḍapāda begins Book IV, unlike the first three ones, with his homage to the 'Greatest of men' and the teacher of the yoga known as *Asparśayoga*, whom the present writer thinks to be no other than the Buddha (IV. 1-2). Introducing his thesis (IV. 3) he says that there are two classes of disputants, one of them holding that it is the existent (*bhūta*) that originates while the other says that which originates is the non-existent (*abhūta*). But the Advayas (= Advayavādins), *i. e.*, Buddhists declaring that there is no origination at all maintain that neither the existent nor the non-existent comes into being (IV. 3-4). Gauḍapāda who is a Vedāntin subscribes to this last view and says (IV. 5): 'We approve of non-origination declared by them; we do not dispute with them, listen as to how there cannot be any dispute.' He then advances (IV. 6-71) various arguments gathered from Buddhist sources in support of the view attacking and refuting the theory of origination in different ways and arrives at the conclusion that non-origination is the highest truth. In the course of it he shows among others that though it is generally believed that a thing which is not born is born, it cannot be so in reality, for in that case it is to be admitted that nature changes; what is unborn must always remain unborn, it is its nature. Yet, if you say that it takes its birth, then evidently it changes. But what is nature does in no way change (IV. 6-10).

The theory that the cause itself is the effect that is born (as held by the Sāṅkhyas) cannot be maintained (IV. 11-13), nor can there be any reasonable relationship or order between the cause and its effect (IV. 14-21). Again, nothing is produced either from itself or from other than itself; nor is there anything produced that is existent, non-existent, or both existent and non-existent (IV. 22). It is not possible to prove the beginning of a cause or of an effect, and as such neither of them comes into being (IV. 24).

G a u ḍ a p ā d a offers here some reasons in his support from the standpoint of the Vijñānavādins (IV. 25-39) showing that the external things are unreal though they appear to be not unreal; they are, however, false as the experience in dream, being cognizable only by mind (*cittadṛśya*). He tells us again (IV. 40-41) that origination cannot be established, for there is no non-existent arising from the non-existent, nor is there any existent arising from the non-existent ; there is no existent arising from the existent, and where is the non-existent arising from the existent ?

It is true that the Buddhas have sometimes said of origination, but it is the instruction meant only for those who are afraid of the doctrine of non-origination (IV. 42). As an elephant called by illusion is said to exist only owing to the perception and the common practice, so it is said that a thing exists (IV. 44). He declares (IV. 45-46) that there is only *vijñāna* without the two (*i.e.*, the percipient and the perceptible), it is quiescent and has no origination (*aja*) ; it does not move, it is not an object (*vastu*), yet, it appears to admit movements, it appears to be an object. Thus the mind and the objects have no origination. As a fire-brand being moved appears to be straight or crooked, even so the mind when it moves appears as the percipient and the perceptible (IV.42). And as the fire-brand when it does not move has no appearance of its being straight or crooked, even so when the mind does not move, it does not appear in the form of the percipient and the perceptible (IV. 48).

We have already seen that causation (*hetuphalabhāva*) is not reasonable. The author explains it further in the following few kārikās (IV. 53-56) for his main purpose of establishing non-origination. With the same object in view he refutes (IV. 57) like the Buddhists theories of eternality (*śāśvata*) and annihilation (*uccheda*), and says (IV. 58) that it is in the empirical truth (*saṃvṛtisatya*) that things are originated, but not in reality. From an illusive seed may come forth an illusive sprout. This sprout is neither eternal, nor has it annihilation. It is to be known with regard to all things. Therefore there is no room for the appellation of 'eternal' and 'non-eternal' of anything (IV. 60). As in dream so in waking it is owing to illusion that the mind which is only one moves having the appearance of the external things. Whatever is experienced in dream is nothing but the mind, similarly whatever we see in the waking state is only the mind. As a creature formed of dream or made of illusion or by some supernatural power takes birth and dies, even so all these creatures exist and do not exist. Therefore there is no Jīva that takes birth, there is no possibility of it. That nothing originates is the highest truth (IV. 61-71). The duality consisting of the subject and the object is only the vibration (*spandita*) of the mind which has, in fact, no object, and consequently has no relation whatsoever to it (IV. 72-74).

Owing to the persistent belief in what is non-existent (*abhūtābhiniveśa*) the mind relates itself to its objects, but when their absence is known it turns back from them having no relation at all (*niḥsaṅga*). Now, when it so turns back and does not move onwards, that position of it is unwavering, it is then free from sorrow, desire and fear. This is the field of the activities of the Buddhas. It shines forth once for all having no origination, nor sleep, nor dream, and is the essence of reality (*dharmadhātu*, IV. 74-81).

This truth is, however, made obscure by the childish with their different notions; yet, one who can realize it attains the state of omniscience free from duality. And if it is so, what is beyond it that one may desire (IV. 82-85)? The author then shows that it is through the 'supra-mundane' (*lokottara*) knowledge by the realization of which one may become omniscient (IV. 86-89). Here he asks us to learn certain things from the A g r a y ā n a (=Mahāyāna) of the Buddhists giving some of its leading thoughts (IV. 90-95).

As the state of detachment (*asaṅgatā*) of our mind or knowledge is absolutely necessary, he tells us what it is and how it can be effected. Both the objects and their knowledge have no origination, and as there is no relation whatsoever between them the knowledge is said to be free from attachment (*asaṅga*). If this state is not achieved, there is no disappearance of the 'cover' or 'obscuration' (*āvaraṇa-cyuti*) from which we suffer. But in reality there is no cover or obscuration of anything, all the elements of existence being naturally unsullied (IV. 96-98). Concluding, the teacher declares that according to the Buddha the knowledge is not related to its objects, and these two things, *i.e.*, the knowledge and its objects, are not mentioned by the Buddha (IV. 99), for, in fact, he has said absolutely nothing.

§ *15. The Philosophy of Gauḍapāda*

Let us now make an attempt to discuss a little the philosophy of Gauḍapāda as it is in our text, though it has already been done to some extent in the preceding section, *i.e., the Conspectus of the Contents.* As some of the philosophical views of our teacher have already been shown incidentally they will not be repeated here. Indeed, much has been written on this by my predecessors, yet when a new annotation is added hereto the subject may be discussed anew according to the light derived from it. In doing so we should keep our minds free from the influence of later thoughts, for it is not always safe to explain an older text by the thoughts in a subsequent work or works.

Now, it goes without saying that our teacher, Gauḍapāda, is a Vedāntist and he mainly deals with the Vedānta in the present work declaring its conclusion (II. 12, 31, 35). Naturally, therefore, as a Vedāntist, he treats his subject in accordance with the scriptures (*śruti*), yet, not without pure reasons. Direct or indirect, his reasonings are in many cases based on scriptures (II. 1-10; III. 24-26). But when there are contradictory scriptures, he says (III. 23) that those which are with reasons (*yukti yukta*) are to be accepted. Besides, throughout the work he has advanced a number of independent grounds which are very cogent. With a view to removing an apparent contradiction in the scripture he would interpret (III 14) a text in its secondary sense saying expressly that the primary one is not reasonable. The well-known practice of explaining Upaniṣadic texts in their secondary senses among the later commentators of the *Brahmasūtras* may be seen first here in Gauḍapāda's interpretation.

Among the Vedāntists Gauḍapāda is an Advaitist, the highest truth to him being *advaita* 'non-duality' (advaitaṃ paramārthataḥ, I. 17; advaitaṃ paramārtho hi, III. 18; advaite yojayet smṛtim, II. 36). He says (II. 31) that according to the Vedānta the universe is like dream or illusion or an imaginary town in the sky (*gandharvanagara*). There is no duality at all, it is mere illusion (I. 17).

The statement of the duality in the scripture is intended for the instruction (of the ignorant), and so when the truth is understood the duality does not exist (I. 18) and its cessation is bliss (I. 29; see also II. 35). He says (I. 17) further that the duality is due to illusion (*māyā*). In order to support this view he quotes scriptures (III. 24) which say 'There is no plurality (neha nānāsti kiñcana, BU, IV. 4. 19; KU, IV. 11)'; and 'Indra appears multiform through *māyās*' (BU, II. 5. 19)'; and he concludes (III. 24) that 'He (Prajāpati) is born variously, though (in fact) he does not take birth (VS, XXX, 19).

Having thus offered the scriptural evidence for maintaining the view that the duality is mere illusion and as such it has no reality, Gauḍapāda gives us some pure reasons. Here, too, first he refers us to a scriptural text (BU, IV. 3. 14) and says (II. 5) that the two states, dream and waking, are the same and one, because of the identity of the nature of the things experienced in them. That the things in dream are unreal is well-known to all and it is said also by the wise (BU, IV. 3. 8 ff), and can be maintained on the following grounds :

The things (such as mountains) in dream are within as they are enclosed or in an enclosed place (II. 1, IV. 33); but if they are real it is impossible. The time being very short, or there being no fixed rule of time, it cannot be said that the dreamer really goes to the distant land dreamt of by him and sees things there. Nor is he seen there when he awakes (II. 2, IV. 34). Again, when he awakes he does not find his friends and others whom he had then in dream grasped (IV. 35). Further, it is said in our scripture (BU, IV. 3. 10) that in dream there are no chariots, etc., yet, they are seen there. Similarly, in the waking state, too, the things we see around us are unreal on account of the fact that they are *within* (II. 4; IV. 33). That which is non-existent at the beginning and at the end is so also in the middle, *i.e.*, at the present. Therefore, being like the unreal (such as mirage) the external things appear as not unreal (II. 6; IV. 31). In both the cases, dream and waking, things are only imagined by the mind. That which is imagined by the mind within is regarded as non-existent (*asat*), while that which is imagined by the mind without is regarded as existent; but the unreality of both of them is reasonable and a matter of experience (II. 9, 10). Whether in dream or waking, whatever is cognizable by the mind is unreal (cittadṛśyam avastukam, IV. 36). Moreover, in both the states the mind though in its own nature is undoubtedly without the two (*i.e.*, the percipient and the perceptible), yet it moves owing to illusion with the appearance of the two (III. 30; IV. 62). This duality comprising the movable and the unmovable is therefore perceptible only by the mind. Hence when the mind becomes non-mind, *i.e.*, when it ceases from its function of thinking, no duality is experienced (III. 31) The cessation of the function of thinking of the mind, or, in other words, the state of non-mind is reached when the mind through its knowledge of the truth of the Ātman does not think anything being non-cognizant owing to the absence of the things to be cognized (III. 32).[1]

We have seen above that the waking experience is as unreal as the dream experience both of them being due to *māyā* or mere imagination of the mind that moves on account of *māyā* (spandate māyayā manaḥ, III. 29 ; cittaṃ calati māyayā (IV. 61).

That all these external things are the creation of

[1] Gauḍapāda seems to have been fond of compromising conflicting views III. 17; IV. 5) and so considering the opinion of the Dvaitins, *i.e.*, those who maintain duality, he says (III. 17 ff.) that they are firmly fixed in their own distinctive conclusions and contend one another, but his view does not conflict with them. In explaining it he says (III. 18) that the supreme reality is non-duality, yet, it is not that we do not admit duality, we do it; so there is no conflict amongst us The only difference amongst us is this that while according to you duality is in reality as well as in appearance we hold that it is only in appearance on account of illusion, and not also in reality (III. 19).

the mind is further said (IV. 72) and described elaborately by G a u ḍ a p ā d a (IV. 47-52) with a very apt illustration of the fire-brand (*alāta*). A fire-brand, only when it is moved, and not when it is not moved, appears to be straight or crooked, or so. Now these appearances are not produced from anything other than the fire-brand. And when it is at rest they are not in a place other than it, nor do they enter into it. Similarly when the *vijñāna*[2] or mind moves and not when it does not move, it appears in the form of the duality consisting of the percipient and the perceptible. These appearances are produced not from anything other than the *vijñāna* ; and when it is at rest they are not in a place other than it, nor they enter into it. He says again (IV. 63-66) that as animals seen in dream are visible to the mind of the dreamer and do not exist apart from it, and as such they are the mind of the dreamer, even so the animals seen in wakefulness are visible to the mind of the waking one and do not exist apart from it, and as such they are the mind of the waking one.

Clearly this is the *Vijñānavāda* ' Idealism ' before us. Now taking here into consideration the passages quoted under IV. 72 from the LA, and comparing the kārikās IV. 47-52 with the corresponding Buddhist passages quoted in the Annotation under IV. 52, one will be struck with the agreement between a Vedāntist and a Vijñānavādin. One will also be in

[2] Mark here the use of the word *vijñāna* in these kārikās, and not of *citta* or *manas*.

a position to understand how far Gauḍapāda is here influenced by the Buddhist thoughts and arguments. It is, however, to be noted that Gauḍapāda, though much influenced by the Buddhist thoughts, maintains his position as a Vedāntist It is true that he advocates the *Vijñānavāda*, but certainly it is originally adopted by him from the Upaniṣadic source, *i.e.*, BU, IV. 3. 14. on which is based his fundamental statement (II. 5) that the two states, dream and waking, are one. This Upaniṣadic seed of idealism being influenced by its elaborate system in Buddhism and the vast literature on it by the Buddhist teachers who flourished before Gauḍapāda, has developed into what we now find in the *Āgamaśāstra*. But when there are the above and the similar germs of idealism in the Upaniṣads[3] it must be accepted that it did not first originate with the Buddhists, though it has much developed in their system later on.

There are thus two schools of Vijñānavādins, (1) Vedāntists headed by Gauḍapāda and (2) Buddhists with Maitreya at the head. In both the schools the external world is the creation or transformation of the mind. But while in the first the cause for that transformation is *māyā* (III. 29; IV. 61) it is *vāsanā* (LA, X. 150)[4] in the second, both of them being without beginning (*anādi*). This *māyā* and *vāsanā*

[3] See *Aitareya Upaniṣad*, III. 2-3; TU. III. 5 : vijñānaṃ brahmeti vyajānāt. vijñānād dhy eva°.

[4] bāhyo na vidyate hy artho yathā bālair vikalpyate |
vāsanair luḍitaṃ cittam arthābhāsaṃ pravartate ||

may, however, be regarded as the same thing. For *vāsanā,* though explained as *pūrva jñāna* 'previous knowledge' is conceived as a cosmical force, transcendental illusion (*The Conception of Buddhist Nirvāṇa,* Leningrad, 1927, p. 209). The real difference then between these two schools in the present case is with regard to the intervention of the Ātman with whom *māyā* is connected in the first, and his denial[5] in the second where the *vāsanā* is with the *citta*.

Now, the *māyā* of the Jīva referred to above like *vāsanā* has no beginning. He sleeps on account of it being himself deluded by it (I. 16; II. 19). He himself imagines himself and various other things through his own *māyā*, some of them being within while others without (II. 13). These things, *i.e.*, those which are within and exist as long as exists the thought (*citta*), as well as those which are without and exist as long as remains the notion of the two, are only imagined (II. 14, 15). In the process of the imagination first he imagines himself as a Jīva 'personal soul' then various things, external and internal (II. 16). Consequently as in the dark, a piece of rope not known determinately is imagined to be a snake or a continuous line of water, etc., even so is imagined the self; but when that piece of rope is known determinately the imagined snake, etc., vanish and there is no duality. So is to be known of the ascertainment of the self (II. 17, 18).

[5] cittamātraṃ na dṛśyo 'sti dvidhā cittaṃ pravartate |
grāhyagrāhakabhāvena ātmātmīyaṃ na vidyate || LA, III. 21

But what is the characteristic of a Jīva ? As we have seen above, G a u ḍ a p ā d a explains it (III.3-9) by an apt illustration of *ākāśa* 'space' or *mahākāśa* 'great space' and *ghaṭākāśas* 'spaces occupied by different jars'. As it is owing to the condition (*upādhi*) of jars that the *ākāsá* is regarded as *ghaṭākāśas*, so it is on account of the conglomerations (of the different parts of the body) that the Ātman is regarded as Jīvas. Consequently as when the jars are destroyed spaces occupied by them are completely merged into the great space (*mahākāśa*), even so are merged the Jīvas into Ātman when the conglomerations are destroyed. The spaces occupied by all jars are in reality only one; yet if the space occupied by one jar is covered by smoke or dust, etc., not all the spaces occupied by all other jars are connected with it. The case is the same also with the Jīvas in regard to their happiness, etc., *i.e.*, if one Jīva feels happiness or suffers pain, not all the Jīvas are subjected to it. There may be different conditions (*upādhis*); their forms, functions and names may differ from one another, but as regards the space occupied by them there is no difference. Similar is the case with reference to the Jīvas. Again, the space occupied by a jar is neither a transformation (*vikāra*), nor a part (*avayava*) of the space (*ākāśa*), similarly a Jīva is neither a transformation nor a part of the Ātman. G a u ḍ a p ā d a says further that the Ātman like the space remains in all the conglomerations or bodies which, too, have no reality as dream being the creation of the illusion of the Ātman (III. 10). The Jīva is the supreme soul of the 'sheaths' (*kośas*) as described in the TU, II. 1-6, and the supreme Brahman or Ātman is shown in the *Madhuvidyā* section of the BU, II, 5. That the identity of the Jīva and the Ātman without distinction is praised and their distinction is censured in the scriptures is reasonable (III. 13), for though in some texts their distinction is to be found, those texts are to be taken in their secondary sense, the primary one being not reasonable (III. 14). Here the distinction is made purposely, it is made out of compassion to help one of inferior vision in one's *upāsanā* which is for such a person impossible without some sort of distinction (III. 11-16). It is not that such a distinction must be a real one.

It is said that the mind becomes non-mind and G a u ḍ a p ā d a is definitely of opinion that Brahman is nothing but the mind that has become non-mind. He says that the mind in the state of *suṣupta* 'deep sleep' falls into a sleeping state (*laya*), but it does not do so when it is suppressed (*nigṛhīta* = *niruddha*), and indeed that is Brahman above fear and radiant with the light of *jnāna* (III. 35). See IV. 77-81, and below. He expresses the same thing in other words saying that when the mind is completely suppressed (*niruddha*) and as such is free from all movements and does not perceive anything else it becomes Brahman (III. 46):

yadā na līyate cittaṃ na ca vikṣipyate punaḥ I
aniṅganam anābhāsaṃ niṣpannaṃ brahma tat tadā II

'When the mind is not in the state of sleep, nor is

distracted again, and as such has no movement, nor any sense-image, then it becomes Brahman.'[6]

It is to be pointed out that here for the first time, so far as goes my information, it is found that Brahman is nothing but the *citta* which by *nirodha* is *anidra* (I. 16; III 36; IV. 81; =*alīna*=*amūḍha*), *asvapna* (I. 16, III. 36; IV. 81; =*avikṣipta*),[7] *aniṅgana* (III. 46; =*akṣipta*), and *anābhāsa* (III. 46; =*nirābhāṣa*=*nirākāra*=*arūpaka*, III. 36). Another appellation of this *citta* is *sanirvāṇa*[8] 'with extinction (III. 37), *i.e.* in this state it is extinct. It is *jñāna* 'knowledge' or 'thought' but *akalpaka* (III. 33; =*nirvikalpa*) 'indeterminate' and consequently *asaṅga* 'having no attachment or relation to any object' (IV. 72, 96; =*niḥsaṅga* IV, 79, see IV.99=*nirviṣaya*, IV. 72).[9] Being as such this *jñāna* is not different from the knowable (*jñeyābhinna*), which is Brahman (III. 33).

6 The first half of the kārikā implies that in this state of the mind, which can be reached by *Asparśayoga* (III. 39-45; IV. 2) it is free from the conditions known in the Yoga systems as *mūḍha* 'stupefied' and *vikṣipta* 'distracted' (Vyāsa on the YS, I. 1). These two are also expressed by our teacher as *anidra* 'sleepless' and *asvapna* 'dreamless' respectively (III, 36: I. 16; IV. 81).

7 Vācaspati (YS, I. 1): mūḍhaṃ tu tamaḥsamudrekān nidrāvṛttimat. kṣiptād viśiṣṭam. viśeṣo' sthemabahulasya kādācitkaḥ sthemā.

8 Here *sanirvāṇa* mind=*amanībhāva* (III. 31; MU, VI. 34; YV, III. 67. 8); =*amanastā* (III. 32; *Mukti UP*. II. 29) =*unmanībhāva* (*Brahmabindu UP*, 4) *manaḥkṣaya* (MU, VI. 20) =*manorāśa* (*Mukti UP*, II. 10, 35, 36, 39) =*manolaya* (*Nādabindu UP*, 47) =*acittatā* (*Mukti UP*, II. 20) =*cittanāśa*(*Op. cit.* II. 32, 34; *Śāṇḍilya UP*. in *One Hundred and Eight Upaniṣads*, Nirnayasagar, 1917, p. 358).

9 See the Annotation on IV. 72.

It is further said that in this state the mind rests in itself (*svastha*, III. 47; = *ātmasaṃstha*, III. 34).[10]

This Brahman of G a u ḍ a p ā d a then points on one side to the state of *kaivalya* 'the state of being not connected with anything else,'[11] or the resting of the Draṣṭṛ or Puruṣa 'Self' in himself (*svarūpa*, i.e., *cinmātra* 'pure thought'), as described in YS, I. 3,[12] and on the other to the resting of the *citta* in the *vijñaptimātratā* of the Yogācāras or Vijñānavādins. According to the latter *citta*, *manas*, *vijñāna* and *vijñapti* are synonyms.[13] Therefore *vijñaptimātratā* is the same as *vijñānamātratā* which means the state of pure and simple *vijñāna* 'intellect' or 'consciousness.' Here in this state there is the highest cessation of the perceiving faculty of the mind.[14] And this is in their opinion *mukti* 'deliverance.'[15] This is also the 'highest place of Viṣṇu' (KU, I. 3. 9; MU, VI. 26; RV, I. 22. 20; 154. 5 with a slight variation), not only according

10 This will remind one of the following in the ChU, VII. 24. 1-2: Yatra nānyat paśyati nānyac chṛṇoti nānyad vijānāti sa bhūmā.° sa bhagavaḥ kasmin pratiṣṭhita iti. sve mahimni. yadi vā na mahimnīti.

11 YS, IV. 34: puruṣārthaśūnyānāṃ guṇānāṃ pratiprasavaḥ kaivalyaṃ svarūpapratiṣṭhā vā citiśakteḥ.

12 tadā draṣṭuḥ svarūpe 'vasthānam.

13 Vk, p. 3; AK, II. 34; MV, p. 303; VM ed. D. K o s a m b i, XIV.82.

14 MSA, XI. 47: parama upalambhasya vigamaḥ; Tk, p. 29: acitto 'nupalambho 'sau; see TSN, 36.

15 viditvā nairātmyaṃ dvividham iha dhīman bhavagataṃ
samaṃ tac ca jñātvā praviśati sa tattvaṃ grahaṇataḥ |
tatas tatra sthānān manasa iha na khyāti tad api
tad akhyānaṃ muktiḥ parama upalambhasya vigamaḥ ||

MSA, 47.

to the Upaniṣadists,[16] but also to the Vaiṣṇavas (BP, II. 1. 19).[17]

One point is to be discussed here. Brahman of the Vedāntists or G a u ḍ a p ā d a (III. 30) is eternal (*nitya*), and if it is so, how can it be suggested, as done before, that Brahman and the *citta* in *Vijñaptimātratā* are the same, for according to Yogācāras *jñāna* is not eternal, but momentary (*kṣaṇika*) ? The following is the solution :—

In the authoritative Buddhist works[18] the following words are used for *nirvāṇa* : *dhruva* 'enduring' *amṛta* 'not dying', *acyuta* 'stable', *akṣara* 'imperishable', *ajarjara* 'not decaying' and *apalokita*[19] 'not broken down.' Certainly these words do not imply momentariness, but on the contrary some kind

The third and the first part of the fourth lines are explained there thus : tatas tatra tattvavijñaptimātrasthānān manasas tad api tattvaṃ na khyāti vijñaptimātram. tad akhyānaṃ muktiḥ.

16 MBU, p. 12 :

yan manas trijagatsṛṣṭisthitivyasanakarmakṛt |
tan mano vilayaṃ yāti tad viṣṇoḥ paramaṃ padam ||

17 tatraikāvayavaṃ dhyāyed avyucchinnena cetasā |
mano nirviṣayaṃ yuktvā tataḥ kiñcana na smaret |
padaṃ tat paramaṃ viṣṇor mano yatra prasīdati ||

18 VM, p. 224 ; SN, IV. 369 ff ; P o u s s i n : *Nirvāṇa*, MCMXXV, pp. 153-4.

19 P o u s s i n has for it in French (*Loc. cit.*) with a query "le Soupçunne" ('suspected' or 'surmised'). But as clear from B u d d h a g h o s a on SN, IV. 370 (apalujjatāya apalokitaṃ) it is derived from *pra-√ruj* and not from *pra √luk* as may appear. And so it can be said in the words of Y a ś o m i t r a (AKV², p, 23) with regard to the derivation of the word *loka* that rujir iha gṛhīto na lokiḥ See my note, *A passage of the Abhidharmakośavyākhyā*, in IHQ, Vol. II, pp. 418 ff., and P o u s s i n ' s *Rejoinder*, p. 656.

of stability. Now the *citta* in the state of *vijñaptimātratā* is described variously according to the vareity of the aspects beginning from the 'Path of Illumination' (*darśanamārga*) in Vasubandhu's Tk, 29-30.[20] It is said there to be *lokottara jñāna* 'super-mundane knowledge,' *āśrayaparāvṛtti* (āśrayasya parāvṛttiḥ) 'the revolution or change of the recipient', *i.e.*, the '*ālaya-vijñāna*,' and *anāsrava dhātu* 'undefiled element' which is *dhruva* 'enduring.'[21] Here by the word *āśrayaparāvṛtti* referred to above we understand, in brief, that owing to the elimination of the two sorts of evil condition (*dauṣṭhulya*), *viz.*, the 'covers' or 'obscurations' (*āvaraṇas*), namely, the knowable (*jñeya*) and the passions (*kleśas*), the recipient (*āśraya*), *i.e.*, *ālayavijñāna*, turns back to its natural state in the form of *advaya jñāna* 'the knowledge free from the two,' *i.e.*, the subject and the object. In other words, the *ālayavijñāna* which was before covered or obscured, the obscurations being now removed, gets its own innate state, *i.e.*, the state of *advaya* (= *lokottara*) *jñāna*. This is called *anāsrava dhātu* 'undefiled element' which is *dhruva*.

20 See our text, IV. 18, foot note 1, where these two kārikās with the introductory line of Sthiramati are quoted.

21 On these words the commentary of Sthiramati may be quoted here:

aparicitatvāt (Tib. ḥdras. par. ma. byas. pa. daṅ, for *anucitatvāt* in the printed text) loke samudācārābhāvāt (for which Tib. suggests *samudayābhāvāt* reading kun. tu. ḥbyuṅ. ba. med. pa. daṅ), nirvikalpatvāt ca lokād uttīrṇam iti jñānaṃ lokottaraṃ ca tad iti°. āśrayo 'tra sarvabījakam ālayavijñānam, tasya parāvṛttir yā dauṣṭhulyavipākadvayavāsanābhāvena parāvṛttiḥ°. nirdauṣṭhulyatvāt sa tu āśrayavigata ity anāsravaḥ°. dhruvo nityatvād akṣayatayā°.

But what is the true significance of the word *dhruva*, that is intended here ? Among the 33 descriptive words for *nirvāṇa* found in SN, IV. 368-373 and 46 synonyms for it in AP. 6-9, we have *dhruva* and never *nitya*. It is true that sometimes the words *nitya*, *dhruva* and *śāśvata* are used as synonyms (Pali *vevecana* = *vivacana* = *paryāya*), as says Buddhaghoṣa himself on SN, I. 142.[22] Yet, there is some difference in their meanings. For while *śāśvata*, according to him, means 'always existing' (sadā vijjamānaṃ) *dhruva* implies 'enduring' (dhuvaṃ'ti thiraṃ ; he writes also on SN, IV. 370 : thiraṭṭhena dhuvaṃ).

Jaina teachers, too, are of the same opinion. In connexion with the definition of *dravya* 'substance'[23] in their system they give the same explanation of the word *dhruva* or *dhrauvya* using the same or similar words.[24]

In the older Upaniṣads *Ātman* or Brahman is *nitya* and not *dhruva*. The word *nitya* implies that it does not admit of any change, while *dhruva* does not do so. Let us give here an illustration. If of a lump of gold a number of different ornaments is made one after another, their forms change, yet, through these changes

22 With regard to pāpaka diṭṭhigata: idaṃ niccaṃ idaṃ dhuvaṃ idaṃ sassataṃ. See also Sthiramati, Tk, 30, explaining *dhruva* as quoted in foot-note 21.

23 *Tattvārthādhigamasūtra*, V. 29: utpādavyayadhrauvyayuktaṃ sat.

24 *Tattvārtharājavārttika* (Sanātana-Jainagranthamālā, 1915), V 29 (*dhruva* = *sthira*) ; *Tattvadīpikā* on *Pravacanasāra* (ed. A. N. Upadhye, 1935) II. 3 (*dhrauvya* = *avasthiti*) ; *Tattvadīpikā* on *Pañcāstisamayasāra* (Rāyacandra Jainaśāstramālā, 2nd ed.), 10: purvottarabhāvocchedotpādayor api svajāter aparityāgo dhrauvyam ; *Sanmatitarka* (Gujarāta-Purātattva-mandira, Ahmedabad, 1940 V.S), Gāthā 12, p. 410 (*dhrauvya* = *sthiti*).

the same gold continues to exist. Owing to this continuance it can be said that gold is here *dhruva* ' enduring ', but not *nitya* ' eternal '.

The Ālayavijñāna is certainly momentary (*kṣaṇika*), as it changes every moment. It does not therefore move forward as one and the same (ekam abhinnam), but continues in an uninterrupted stream (*santati*) as the flood with its currents (srotasā oghavat). This continuity has no beginning, nor has it an end (*anādi-nidhana*) till *nirvāṇa*. Now as through all the moments the Ālayavijñāna continues it is *dhruva* and not *nitya*.

It may be pointed out here that there is more than one kind of *nityatā* ' eternity ' according to the primary and the secondary senses of the word; *viz.*, (*i*) *kūṭasthanityatā* ' eternity as unchangeability ' as of Ātman or Brahman of the Vedāntists; (*ii*) *pariṇāmanityatā* ' eternity as transformation ' as held by the Sāṅkhyas and the Jainas. To these two may be added, according to the Buddhists, (*iii*) one more, *viz.*, *santatinityatā* ' eternity as continuance.' It may, however, be the same as *pariṇāma-nityatā*. Where in such cases in Buddhist texts the word *nitya* is employed it is to be taken in this light.

Now in support of the main problem we are here concerned with, the following couplet may be taken into consideration:

> prabhāsvaram idaṃ cittaṃ prakṛtyāgantavo malāḥ |
> teṣām apāye sarvārthaṃ taj jyotir avinaśvaram || [25]

[25] Quoted by Jayatīrtha representing the views of the Vijñānavādins in his ṭīkā (śl. 30, on TAK, III, p. 35). It is already cited once more on p. 70 of our text.

Mark that *citta* is said here to be *avinaśvara jyotis* 'the light that is not liable to be destroyed'.[26]

It may therefore be safely concluded that G a u ḍ a-p ā d a 's Brahman and the *citta* in *vijñaptimātratā* of the Yogācāras are in fact the same thing with the only one difference that while the former is *nitya* the latter is *dhruva*.

Let us remember here what G a u ḍ a p ā d a says about Brahman (III. 35-36, 46-47),[27] as we have seen just now from the Vedāntic point of view, and compare it with what he says in IV. 76-81[28] of the 'field of the activities (*viṣaya*) of the Buddhas' describing

26 See also the following :

(i) tatrotpannapradhvaṃsi vijñānam anutpannapradhvaṃsi jñānam. LA, p. 157. See our text p 85, foot-note 2.

(ii) *Jñānasiddhi* (*Two Vajrayāna Texts*, GOS, p. 85), XV, 50, referring to *cittadhārā* 'current of thought' (in the text read *cittadhāraiva* for *chittadhāreva* in 48) :

anādinidhanā śāntā sarvadharmeśvarī ca sā |
bibharti sarvarūpāṇi satyadvayasamāśritā ||

(iii) *Op. cit.*, p. 75 : anādinidhanaṃ śāntaṃ bodhicittaṃ.

(iv) *Op. cit.*, p. 86 : jñānam amaraṇam° anabhilāpyam.

(v) S u z u k i writes in his *Outlines of Mahāyāna Buddhism*, 1907, p. 348 : "Nirvāṇa is sometimes spoken of as possessing four attributes; (1) eternal (*nitya*), (2) blissful (*sukha*), (3) self-acting (*ātman*), and (4) pure (*śuci*). It is eternal, because it is immaterial; it is blissful, because it is above all sufferings; it is self-acting, because it knows no compulsion; it is pure, because it is not defiled by passion and error."

27 Brahman is that *citta* which is unwavering and has no sense-image nor origination, nor sleep, nor dream : aniṅganam anābhāsam (III. 46) and ajam anidram asvapnaṃ cittam (III. 36).

28 The field of activities or the aim of the Buddhas is the unwavering position of the mind having no origination, nor sleep, nor dream : cittasya anutpattiḥ (IV. 77) and niścalā sthitiḥ (IV. 80), and ajam anidram asvapnaṃ cittam (IV. 81).

and approving the views of the Buddhists ; it will then be clear that the same thing has been said by G a u ḍ a p ā d a in two places almost in the same words though from the two different standpoints.

We have already discussed the *Vijñānavāda* as it is in our text. It may be noted here in this connexion that it is treated here by G a u ḍ a p ā d a only with a view to the establishment of the *Ajātivāda* 'the Theory of Non-origination' which is one of the most important topics of the philosophy of G a u ḍ a p ā d a. Having proposed to show what it is first in III. 2 and then in IV. 5 he declares (III. 48) and affirms (IV. 71) that the highest truth is that nothing originates. For details the reader is referred to the *Conspectus of the Contents* (pp. cxiii-cxxvi) and the work itself, we should like to point out here only a few important aspects of it.

The subject is dealt with by our author as a Vedāntist separately in two places, Book II and Book IV. In the former he does so purely from the Vedāntic point of view supporting his thesis by scriptures and grounds based on them or in favour of them, some of these grounds being strikingly similar to those offered by the Buddhists for the same purpose ; while in the latter he expresses his approval on behalf of his schcol regard ng *ajāti* as declared by the Advayas or Buddhists saying that he does not dispute with them onthis point and asking his followers or the people at large to listen to him as to how there cannot be any dispute. He proceeds then to show throughout the Book IV the arguments of the Buddhists taking even the actual words from their authoritative works in a number of cases. Readers are here referred to our text with Annotation.

One point may be pointed out here. In Book IV G a u ḍ a p ā d a has discussed nothing directly of the Vedānta,[29] as nothing Vedāntic will be found therein. In explaining the Vedānta in accordance with his own light he establishes the *Ajātivāda* in Book III, as we have seen above. Then in Book IV he supports that theory referring to the Buddhists who also hold the same view independently of the Vedāntists. G a u ḍ a p ā d a says here that his school approves of what they say on this point and shows their arguments one by one.

From this it may appear that whatever is said by G a u ḍ a p ā d a as the opinion of the Buddhists in that Book is approved or accepted by him. But can it be said strictly ? The Buddhists being the follower of the Middle Path (*madhyama pratipad*) reject both the extreme views of 'eternity' and 'annihilation' (*śāśvata*- and *uccheda-vādas*). This is alluded to in our text in IV. 57-60. But how can G a u ḍ a-p ā d a as a Vedāntist accept it when his Brahman in his own word (III. 33) is eternal (*nitya*)? Nevertheless, in the present case, G a u ḍ a p ā d a seems to have accepted the middle theory, for, as the case is put here, there may not be raised any objection. Or it may be that G a u ḍ a p ā d a has here simply mentioned the views

29 Even such words as Brahman and Ātman are not to be found there.

of the Buddhists as he has done it in some other cases in this Book. For instance, see IV. 90.

It is a very striking fact that some of the most remarkable doctrines as discussed and established by Gauḍapāda have not been appreciated in subsequent works on the Vedānta even of the Advaita school; for instance, the peculiar conception of Brahman, the *Ajātivāda*, the *Sarvajñatvavāda* (IV. 85, 89) and the *Vijñānavāda*, besides what Gauḍapāda approves of the views of the Advayavādins or Buddhists in Book IV. Even the great Śaṅkara himself does not appear to subscribe to the above doctrines of our teacher. It need not, however, be said that his *Māyāvāda* has undoubtedly got strong impetus from the first three Books of the ĀŚ. His *Adhyāsavāda* as explained by him in his *Śārīrakabhāṣya* and other works has no mention in the ĀŚ, though a distant relationship may be found out. Here he is undoubtedly influenced by the Buddhist Vijñānavādins specially in explaining their doctrine of *Trisvabhāva* or *Trilakṣaṇa* 'three characteristics' (IV. 74, pp. 175 ff).

Of the philosophy of Gauḍapāda there is much more that deserves to be discussed separately, but in order to avoid prolixity readers are referred to the text itself, specially to its Book IV together with the new Annotation of the present writer, in which he has tried to explain many an important and hitherto obscure point of the work. From this, it is hoped, readers will be in a position to form their own judgements as to how much G a u ḍ a p ā d a is influenced by Buddhist thoughts and how much of them he has adopted into his own system of the Vedānta.[30]

---

30 One may consider here the following words in the *Bhāvaprakāśa* (TM, Vol. II, p. 415) referring to ĀŚ, IV. 11-23 :

nanu māṇḍūkyakārikāsu Gauḍapādācāryaiḥ mādhyamikoktayuktibhiḥ kāryakāraṇa- (for wrongly printed *kāryākāraṇa-*) bhāvasya sāṃvṛtatvam sthāpitam.

BOOK I

1

bahiṣprajño vibhur viśvo hy antaḥprajñas tu taijasaḥ ।
ghanaprajñas tathā prājña eka eva tridhā sthitaḥ ॥

'The all-pervading one is V i ś v a 'all' when he has the consciousness of outside; he is T a i j a s a 'brilliant' when he has the consciousness of inside and when his consciousness is concentrated[1] he is P r ā j ñ a 'intelligent'. The one exists in three forms.'[2]

[1] Literally 'condensed' (*ghana*), in other words, when consciousness does not admit of any distinction within itself, as is the case in wakefulness and in dream.   [2] See I. 2.

2

dakṣiṇākṣimukhe viśvo manasy antas tu taijasaḥ ।
ākāśe ca hṛdi prājñas tridhā dehe vyavasthitaḥ ॥

'V i ś v a is in the front of the right eye,[1] within the mind is T a i j a s a, while P r ā j ñ a is in the sky in the heart.[2] Thus he remains in the body in three ways.'[3]

[1] KtU, IV. 17; MU, VII. 11; ChU, IV. 15. 1, VII. 7. 4; BU, II. 3. 5, IV. 2. 2, V. 5. 2, 4.

[2] BU. II. 1. 17, IV. 2. 3.

[3] See pp. lxxxxiv-lxxxxviii and I. 3.

*

3

viśvo hi sthūlabhuṅ nityaṃ taijasaḥ praviviktabhuk |
ānandabhuk tathā prājñas tridhā bhogaṃ nibodhata ||

'V i ś v a enjoys what is gross, T a i j a s a what is fine, and P r ā j ñ a bliss. (Thus) know enjoyment to be of three kinds.'

4

sthūlaṃ tarpayate viśvaṃ praviviktaṃ tu taijasam |
ānandaś ca tathā prājñaṃ tridhā tṛptiṃ nibodhata ||

'The gross satisfies V i ś v a, the fine T a i j a s a, and bliss P r ā j ñ a. (Thus) know satisfaction to be of three kinds.'

5

triṣu dhāmasu yad bhojyaṃ bhoktā yaś ca prakīrttitaḥ |
vedaitad ubhayaṃ yas tu sa bhuñjāno na lipyate ||

'One who knows both what is said to be enjoyable, and what is said to be the enjoyer in three stages, is not tainted through enjoying.'

6

prabhavaḥ sarvabhūtānāṃ satām iti viniścayaḥ |
sarvaṃ janayati prāṇaś ceto'ṃśūn puruṣaḥ pṛthak ||

'The settled opinion of sages is that all things have their origin. (Some hold that) the Breath,[1] the Puruṣa (self), creates all -the rays of the mind differently.'

[1] For the creation by Prāṇa see BS. I. 1. 23. Prāṇa is here Brahman.

The objective world is the vibrations of one's mind (*citta-spandita*, see IV. 72) which shines inside. These vibrations are called here rays (*aṃśu*) and assume different forms just like the rays of the sun on the clouds appearing in the form of the rainbow.

7

vibhūtiṃ prasavaṃ tv anye manyante sṛṣṭicintakāḥ |
svapnamāyāsvarūpeti sṛṣṭir anyair vikalpitā ||

'Other theorisers about creation assert dogmatically that the creation (of the world) is (his) expansion,[1] while others imagine that creation is of the nature of dream and magic.'[2]

[1] As in the Upaniṣads. TU, II. 6. 1: so 'kāmayata bahu syāṃ prajāyeya.

[2] This view is held by some of the Vedantists including our teacher (see II. 31) and the Buddhists, Mādhyamikas and Yogācāras.

8

icchāmātraṃ prabhoḥ sṛṣṭir iti sṛṣṭau viniścitāḥ |
kālāt prasūtiṃ bhūtānāṃ manyante kālacintakāḥ ||

'Those who are assured about creation say that creation is the mere volition of the Lord,[1] and those who theorise about Time consider the creation of beings to be from Time.'[2]

[1] See note on I.7. Kūranārāyaṇa, a follower of Rāmānuja, says that they are *Aupaniṣadas* or the followers of the *Upaniṣads*, who say He is *satyasaṅkalpa* 'one whose purpose is true or fulfilled' (ChU, 3.14.2).

[2] They are Astronomers, See SU, 1. 1; MU, 7; MB, XII. 224, 227; ṢS. pp. 10-11 and specially the hymns on Kāla in the AV, XIX. 53, 54.

*

Now as regards the object of the creation the author says:

9

bhogārthaṃ sṛṣṭir ity anye krīḍārtham iti cāpare |
devasyaiṣa svabhāvo 'yam āptakāmasya kā spṛhā ||

'Some (say) that the creation is for the sake of (his) enjoyment,[1] while others (are of opinion) that it is for the sake of his sport.[2] It is, however, the nature of the Shining One, for how can desire be in one for whom every object of desire is (already) secured.[3]

Kūranārāyaṇa says here in his ṭīkā: harer atṛptasyaiva bhogārthaṃ sṛṣṭir ity anye. Śrīnivāsatīrtha, an annotator of Madhvācārya's commentary on MāU, clearly says that this view is held by Rāmānuja or his followers (kecid rāmānujāḥ).'

1 See BU, 1.4.17; ātmaivedam agra āsīd eka eva. so 'kāmayata jāyā me syād atha prajāyeya vittam me syād atha karma kurvīyeti.

2 See BS, II. 1. 33: lokavat tu līlākaivalyam; MU, VI. 1: viśvakrīḍāratiprabhuḥ.

3 The second half of the kārikā is quoted as *śruti* in the *Mādhvabhāṣya* on BS, II. 1, 33.

10

nivṛtteḥ sarvaduḥkhānām īśānaḥ prabhur avyayaḥ |
advaitaḥ sarvabhāvānāṃ devas turyo vibhuḥ smṛtaḥ ||

'The Turya 'fourth one'[1] is said to be all-pervading, efficient in removing all miseries, the shining one, changeless, and of all things without a second.'

1 The other three are already mentioned: Viśva, Taijasa and Prājña.

11

kāryakāraṇabaddhau tāv iṣyete viśvataijasau ।
prājñaḥ kāraṇabaddhas tu dve tu turye na sidhyataḥ ॥

'It is held that those two, Viśva and Taijasa, are bound with cause and effect, Prājña is bound with cause, but in Turya neither of them can be asserted.'

Here according to the commentator 'cause' (*kāraṇa*) is non-grasping of the truth (*tattvāgrahaṇa*), while 'effect' (*kārya*) is grasping the truth otherwise (*anyathāgrahaṇa*). See I. 15. These two are common to both Viśva and Taijasa. In Prājña there is only *tattvāgrahaṇa*, while in Turya there is neither of them, Cf. PS[1], 31 ; PS[2], 34, 35.

[1] This kārikā is quoted in the NSi, IV. 41.

12

nātmānaṃ na parāṃś caiva na satyaṃ nāpi cānṛtam ।
prājñaḥ kiñcana saṃvetti[1] turīyaḥ sarvadṛk[2] sadā ॥

'Prājña knows nothing—neither himself nor others, neither truth nor falsehood; but Turīya is always all-seeing.'[1]

As to why Prājña is bound with cause (*tattvāgrahaṇa*) and Turīya is not bound with either of cause and effect (*anyathāgrahaṇa*) is stated in the following kārikā.

[1] See BU, IV. 3. 21.

[2] See IV. 84; Cf *sarvajña*, III. 36, 47.

*

As P r ā j ñ a does not know anything he is regarded as bound with the cause (*tattvāgrahaṇa*) which is just like darkness (*tamas*).[3] As regards T u r ī y a there being nothing except himself he is all-seeing and thus in the absence of all ignorance he is not bound in any way.

[3] See US, XVIII, 26.

13

dvaitasyāgrahaṇaṃ tulyam ubhayoḥ prājñaturyayoḥ I
bījanidrāyutaḥ prājñaḥ sā ca turye na vidyate II

'Non-recognition of duality is common to both P r ā j ñ a and T u r y a ; but P r ā j ñ a is with sleep which is a seed (*i.e.*, cause of specific cognition), while it does not exist in T u r y a.'

In this kārikā the difference between P r ā j ñ a and T u r y a is shown. In the text *nidrā* 'sleep' implies *tattvāpratibodha* 'non-realization of truth' (I. 15), and as it is the cause of specific cognition in dream and waking it is called *bija* 'seed'.

14

svapnanidrāyutāv ādyau prājñas tv asvapnanidrayā I
na nidrāṃ naiva ca svapnaṃ turye paśyanti niścitāḥ II

'The first two (V i ś v a and T a i j a s a) are with sleep and dream,[1] P r ā j ñ a is with dreamless sleep, while those who are certain (about the truth) see neither sleep nor dream in T u r y a.'

It follows, therefore, from the above that T u r y a is not bound either with cause or with effect.

[1] Dream (*svapna*) is 'knowing otherwise' (*anyathāgrahaṇa*) and sleep (*nidrā*), as said before, is 'non-cognition of truth' (*tattvāpratibodha*). See I. 15.

15

anyathā gṛhṇataḥ svapno nidrā[1] tattvam ajānataḥ |
viparyāse tayoḥ kṣīṇe turīyaṃ padam aśnute ||[2]

'Dream is for him who takes the truth otherwise, and sleep is for him who does not know the Reality. The error in these two (*svapna* and *nidrā*) being destroyed one attains the stage of T u r ī y a.'

[1] See YS, I. 10. [2] See NSi, IV. 42; US, xviii. 26,

16

anādimāyayā supto yadā jīvaḥ prabudhyate |
ajam anidram asvapnam advaitaṃ budhyate tadā ||

'When the Jīva sleeping on account of illusion[1] which has no beginning is awakened, he realizes (the state of T u r y a) which is unborn and in which there is neither sleep nor dream,[2] nor duality.'

[1] The commentator says that this *māyā* is in the form of *tattvāpratibodha* and *anyathāgrahaṇa*.
[2] See I. 14, III. 36, IV. 81.

17

prapañco yadi vidyeta nivarteta na saṃśayaḥ |
māyāmātram idaṃ dvaitam advaitaṃ paramārthataḥ ||

'If the expansion of the (visible) universe (*prapañca*) were (really) existing it would have to cease to exist, no doubt, but this duality is mere illusion, in absolute truth there is non-duality.'

*

For the meaning of *prapañca* see Candrakīrtti on MV, p. 350:

te ca vikalpā anādimatsaṃsārābhyastāj jñānajñeya-vācya-vācaka-kartṛkarmakriyā-ghaṭa-paṭa-mukuṭa-ratha-rūpa-vedanā-strī-puruṣa-lābhālābha-sukha-duḥkha-yaśo-'yaśo-nindā-praśaṃsādi-lakṣaṇād vicitrāt prapañcād upajāyante.

Op. cit., p. 373:

prapañco hi vāk prapañcayaty arthān iti kṛtvā.

18

vikalpo vinivarteta kalpito yadi kenacit ।
upadeśād ayaṃ vādo jñāte dvaitaṃ na vidyate ॥

'False creation (*vikalpa*)[1] would cease if it were created[2] by some one. This statement (of *vikalpa*) is for the sake of instruction. When (the Reality) is known there is no duality.'

It means that if it is held, as we hold, that the *vikalpa* (=*prapañca* in the preceding kārikā) 'false creation', *i.e.*, duality, is made by some one it must disappear. We say that it is said so in order to instruct the ignorant or stupid people, so that they may gradually arrive at the truth (*ajñānām avabodhārtham.*—YV, III. 84.24). This will be clear from YV (III. 84.19-27), from which a few lines are quoted below.

The second half of the kārikā is identical with YV. III. 84.25*a* and 27*b* with the single variation that in 26*a* there is *avibodhād* for our *upadeśād*. The reading *avibodhād*, however, seems to have actually been *avabodhād*. See the following from YV, III.84:

upadeśāya śāstreṣu jātaḥ śabdo'thavārthajaḥ ।
pratiyogivyavacchedasaṃkhyālakṣaṇapakṣavān ॥ 19
bhedo dṛśyata evāyaṃ vyavahārān na vāstavaḥ ।
vetālo bālakasyeva kāryārthaṃ parikalpitaḥ ॥ 20

[1] That is, duality which is only imaginary.

[2] Lit. imagined.

e... mādimayī mithyāsaṅkalpakalpanā matā ।
ajñānām avabodhārthaṃ na tu bhedo 'sti vastuni ॥ 24
avibodhād ayaṃ vādo jñāte dvaitaṃ na vidyate ।
jñāte saṃśāntakalanaṃ maunam evāvaśiṣyate ॥ 25
vivadante hy asaṃbudhāḥ svavikalpavijṛmbhitaiḥ ।
upadeśād ayaṃ vādo jñāte dvaitaṃ na vidyate ॥ 27

In *a* of the kārikā KN reads *na nivarteta* for *vinivarteta*. Accordingly it would give the following meaning: *vikalpa* would not cease if it is created by some one, but the fact is not so, for it is mentioned only for one's instruction. KN, however, explains it differently.

19

viśvasyātvavivakṣāyām ādi sāmānyam utkaṭam ।
mātrāsampratipattau syād āptisāmānyam eva ca ॥

'In the desire of saying that V i ś v a is A and in knowing the measure[1] the common quality 'first' (*ādi*) as well as 'pervading' (*āpti*) is quite apparent.'

Ātman is to be meditated through the symbol Om, and for doing so these two must be regarded as identical. This identification of Ātman and Om is described in this and the following two kārikās. In the present kārikā the first part (*pāda*) of Ātman, *viz.*, V i ś v a, is identified with the first part or measure (*mātrā*) of Om, *viz.*, the letter A. It is to be noted that Om results from the euphonic combination of the three letters (*mātrās*), A, U and M. In such identification there must be some common quality (*sāmānya dharma*) of the things to be

[1] That is, in knowing the identity of the first *mātrā* of Om, *i.e.*, A, with the first *pāda* of Ātman, *i.e.*, V i ś v a. See I, 20, 21, note 1.

meditated as identical.[2] In the present case there are two common qualities, 'first' (*ādi*) and 'pervading' (*āpti*). As V i ś v a is the first of the four *pādas* of Ātman, so A is the first of all the letters of which Om is composed. And, again, as the reward of one who understands this identity of V i ś v a and A is far-reaching (for one attains thereby everything that one may desire), so is far-reaching A, for, as said in the *śruti*, A is all speech, as it manifests itself in different letters.[3]

2 See *bhaktivāda* in Vedic texts; *Nirukta*, VII. 24: bahubhaktivādīni brāhmaṇāni bhavanti; and the present writer's *Vedic Interpretation and Tradition* in the *Proceedings of the Sixth Oriental Conference* held at Patna, p. 498.

3 S ā y a ṇ a says in his commentary on the TA, VII: etad apy aitareyake samāmnātam akāro vai sarvā vāk. saiṣā sparśoṣmabhir vyajyamānā bahvī nānā-rupā bhavati. This passage is quoted by commentators on the BG, X. 33. See AĀ. III. 2.3 with S ā y a ṇ a : tasyaitasyākāro rasaḥ.

20

taijasasyotvavijñāna utkarṣo dṛśyate sphuṭam ।

mātrāsampratipattau syād ubhayatvaṃ tathāvidham ॥

'In understanding that T a i j a s a is (the letter) U and in knowing the measure,[1] the common quality 'subsequence' (*utkarṣa*) as well as the state of being in (the middle of) both (*ubhayatva*) is clearly seen.'

The common qualities required for identification of T a i j a s a with U are *utkarṣa* 'subsequence' and *ubhayatva* which is the same as *madhyasthatva* 'intermediate position.'

1 That is, in understanding that the second *mātrā* of Om, *i.e.*, U, and the second *pāda* of Ātman, *i.e.*, T a i j a s a, are identical. See I, 19, note 1. and 21, note 1.

T a i j a s a is subsequent to V i ś v a and U is subsequent to A ; therefore there is *utkarṣa*. T a i j a s a and U both are in the middle being between V i ś v a and P r ā j ñ a and A and M respectively.

21

makārabhāve prājñasya mānasāmānyam utkaṭam I
mātrāsampratipattau tu layasāmānyam eva ca II

'In the identity of P r ā j ñ a with (the letter) M and in understanding the measure the clear common quality is 'measure' (*māna*) as well as 'disappearance' (*laya*).'

The commentator's explanation of the kārikā, as I understand it, is as follows: In involution V i ś v a and T a i j a s a enter into P r ā j ñ a, while in evolution they come out of it ; and as such they, as it were, are measured with P r ā j ñ a, just as grains of barley are measured with *prastha* 'a special standard of measure,' generally a basket made of bamboo or cane of particular capacity. In measuring the grains they are first put into the basket and then they are taken out. Now as V i ś v a and T a i j a s a enter into and come out of P r ā j ñ a, so in pronouncing Om continually, A and U, as it were, merge into and emerge from M This is the first common quality, called 'measure' (*māna*) for the identification of P r ā j ñ a and M. The second common quality called 'disappearance' (*laya*) is this: In *suṣupti* 'profound, deep and undisturbed sleep' V i ś v a and T a i j a s a disappear in P r ā j ñ a. Similarly in pronouncing Om, A and U seem to disappear in M.

22

trișu dhāmasu yas tulyaṃ sāmānyaṃ vetti niścitaḥ ।
sa pūjyaḥ sarvabhūtānāṃ vandyaś caiva mahāmuniḥ ॥

'One who knows what is equal and common in the three stages and is certain (about it) is a great sage worthy of veneration and praise of all beings.'

23

akāro nayate viśvam ukāraś cāpi taijasam ।
makāraś ca punaḥ prājñaṃ nāmātre vidyate gatiḥ ॥

'A leads to Viśva, U to Taijasa, and M to Prājña; there is no going to that which has no measure (*mātrā*).'[1]

This is the consequence of one's meditating upon the symbol Om consisting of three *mātrās*, A, U and M. The last *pāda* of the kārikā speaks of the consequence of the meditation on 'the fourth' (Turya). In this state none is led to anywhere, it itself being the cessation of all duality (*dvaitasya upaśamaḥ*).[2]

[1] That is, Turya. [2] See I. 29.

24

oṅkāraṃ pādaśo vidyāt pādā mātrā na saṃśayaḥ ।
oṅkāraṃ pādaśo jñātvā na kiñcid api cintayet ॥

'One should understand Om with each of the *pādas* 'quarters'; no doubt, the *pādas* are the *mātrās* 'measures.'[1]

[1] It is said in the original Up, 8 : pādā mātrā mātrāś ca pādāḥ, which means that the quarters (*pādas*) of ātman are to be regarded as identical with the measures (*mātrās*) of Om.

And having understood Om with each of the *pādas* one should not think of anything else. [2]

[2] For *d* cf. BG, VI. 25 : *ātmasaṃstham manaḥ kṛtvā na kiñcid api cintayet.* See BP, II. 1.19.

25

yuñjīta praṇave cetaḥ praṇavo brahma nirbhayam ।
praṇave nityayuktasya na bhayaṃ vidyate kvacit ॥

'One should apply[1] the mind to Om, for Om is Brahman in whom there is no fear. And nowhere is fear for him who is always fixed[2] upon Om.'

[1] That is, concentrate.

[2] That is, whose mind is always fixed.

26

praṇavo hy aparaṃ brahma praṇavaś ca paraṃ smṛtaḥ ।
apūrvo 'nantaro 'bāhyo 'naparaḥ praṇavo 'vyayaḥ ॥

'Om is said to be the lower, as well as the higher Brahman. Om is without any antecedent and unchanging, and it has nothing other than itself, nor has it inside or outside.'[1]

[1] BU, IV. 5. 83 : anantaro'bāhyaḥ.

27

sarvasya praṇavo hy ādir madhyam antas tathaiva ca ।
evaṃ hi praṇavaṃ jñātvā vyaśnute tad anantaram ॥

'Om is the beginning, middle, and end of all. Having known Om in this way one attains it[1] immediately.'

[1] Original *tad*. It seems to refer to Brahman in the preceding kārikā. The commentator takes it to refer to *ātmabhāva*.

28

praṇavaṃ hīśvaraṃ vidyāt sarvasya hṛdi saṃsthitam[1] ।
sarvavyāpinam oṅkāraṃ matvā dhīro na śocati[2] ॥

'One should know Om to be the Lord present in the heart of all. Having understood the all-pervading Om a wise man does not grieve.'

[1] BG, XIII. 17 : hṛdi sarvasya dhiṣṭhitam ; KU, II. 3. 17 : sadā janānāṃ hṛdaye sanniviṣṭaḥ.
[2] KU, I. 2. 22 ; II. 1. 4, 3. 6.

29

amātro 'nantamātraś ca dvaitasyopaśamaḥ śivaḥ ।
oṅkāro vidito yena sa munir netaro janaḥ ॥

iti gauḍapādīya āgamaśāstra āgamākhyaṃ
prathamaṃ prakaraṇaṃ samāptam.

'He and no other person is a sage (*muni*)[1] who knows Om which has no measure, and yet has an unlimited measure, and which is the cessation of duality, and which is bliss.'

'Here ends, in the *Āgamaśāstra* of Gauḍapāda, Book One, called Traditional Doctrine.'

[1] I. 22.

BOOK II

1

vaitathyaṃ sarvabhāvānāṃ svapna āhur manīṣiṇaḥ ।
antaḥsthānāt tu bhāvānāṃ saṃvṛtatvena hetunā ॥

'The wise say that all things in a dream are unreal, for they are within owing to the fact that they are enclosed.'

See II. 4, IV. 33.

Things such as mountains, elephants, etc., which are seen in a dream are not outside but inside the body. But as in reality they cannot exist within the body they must be regarded as unreal. Literally the kārikā means that owing to the fact that the things in a dream are enclosed (*saṁvṛta*) they are inside (*antaḥśthāna*), and hence they are unreal (*vitatha*). But it will be evident from kārikā IV. 33 in which this very thought is expressed in almost identical words, that the state of being enclosed (*saṁvṛtatva*) is not with reference to things (*bhūtas*), but to the place (*pradeśa*). This explanation of the author himself may rightly be accepted here and also in kārikā II. 4. See II. 2.

That the things seen in a dream are inside the body is explained in the following kārikā :

2

adīrghatvāc ca kālasya gatvā deśān na paśyati ।
pratibuddhaś ca vai sarvas tasmin deśe na vidyate ॥

'The time being not long one does not see the things

dreamt) by going to (different) places ; and no person, on waking, is in the place (where he dreamt himself to be).'

It cannot be held that in a dream one goes to different places and sees things in those places, for one may see things in a dream in a very distant land, but the time being short it is impossible to think that the dreamer travels to that distant land and sees the things there. Moreover, it is found that a dreamer, on waking, does not see himself in the country where he dreamt himself to be.

Thus it follows that the things seen in a dream do not exist in the external world.

In support of this view the author refers in the next kārikā to the BU, IV. 3. 10 :

3

abhāvaś ca rathādīnāṃ śrūyate nyāyapūrvakam |

vaitathyaṃ tena vai prāptaṃ svapna āhuḥ prakāśitam ||

'The non-existence of chariots, etc. (seen in a dream), with the reason therefor, is learnt from the *śruti*.[1] Therefore, it is

[1] See BU, IV. 3. 10 which runs as follows : na tatra rathā na rathayogā na panthāno bhavanty atha rathān rathayogān pathaḥ sṛjate. In this passage *tatra* refers to *svapna*. See also IV. 3. 13 :

svapnānta uccāvacam īyamāno
rūpāṇi devaḥ kurute bahūni |
uteva strībhiḥ saha modamāno
jakṣad utevāpi bhayāni paśyan ||

As regards the *nyāya* 'reason' referred to here, Puruṣottama writes: svapnānta uccāvacamīyamāna—iti mantreṇānekarūpakaraṇam uktvā tasmān nāyataṃ bodhayed durbhiṣajyaṃ hāsmai bhavatity anena suptasya nirbandhena jāgaraṇe kaṣṭam āha yady anyatra gato bhavet tatkaraṇaṃ na vaded (?) durbhaiṣajyaṃ ca. yatra suptas tatraiva striyā svapne ramamāṇaḥ skhalite jāgrat tāṃ bahiḥ paśyet. yato na paśyati tataḥ karoti. yataḥ karoti tato rathādyabhāvāḥ. evaṃ ca svapne pūrvaṃ rathādyabhāvaḥ paścāt karaṇād ityādinyāyapūrvakam.

said that the unreality (of things seen) in a dream, as follows (from the foregoing arguments), is evident.'

In the next kārikā the author proceeds to show the unreality of things in the waking state also applying the same reasons :

4

antaḥsthānāt tu bhedānāṃ tathā jāgarite smṛtam ı
yathā tatra tathā svapne saṃvṛtatvaṃ na bhidyate[1] ıı

'The same [2] is declared of the things [3] in waking on account

[1] The actual reading of *d* in all printed texts and MSS. examined is *saṃvṛtatvena bhidyate* which hardly gives any proper sense. The commentary does not help us on this point. It explains : antaḥsthānāt saṃvṛtatvena ca svapnadṛśyānāṃ bhāvānāṃ jāgraddṛśyebhyo bhedaḥ—'on account of being inside as well as of being covered the phenomena in a dream are different from those in waking.' But this explanation is hardly possible, for one naturally expects here to know the non-difference (*abheda*) and not the difference between the things in waking and in dream. Accordingly one might disjoin the *sandhi* in *jāgraddṛśyebhyo bhedaḥ* in the commentary taking the last word as *abhedaḥ* and not *bhedaḥ*, though Ānandagiri evidently accepts the latter. Apart from the propriety of that explanation the question is : How should one construe the second half of the kārikā ? What is the nominative of the verb *bhidyate*? According to the commentator it must be *svapnadṛśya bhāva*, but it is not in the text, nor can it be understood or supplied from any of the preceding kārikās.

One may, however, take the line as *saṃvṛtatve na bhidyate*. In this case the nominative is *vaitathya* 'unreality' which is to be supplied from the preceding kārikā. The author wants here to show the unreality of the phenomena in the waking state just like that of those in a dream on the same ground, *i.e.*, *antaḥsthāna* which is due to *saṃvṛtatva* of the place. Thus it is said that the *vaitathya* of the things in waking does not differ from that of the things in a dream, for in both the cases *saṃvṛtatva* is the same, there being no difference whatsoever.

[2] That is, *vaitathyam* already described in the preceding kārikā.

[3] The words *bhūta* (IV. 33), *bhāva* (II. 13, 16, 17, 19, 33 ; III. 20, 22), and *bheda* (II. 4, 5, 11, 12) are the same as regards the meaning.

of the fact that they are inside ; for, as there (*i.e.*, in waking) so in a dream the state of being enclosed does not differ.'[4]

See II. 1, IV. 33.

I should, however, like to suggest the reading as *saṃvṛtatvaṃ na bhidyate* which makes the sense very clear.

As to how the state of being enclosed (*saṃvṛtatva*) does not differ in waking and dream, is discussed and shown in some of the following kārikās (II. 9, 10, 13, 14, 15 ; III. 29, 30 ; IV. 61, 62, 64-66), where it is fully explained, as the Vijñānavādins would say, that there being no external thing in reality, whatever we see around us either in waking or in dream is only imagined (*kalpita*) by mind which is inside our body and inside of a body is covered (*samvṛta*). Says Diṅnāga in his *Ālambanaparīkṣā*, 6 : yad antar jñeyarūpaṃ tad bahirvad avabhāsate.

Puruṣottama writes here: jāgarita iti. bahir anubhavāt katham antaḥsthatvam ity ākāṅkṣāyāṃ svapnatulyatvād iti vaktuṃ svapnasyaitattaulyam āha yathā tatreti. yathā jāgarite manodhyāto 'rthaḥ śarīrasaṃvṛtatvena bāhyebhyo bhidyata iti śarīrāntaḥsthatvaṁ tathā svapne 'pi pūrvaṁ uktam. atas tattulyatvāt tathety arthaḥ.

[4] The commentary reads in explaining the kārikā : jāgraddṛśyānāṃ bhāvānāṃ vaitathyam iti pratijñā. dṛśyatvād iti hetuḥ. svapnadṛśyabhāvavad iti dṛṣṭāntaḥ. yathā tatra svapne dṛśyānāṃ bhāvānāṃ vaitathyaṃ tathā jāgarite 'pi dṛśyatvam aviśiṣṭam iti hetūpanayaḥ. tasmāj jāgarite 'pi vaitathyaṃ smṛtam iti nigamanam.

Now the author goes to show further in the next kārikā that there is no difference between the two states, waking and dream ; in fact they are one :

5

svapnajāgarite sthāne hy ekam āhur manīṣiṇaḥ I
bhedānāṃ hi samatvena prasiddhenaiva hetunā II

'The wise say that the two states, dream and waking, are

one, on account of the identity of things (in those two states), for the reason that has been well established.'

The first half of the kārikā refers to BU, IV. 3. 14 :

atho khalv āhur jāgaritadeśa evāsyāiṣa iti yāni hy eva jāgrat paśyati tāni supta iti.

Here *eṣaḥ* refers to *svapna*, as says Śaṅkara: *eṣaḥ svapnaḥ*.

For *svapnajāgarite sthāne* cf. BU, IV. 3. 9 : dve eva sthāne bhavataḥ.

'The reason that has been well established' (*prasiddhenaiva hetunā*) refers to *antaḥsthāna* already explained (II. 1, 4),

Though in fact the objects of waking experience appear as real, still they are unreal. How it may be so the author proceeds to say in the following kārikās:

6

ādāv ante ca yan nāsti vartamāne'pi tat tathā ।
vitathaiḥ sadṛśāḥ santo'vitathā iva lakṣitāḥ ॥

See IV. 31.

'That which is non-existent at the beginning, and at the end, is so also at the present (*i.e.*, in the middle); being like the unreal[1] things still appear as not unreal' ;

For a full discussion see IV. 31, which is identical with the present kārikā.

1 That is, being like mirage, etc., which are acknowledged to be unreal by all.

7

saprayojanatā teṣāṃ svapne 'pi pratipadyate[1] ।
tasmād ādyantavattvena mithyaiva khalu te smṛtāḥ ॥

1 The reading of *b* generally found in editions and MSS. examined is *svapne vipratipadyate* ; but as the sense requires it should be *svapne 'pi prati-*

'that the things have some purpose also in dream is known. Hence owing to their having a beginning and an end, indeed, they are regarded as unreal.'

For particulars see IV. 32 which is a repetition of the present kārikā.

padyate which is actually found in a MS., D[2]. in IV. 32 which is identical with the present kārikā. Here, too, MS. Vn. reads *svapne ca prati°*. It is supported also by MS. Ch (क) of the Comm. in Ānandāsrama ed. which has *svapne prati°* for *svapne viprati°*.

8

apūrvāḥ sthānidharmā hi yathā svarganivāsinām ।
tān ayaṃ prekṣate gatvā yathaiveha suśikṣitaḥ ॥

'(The phenomena of dream) are strange, like (the characteristics) of the inhabitants of the heaven; they are the characteristics of the person in the place (of dream, *i.e.*, the dreamer himself). Just like one who is well trained here, he goes and sees them (in dream).'

I confess this kārika is not quite clear to me. I simply write what I have been able to gather from it in the light of the commentator.

It is to be noted that in *a* I suggest the reading *apūrvāḥ sthānidharmāḥ* for *apūrvaṃ sthānidharmaḥ*, so that the former can be connected with *tān* in *c*. For other readings see the commentary and the Appendix.

The kārikā seems to say as follows: The phenomena of dream, on the analogy of which the objects of the waking experience are held to be unreal, are sometimes strange, as the characteristics of some gods, such as the thousand eyes of Indra, and this is the nature of the dreamer (*sthānin* 'one in the place' of dream) himself. And just as a man who is well trained goes to a place and sees there strange things, so he sees strange things in a dream.

The next two kārikās seek to establish the unreality of dream and waking experience alike :

9

svapnavṛttāv api tv antaś cetasā kalpitaṃ tv asat |
bahiś cetogṛhītaṃ sad dṛṣṭaṃ vaitathyam etayoḥ ||

'Even in the state of dream that which is imagined by mind within is (regarded as) non-existing (*asat*), while that which is cognized by mind without is (regarded as) existing (*sat*) ; (but) the unreality of (both of) them is a matter of experience.'

10

jāgradvṛttāv api tv antaś cetasā kalpitaṃ tv asat |
bahiś cetogṛhītaṃ sad yuktaṃ vaitathyam etayoḥ ||

'In the waking state also, that which is imagined by mind within is regarded as non-existing (*asat*), while that which is cognized by mind without is regarded as existing, (*sat*); the unreality of (both of) them is reasonable.'

Cf. these two kārikās with IV. 63-66.

The opponent here says that it cannot be said that everything in the waking experience and dream is unreal, for there must be at least one thing real without which we cannot go on:

11

ubhayor api vaitathyaṃ bhedānāṃ sthānayor yadi |
ka etān budhyate bhedān ko vai teṣāṃ vikalpakaḥ ||

'If in both the states the different things are unreal, well, then who is it that cognizes these things? Who is it that imagines them?'

The answer is given in the following kārikā :

12

kalpayaty ātmanātmānam ātmā devaḥ svamāyayā |
sa eva budhyate bhedān iti vedāntaniścayaḥ ||

'It is the self, the shining one, that imagines the self by the self through its own illusion (*māyā*), and verily it is that (self) which cognizes the things. This is the conclusion of the Vedānta.'

For such use of the word *ātman* in the sense of self see BG, II. 55; V. 17 ; VI. 5, 6.

The word *deva* here and in similar cases (I. 1 ; II. 19, 21) does not mean a 'god'. Its literal sense is 'a shining one' and it is used to denote anything that shines in any way, or that which has some sort of glory or power For instance, in Upaniṣadic texts see PU, II. 1, 2 (where the following are called *devas* : *ākāśa*, *vāyu*, *agni*, *pṛthvī*, *vāc*, *manas*, *cakṣus* and *śrotra*); 5 (*vāyu*); 8 (*prāṇa*); IV. 1, 2, 5, 6 (*manas*); 11 (*agni*, etc.) ; BU, IV. 3. 13 (Śaṅkara: *devo dyotamānaḥ*). Puruṣottama would take the word in the sense of 'a playing one' : atra deva iti krīḍāparatvam uktam teneyaṃ kalpanā krīḍāpareti phalati.

It may be noted incidentally that the words *prabhu* (I. 8, 10 ; II. 13) and *vibhu* (I. 1, 10) in such cases are not to be connected with the sense of 'god', they simply mean 'powerful'. See BG, V. 14, 15.

See also our text II. 19; ŚU, IV. 9.

In what manner the Ātman imagines so, is shown in the next kārikā :

13

vikaroty aparān bhāvān antaś citte 'vyavasthitān |
niyatāṃś ca bahiś citta evaṃ kalpayate prabhuḥ ||[1]

'It brings about some things in the mind within, which are not fixed, also some other things in the mind without, which are fixed. Thus brings about the powerful one.'

vikaroti 'brings about' (lit. 'makes variously', Com. *nānā karoti*) = *kalpayati* (II. 12) or *kalpayate* (II, 13, 16; see 14, 30, 33 ; I. 18, II. 9).

There are two kinds of things, things in dream, and those in wakefulness, and both of them are imagined in mind. The only difference between them is that the former are imagined inside and are not fixed vanishing at once, while the latter are imagined outside and are fixed, for they serve our practical purposes.

The next kārikā seeks to show that in fact there is no difference between them :

[1] In *b* the commentator with a number of editions and MSS. reads *vyavasthitān* for *avyavasthitān* which is clearly supported by P u r u ṣ o t t a m a. The sense of the kārikā demands in the first half a term opposite to *niyata* in the second half, and it is *avyavasthita* (= *aniyata*) and not *vyavasthita*. In the phrase *bahiścitta evam* (in *c* and *d*) the commentator takes the first word as *bahiścittaḥ*. But it must be *bahiścitte*. P u r u ṣ o t t a m a clearly reads the latter. Cf. *antaścitte* in *b*.

14

cittakālāś ca ye 'ntas tu dvayakālāś ca ye bahiḥ |
kalpitā eva te sarve viśeṣo nānyahetukaḥ ||

'Those which are within and exist as long as exists the thought (*citta*), and those which are without and exist as long as remains (the notion of) the two (*i.e.*, *grāhya* 'perceptible' and *grāhaka* 'percipient'), are all merely imagined. And (in this respect) there is no difference on any other ground.'

For *dvaya* see III. 29, 30 ; IV. 4, 24, 61, 62, 72, 75, 87.

That in such cases *dvaya* 'twofold' means *grāhya* and *grāhaka*, 'perceptible' and 'percipient' respectively, is quite clear from the words of the author himself (IV. 72*b*) : grāhyagrāhakavad dvayam. It is also well known throughout the Buddhist literature, for instance, MS, XIV. 28 (p. 94) :

dvayagrāhavisaṃyuktaṃ lokottaram anuttaram |
nirvikalpaṃ malāpetaṃ jñānaṃ sa labhate punaḥ ||

°dvayagrāhavisaṃyuktaṃ grāhyagrāhagrāhakagrāhavisaṃyogāt. *Op. cit.* XI. 32 (p. 63) :

svadhātuto dvayābhāsāḥ sāvidyākleśavṛttayaḥ |
vikalpāḥ sampravartante dvayadravyavivarjitāḥ ||

°dvayābhāsā iti grāhyagrāhakābhāsāḥ. dvayadravyavivarjitā iti grāhyadravyeṇa grāhakadravyeṇa ca.

See also the following quoted from the *Āryadṛḍhāśayaparipṛcchā* in MV, p. 463 :

na hi kulaputra dvayaprabhāvitā tathāgatadharmatā· tatra ye dvaye caranti na te samyakprayuktā mithyāprayuktās te vaktavyāḥ· katamac ca kulaputra dvayaṃ. ahaṃ rāgaṃ prahāsyāmīti dvayam etat. ahaṃ dveṣaṃ prahāsyāmīti dvayam etat. ahaṃ mohaṃ prahāsyāmīti dvayam etat.

TS, 3,538 :

prakṛtyā bhāsvare citte dvayākārākalaṅkite ।
dvayākārāvimūḍhātmā kaḥ kuryād anyathāmatiḥ (tim) ॥
dvayākārāvimūḍhātmeti prahīṇagrāhyagrāhakābhiniveśaḥ.

—*Pañjikā*.

Though both of the experiences, *i.e.*, the experiences in dream and waking, are mere imaginations, and as such are not different, yet there is some difference between them with regard to the means of their cognition. This is shown in the next kārikā :

15

avyaktā eva ye 'antas tu sphuṭā eva ca ye bahiḥ ।
kalpitā eva te sarve viśeṣas tv indriyāntare ॥

'Those which are unmanifest within and those which are manifest without are all imagined indeed, but there is some difference owing to the difference of the organs of sense (with which they are cognized).'

The experiences of dream being related only to the mind (*manomātrasambandhāt*) are unmanifest (*avyakta=asphuṭa*); while those of waking being related to external senses, such as eyes, etc. (*cakṣurādibhir indriyasambandhāt*) are manifest (*sphuṭa*). Hence it is to be admitted that there is some difference between them. But this difference is not due to any reality (*astitvakṛta*) of external things; for the phenomena of dream, too, appear for the time being to be as real as those of waking. Therefore this difference lies in the fact that while the things within are cognized by mind, those without are cognized by external senses. The following line of Ānandagiri is to be noted here specially: ye manasy antarbhāvanārūpatvād asphuṭā ye ca manaso bahir upalabhyamānāḥ sphuṭā bhavanti te sarve manaḥspandanamātratvena kalpitāḥ. Mark here *manaḥspandana* and compare the views of the Vijñānavādins which will be more and more evident as we proceed. See IV. 72.

The creation of internal and external things are effected thus:

16

jīvaṃ kalpayate pūrvaṃ tato bhāvān pṛthagvidhān |
bāhyān ādhyātmikāṃś caiva yathāvidyas tathāsmṛtiḥ ||

'First one[1] imagines a personal soul (*jīva*)[2], and then various things,[3] external and internal.[4] As one knows so one recollects.'

Mark that it is a personal soul (*jīva*) that is first imagined, and then the other things. And it is so, because the imagination of the latter depends entirely on that of the former. Says the commentator (II. 17) : *jīvakalpanā sarvakalpanāmūlam* 'the imagination of *jīva* is the root of other imaginations.' This imagination of a personal soul is what is called *satkāyadṛṣṭi*[5] or *svakāyadṛṣṭi* (MK. XXIII. 5), Pali *sakkāyadiṭṭhi*, 'theory of individuality' in Buddhism. It is generally known as *ātmadṛṣṭi*, Pali *attadiṭṭhi*, or *ātmavāda*, Pali *attavāda*. This *satkāyadṛṣṭi* is fourfold : thinking that (*i*) *rūpa* (so also *vedanā*, *saṃjñā*,

[1] It refers to *ātman* 'self,' II. 12, 13.

[2] ātman, sattva, jīva, jantu, puruṣa, pudgala, etc., are synonyms, MVt[1], §207 ; *Abhidhānappadīpikā*, 93 ; ŚS, pp. 172, 236 ; NS, Commentary I. 1.2.

[3] Such as *prāṇa* 'breath,' etc., See II. 19-28.

[4] MS, XI.5 (p. 55) : tatra grāhakabhūtaṃ kāyādikam ādhyātmikaṃ grāhyabhūtaṃ bāhyam. See also Vācaspati Miśra on the *Sāṅkhyakārikā*, I.

[5] See ZDMG, Vol. 64, pp. 581 ff ; AK. V. 7 ; *The Basic Conception of Buddhism*, pp. 77 ff.

saṃskāra and *vijñāna*) is ātman, (*ii*) *ātman* has *rūpa*, (*iii*) *rūpa* is in *ātman*, and (*iv*) *ātman* is in *rūpa* [6]

This *satkāyadṛṣṭi* is the source of all sorts of miseries in the world and consequently their cessation is effected only by giving it up (MK, XVIII, 2; MV. pp. 346,361; ŚS, p. 247).

As to how the imagination of all other things is dependent on the *satkāyadṛṣṭi* the following may be quoted from the BAP, pp. 491-92 :

tathā hy ātmānaṃ paśyataḥ saṃskṛteṣu skandhadhātv āyataneṣv ahaṃ iti dṛḍhataram utpadyate snehaḥ. tatas tadduḥkhapratikārecchayā sukhābhilāṣī doṣān pracchādya tadarthitayā guṇādhyāropāt tatsādhaneṣu pravartate svopakāriṇi vayam iti buddhir upajāyate ahaṃ mameti ca darśanāt. paripanthini vidveṣaḥ. tataḥ samastaduḥkhanidānaṃ sarva eva kleśopaklesā labdhaprasārāḥ pravartante. ity ātmamohapravartito duḥkhahetur ahaṅkāro bhavati. tad uktam ācāryapādaiḥ :

yaḥ paśyaty ātmānaṃ tatrāsyāham iti śāśvatasnehaḥ ।
snehāt sukheṣu tṛṣyati tṛṣṇā doṣāṃs tiraskurute ॥
guṇadarśī paritṛṣyan mameti tatsādhanāny upādatte
tenātmābhiniveśo yāvat tāvat sa saṃsāraḥ ॥
ātmani sati parasaṃjñā svaparavibhāgāt parigrahadveṣau ।
anayoḥ sampratibaddhāḥ sarve doṣāḥ prajāyante ॥[7]

6 To mention only a few see DSṇ, pp. 182-183, § 1003; MN, I, 300; SN, III. 16 ff. 42, 44, 46, 56, 102, etc.; MVt², § 208: rūpam ātmā svāmivat, rūpavān ātmā alaṅkāravat, ātmīyaṃ rūpaṃ bhṛtyavat, rūpe ātmā bhājanavat. The following may be quoted here which refutes the above view :

rūpaṃ nātmā rūpavān naiva cātmā
rūpe nātmā rūpam ātmany asac ca ।

This is quoted in SS, p. 20; MV, p. 355.

7 These stanzas are from PV, II. 217-19. BAP reads *tasyātrāha*° for *tatrāsyāha*°, *paritṛṣan* for °*tṛṣyan* and *tu* for *sa* in kārikā 1[b], 2[a] and 2[d] respectively. The last verse is quoted in AAA, p. 67; NK, p. 279. *Cf.* the views

yāthāvidyas tathāsmṛtiḥ 'as one knows so one recollects' implies here that one's imagination of different things follows the recollection of one's experience.

of the Kāpilas (Sāṃkhyas) quoted here. See A n i r u d d h a ' s *Vṛtti* on the SāS, V. 79; JA, 1902, Sept.-Oct., p. 291, AK, IX 230 :

sāhaṅkāre manasi na śamaṃ yāti janmaprabandho
nāhaṅkāraś calati hṛdayād ātmadṛṣṭau tu satyām |
anyaḥ śāstā jagati ca yato nāsti nairātmyavādī
nānyas tasmād upaśamavidhes tvanmatād asti mārgaḥ ||

See also the *Basic Conception of Buddhism*, p. 72.

17

aniścitā yathā rajjur andhakāre vikalpitā |
sarpadhārādibhir bhāvais tadvad ātmā vikalpitaḥ ||

'As in the dark a rope which is not determinately known is imagined to be a snake or a continuous line of water,[1] etc., so is imagined the soul (*ātman*=*jīva*).'[2]

[1] See note 2.

[2] In the commentary on śloka 93 of his *Madhyamakālaṅkāra* which is now available only in its Tibetan version, Tanjur(Mdo, sa=XXVIII, 52^b.1—84^a 7; C o r d i e r: III. p. 311), Ś ā n t i r a k ṣ i t a quotes some kārikās from Books II and III of our work. The following is the Tibetan version of the present kārikā :

ji. ltar. mun. khuṅ. ma. rtogs. te |
thag.pa. sbrul.gyi.rgyun.la.sogs |
dṅos.por.rnaṃ par. brtags pa ltar |
de.bžin bdag. kyaṅ rnam.par.brtags |

In *a* Tib. has *andhakārabile* (mun. khuṅ) for *andhakāre* and in *b* it takes *sarpadhārā* as *sarpasya dhārā* (sbrul. gyi. rgyun), and not as *sarpa* 'snake' and *dhārā* 'continuous line'.

18

niścitāyāṃ yathā rajjvāṃ vikalpo vinivartate |
rajjur eveti cādvaitaṃ tadvad ātmaviniścayaḥ ||

'As the rope being determinately known the thing imagined vanishes and there is non-duality—it is nothing but the rope, so is the ascertainment of ātman '

According to Tib.[1] the reading *rajjur eveti* in *c* is *rajjur ekaiva* (thag. pa. gcig. ñid), and it appears to be better. In *d* Tib. literally reads *ātmāpi niścitaḥ* (bdag. kyaṅ. ṅes pa. yin) for *ātmaviniścayaḥ*.

[1] It runs thus:

ji.ltar. thag.pa ṅes.rtogs na |
rnam.par.rtog.pa.ldog.ḥgyur.te |
thag.pa.gcig.ñid.gñis.min.pa |
de.ltar.bdag.kyaṅ.ṅes.pa.yin ||

19

prāṇādibhir anantais tu bhāvair etair vikalpitaḥ |
māyaiṣā tasya devasya yayāyaṃ mohitaḥ svayam ||[1]

'It (Ātman) is imagined as Prāṇa 'breath' or 'life' and other innumerable things.[2] This is an illusion of it, the shining one,[3] by which it itself is deluded.'[4]

[1] See II. 12.

[2] See II. 20 ff.

[3] See BU, IV. 4. 15 : yadaitam anupaśaynty ātmānaṃ devam añjasā.

[4] The following is the Tib. version :

srog.la.sogs.pa mthaḥ.yas.paḥi |
dṅos po.de.dag.rnam.par.bratags |
gaṅ.gis.de.bdag.ñid.rmoṅs |
de.ni.lha.deḥi.sgyu.ma. yin ||

In c the actual reading is *dag* for *bdag* and in *d* there is *rgyu* for *sgyu*. In c there are only six syllables instead of seven. One may, however, add here *pa* after *rmoṅs*.

It is said that Ātman is imagined as Prāṇa and such other things. But what these things are is stated in the following kārikās (20-28) :

20

prāṇā iti prāṇavido bhūtānīti ca tadvidaḥ ।
guṇā iti guṇavidas tattvānīti ca tadvidaḥ ॥[1]

'Those who know *prāṇa* 'breath' or 'life' (imagine) it as *prāṇa*; those who know *bhūtas* 'elements' as *bhūtas* ; those who know *guṇas* 'ingredients' as *guṇas*, and those who know *tattvas* 'categories,' as *tattvas*.'

The knowers of *prāṇa* are some followers of Upaniṣads; their view is found in the following : MnU, III. 4 : prāṇo hy eṣa yaḥ sarvabhūtair vibhāti; PU. II. 4 : prāṇe sarvaṃ pratiṣṭhitam ; ChU, I. 11. 4-5 ; BU, IV. 4. 18 ; BS, I. 1, 13. Ā n a n d a g i r i says that they are the votaries of Hiraṇyagarbha, etc., Vaiśeṣikas and others.

The *bhūtas* 'elements' are nve, *viz.*, earth, water, fire, air and sky (or ether). According to Mādhyamikas and the Sautrāntikas there are only four elements excluding the sky (CŚ, IX. 3, 5). The Vaibhāṣikas, however, admit it as *bhūia* (AK, 1.8). Ā n a n d a g i r i says that the view referred to here is held by the Lokāyatikas who maintain that the first four elements are the origin of the world.

[1] The following is the Tib. version :

srog du. rig.pas.srog.ces.brjod ।
ḥbyuṅ.po.yin.žes.de.rig.rnams ।
yon.tan.rig.rnams. yon.tan.sñam ।
yaṅ.dag.yin. žes. de.rig.rnams ।

Tib. *yaṅ, dag* is generally used for Skt. *samyak* and sometimes for *bhūa*, and *paramārtha*; but it is only here in *d*, so far as I have noticed, that it is employed for *tattva*.

The *guṇas* are the three constituent elements of *Prakṛti* of the Sāṅkhya philosophy, *viz*., *sattva*, *rajas* and *tamas*.

As regards the *tattvas* Ā n a n d a g i r i says that the Śaivas are referred to here, according to whom there are three *tattvas*, *viz*., *ātman*, *avidyā* and *Śiva*.

21

pādā iti pādavido viṣayā iti tadvidaḥ ।
lokā iti lokavido devā iti ca tadvidaḥ ॥

'Those who know *pādas* 'quarters' (imagine it) as *pādas;* those who know *viṣayas* 'objects' as *viṣayas* ; those who know *lokas* 'worlds' as *lokas;* and those who know *devas* 'gods' as *devas*.'

Pāda may refer to what is known from such passages as the following : RV. X. 90. 3 pādo 'sya viśvā bhūtāni tripād asyāmṛtaṃ divi ; ChU, III. 12.6 : pādo 'sya sarvā bhūtāni. 18.2; vāk pādaḥ prāṇaḥpādaś cakṣuḥ pādo 'gniḥ pādo vāyuḥ pādaḥ; also IV. 6.3, 8.3. Ā says it alludes to the four *pādas* of *ātman*, *viz*., V i ś a, T a i j a s a, etc., described above.

According to Ā the *viṣayas* are the objects of senses (*indriyas*). They are five, *viz*., sound (*śabda*), the tangible (*sparśa*), colour (*rūpa*), savour (*rasa*), and odour (*gandha*). These are to be enjoyed again and again, and as such are regarded as *tattva* 'principle'. This view is, as Ā tells us, held by V ā t s y ā y a n a and others (*vātsyayana-prabhṛti*). This V ā t s y ā y a n a appears to be the author of the *Kāmaśāstra*. By 'others' we may take the Lokāyatikas and some Tāntrikas, Buddhist and Brāhmanic. See *The Basic Conception of Buddhism*, pp. 62 ff.; SS, pp. 37 ff.; *Cittaviśuddhiprakaraṇa*;

Visvabharati, 1933, p. 2. The following is quoted from the last mentioned work :

svādhidaivatayogātmā jagadarthakṛtodyamaḥ ।
bhuñjāno viṣayān bhogī mucyate na ca lipyate ॥ 17
yathaiva viṣatattvajño viṣam ālokya bhakṣayan ।
kevalaṃ mucyate nāsau rogamuktaś ca jāyate ॥

The *lokavids* are, according to Ā, the followers of the Purāṇas holding that there are three *lokas* 'worlds,' *viz.*, *bhū* 'earth', *bhuvas* (*bhuvar*) 'atmosphere,' and *svar* 'heaven.'

The *devavids* are, as says Ā, the followers of the *Devatākāṇḍa*, *i.e.*, that part of the Veda (*cf.* *Nighaṇṭu* or *Nirukta*, VII) which deals with *devatās* 'deities.' They hold that *karmaphala* 'consequence of action' is given by Devatās, Agni, Indra and others, and not by God.

22

vedā iti vedavido yajñā iti ca tadvidaḥ ।
bhokteti ca bhoktṛvido bhojyam iti ca tadvidaḥ ॥

'The knowers of the Vedas (imagine it) as the Vedas, the knowers of *yajñas* 'sacrifices' as *yajñas*, the knowers of the *bhoktṛ* 'enjoyer' as *bhoktṛ*, and those who know *bhojya* 'enjoyable' as *bhojya*.'

According to Ā *yajñavids* are Baudhāyana and others. The *bhoktṛvids* are the Sāṅkhyas who maintain that *ātman* is only enjoyer (*bhoktṛ*) and not also doer (*kartṛ*). Or see BG, V. 29: bhoktāraṃ yajñatapasām; IX. 24: bhoktā ca prabhur eva ca; XIII. 22: bhartā bhoktā maheśvaraḥ. See also our text, I. 9.

In accordance with the same authority *bhojyavids* are the cooks (*sūpakāras*), for in their opinion food (*bhojyaṃ vastu*) is the principle. *Cf.* TU, III. 2-1 : annaṃ brahmeti vyajāṇāt; ChU, I. 3. 6: anne hīdaṃ sarvam sthitam.

23

sūkṣma iti sūkṣmavidah sthūla iti ca tadvidaḥ ।
mūrta iti mūrtavido 'mūrta iti ca tadvidaḥ ॥

'Those who know what *sūkṣma* 'a subtle thing' is (imagine it) as *sūkṣma*, those who know what *sthūla* 'a gross thing' is as *sthūla*, those who know what *mūrta* 'an embodied thing' is as *mūrta*, and those who know what *amūrta* 'non-embodied' is as *amūrta*.'

Sūkṣmavids are those who hold that the dimension of ātman is like that of an atom (*aṇu*). Accordingly they would refer to all the Vaiṣṇava teachers, such as Rāmānuja, Nimbārka, Madhva, and Vallabha. For the discussion see BS, II. 3. 19-32. See also MuU, III. 1 : sūkṣmāc ca tat sūkṣmataraṃ vibhāti ; 9: eṣo 'ṇur ātmā cetasā veditavyaḥ; MU, II. 5 : sa vā eṣa sūkṣmo 'grāhyaḥ.

Sthūlavids refer to a class of Lokāyatikas holding that the gross body is ātman.—Ā.

Mūrtavids are Āgamikas, followers of *Āgamas* (*Śaivas* and *Vaiṣṇavas*). mūrtas triśūlādidhārī maheśvaraś cakrādidhārī vā paramārtho bhavati.—Ā. The following passage (BU, II. 3. 1) may here be cited: dve vāva brahmaṇo rūpe mūrtaṃ caivāmūrtaṃ ca.

Ā says *Amūrtavids* are Śūnyavādins. But see the passage quoted above from the BU.

24

kāla iti kālavido diśa iti ca tadvidaḥ ।
vādā iti vādavido bhuvanānīti tadvidaḥ ॥

'Those who know *kāla* 'time' (imagine it) as *kāla*, those who know *diś-es* 'directions' or 'quarters' as *diś-es*, those who know *vādas* 'discussions' as *vādas*, and those who know *bhuvanas* 'worlds' as *bhuvanas*.'

Kālavids are astronomers. *Kāla* is the cause of all existence. See AV, XIX. 53, 54; ŚU, I. 2, VI. 1 ; ṢS with Guṇaratna, pp. 10 ff.

The knowers of *diś-es*, as says Ā, are *svarodayavids*, *i.e.*, those who know good or bad omens by voices of birds, etc., holding that the *diś-es* are the highest reality.

Vādavids are, according to the same authority, those who hold *dhātuvāda* 'alchemy', *mantravāda* 'formulas of sacred texts,' or 'the science of magic,' and so on. Here *vāda* may, however, refer to 'discussion' as in NS, I. 1.1, 2. 1.

The knowers of *bhuvanas* are those who know the system of the worlds (*bhuvanakośa*) and say that there are in all fourteen of them. See ViP, XXXIII-LX (*Bhuvanavinyāsa* and *yotiṣpracāra*).

25

mana iti manovido buddhir iti ca tadvidaḥ I
cittam iti cittavido dharmādharmau ca tadvidaḥ II

'Those who know *manas* 'mind' (imagine it) as *manas*, those who know *buddhi* 'intellect' as *buddhi*, those who know *citta* 'thought' or 'consciousness' as *citta*, and those who know *dharma* 'duty' and *adharma* 'non-duty' as *dharma* and *adharma*.'

Ā says that a particular section of the Lokāyatikas who opine that *manas* is the self (ātman) is referred to by the word *manovid*, and the knowers of *buddhi* are Buddhists who maintain that the intellect is the self (*ātman*). The knowers of *citta* are evidently Yogācāras or Vijñānavādins. The knowers of *dharma* and *adharma* are the Mīmāṃsists.

26

pañcaviṃśaka ity eke ṣaḍviṃśa iti cāpare I
ekatriṃśaka ity āhur ananta iti cāpare II

'Some say it to be consisting of twenty-five, some consisting of twenty-six, some consisting of thirty-one, while others to be endless in number.'

Here *pañcaviṃśaka* refers to the opinion of the Sāṅkhyas, according to whom there are twenty-five *tattvas* 'principles,' *viz.*, 1. *prakṛti*, 2. *mahat*, 3. *ahaṅkāra*, 4-8. five *tanmātras*, 9. *manas*, 10-14. five *jñānendriyas*, 15-19. five *karmendriyas*, 20-24. five *mahābhūtas*, and 25. *puruṣa*.

By *ṣaḍviṃśa* we are to understand the view of Pātañjalas or the followers of the Yoga system. Their *tattvas* are the same as those of the Sāṅkhyas enumerated above *plus* Īśvara, the twenty-sixth.

The word *ekatriṃśaka* refers to the view held by the Pāśupatas. There are, in fact, thirty-six *tattvas*, *viz.*, 1. *śiva*, 2. *śakti*, 3. *sadāśiva*, 4. *īśvara*, 5. *vidyā*[1], 6. *puruṣa*, 7. *māyā*, 8. *kāla*, 9. *niyati*, 10. *kalā*, 11. *avidyā*[2], 12. *rāga*[3], 13. *prakṛti or avyakta*, 14. *mahat*, 15. *ahaṅkāra*, 16. *manas*, 17-21. five *jñānendriyas*, 22-26. five *karmendriyas*, 27-31. five *tanmātras*, and 32-36. five *bhūtas*.[4]

As Nos. 8-12 are merely the manifestations (*vibhūtis*) of *māyā*, as said by the commentator of the MM, p. 50, one may

1 Nos. 1-5 constitute the *tattva* called *pati*.

2 This is according to MM, p. 50; but TP, III. 8 clearly reads *vidyā* and the commentator explains it as *aśuddhavidyā*.

3 Nos. 6-12 constitute the *tattva* known as *paśu*.

4 Nos. 13-36 are included in the *tattva* named pāśa. See MM, verses 13-25; TP. II 5-11, III. 4, 12.

exclued these five, thus making the number thirty-one as required in our text.

There is one point to be noted here. According to TP, IV. 2, between *avyakta* and *buddhi* or *mahat* there is an additional *tattva* called *guṇa*, but in MM it is not mentioned.

27

lokāllokavidaḥ prāhur āśramā iti tadvidaḥ ।
strīpuṃnapuṃsakaṃ laiṅgāḥ parāparam athāpare ॥

'Those who know *lokas* 'people' (imagine it) as *lokas*, those who know *āśramas* 'stages of religious life' as *āśramas*, those who know *liṅgas* 'sexes' as a male, a female, or a eunuch, while others as *para* 'higher' and *apara* 'lower'.'

The *lokavids* or *laukikas* are those who hold that the pleasing of people (*lokānurañjana*) is the real thing.—Ā. See II. 21.

The *āśramavids* are, as says Ā, D a k ṣ a and others. Probably they are the writers on religious laws (*dharmaśāstrakāras*).

Laiṅgas are grammarians, as says Ā.

Here *parāpara* refers to those who say that two *Brahmans* are to be known, the higher and the lower. MU, VI. 1 : dve brahmaṇī veditavye paraṃ caivāparaṃ ca.—Ā.

28

sṛṣṭir iti sṛṣṭivido laya iti ca tadvidaḥ ।
sthitir iti sthitividaḥ sarvaṃ ceha tu sarvadā ॥

'Those who know *sṛṣṭi* 'creation' (imagine it) as *sṛṣṭi*,[1] those who know *laya* 'destruction' as *laya*, and those who know *sthiti* 'continued existence' as *sthiti*.[2] All (these imaginations) are always here.'[3]

1 See I. 7.

2 The knowers of *sṛṣṭi*, *laya* and *sthiti* are, according to Ā, the Paurāṇikas 'knowers of *Purāṇas*.'

3 It (*iha*) refers to Ātman.

29

yaṃ bhāvaṃ darśayed yasya taṃ bhāvaṃ sa tu paśyati |
taṃ cāvati sa bhūtvāsau tadgrahaḥ samupaiti tam ||

'Whatever thing is presented to him, he sees it; that (*ātman*) becomes it (*i.e.*, the thing presented), and satisfies him. And the strong attachment to it (*i.e.*, to the idea that herein lies the truth) takes possession of him.'

30

etair eṣo 'pṛthagbhāvaiḥ pṛthag eveti lakṣitaḥ |
evaṃ yo veda tattvena kalpayet so 'viśaṅkitaḥ ||

'Verily it (ātman) is considered different through these things that are not different from it. One who knows it in fact may imagine without any hesitation.'

When one sees a piece of rope as a snake, in fact, there is no difference between these two things, for the snake is nothing but the piece of rope which simply appears as a snake. Thus there is only the piece of rope and not the snake which is merely imposed thereon. In the same way there is only ātman, all things other than that being mere imagined.

The imagination referred to in *d* of the kārikā is with reference to the practical view of the things. There is no harm to the man in doing so when he knows the truth.

31

svapnamāye yathā dṛṣṭe gandharvanagaraṃ yathā ।
tathā viśvam idaṃ dṛṣṭaṃ vedānteṣu vicakṣaṇaiḥ ॥

'As dream and illusion are seen, and as is the town of Gandharvas, so is seen all this universe by those who are well-versed in the Vedāntas.'

The word *gandharvanagara* 'an imaginary town in the sky'[1] is not pre Buddhist and is frequently used in Buddhist works. The thought, too, of the kārikā has often found expression in them. For instance, SR, IX (p. 29):

yathaiva gandharvapuraṃ marīcikā,
yathaiva māyā supinaṃ yathaiva ।
svabhāvaśūnyā tu nimittabhāvanā
tathopamān jānatha sarvadharmān ॥

See MV, p. 178; MK, XVII. 33:

gandharvanagarākārā marīcisvapnasannibhāḥ ।

LA, X. 144 (p. 283):

gandharvanagarasvapnamāyānirmāṇasādṛśāḥ ।

Op. cit. 875 (p. 374):

māyāsvapnanibhā bhāvā gandharvanagaropamāḥ ।
marīcyudakacandrābhāḥ svavikalpaṃ vibhāvayet ॥

1 Tissendar writes in his *Popular Scientific Recreations*: The mirage or Fata Morgana is a very curious but sufficiently common phenomenon and in the Asiatic and African plains it is frequently observed. * * * The Fata Morgana and the inverted images of ships at sea are not uncommon on European coasts. Between Sicily and Italy, this effect is seen in the Sea of Riggio with fine effect. Palaces, towers, fertile plains with cattle grazing on them are seen with many other terrestrial objects upon the Sea.—*The Palaces of Fairy Morgana*, p. 649.

See also 279, 291 (pp. 301, 303).

In showing the Buddhist view Śaṅkara quotes the following in his commentary on BS. II. 2, 28:

svapnamāyāmarīcyudakagandharvanagarādipratyayā vinaiva bāhyenārthena grāhyagrāhakakārā bhavanti.

The author says in the kārikā that this view is of the Vedāntins. Śaṅkara follows it, but Rāmānuja with others is of the opposite opinion saying (B.S., I. 1. 1): jagad api pāramārthikam eva jñāyate.

The following two kārikās show the conclusion:

32

na nirodho na cotpattir na baddho na ca sādhakaḥ ।
na mumukṣur na vai mukta ity eṣā paramārthatā ॥

'There is no disappearance,[1] nor origination; no one in bondage, no one who works for success; no one who is desirous of emancipation, no one who is emancipated.--This is the highest truth.'

This is what is the essence of Mahāyāna Buddhism. For the wording of na nirodho na cotpattiḥ *cf.* the opening kārikā of Nāgārjuna's MK, p. 3: anirodham anutpādam. See also BA, IX. 150:

evaṃ ca na nirodho 'sti na ca bhāvo 'sti sarvadā ।
ajātam aniruddhaṃ ca tasmāt sarvam idaṃ jagat ॥

LA, p. 191: aniruddhā anutpannāś ca bhagavatā sarvadharmā deśyante.

See also LA, II. 1, X. 1:

utpādabhaṅgarahito lokaḥ khapuṣpasannibhaḥ ।

[1] Lit. 'suppression.'

*

For *bandha* and *mokṣa* compare the following: CŚ. 179:

kasyacit kenacit sārdhaṃ bandho nāma na vidyate ।
pareṇa saha bandhasya viprayogo na yujyate ॥

LA. 79*b*:

nātra kaścin mahāmate badhyate na ca mucyate.

Op. cit. X. 275:

na mokṣo na ca bandhanaṃ ।

See also the *Āryaratnakūṭa* quoted in MV. pp. 49, 339 and the Chapter called *Bandhanamokṣaparīkṣā* of MK with MV. XVI from which we quote the following (5):

atrāha. yady api tvayā saṃsāranirvāṇe pratiṣiddhe tathāpi bandhamokṣau vidyete. na cāvidyamānasya bhāvasvabhāvasya bandhamokṣau sambhavataḥ. tasmād bandhamokṣasadbhāvād vidyata eva bhāvānāṃ svabhāva iti. ucyate. syād bhāvānāṃ svabhāvo yadi bandhamokṣāv eva syātāṃ. na tu sta ity āha—

na badhyante na mucyanta udayavyayadharmiṇaḥ ।

Āryaratnakūṭa in MV. p. 49 :

athāyuṣmān subhūtis tān bhikṣūn etad avocat kutrāyuṣmanto gatāḥ kuto vāgatāḥ. te 'vocan. na kvacid gamanāya na kutaścid āgamanāya bhadanta subhūte bhagavatā dharmo deśitaḥ. āha. ko nāmāyuṣmatāṃ śāstā. āhuḥ. yo notpanno na parinirvāsyati. āha. kathaṃ yuṣmābhir dharmaḥ śrutaḥ. āhuḥ. na bandhanāya na mokṣāya.

Cf. Sāṅkhyakārikā. 62 :

tasmān na badhyate nāpi mucyate nāpi saṃsarati kaścit ।
saṃsarati badhyate mucyate ca nānāśrayā prakṛtiḥ ॥

We read in the MSA, VI. 2 (p. 22):

na san na cāsan na tathā na cānyathā
na jāyate vyeti na cāvahīyate ।
na vardhate nāpi viśudhyate punar
viśudhyate tat paramārthalakṣaṇaṃ ॥

The present kārikā is widely quoted in minor Upaniṣads and other religious and philosophical works of the country sometimes with slight variations. For instance, see *Avadhūtopaniṣad*, 8; *Ātmopaniṣad*, 31; *Tripurātāpanyupaniṣad*, V. 10; *Brahmabindūpaniṣad*, 10.

The reason for what is said above is advanced in the following kārikā:

33

bhāvair asadbhir evāyam advayena ca kalpitaḥ |
bhāvā apy advayenaiva tasmād advayatā śivā ||

'It is (ātman) imagined in the form of things which are really non-existent through that which is non-dual, and the things (themselves), too, are imagined through what is non-dual. Therefore non-duality is blissful.'

The word *advaya* 'non-dual' means 'one free from both the perceiver and perceptible (*grāhyagrāhakarahita*).'

The imagination of ātman as different things, such as *prāṇa*, etc., which have no existence, is through the *advaya*. For the imagination mainly depends on it, just like the imagination of a snake on a piece of rope; no imagination of a snake is possible, if there is no rope. Similarly things are imagined through the *advaya*, ātman. It is the *advaya* through which there are both the imaginations, the imagination of ātman as different things, and the imagination of the things themselves. Thus *advayatā* 'the state of non-duality' being real is blissful.

34

nānyabhāvena nānedaṃ na svenāpi kathañcana |
na pṛthaṅ nāpṛthak kiñcid iti tattvavido viduḥ ||

'It (the world) is not manifold either through its own nature or through that of another; there is not either the different or the non-different—the knowers of truth know this.'

Here in the beginning of *a* I should like to propose to read *nānyabhāvena*, as I have done, for *nātmabhāvena* accepted by all, though the former is not supported by any edition or MS. known to me. My reason is this: The words *ātmabhāvena* (*a*) and *svena* (*b*) are in fact, one and the same in sense; they do not convey any difference in their meanings which is evidently required here. I am afraid, Ś's explanation[1] can hardly be accepted being unwarranted and far-fetched, as it seems to me. Here *ātmabhāvena* appears to be inexplicable.

Having modified the reading as above, I think the words *anyabhāva* and *sva* are actually the same as *parabhāva* 'nature of other' and *svabhāva* 'nature of one's own' respectively, as thoroughly attacked, discussed, and finally refuted in MK and MV, XV (*svabhāvaparīkṣā*), pp. 259 ff. *Cf.* Nāgārjuna's *pratītyasamutpāda* which is (MV, p. 3) anekārtham anānārtham. Candrakīrti comments: ekaś cāsāv arthaś caikārtho 'bhinnārthaḥ. na pṛthag ity arthaḥ, nānārtho bhinnārthaḥ. pṛthag ity arthaḥ. See MK. X. 16:

ātmanaś ca satattvaṃ ye bhāvānāṃ ca pṛthak pṛthak ।
nirdiśanti na tān manye śāsanasyārthakovidān ॥

See our text IV. 91 with notes.

[1] ātmabhāvena paramārthasvarūpeṇa. svena prāṇādyātmanā.

35

vītarāgabhayakrodhair munibhir vedapāragaiḥ ।
nirvikalpo hy ayaṃ dṛṣṭaḥ prapañcopaśamo 'dvayaḥ ॥

'This cessation of the expansion of the universe, devoid of duality and imagination, is seen by the sages who have reached the other shore of the (ocean of the) Vedas and are free from attachment, fear and anger.'

The word *prapañcopaśama* is nowhere found in the pre-Buddhist Brahmanic works. It is met with only in later and minor Upaniṣads (NPU, 4. 1; NUU, 1; RUU, 2; for *prapañca* see ŚU, 6.6; KlU, 17), including the MāU, 7, the existence of which before Ś is doubtful.

The word *prapañca* of *prapañcopaśama* is from *pra-√pac* or √*pañc* 'to spread out, make clear, or evident.' With this is connected √*pajpañj* from which *pañjikā* 'a commentary.' R ā j a ś e k h a r a writes in his *Kāvyamīmāṃsā*, GOS, 1916, p. 5: *viṣamapadabhañjikā pañjikā*; and we read in H e m a c a n d r a's *Abhidhānacintāmaṇi*, II. 168, 170: *niruktaṃ padabhañjanam, pañjikā padabhañjikā*. From this it appears that *pañjikā* is from *bhañjikā* (from √*bhañj*; *cf*. *vibhaṅga* from this root in the sense of 'thorough explanation' used in Buddhist Sanskrit and Pali works). But philologically it can hardly be supported.

Let it be as it may, the meaning of *prapañca* used frequently in subsequent Vedantic works is, according to that system, 'expansion of the universe' or the 'visible world' (*prapañcyata iti prapañcaḥ*). But in accordance with the Buddhists it means 'verbal designation,' 'expression,' 'word' (*prapañcyate 'nena* or *prapañcayatīti prapañcaḥ*). Thus anything that is expressed by a word or the word itself is *prapañca* according to the Buddhists. (See *The Conception of Buddhist Nirvāṇa*, pp. 48, 91, 156, 209.) C a n d r a k ī r t t i writes in his MV, p. 373:

prapañco hi vāk prapañcayaty arthān iti kṛtvā. prapañcair aprapañcitaṃ (MK, XVIII. 9) vāgbhir avyākṛtam ity arthaḥ.

These words (*vāc*) are naturally various as said in the same work, p. 350. See the passage quoted in our text, I. 17.

prapañcopaśama which is the same as *prapañcoparama* (MV, p. 11) and *prapañcavilaya* (discussed by Ś in his commentary on BS, III. 2. 21) is *mokṣa* of the Vedāntists belonging to the school of G a u ḍ a p ā d a followed by Ś. and *nirvāṇa* of the

Mādhyamikas, and the object in view of N ā g ā r j u n a in writing his MK as said in MV, p. 4: sarvaprapañcopaśamaśivalakṣaṇaṃ nirvāṇaṃ śāstrasya prayojanaṃ nirdiṣṭam. He himself says (MV, p. 11):

anirodham anutpādam anucchedam aśāśvatam ।
anekārtham anānārtham anāgamam anirgamam ॥
yaḥ pratītyasamutpādaṃ prapañcopaśamaṃ śivaṃ ।
deśayāmāsa saṃbuddhas taṃ vande vadatāṃ varam ॥

For a fuller explanation of *prapañcopaśama* (and *śiva*, MāU, 7) from the Buddhist point of view see MK, XXV. 24 with MV, p. 538:

sarvopalambhopaśamaḥ prapañcopaśamaḥ śivaḥ ।

iha hi sarveṣāṃ prapañcānāṃ nimittānāṃ ya upaśamo 'pravṛttis tan nirvāṇaṃ. sa eva copaśamaḥ. prakṛtyaivopaśāntatvāc chivaḥ. vācām apravṛtter vā prapañcopaśamaś cittasyāpravṛtyā śivaḥ. kleśaprahāṇena vā prapañcopaśamo niravaśeṣavāsanāprahāṇena śivaḥ. jñeyānupalabdhyā vā prapañcopaśamo jñānānupalabdhyā śivaḥ.

LA, X. 230 (p. 295):

sarvaprapañcopaśamād bhrānto nābhipravartate
prajñā yāvad vikalpante bhrāntis tāvat pravartate ॥

For *nirvikalpa* see MV, p. 374:

nirvikalpaṃ hi tat (referring to *tattva*, MK, XVIII. 9). vikalpaś cittapracāraḥ. tadrahitatvāt tattvaṃ nirvikalpam. yathoktaṃ sūtre. paramārthasatyaṃ katamat. yatra jñānasyāpracāraḥ kaḥ punarvādo 'kṣarāṇām iti. evaṃ nirvikalpam.

It is to be noted that it is *vikalpa* from which spring up *rāga*, *dveṣa*, *moha*, etc.

The word *vedapāraga* in the text may be taken here as *vedapāra-ga* and not *veda-pāraga* as above meaning 'one conversant with Vedānta (*Veda-pāra*).' *Cf*. *vedānteṣu vicakṣaṇaih* (II. 31).

36

tasmād evaṃ viditvainam advaite yojayet smṛtim ।
advaitaṃ samanuprāpya jaḍaval lokam ācaret ॥

'Therefore having thus known it (*i.e.*, *prapañcopaśama*) one should fix one's memory on non-duality, and having realized non-duality should behave as a fool among people.'

The word *smṛti*, Pali *sati*, means one of the five *balas* 'strengths or powers,' or one of the seven requisites for attaining supreme knowledge (*bodhyaṅgas*, Pali *bojjhaṅgas*). See DS, LXVIII, XLIX; MVT[2] §§ 38, 39, *Cf.* ChU, VII. 26. 7: āhāraśuddhau sattvaśuddhiḥ. sattvaśuddhau dhruvā smṛtiḥ. smṛtilambhe sarvagranthīnāṃ vipramokṣaḥ. Here Ś explains *dhruvā smṛti* as continuous absence of forgetting (*avicchinna avismaraṇa*). This is nothing but *dhyāna* 'meditation.' Rāmānuja in his commentary on BS, I.1.1 (ed. Narasiṃhācārya, Ananda Press, 1909, pp. 9ff.), supports it; and Vācaspatimiśra, YS, I. 20, expressly says that *smṛti* is steady and undisturbed meditation (*smṛtir dhyānam anākulam avikṣiptam*). The word *smṛti* in the present kārikā should be taken in this sense.

For *d* see Ś on BS, III. 4. 50, where he says: 'Let him be free from guile, pride and so on, not manifesting himself by a display of knowledge, learning and virtuousness, just as a child whose sensual powers have not yet developed themselves does not strive to make a display of himself before others (SBE).' He quotes here the following from a work (*smṛti*):

gūḍhadharmāśrito vidvān ajñātacaritaṃ caret ।
andhavaj jaḍavac cāpi mūkavac ca mahīṃ caret ॥

See *Jābāla Up*, 6; *Āśrama Up*, 4; *Minor Upaniṣads*, Adyar Library, 1921, Vol. I, pp. 154, 161, 184.

37

nistutir nirnamaskāro niḥsvadhākāra eva ca |
calācalaniketaś ca yatir yādṛcchiko bhavet ||

'Giving no praise, paying no homage, nor pronouncing *svadhā*, with an unfixed home and acting at random, one should become an ascetic.'

The word *svadhā* (originally *svadhā'* 'self-position,' 'self-power,' 'inherent power') is a Vedic exclamation mostly used in offering food to *pitṛs* 'deceased ancestors.' It also means the food for *pitṛs*. In this case *svadhākāra* would mean 'offering food to *pitṛs*.'

Calācalaniketa is, in fact, *aniketa* of BG, XII. 9, and *anilaya* of BA, VIII. 29, 88, both meaning 'homeless.' *Cf*. apūrva iva sarvatra in BA, VIII. 16 ; *anagāra* 'homeless' or 'a homeless wanderer' in Buddhist literature, and in Jaina works (*Aupapātikasūtra*, ed. Leumann, 1883, §§. 27, 57, etc.).

Here *calācala* in the compound *calācalaniketa* is taken by Ś as two words *cala-* and *-acala-*, and consequently he has fallen into a great confusion in explaining it. The fact is that *calācala* is one word meaning *cañcala* 'intensely moving' *i.e.*, 'absolutely not fixed.' See the *Vārtika*, 6 ('*caricali*°') in the *Mahābhāṣya* on Pāṇini, VI 1. 12. For example, the following may be quoted : *Śiśupālavadha*, XVII. 53 : calācalair anupadam āhatāḥ khuraiḥ ; *Kirātārjunīya*, XI. 30 : janmino 'sya sthitiṃ vidyāl lakṣmīm iva calācalam; *Cāṇakyanītidarpaṇa* (Bombay, 1867), V. 20 : calācale ca saṃsāre dharma eko hi niścalaḥ.

The word *yādṛcchika* does not imply absolutely unrestrained movements, for that is impossible for such a man. See Ś on BS, III. 4. 28-31, 47-50. Mark the significance of the word *yati* lit. 'one who strives to restrain one's passions.' The following occurs in the NPU in the *Minor Upaniṣads*, Adyar, Vol. I, pp. 147, 153 :

nirdvandvo nirnamaskāro niḥsvadhākāra eva ca.

kasyāpi vandanam akṛtvā na-namaskāro na-svāhākāro na-svadhākāro na-nindāstutir yādṛcchiko bhavet.

38

tattvam ādhyātmikaṃ dṛṣṭvā tattvaṃ dṛṣṭvā tu bāhyataḥ ।
tattvībhūtas tadārāmas tattvād apracyuto bhavet ॥

iti gauḍapādīya āgamaśāstre vaitathākhyaṃ
dvitīyaṃ prakaraṇaṃ samāptam.

'Having realised the truth inward, having also realised the truth outward, one becomes the truth (itself), delighting therein and being such one should be unmoved from it.

Here ends in the *Āgamaśāstra* of Gauḍapāda
Book Two called Unreality.'

The *tattva* referred to in the kārikā is nothing but *prapañcopasama* (II. 35) and this is for Vedantists *mokṣa* and for Buddhists *nirvāṇa*=*pratītyasamutpāda*=*śūnya*.

The words *ādhyātmika* and *bāhya* are two opposite terms and can respectively be translated by 'subjective' and 'objective', or in some cases by 'inward' and 'outward' respectively, *ātman* meaning 'body' and, according to those who believe in the existence of a separate soul, 'soul' as well. Here *bāhyataḥ* is an adverb, and so *ādhyātmika*, too, may be taken as such. Or both of them are to be construed as adjectives.

For the thought and wording of the kārikā see the following couplet quoted as a speech of Bhagavat in MV, p. 348 (Poussin JRAS, 1910, p. 137) :

śūnyam ādhyātmikaṃ paśya paśya śūnyaṃ bahirgataṃ ।
na vidyate so 'pi kaścid yo bhāvayati śūnyatām ॥

BOOK III

1

upāsanāśrito dharmo jāte brahmaṇi vartate I

prāg utpatter[1] ajaṃ sarvaṃ tenāsau kṛpaṇaḥ smṛtaḥ II

'The *dharma* 'duty' relating to *upāsanā* 'worship' arises when Brahman is born, but before birth all is unborn; therefore, that (*dharma*) is regarded as miserable.'

Ś takes *dharma* to signify a worshipper (*upāsaka*, *sādhaka*). A simply follows him explaining: dehasya dhāraṇād dharmo jīvaḥ.

Upāsanā depends upon the duality of an *upāsaka* 'worshipper' and an *upāsya* 'one to be worshipped.' This duality also in its turn is possible only when that one Brahman is *jāta* 'born', *i.e.*, manifests himself in the form of this universe. His *jāti* or *prajāti* 'birth' or 'growing forth' or *bahubhāva* 'becoming many' is often found in the Upaniṣads : TU, II. 6: so 'kāmayata bahu syāṃ prajāyeya; ChU, VI. 2.1-3: tad aikṣata bahu syāṃ prajāyeya, 3.23: seyaṃ devataikṣata hantāham imās tisro devatā anena jīvenātmanānupraviśya nāmarūpe vyākaravāṇi. See BS with Ś, I. 1. 2, 5.

Upāsanā literally means 'sitting near,' *i.e.*, 'sitting near one who is to be worshipped.' In fact, *upāsanā*, as Ś explains it, is a continuous course of thought (*i.e.*, meditation), not disturbed by any other dissimilar thought upon an object supported by the scripture. So says Ś in his Introduction to ChU, I. 1. 1: upāsanaṃ tu yathāśāstrasamarthitaṃ kiñcid ālambanam upādāya tasmin samānacittavṛttisantānakaraṇaṃ tadvilakṣaṇapratyayānantaritam. See his Com. PU, 5, and BS, I. 1.11.

[1] This phrase, *prāg utpatteḥ*, is used not less than eight times by Ś in his comm. on the ChU, VI. 2. 1.

2

ato vakṣyāmy akārpaṇyam ajāti samatāṃ gatam ।
yathā na jāyate kiñcij jāyamānaṃ samantataḥ ॥

'I shall, therefore, so speak of that state of non-miserableness in which there is no origination (*jāti*), and which (on that account) is the same throughout, as to show that the things which are (apparently) being born on all sides are none of them born at all.'

The highest truth (*paramārtha*), according to our author and the Mādhyamikas as well, is that there is nothing that comes into being (*jāyate*, III. 48). This *ajāti* or *anutpāda* (so frequently used in Buddhist texts) 'non-origination' is the main subject which the author takes up and discusses throughout the remaining portion of his book. See II. 32; III. 20, 38, 48; IV. 5,71. The word *ajāti* occurs nine times in the work: III. 2, 38; IV. 4, 5, 19, 21, 29, 42, 43.

The sameness (*samatāṃ gata*, *samatā*, *sāmya*) of things is owing to their common quality of non-origination (*ajāti*). The following is from the *Āryasatyadvayāvatāra* quoted in MV, p. 374: paramārthataḥ sarvadharmānutpādasamatayā paramārthataḥ sarvadharmātyantājātisamatayā paramārthataḥ samāḥ sarvadharmāḥ. tat kasmād dhetoḥ. paramārthato nirvāṇā-(nānā)karaṇā hi devaputra sarvadharmā atyantanirutpādatām upādāya. tad yathāpi nāma devaputra yac ca mṛdbhājanasyābhyantaram ākāśaṃ yac ca ratnabhājanasyābhyantaram ākāśaṃ ākāśadhātur evaiṣaḥ. tat paramārthato na kiñcin nānākaraṇam. evam eva devaputra yaḥ [saṃ]kleśa[ḥ sa] paramārthato 'tyantānutpādatā. yad api vyavadānaṃ tad api paramārthato 'tyantānutpādatā. saṃsāro 'pi paramārthato 'tyantānutpādatā. yāvan nirvāṇam api paramārthato 'tyantānutpādatā. nātra paramārthato nānākaraṇaṃ. tat kasmād dhetoḥ. paramārthato 'tyantānutpādatvāt sarvadharmāṇām. See SP, IV. 83 (p. 143):

sarvadharmān samāñ śūnyān nirnānākaraṇātmakān ।
na caitān prekṣate nāpi kiñcid dharmaṃ vipaśyati ॥
sarvadharmāḥ samāḥ sarve samāḥ samasamāḥ sadā ।
evaṃ jñātvā vijānāti nirvāṇam amṛtaṃ śivaṃ ॥

For *b* of the kārikā see III. 38*a*; IV. 93*c-d*, 95*a*, 100*b*.

In the first kārikā of this chapter mention of origination (*jāti*) of Brahman is made. Non-origination (*ajāti*) is, however, said in the second, and the author promises here to explain it. Now from the following kārikā he proceeds to do so showing the real sense of origination and non-origination:

3

ātmā hy ākāśavaj jīvair ghaṭākāśair ivoditaḥ ।
ghaṭādivac ca saṅghātair jātāv etan nidarśanam ॥

'Ātman has sprung up in the forms of Jīvas 'individual selves,' just like the springing up of the *ākāśa*[1] 'space' in the form of *ghaṭākāśas* 'spaces occupied by jars,' the conglomerations (of different limbs, organs of sense, etc.) being like jars and others. This is the illustration of origination.'

It is with *ghaṭas* that *ghaṭākāśas* are formed from the *mahākāśa*. In the same way, it is with the conglomerations that Ātman is born in the form of Jīvas.

On the origination of Ātman see BU, II. 1. 20; MuU, II. 1.1; MnU, 1.4; BS, II. 3.17 with Ś's Com.

It is evident from the kārikā that the origination in both of the cases is not real, but imaginary.

See TJ, VIII. 10, and cf. :

ghaṭasaṃvṛtam ākāśaṃ nīyamāne ghaṭe yathā ।
ghaṭo nīyeta nākāśaṃ tathā jīvo nabhopamaḥ ॥

TIU, V. 3.

1 This is generally called *mahākāśa* in Vedantic and other works

This is further explained in the following kārikā :

4

ghaṭādiṣu pralīneṣu ghaṭākāśādayo yathā ।
ākāśe sampralīyante tadvaj jīvā ihātmani ॥

'As the jars, etc., being destroyed the spaces of jars, etc., are completely merged into space, so are (completely merged) the Jīvas into Ātman.'

This kārikā is quoted by Śāntirakṣita in his commentary on MAK, 93, and it runs as follows in its Tibetan version:

bum.pa.la. sogs. shig.[1] pa.ni ।
[bum. paḥi. nam. mkhaḥ.la.sogs. pa ।]
ji.ltar. nam.mkhaḥ.ḥdu.ḥgyur. ba ।
de.bshin. srog.kyaṅ. ṅes.pa.yin ॥

The second line of the verse is left out in Tib., and is reconstructed from Sanskrit by Wallesser: *Der älter Vedānta*, p. 20.

1 Read *bshig* for *shig*.

The following kārikā meets the objection that the Ātman that springs up as different Jīvas being one, if one jīva feels happiness or suffers pain, all the Jīvas should have the same state of mind. But in fact it is not so :

5

yathaikasmin ghaṭākāśe rajodhūmādibhir yute ।
na sarve saṃprayujyante tadvaj jīvāḥ sukhādibhiḥ ॥

'As one *ghaṭākāśa* 'space occupied by a jar' being connected with dust, smoke, etc., not all (*ghaṭākāśas*) are connected with them, so are the jivas with reference to happiness, etc.

The kārikā is quoted by Bhavya in his MHK, VIII. 13, the Tibetan version being as follows:

ji.ltar.bum.paḥi.nam.mkhaḥ.gcig ।
rdul.daṅ.du.bas.bsgribs.pa.na ।
thams.cad.de.bshin.ma.yin.ltar ।
bde.sogs.de.bshin.bdag.la.min ॥

Literally reconstructed it would read in Sanskrit:

yathaikasmin ghaṭākāśe rajodhūmaiḥ [sam]āvṛte ।
na bhavanti tathā sarve na sukhādi tathātmani ॥

The present kārikā is quoted with the reading *na ca sarve prayujyante* for *c* and is attributed to the ViP by Vijñānabhikṣu in his comm. on the SāS, I. 152; but it is not to be found there. See Ś's comm. on the VSN, p. 16.

6

rūpakāryasamākhyāś ca bhidyante tatra tatra vai ।
ākāśasya na bhedo 'sti tadvaj jīveṣu nirṇayaḥ ॥

'Indeed forms, functions and names differ here and there, but there is no difference of the space; similar is the conclusion with regard to jīvas.'

There are different things, earthen pots, cloths, etc., their forms, functions, and names all differing from one another, yet the *ākāśa* intercepted by them is in itself not different in fact. In the same way though jīvas corresponding to *ghaṭākāśas*, etc., are different, Ātman correspnnding to *ākāśa* or *mahākāśa*, etc., is not different.

Cf. TJ, VIII. 12:

ji.ltar.bum.sogs.tha.dad.kyaṅ ।
sa.la.tha.dad.ḥgah.yaṅ.med ।
de.bshin.lus.ni.tha.dad.kyaṅ ।
bdag.la.tha.dad.hgaḥ.yaṅ.med ॥

It may thus be translated into Sanskrit:

bhinneṣv api ghaṭādyeṣu mṛdi bhedo na kaścana ।
tathā deheṣu bhinneśu na kaścid bheda ātmani ॥

7

nākāśasya ghaṭākāśo vikārāvayavau yathā ।
naivātmanaḥ sadā jīvo vikārāvayavau tathā ॥

'As the *ghaṭākāśa* is neither a transformation, nor a part of the *ākāśa*, so is always a Jīva neither a transformation, nor a limb of Ātman.'

8

yathā bhavati bālānaṃ gaganaṃ malinaṃ malaiḥ।
tathā bhavaty abuddhānām ātmāpi malino malaiḥ ॥

'As the sky appears to be soiled with dirt[1] to the ignorant, so appears Ātman, too, with impurities, to those who are not enlightened.'

For *a* and *b* see Ś on BS, I. 1. 1 : ākāśe bālās talamalinatādy adhyasyanti.

This kārikā is quoted by Śāntirakṣita, *loc. cit.* The Tib. version is as follows :

ji. ltar.byis.pa.rnams.la. ni ।
nam.mkhaḥ.dri.mas. dri.can. ḥgyur ।
de.bshin. mi. mkhas.rnams.la.yaṅ ।
bdag.ni. dri.mas.dri.can. ḥgyur ॥

1 Such as dust, smoke, etc., See III. 5: *rajodhūmādibhiḥ.*

9

marane sambhave caiva gatyāgamanayor api ।
sthitaḥ[1] sarvaśarīreṣu ākāśenāvilakṣaṇaḥ ॥

In death and in birth, in moving forward and backward, (Ātman) in all bodies exists just like the space.'

In the origination and destruction of the *ghaṭākāśa* the *mahākāśa* is not affected. So is the case with Ātman in regard to death, birth, etc., which are connected only with the bodies. See ChU. VI. II. 3 : jīvāpetaṃ vāva kiledaṃ mriyate na jīvo mriyate.

1 This is found in only one MS., the reading which is generally known is *sthitau* 'in standing.'

10

saṅghātāḥ svapnavat sarve ātmamāyāvisarjitāḥ ।
ādhikye sarvasāmye vā nopapattir hi vidyate ॥

'All conglomerations (of limbs, etc.) are like dream being projected by the illusion of Ātman. As regards their superiority or the equality of all of them there is no ground.'

The *saṅghātas*, *i.e.*, the bodies, having which the Ātman is born in the form of Jīvas, are like the *ghaṭas* of *ghāṭākāśas*. These *saṅghātas* have, however, no real existence, nor is there, therefore, any ground for thinking of their superiority or equality among them.

In discussing what Jīva is the author says further:

11

rasādayo hi ye kośā vyākhyātās taittirīyake ।
teṣām ātmā paro jīvaḥ sa-yathā[1] samprakāśitaḥ ॥

'The seaths such as consisting of the essence (of food)

are described in the *Taittirīyaka*, i.e., *Taittirīya Upaniṣad* (II. 1-6), the supreme soul of them is Jīva, as it is made there clear.'

'There are five *kośas* 'seaths,' *viz.*, *annarasamaya* or simply *annamaya*, *prāṇa*°, *mano*°, *vijñāna*°, and *ānanda*°, *i.e.*, consisting of the essence of food, breath, mind, understanding, and bliss respectively. These are explained in the TU, II, 2 ff. According to the five divisions of *kośas* Ātman is also divided into five and are called after them, the last of them *i.e.*, *ānandamaya*, or in accordance with a different authority (see BS, I. 1. 12-19), the one on which rests the last of them is real Ātman. This is referred to in the present kārikā by *para ātman*. And the author says that this is Jīva.

[1] With some MSS. I read *sa-yathā* for *khaṃ yathā* accepted by Ś and found in other MSS. In favour of the second reading compare *d* of the next kārikā, which is in fact identical. The word *sayathā*, Pali *seyyathā*, in the sense of *tad yathā*, is often used in Brāhmaṇas and Upaniṣads. See PU, IV. 7, VI 5 ; MuU, III. 2. 8; ŚB, I. 2. 5. 24; 7. 3. 2; BU, II. 1. 20. Cf. in this connexion *sa-yadi* (=*tad yadi*), PU, V. 1, and Pali *sa-ce* for *sa-cet* (see p. 72, l.2) in the same sense (Skt. *tac cet*).

12

dvayor dvayor madhujñāne paraṃ brahma prakāśitam I
pṛthivyām udare caiva yathākāśaḥ prakāśitaḥ II

'In the *madhuvidyā* (*i.e.*, the *Madhubrāhmaṇa* section of the BU, II. 5) in each of the pairs, (such as) the earth and the inside (of the body), the supreme Brahman is made manifest, as is made manifest the sky (III. 3 ff.).'

BU, II. 5, is called *Madhubrāhmaṇa* owing to the fact of its dealing with a particular *Brahmavidyā* which is named *madhuvidyā* or *madhujñāna* (as in our text) on account of the frequent use of the word *madhu* which is very important in this connexion. Here there are some pairs of things, such as the earth and all beings (*pṛthivī* and *sarvāṇi bhūtāni*), and in these pairs it is shown that the person outside the body in the earth, etc., and the person inside the body are identical with Ātman, Brahman. Let the following passage be quoted here (BU, II. 5. 1):

iyaṃ pṛthivī sarveṣāṃ madhv asyai pṛthivyai sarvāṇi bhūtāni madhu. yaś cāyam asyāṃ pṛthivyāṃ tejomayo 'mṛtamayaḥ puruṣo yaś cāyam adhyātmaṃ śārīras tejomayo 'mṛtamayaḥ puruṣo 'yam eva sa yo 'yam ātmedam amṛtam idaṃ brahmedaṃ sarvam.

'This earth is the honey (*madhu*, the effect) of all beings, and all beings are the honey of this earth. Likewise this bright immortal person in this earth, and the bright immortal person incorporated in the body (both are *madhu*). He indeed is the same as the self, that immortal, that Brahman, that All.[1]

[1] Tr. Max Müller, SBE.

13

jīvātmanor ananyatvam abhedena praśasyate |
nānātvaṃ nindyate yac ca tad evaṃ hi samañjasam ||

'That the identity without any distinction of Jīva and Ātman is praised, and that their distinction is censured, this becomes reasonable only on this hypothesis.'

As regards the identity of Jīva and Ātman see ChU, VI. 8.7 (tat tvam asi); BU, I. 4. 10 (ahaṃ brahmāsmi), II. 5. 19 (ayam ātmā brahma); MuU, III. 2. 9 (sa yo ha vai tat paramaṃ brahma veda brahmaiva bhavati). As for the difference see BU, I. 4. 2 (dvitīyād vai bhayam bhavati), IV. 4. 19, KU, IV. 10, 11 (mṛtyoḥ sa mṛtyum āpnoti ya iha nāneva paśyati); TU II. 7 (yadā hy evaiṣa etasminn u daram antaraṃ kurute atha tasya bhayaṃ bhavati).

14

jīvātmanoḥ pṛthaktvaṃ yat prāg utpatteḥ prakīrttitam I
bhaviṣyadvṛttyā gauṇaṃ tan mukhyatvaṃ na hi yujyate II

'The difference of Jīva and Ātman before creation, which is declared (in texts[1]), is attributive with reference to the future state; its primary sense is certainly not reasonable.'

It is only after creation that there is a distinction between Ātman and Jīva, but before it there is no distinction whatsoever. When there is no production of *ghaṭa* 'jar,' and consequently no *ghaṭākāśa*, there is no distinction between *mahākāśa* and *ghaṭākāśa*. Yet, one sometimes speaks of that distinction at that time, simply anticipating what is going to happen in the near future, that is, thinking of the imminent production of the *ghaṭa*.

In his explanation of the kārikā Ś gives an apt example. He says that it is like the use of the following sentence which is very common: *odanaṃ pacati*. The word *odana* means 'cooked or boiled rice.' Therefore literally the sentence means 'one cooks cooked rice.' But the rice which was already cooked or boiled does not require to be cooked again. Yet, the people say, 'He cooks *cooked* rice.' Clearly here this use is attributive and has reference to the *future* state of the unboiled rice. The people assume the future state as present. So is here the statement of difference of Ātman and Jīva.

Ś says that in passages of the Upaniṣads about evolution and dissolution it is the unity of Ātman and Jīva, which is sought to be established. This unity will be demonstrated in the text. First there is shown difference and then unity which is the conclusion. It is, therefore, in view of this future

[1] Such as RV. X. 121.1:

sa dādhāra pṛthivīṃ dyām utemāṃ |
kasmai devāya haviṣā vidhema||

sense or state that the difference is stated. Thus it is only in its secondary, and not in its primary sense.

The author wanted (III. 2) to show that there is no origination (*jāti*), nor is there anything that comes into being (*jāyate*). Having done so to some extent he now meets, in the next kārikā, the objection that may be raised against this view, showing thereby also that there is, in fact, no distinction between Ātman and Jīva :

15

mṛllohavisphuliṅgādyaiḥ sṛṣṭir yā coditānyathā ।
upāyaḥ so 'vatārāya nāsti bhedaḥ kathañcana ॥

'The creation which is urged in different manners with the illustrations of earth, metal, sparks, etc., is only a means for an introduction (to the truth). There is in no way any distinction (between Ātman and Jīva).'

For details see IV. 42.

For the creation referred to see ChU, VI. 1. 4-5; BU, II. 1.20, VI. 2. 14 ; MuU, II. 1-1; MU, VI. 26.

As to how that creation and consequently the distinction between Ātman and Jīva, though unreal, are a means for introducing one to truth is explained in the next kārikā :

16

āśramās trividhā hīnamadhyamotkṛṣṭadṛṣṭayaḥ ।
upāsanopadiṣṭeyaṃ tadartham anukampayā ॥

'There are three spiritual stages, *viz.*, of lower vision, of middle vision, and of higher vision ; and this *upāsanā* 'worship' is laid down for them out of kindness.'

In fact there is no distinction between Ātman and Jīva, yet some distinction is attributed there, only to help people in realizing the truth by prescribing different *upāsanās* according to their respective powers of vision. See III. 1.

The word *āśrama* in the text is explained by Ś as *āśramin* 'one with *āśrama* or religious state of life,' *i.e.*, *adhikṛta* 'an entitled one.' In all probability the original word was *āśraya* 'a recipient, a person or thing in which any quality or article is inherent or retained or received,' *i.e.*, an *adhikārin* or *adhikṛta* 'an entitled one.' See the use of the word in the following line from MSA, XVI. 69 :

nikṛṣṭamadhyottamavīryam anyad
yānatraye yuktajanāśrayeṇa ।
atra āśrayabhedena vīryabhedo nirdiṣṭaḥ.

The author now mentions the opinions of the dualists, such as the Vaiśeṣikas, the Sāṅkhyas, etc., and shows that the decision arrived at by him, *i.e.*, non-distinction (*abheda*), does not conflict with the views held by them :

17

svasiddhāntavyavasthāsu dvaitino niścitā dṛḍham ।
parasparaṃ virudhyante tair ayaṃ na virudhyate ॥

'The dualists are firmly fixed in their own distinctive conclusions and contend with one another, but this (our view) does not conflict with them.'

18

advaitaṃ paramārtho hi dvaitaṃ tadbheda ucyate ।
teṣām ubhayathā dvaitaṃ tenāyaṃ na virudhyate ॥

'The supreme reality is non-duality, and duality is said

to be of it a particular state or effect of it,[1] while according to them (*i.e.*, dualists) there is duality in both ways.[2] Therefore it does not conflict.'

So far as mere duality is concerned, it is not that we do not admit it at all, as you do; we do accept it. Hence there is no conflict. Between cause and effect there is, in fact, no difference (*kāryakāraṇayor abhedaḥ*), the effect being merely a particular state of its cause. So there is no independent existence of the effect apart from that of its cause. In the same way duality is a particular state or effect of non-duality, being an illusion (II. 10). The only difference between us is that according to you duality is in both ways, in reality and also in appearance, while we say that though there is duality, no doubt, it is not in reality, it exists only in appearance.

See next kārikā.

[1] Cf. *bheda* with *bhidyate* in the following kārikā.

[2] Ś: paramārthataś cāparamārthataś ca 'in reality and not in reality,'

19

māyayā bhidyate hy etan nānyathājaṃ kathañcana |
tattvato bhidyamāne hi martyatām amṛtaṃ vrajet ||

'It (*advaita*) becomes different only through illusion, as the unborn (*aja*) can in no other way become different, for if it becomes in reality different the immortal would become mortal.'

See IV. 6.

20

ajātasyaiva bhāvasya jātim icchanti vādinaḥ |
ajāto hy amṛto bhāvo martyatāṃ katham eṣyati ||

'The disputants seek to establish the birth of an unborn

thing. Now a thing which is unborn is immortal, and that being the case, how can it become mortal ?

See IV. 6.

21

na bhavaty amṛtaṃ martyaṃ na martyam amṛtaṃ tathā ।
prakṛter anyathābhāvo na kathañcid bhaviṣyati ।

'The immortal does not become mortal, nor likewise the mortal immortal. In no way can nature change.'

See IV. 7, 29.

22

svabhāvenāmṛto yasya bhāvo gacchati martyatām ।
kṛtakenāmṛtas tasya kathaṃ sthāsyati niścalaḥ ॥

'How can he, according to whom a thing which is naturally immortal becomes mortal, maintain that an immortal thing, when it becomes artificial, will remain changeless ?

See IV. 8.

23

bhūtato 'bhūtato vāpi sṛjyamāne samā śrutiḥ ।
niścitaṃ yuktiyuktaṃ ca yat tad bhavati netarat ॥

'As regards creation there are equal sacred texts (stating

creation to be) from the existent[1] or from the non-existent.[2] But that which is ascertained and reasonable is (acceptable), and not the other.'

See IV. 3.

It says that in reality there is no *jāti* 'origination' either from the existent or the non-existent, though there are *śrutis* supporting both the views equally. Therefore the author says that what is reasonable is to be accepted, as certain And what is reasonable is pointed out in the next kārikā.

According to Śaṅkara *bhūtataḥ* is *paramārthataḥ*, and *abhūtataḥ māyayā*. But in IV. 3 he explains the same words saying *bhūtasya vidyamānasya°*, *abhūtasya avidyamānasya*.

1 sad eva somyedam agra āsīt°. ChU, VI. 2.1.

2 asad vā idam agra āsīt. tato vai sad ajāyata. TU, II. 7. 1.

24

neha nāneti cāmnāyād indro māyābhir ity api ।
ajāyamāno bahudhā māyayā jāyate tu saḥ ॥

'From the sacred text[1] "there is no plurality here"[2] and also from "Indra through *māyās*, etc.,"[3] (it is to be known

1 In the original *āmnāya* means *śruti*.

2 neha nānāsti kiñcana. BU, IV. 4. 19; KU, IV. 11.

3 rūpaṃrūpaṃ pratirūpo babhūva
tad asya rūpaṃ praticakṣaṇāya ।
indro māyābhiḥ pururūpa īyate
yuktā hy asya harayaḥ śatā daśa ॥
RV, VI. 47. 18; BU, II. 5. 19.

that) it is through illusion that he[4] is variously born, though (in fact) he does not take birth.'[5]

[4] It refers to Puruṣa, Prajāpati.

[5] The sentence ajāyamāno bahudhā jāyate in the text is taken from the VS. XXXI. 19 (=TA, III. 13.1) which runs as follows:

prajāpatiś carati garbhe antar
ajāyamāno bahudhā vijāyate |
tasya yoniṃ paripaśyanti dhīrās
tasmin ha tasthur bhuvanāni viśvā ||

The preceding stanza (18) is:

vedāham etaṃ puruṣaṃ mahāntam
ādityavarṇaṃ tamasaḥ parastāt |
tam eva viditvātimṛtyum eti
nānyaḥ panthā vidyate 'yanāya ||

25

sambhūter apavādāc ca sambhavaḥ pratiṣidhyate |
ko nv enaṃ janayed iti kāraṇaṃ pratiṣidhyate ||

'By the denial of *sambhūti* 'birth' (in the *śruti*)[1] birth is negatived; and (by the *śruti*) "who indeed would produce him"[2] the cause of birth is denied.'

Here for the first time we have the oldest interpretation of the words *sambhūti* or *sambhava* and *asambhūti* or *asambhava* in IU, 12, 13, 14, which are so differently explained

[1] tato bhūya iva te tamo ya u sambhūtyāṃ ratāḥ. IU, 12. This is the second half of the verse the first half being: andhaṃ tamaḥ praviśanti ye 'sambhūtim upāsate.

[2] jāta eva na jāyate ko nv enaṃ janayet punaḥ. BU, III. 9. 28.

by Ś and others.[3] Evidently G a u ḍ a p ā d a takes here *sambhūti* (*sambhava*) in the sense of *utpatti* or *jāti*, 'birth,' 'production,' 'origination.' This origination is negatived (*ajāti*) here, and that is one of the main points of the work of G a u ḍ a p ā d a. For his use of the word *sambhava* see III. 9, 48; IV. 16, 38.

[3] The following may be read with interest. Here the meanings of the words *asambhūtiḥ*, etc., are given according to Ś and others.

The figures refer to the stanzas of IU, while those in brackets to the stanzas of the VS.

Ś a ṅ k a r a

12	asambhūtiḥ	prakṛtiḥ, kāraṇam avidyā avyākṛtākhyā.
	sambhūtiḥ	kāryabrahma, hiraṇyagarbhaḥ.
13	sambhavaḥ	sambhūtiḥ, kāryabrahma.
	asambhavaḥ	asambhūtiḥ, avyākṛtam.
14	vināśaḥ	vināśavat kāryam.
	sambhūtiḥ (once taken as asambhūtiḥ)	avyākṛtam, avyākṛtopāsanā.

U v a ṭ a

12 (9)	asambhūtiḥ	mṛtasya sataḥ sambhavo nāsti. mṛta ātmano 'bhāvaḥ.
	sambhūtiḥ	ātmāstitvam.
13 (10)	sambhavaḥ	sambhavaparijñānam (= sambhūti°)
	asambhavaḥ	0
14 (11)	sambhūtiḥ	jagataḥ sambhavaikahetuḥ paraṃ brahma.
	vināśaḥ	vināśi śarīram.

M a h ī d h a r a

12 (9)	asambhūtiḥ	asambhavam° mṛtasya punaḥ sambhavo nāsti.
	sambhūtiḥ	ātmā.
13 (10)	sambhavaḥ	kāryabrahma.
	asambhavaḥ	avyākṛtam.
14 (11)	sambhūtiḥ	paraṃ brahma.
	vināśaḥ	vināśadharmakaṃ śarīram.

For the explanation given by the followers of R ā m ā n u j a and M a d h v ā c ā r y a see their respective works: commentary by R a ṅ g a r ā m ā n u j a, Anandashrama Sanskrit Series; by M a d h v ā c ā r y a, in the *Sacred Books of the Hindus*.

26

sa eṣa neti netīti vyākhyātaṃ nihnute yataḥ |
sarvam agrāhyabhāvena hetunājaṃ prakāśate ||

'(The *śruti*) "This is No, No" denies what is explained. Therefore by the reason of incomprehensibleness it is evident that all is unborn.'

The *śruti* "This is No, No" refers to sa eṣa neti nety ātmāgṛhyo na hi gṛhyate (BU, III. 9. 26; IV. 2. 4, 4. 22, 5. 15) —'That (Ātman) is (to be described by) No, No. He is incomprehensible, for he cannot be comprehended.' But it appears, as thinks also the commentator himself, it alludes to the following *śruti*, too: athāta ādeśo neti neti (BU, II. 3. 6) 'Now follows the teaching by No, No.' For it is that *śruti* which denies both the forms of Brahman, *viz.*, that which has form (*mūrta*) and that which has not form (*amūrta*). These two forms have already been described or explained in the text (BU, II. 3. 1).[1] Things are either with or without a form, so when both of them are denied they cannot be comprehended. Thus it becomes evident that there is nothing that may have origination, in other words, all is 'unborn' (*aja* 'without generation)'.

[1] dve vāva brahmaṇo rūpe mūrtaṃ caivāmūrtaṃ ca°.

Now *jāti* or origination may be either of the existent (*sat*) or of the non-existent (*asat*). But both the cases are impossible. The author shows it in the next kārikās :

27

sato hi māyayā janma jujyate na tu tattvataḥ |
tattvato jāyate yasya jātaṃ tasya hi jāyate ||

'The birth of that which exists can be reasonable only

through illusion, but not in reality. He who holds that one is born in reality has to accept (the position) that what is born had, indeed, been born.'

See IV. 58. See also IV. 13 with its explanation. Cf. CŚ, XI. 10 (260) with the note :

> sambhavaḥ kriyate yasya prāk so' stīti na yujyate |
> sato yadi bhavej janma jātasyāpi bhaved bhavaḥ ||

28

> asato māyayā janma tattvato naiva yujyate |
> vandhyāputro na tattvena māyayā vāpi jāyate ||

'The birth of that which does not exist is not reasonable at all through illusion or in reality. The son of a barren woman is not born either through illusion or in reality.'

The author now proceeds to show that the birth of the existent is possible only through *māyā* as said before (III. 27) :

29

> yathā svapne dvayābhāsaṃ spandate māyayā manaḥ |
> tathā jāgrad dvayābhāsaṃ spandate māyayā manaḥ ||

'As owing to *māyā* the mind in dream moves with appearance (or image) of the two (*viz.*, the percipient and the perceptible, or in other words, the subject and the object), so owing to *māyā* the mind in the waking state[1] moves with the appearance of the two.'

See IV. 61.

[1] See IV. 40.

30

advayaṃ ca dvayābhāsaṃ manaḥ svapne na saṃśayaḥ ।
advayaṃ ca dvayābhāsaṃ tathā jāgran na saṃśayaḥ ।

'There is no doubt that in dream the mind which is without a second is with the appearance of the two; so there is no doubt that in the waking state the mind which is without a second is with the appearance of the two.'

See IV. 62.

31

manodṛśyam idaṃ dvaitaṃ yat kiñcit sacarācaram ।
manaso hy amanībhāve dvaitaṃ naivopalabhyate ॥

'This duality in whatever form, comprising the movable and the unmovable is perceived by the mind, but when the mind becomes non-mind (*i.e.*, when it loses its own function of thinking, *manana*) duality is not experienced.

See IV. 47, 48, 72. It means that the appearance of duality is nothing but the vibration of the mind (*citta-* or *vijñāna-spandita*), and when this vibration is stopped there is no duality at all.

When the state of non-mind is reached is said in the following kārikā:

32

ātmasatyānubodhena na saṅkalpayate yadā ।
amanastāṃ tadā yāti grāhyābhāve tadagrahāt ॥

'When by the knowledge of the truth of *ātman* it the mind) ceases from imagining it goes to the state of non-mind being non-cognizant in the absence of the things to be cognized.'

See IV. 72, 79, 99.

Mark here that *d* (*grāhyābhāve tadagrahāt*) is identical with that of Tk, 28. See Vis, p. 584 ; LA, p. 169 ; and the note on III. of our text.

The next kārikā says that the mind which becomes non-mind 38 as described above, is, in fact, identical with Brahman :

33

akalpakam ajaṃ jñānaṃ jñeyābhinnaṃ pracakṣate I
brahma jñeyam ajaṃ nityam ajenājaṃ vibudhyate II

'The *jñāna* that does not imagine (*i.e.*, indeterminate) and is (consequently) unborn is, they say, not different from the knowable. The knowable is Brahman, the unborn and eternal one. So the unborn (Brahman) becomes manifest through the unborn (*jñāna*).'

Here *jñāna* which the commentator explains as *jñaptimātra* is in reality *vijñāna* or *citta* 'mind' as spoken of above. See Vk, p. 3 : cittaṃ mano vijñānaṃ vijñaptiś ceti paryāyāḥ; MV, XVII. 1 (p. 308) : cittaṃ mano 'tha vijñānam iti tasyaiva (=cittasyaiva) paryāyāḥ ; AK, II. 34 : cittaṃ mano 'tha vijñānam ekārtham; DN, I. 121; SN, II. 94. See III. 38, IV. 96.

For *ajaṃ vibudhyate cf.* I. 16 : *advaitaṃ budhyate tadā* ; III. 26 : *ajaṃ prakāśate*. For the whole thought see III. 35, 46. *ajenājaṃ vibudhyate*=ajena jñānena (=*cittena*) ajaṃ jñeyaṃ (Brahman) vibudhyate prakāśate. The unborn knowable Brahman is manifest through the unborn knowledge (*i.e.*, the mind when it ceases from its function), there being no difference between them. See III, 46, 47.

akalpaka=*nirvikalpa* (III. 34)=*asaṅga* (IV. 72). See LA, p. 157: *asaṅgalakṣaṇaṃ jñānam*.

For *jñeyābhinna* 'not different from the knowable see IV. 1.

The author now goes to speak about the state of the mind described above :

34

nigṛhītasya manaso nirvikalpasya dhīmataḥ ।
pracāraḥ sa tu vijñeyaḥ suṣupte 'nyo na tatsamaḥ ॥

'That state (*pracāra*) of the mind of a wise man which is suppressed and (thus) indeterminate is to be known; (the state of the mind) in deep sleep is different from that, it is not like that.'

It is said here that the state of the suppressed and indeterminate mind is different from that in *suṣupti*. Why it is so is stated in the following kārikā (III. 35).

The word *pracāra* which is the same as *vihāra* or *bhūmi*, as the yogins and the Buddhists would express, means in such cases *avasthā* 'state.' Our author uses (IV. 80) for it also *viṣaya*.

By *nirvikalpa manas* 'indeterminate mind' we are to understand that it recognises no such distinction as that of subject and object, etc.

In Buddhist works *dhīmat* is a synonym for Bodhisattva (MSA, XIX. 73).

The reason for what is said above is now offered as follows :

35

līyate hi suṣupte tan nigṛhītaṃ na līyate ।
tad eva nirbhayaṃ brahma jñānālokaṃ samantataḥ ॥

'For in deep sleep it (*manas*) falls into a state of oblivion,[1] but it does not do so when suppressed. Indeed, that is

[1] Or, into a sleeping state, *laya*, see III. 41, 42.

Brahman, free from fear and radiant as *jñāna*[2] on all sides.'

It is clear here that the mind when suppressed, *i.e.*, ceases from all of its activities, becomes Brahman. See III. 46.

Cf. the following quoted by Jayaratha in his commentary on śloka 30 of TA (Vol, III, p. 23) presenting the views of the Vijñānavādins :

prabhāsvaram idaṃ cittaṃ prakṛtyāgantavo malāḥ ।
teṣām apāye sarvārthaṃ taj jyotir avinaśvaram ॥

[2] On *jñānāloka* Śaṅkara writes: jñaptir jñānam ātmasvabhāvacaitanyaṃ tad eva jñānam ālokaḥ prakāśo yasya tad brahma jñānālokam. For *āloka* see *vibhāta* (III. 36, IV. 81), and *jyotis* (III. 37).

Brahman referred to above is now further described in the following kārikā :

36

ajam anidram asvapnam[1] anāmakam arūpakam ।
sakṛdvibhātaṃ[2] sarvajñaṃ[3] nopacāraḥ kathañcana ॥

'It is unborn, and has no sleep, nor dream ; nor has it name and form ; it is illumined once for all, and is all-knowing. And in no way is there access-concentration (*upacāra*).'

The state, *i.e.*, the state of becoming Brahman as stated above, is, in fact, the state of *samādhi* 'intense abstract meditation,' as we shall see presently in the following two kārikās.

[1] See I. 16ᵃ ; IV. 81ᵃ.

[2] See III. 37ᵃ ; IV. 81ᶜ with the note ; ChU, VIII. 4. 1-2 : sakṛd vibhāto hy eṣa brahmalokaḥ.

[3] III. 47.

Now, there are two kinds or stages of *samādhi*, *upacāra samādhi* and *arpaṇā*° (Pali *appanā*). In the first the mind is concentrated on its object, but not uninturruptedly, for now it is so and the next moment it is not so. simply moving near (*upacarati*) the object just like a bee sitting gently inside a lotus in search of its honey. In the second, the mind is firmly and uninturruptedly fixed on the object. Because this state of *samādhi* 'gives (*arpayati*)' the one-pointed mind to the object it is called *arpaṇā*, as B u d d h a g h o ṣ a explains in his AS, p. 142 : ekaggaṃ cittaṃ ārammaṇe appetīti appanā. Cf. p. 143 : upagantvā vicaraṇavasena upavicāro. Cf. also *vicāra* as explained in the *Vibhāvanī Ṭīkā* on the AAS, I. 17 :

santavutti vicāro cittassa nātipphandabhūto ākāse uppatitassa sakuṇassa pakkhapasāraṇaṃ viya, padumassa uparibhāge paribbhamaṇaṃ viya ca padumābhimukhapatitassa bhamarassa.

The difference between *upacāra* and *appanā* is thus shown in VM, p. 126 :

duvidho hi samādhi upacārasamādhi ca appanāsamādhi ca. dvīh'ākārehi cittaṃ samādhīyati upacārabhūmiyaṃ (=upacārāvatthāyaṃ—Ṭīkā) vā parilābhabhūmiyam (=jhānassa adhigamāvatthāyaṃ—Ṭīkā).° dvinnaṃ pana samādhīnaṃ idaṃ nānākaraṇaṃ°. yathā nāma daharo kumārako ukkhipitvā ṭhapiyamāno punappunaṃ bhūmiyaṃ patati evam eva upacāre uppanne cittaṃ kālena nimittaṃ ārammaṇaṃ karoti kālena bhavaṅgaṃ otarati.° yathā nāma balavā puriso āsanā vuṭṭhāya divasam'pi tiṭṭheyya evam eva appanāsamādhimhi uppanne cittaṃ saki bhavaṅgavāraṃ chinditvā kevalam'pi rattiṃ kevalam'pi divasaṃ tiṭṭhati.

The *d* of the kārikā may be explained in another way. Brahman is described here by such words as *aja*, *anidra*, etc., but being beyond speech and mind it cannot be done so. This is said : nopacāraḥ kathañcana '(But) in no way there is any figurative (or metaphorical) expression (*upacāra*). See BSB, p. 44 :

sa punaḥ pāramārthikaḥ svabhāvaḥ sarvadharmāṇām nirvikalpasyaiva jñānasya gocaro veditavyaḥ. sacet punar yathaivābhilāpo yeṣu dharmeṣu yasmin vastuni pravartate tadātmakās te dharmās tad vastu syāt. evam sati bahuvidhā bahavaḥ svabhāvā ekasyaikasya vastuno bhaveyuḥ. tat kasya hetoḥ. tathāhy ekasmin dharma ekasmin vastuni bahuvidhā bahavo bahubhir abhilāpaiḥ prajñaptaya upacārāḥ kriyante.°

The following two kārikās say that this state of becoming Brahman is *samādhi* :

37

sarvābhilāpavigataḥ sarvacintāsamutthitaḥ ।

supraśāntaḥ sakṛjjyotiḥ samādhir acalo 'bhayaḥ ॥

'It is intense abstract concentration (*samādhi*) which is beyond all expression,[1] and above all thoughts,[2] very calm and full of light burning once for all,[3] unwavering and without fear.'

In Buddhism there is a particular *samādhi* called *acala* (MVt,[1] 580).

[1] *anabhilāpya*=*akathya*, AK, ii. 243. See IV. 24.

[2] III. 38[b] : cintā yatra na vidyate.

[3] III. 36[c], IV 81 with note.

38

graho na tatra notsargaś cintā yatra na vidyate ।

ātmasaṃsthaṃ tadā jñānam ajāti samatāṃ gatam ॥

'Where there is no thought[1] there is neither apprehension or abandonment (of any object). At that time the mind

[1] III. 37[b].

(*jñāna*=*citta*)[2] rests in itself, is unborn and attains to the state of sameness.'[3]

In this state the mind does not apprehend or abandon any of its objects and as such rests in itself (*ātmasaṃstha*).

The word *ātman* in *ātmasaṃstha* here means 'itself' (*svarūpa*) and not 'soul' (*paramātman* or Brahman) as distinct from the mind (*jñāna*). Cf. BG, VI. 25: ātmasaṃsthaṃ manah kṛtvā na kiñcid api cintayet 'having made the mind resting in itself one should not think of anything.' Nīlakaṇṭha writes here in his ṭikā on the word *ātmasaṃstha*: ātmani svarūpe saṃsthā sthitir yasya.

This *ātmasaṃstha jñāna* is, in fact, in other words, *vijñaptimātra* or *vijñānamātra* of the Buddhist Vijñānavādins. The word *vijñānamātra* means 'simply *vijñāna*,' and the state of being so is *vijñānamātratā*. When the *vijñāna* does not apprehend any object whatsoever and as such rests only in itself this state is called *vijñānamātratā*. Says Vasubandhu (Tk. 28, ViS, p. 584):

> yadā tv ālambanaṃ jñānaṃ naivopalabhate tadā ı
> sthitaṃ vijñānamātratve grāhyābhāve tadagrahāt ıı

LA, p. 169:

yadā tv ālambyam arthaṃ nopalabhate jñānaṃ tadā vijñaptimātravyavasthānaṃ bhavati. vijñapter grāhyābhāvād grāhakasyābhāvaḥ. tadagrahaṇān na pravartate jñānaṃ.

This is referred to in the following stanza of the KU, II. 3.10:

> yadā pañcāvatiṣṭhante jñānāni manasā saha ı
> buddhiś ca na viceṣṭate tām āhuḥ paramāṃ gatim ıı

2 See III. 32, IV. 96, with notes.

3 See III. 2; IV. 77, 80, 93, 95, 100. It is to be noted in these kārikās that *ajāti* or *anutpatti* and *sama*, or *sāmya* or *samatā* are always used together. Cf. this with the quotation of MV in the note on III. 2

In the Upaniṣads it is well-known that Brahman is *vijñāna* (BU, III. 9. 28; TU, II. 5 1, III. 5. 1., etc., *vijñānamaya*=vijñāna) or jñāna (TU, II. 11). This *vijñāna* or *jñāna* is *ātmasaṃstha jñāna* or vijñānamātra.

For *ātmasaṃstha jñāna* see ChU. VII. 24. 1-2 :

"Where one sees nothing else, hears nothing else, understands nothing else, that is the Infinite (*bhūman*).

'Sir, in what does the Infinite rest?'

'In its own greatness,—or not even greatness.'"[4]

It is to be noted that in the beginning of the present chapter (III. 2) the author proposed 'ato vakṣyāmy akārpaṇyam ajāti samatāṃ gatam,' here in the present kārikā he concludes the subject.

[4] See my paper *Evolution of Vijñānavāda* in IHQ, X, 1934, pp. 1 ff.

That *samādhi* which is *nirvikalpa* is further described in the next kārikā :

39

asparśayogo nāmaiṣa durdarśaḥ sarvayogibhiḥ |
yogino bibhyati hy asmād abhaye bhayadarśinaḥ ||

'This is what is called 'contactless concentration' (*asparśa-yoga*), very difficult to be realized by all yogins; the yogins shrink from it seeing fear where (in fact) there is no fear.'

For *asparśayoga* see IV. 2.

The Commentator explains the second half of the kārikā saying that though there is no fear in this yoga yogins (of lower order) are afraid of it thinking it to be one's own destruction (*ātmanāśarūpa*). These people have no discrimination (*avivekin*), and so they have fear though there is no fear.

Vidyāraṇya quotes this kārikā in his PD, II. 29, introducing it (II. 28) thus :

gauḍācāryā nirvikalpe samādhāv anyayoginām ।
sākārabrahmaniṣṭhānām atyantaṃ bhayam ūcire ॥

Now the author proceeds to say that for the yoga referred to the control of mind is absolutely necessary, on which depend the absence of fear, and such other things :

40

manaso nigrahāyattam abhayaṃ sarvayoginām ।
duhkhakṣayaḥ prabodhaś cāpy akṣayā śāntir eva ca ॥

'The absence of fear, the destruction of misery, the awaking, as well as the eternal peace of all yogins depend on the control of mind.'

The next kārikā shows how the mind can gradually be controlled without difficulty :

41

utseka udadher yadvat kuśāgreṇaikabindunā ।
manaso nigrahas tadvad bhaved aparikhedataḥ ॥

'The control of mind without great pains is like the draining out of a sea by drops with the point of a *kuśa* grass.'

The first half of the kārikā refers, according to Madhusūdana Sarasvatī (BG, VI. 23) and Rāmakṛṣṇa, a commentator of PD (XI. 109), where this kārikā is quoted, to an old story, (cf. *Ṭiṭṭibhopākhyāna*, HU, pp. 78-79) which runs, as given by Madhusūdana Sarasvatī, as follows :

Once upon a time the sea carried off with its waves the eggs of a bird which were laid on the beach. The bird got angry and determined to dry it up. He began to take out the water drop by drop with the tip of his beak and he could not be dissuaded from it by the birds related to him. In the mean time the divine sage Nārada came there. He, too, asked him to turn back, but in vain. The bird said that anyhow he would dry up the sea either in this or in the future life. Fortunately Nārada became very kind to him, and sent there Garuḍa, the lord of birds, for his help. Owing to the wind produced by the flapping of the wings of Garuḍa the sea began to dry up and thus being frightened gave back the eggs to the bird.

The substance of the kārikā is that it is with determination and perseverance that mind is gradually controlled.

The author now suggests the means for controlling the mind :

42

upāyena nigṛhṇīyād vikṣiptaṃ kāmabhogayoḥ |

suprasannaṃ laye caiva yathā kāmo layas tathā ||

'By the means[1] one should control it (mind) when it is distracted in desire and enjoyment, and also when it remains at ease in the sleeping state, for the sleeping state is as (bad) as desire is.'

Kārikās III. 42-46 are quoted and explained by Madhusūdana Sarasvatī in the commentary on the BG,

[1] See III. 43-45.

VI. 26, and III. 44-45 *a-b* by Sadānanda in his VeS, §§32-33. According to the former *kāma* 'desire' is the state of thinking of, or longing for enjoyment (*cintyamānāvasthā*), while *bhoga* 'enjoyment' is the state of enjoying the desired things (*bhujyamānāvasthā*). *Laya* 'sleeping state' is, in his opinion, deep sleep (*suṣupti*), as supported by Gauḍapāda himself (III. 35), but Sadānanda explains it by 'sleep' (*nidrā*). *Laya* causes mental inactivity, and corresponds to the state called *mūḍha* 'infatuated' in the yoga philosophy. See Vyāsa on YS, I. 1.

The means referred to above are as follows :

43

duḥkhaṃ sarvam anusmṛtya kāmabhogān nivartayet |
ajaṃ sarvam anusmṛtya jātaṃ naiva tu paśyati ||

'Repeatedly remembering that all is misery one should turn back (one's mind) from desires and enjoyments.[1] Indeed repeatedly remembering that all is unborn one does not see anything born.'

The second half of the kārikā implies that when everything is unborn and consequently has no existence in reality there is no object for one's desire and enjoyment.

[1] Or we may write for 'one should, etc.,' 'one should keep back (from the mind) desires and enjoyments.' Thus, as says Madhusūdana Sarasvatī (BG, VI. 26), *kāmabhogān* in the kārikā may be explained as accusative plural or ablative singular.

44

laye sambodhayec cittaṃ vikṣiptaṃ śamayet punaḥ |
sakaṣāyaṃ vijānīyāc chamaprāptaṃ na cālayet ||

'One should awaken the mind when it is in the state of

sleep; when distracted one should pacify it again. One should also investigate if it is with the evil passions (*sakaṣāya*). And (finally) when it reaches the state of equanimity one should not cause it to move.'

As regards the control of mind there are four impediments enumerated in our kārikās (III. 42-45) of which *vikṣepa* 'distraction' and *laya* 'sleep' have already been mentioned also in kārikā 42, the other two being *kaṣāya* and *sukha-*, or according to some (VeS, §33) *rasa-āsvāda*. The last term will be explained in the next kārikā (45). We are concerned here with *kaṣāya*. It means here *stabdhībhāva* 'becoming stiffened' of mind as Madhusūdana Sarasvatī and Sadānanda would explain (*loc. cit.*). The primary meaning of *kaṣāya* is 'decoction,' so to say, of evil passions (*rāga, dveṣa, moha*). Śaṅkara explaining *mṛditakaṣāya* in ChU, VII. 26. 2, writes: vārkṣādir iva kaṣāyo rāgadveṣādidoṣaḥ. It causes the stiffness of mind, owing to which it cannot be fixed on the object. Thus the *kaṣāya, i.e.*, the evil passions, being the cause of *stabdhībhāva*, is explained by those authors to mean *stabdhībhāva*. We may, however, take the word in its actual sense, *i.e.*, the evil passions.

Cf. MSA, XIV. 9[c-d]—10[a-b] :

līnaṃ cittasya gṛhṇīyād uddhataṃ śamayet punaḥ ॥
śamaprāptam upekṣeta tasmin nālambane punaḥ ।

See also XIV. 11.

For *śamaprāpta* in *d* which gives better sense (cf. *śamayet* in *d* of the *kārikā*) and is supported by VeS, with its Ṭīkā *Vidvanmanorañjanī*, §33 and MSA quoted above, the reading found in editions and a very large number of MSS is *samaprāpta*. It means one that has reached the state of equilibrium. Madhusūdana Sarasvatī takes the word *sama* in the sense of Brahman.

45

nāsvādayet sukhaṃ tatra niḥsaṅgaḥ prajñayā bhavet |
niścalaṃ niścarac cittam ekīkuryāt prayatnataḥ ||

'There (in practising yoga) he should not enjoy happiness.[1] By wisdom[2] he must be (then) free from all attachment. If the mind which is (thus) fixed goes out, by endeavour he should so do as to make it remain only in itself.'

On *ekīkuryāt* 'should make one' the Commentator says: citsvarūpasattāmātram evāpādayet. Cf *ekībhavati*, BU, IV. 4.2; *ekibhūta*, MāU, 5.

[1] There is a feeling of happiness from that condition of mind in practising yoga, and it should be avoided as it is an impediment.
[2] Or, discrimination.

The next kārikā says that when the mind is thus completely controlled or suppressed (*niruddha*) and as such is free from all movements and does not perceive anything it becomes Brahman:

46

yadā na līyate cittaṃ na ca vikṣipyate punaḥ |
aniṅganam anābhāsaṃ niṣpannaṃ brahma tat tadā ||

'When the mind is not in the state of sleep, nor is distracted again, and as such has no movement nor any senses-image, then it becomes Brahman.'

See III. 35.

The first half refers to two states *laya* corresponding to *mūḍha* and *vikṣepa* corresponding to *vikṣipta* in the Vyāsa's commentary on YS, I. 1. See III. 42. See also *anidra* and *asvapna* in III. 36. The Commentator explains *anābhāsa* saying that it does not appear in the form of any of its objects which are imaginary (na kenacit kalpitena viṣayabhāvenāvabhāsate). *Ābhāsa* is *praticchāyā* 'reflection'. See BAP, V. 36. Or it may be taken in the sense of 'appearance,' namely, the appearance of any object.

On *d* the Commentator says : yadaivaṃlakṣaṇaṃ cittaṃ tadā niṣpannaṃ brahma brahmasvarūpeṇa niṣpannaṃ cittaṃ bhavatīty arthaḥ. Cf. IV. 77 where he writes : cittasyeti yā mokṣākhyā-'nutpattiḥ and on IV. 80 cittasya niścalā calanavarjitā brahmasvarūpaiva tadā sthitir yaiṣā brahmasvarūpā sthitiś cittasyādvayavijñānaikarasaghanalakṣaṇā.

In this connexion the following may be quoted from the BA, IV. 15 : *cittasya brahmatādikam* which BAP explains : cittasya phalaṃ brahmabhūyādikam.

It is said here that the *aniṅgana* and *anābhāsa citta* becomes Brahman. With this compare the following :

MU. VI. 24 (p. 143) :

mānase ca vilīne tu yat sukhaṃ cātmasākṣikam ।
tad brahma cāmṛtaṃ śukraṃ sā gatir loka eva ca ॥

Mṛtyujidbhaṭṭāraka as quoted in ŚV, p. 99 :

nirābhāsaṃ padaṃ tat tu tat prāpya vinivartate

LA : IV. 16 :

cittamātraṃ nirābhāsaṃ vihāro baddhabhūmi ca ।
etad dhi bhāṣitaṃ buddhair bhāṣante bhāṣayanti ca ॥

X. 105 (p. 278).

cittamātram atikramya nirābhāse sthitaṃ phalam ।

X. 110 (p. 279).

cittamātram atikramya nirābhāsam atikramet ।
nirābhāsasthito yogī mahāyānaṃ na paśyate ॥

X. 257 (p. 299).

tadā yogī hy anābhāsaṃ prajñayā paśyate jagat ।
nimittaṃ vastu vijñaptir manovispanditaṃ ca yat ।
atikramya tu putrā me nirvikalpāś caranti te ॥

X. 94 (p. 277).

etad vibhāvayan yogī nirābhāse pratiṣṭhate ।

X. 235 (p. 296).

ālambālambayvigataṃ yadā paśyati saṃskṛtam ।
niścitaṃ cittamātraṃ hi cittamātraṃ vadāmy aham ॥
mātrāsvabhāvasaṃsthānaṃ pratyayair bhāvavarjitam ।
niṣṭhābhāvaḥ paraṃ brahma etāṃ mātrāṃ vadāmy aham ॥

III. 25,26.

See also LA, p. 126 : matpravacane punar mahāmate vikalpakasya manovijñānasya vyāvṛttir nirvāṇam. Ś a ṅ k a r a on BU, IV. 3.7 (p. 587) : vijñānasya nirvāṇaṃ puruṣārthaḥ.

See III. 35, IV. 29 (comm. : ajātaṃ yac cittaṃ brahmaiva jāyate), 48, 77, 80.

The *citta* that becomes Brahman is described in the next kārikā :

47

svasthaṃ śāntaṃ sanirvāṇam akathyaṃ sukham uttamam ।
ajam ajena jñeyena sarvajñaṃ paricakṣate ॥

'They say it rests in itself [1] and is calm having *nirvāṇa* ; it is unspeakable and the highest bliss, unborn, and (identical) with the knowable, which is also unborn, and is all-knowing.'

See III. 33, IV. 1.

The word *nirvāṇa* has different meanings, such as 'delight', 'extinction', 'cessation', 'disappearance', 'calmed', 'quieted'.

[1] Here *svastha* is *ātmasaṃstha*, III. 38.

We may take it here in the sense of 'extinction'. The extinction of mind means the disappearance of its function of thinking (*manana* or *cintana*), in other words, the *amanībhāva* of *manas* referred to above (III. 31), and in MU, VI. 34, or *vilaya* of *manas* in MBU p. 12. This is also called *unmanībhāva* (BBU, 4), *vṛttikṣaya* of *citta* (MU, VI. 34, p. 178), and the *nirodha* of *vijñāna* (=*nirvāṇa*) in DN, I. 223 (viññānassa nirodhena).

Cf. YV, III. 67.8 :

spandād bhavati citsargo niḥspandād brahma śāśvatam ।

See also MU, VI. 24 (p. 143) :

mānase ca vilīne tu yat sukhaṃ cātmasākṣikam ।
tad brahma cāmṛtaṃ śukraṃ sā gatir loka eva ca ॥

For *sarvajña* see III. 36.

The author proposed in the beginning of this chapter (III. 2) to speak of non-origination (*ajāti*). Now having done so mainly with regard to Jīva and partly also to other things he concludes thus :

48

na kaścij jāyate jīvaḥ sambhavo 'sya na vidyate ।
etat tad uttamaṃ satyaṃ yatra kiñcin na jāyate ॥[1]

iti gauḍapādīya āgamaśāstre 'dvaitākhyaṃ tṛtīyaṃ prakaraṇaṃ samāptam.

'No individual soul is born, nor is there any possibility of it. This is that highest reality where nothing is born.

Here ends, in the *Āgamaśāstra* of Gauḍapāda, Book Three called 'Non-duality'.

---

[1] See IV. 71.

BOOK IV

The proposition was enunciated (III. 2), discussed (III), and finally established in the last line of the last kärikā of the last Book, and it will further be affirmed later on (IV.71) that there is nothing that originates, and this is the highest truth. In order to further elucidate this view the author now begins the present Book of his *Āgamaśāstra*.

Its first two kārikās form what is known in later Sanskrit works as *maṅgalācaraṇa* 'salutation, benediction, or prayer for success.' The first kārikā is as follows :

1

jñānenākāśakalpena [1] dharmān yo gaganopamān [2] ।
jñeyābhinnena[3] sambuddhas taṃ vande dvipadāṃ varam ॥

'Who has perfectly understood the elements of existence (*dharma*) that are like the sky, through the knowledge (*jñāna*) which is not different from its object (*jñeya*) and is also like the sky, to him, to the greatest of men, I pay my homage.'

The author here pays his homage to *dvipadāṃ vara* 'the greatest of men.' Who is this *dvipadāṃ vara* ? The word *dvipad* (RV, X. 165.1: *śaṃ no astu dvipade śaṃ catuṣpade*) or *dvipada* literally 'biped' means in such cases 'man.' Words such as *dvipadāṃ vara* or *dvipadānām uttama* (or *agra*) or *dvipadottama* (Pali *dvipad'uttama*) in compound are all synonymous. They are used both as adjectives and nouns.

[1] IV.96 with Ś.
[2] IV.91.
[3] III.33; IV.88.

As an adjective *dvipadāṃ vara* is found in MB, Vanaparvan, 54.45 (: *naiṣadho dvipadāṃ varaḥ*) and also in Ādiparvan, 220.36 (with reference to D h ṛ t a r ā ṣ ṭ r a : *abhiṣṭauṣi ca yat kṣattuḥ samīpe dvipadāṃ vara).*[4] In Buddhist literature, both Sanskrit and Pali, *dvipadottama* or *dvipad'uttama* in Pali or any one of the synonyms mentioned above is used to mean the B u d d h a (AP, 1; MSt, p. 60, l. 25; SNt, 83, 995, 998; MVt², § 267; SS, p. 8, 57, here in the last place not less than thirteen times). *Narottama* (Pāli *nar'uttama*) and *puruṣottama* (Pali *puris'uttama*) are also used specially for the B u d d h a [SNt, 544 (see DP, 78) 1021; MVt,² § 1,40; MVu, Vol. II, pp. 194, 199, 232, 266].

On the other hand Ś takes *dvipadām vara* to mean *puruṣottama* in the sense of N ā r ā y a ṇ a.[5]

Now, which of them, the B u d d h a or N ā r ā y a ṇ a, is really meant by the author himself can be decided if we consider the subject matter of the kārikā.

There are mainly two points to be discussed here. First, *jñāna* 'knowledge' is said to be *ākāśakalpa* 'like the sky,' and again it is not different from the *jñeya* 'the knowable,' *i.e.*, the object of knowledge. And second, the *dharmas*, 'elements of existence' or 'things or objects,' are also *gaganopama* 'like the sky.'

What are we to understand by the statement that *jñāna* is like the sky? One characteristic of *jñāna*, according to both our author and the Vijñānavādins, is that it is *asaṅga* (IV. 72, 96) 'having no attachment, contact, or relation,'

Such instances are there many. See I. 50.27.

[5] It may be noted that so far as I know no word compounded with *dvipad* or *dvipada* is found in Brahmanic literature to mean N ā r ā y a ṇ a. But thanks to a friend who points out that *dvipadāṃ variṣṭha* which, in fact, is the same as *dvipadāṃ vara* is applied at least once to N ā r ā y a ṇ a (MB, *Śāntiparvan*, 343. 1). But it is to be noted that though here it refers to N ā r ā y a ṇ a, no doubt, this N ā r ā y a ṇ a is not God (*īśvara*), but a *sage* (*ṛṣi*) and hence a *man*, though an incarnation of the former.

i.e., it does not relate itself to its object, it does not cognize any object (*agraha*, III. 32), there being no object whatsoever. See IV. 26, 27, 72, 96, 99, and the following from LA, p. 157: *asaṅgalakṣaṇaṃ jñānaṃ.*[6] Now jñāna being *asaṅga* is compared here with the sky which is also *asaṅga*. See BAP, p. 359: evam° niṣprapancatvād ākāśavad asaṅgam anāspadam[7] aśeṣaṃ viśam utpaśyāmaḥ.[8]

As regards the absence of difference between *jñāna* and *jñeya* it is a well-known fact that this view is maintained by Vijñānavādins. According to them there is no reality in external things. Knowable is, in fact, inside being the transformation of *vijñāna*, and *only appears* to be outside. Diṅnāga says in his *Ālambanaparīkṣā*, 6 (quoted by Śaṅkara in his commentary on BS, II. 2. 28 and by Kamalaśīla in his *Pañjikā* on TS, p. 582 : yad antarjñeyarūpaṃ tad bahirvad ababhāsate[9]. And Dharmakīrtti formulates it in his PV,[10] fol. 274a, l. 7 in the following

[6] Sometimes there is made a difference between *jñāna* and *vijñāna* as the following passages of the same work (LA) will show saying that *jñāna* is *asaṅga*; p. 157: tatrotpannapradhvaṃsi vijñānam anutpannapradhvaṃsi jñānam; asaṅgalakṣaṇam jñānaṃ viṣayavaicitryasaṅgalakṣaṇaṃ ca vijñānam; asaṅgasvabhāvalakṣaṇaṃ jñānam; aprāptilakṣaṇaṃ jñānam; ASP, p. 399: asaṅgalakṣaṇā subhūte prajñāpāramitā. See also MV, p. 533; nimittālambanaṃ vijñānaṃ, jñānena hi śūnyatālambanena bhavitavyaṃ, taccānutpādarūpam eveti. See IV. 96, notes.

[7] As the editor, Poussin, has pointed out, this reading is supported by the Tibetan version where we have: lhag.pa.med.pa(*asaṅga*). gnas.med (*anāspada*).

[8] See also BA with BAP, IX. 155.

[9] The other half runs as follows: so 'rtho vijñānarūpatvāt tatpratyayatayāpi ca. See also TS, p. 582 :

nīlapītādi yaj jñāne bahirvad ababhāsate |
tatra satyam ato nāsti vijñeyaṃ tattvato bahiḥ ||

[10] The book in its original Sanskrit is not yet found, but there is a Tibetan translation called *Tsad.ma.rnam.par.ṅes.pa* (*Pramāṇaviniścaya*) in Tanjur, Mdo, G, fols. 250*b*. 6--329*b*.1. Cordier, III, p. 437.

line which is widely quoted[11] in Brāhmanical works in discussing *vijñānavāda*, a common subject for philosophical discussions found in them[12]:

sahopalambhaniyamād abhedo nīlataddhiyoḥ ।[13]

'On account of the regularity of the simultaneous perception of the blue and its knowledge there is no difference between them.'

This theory is based on such utterances of the Buddha as the following :

cittamāttaṃ bho jinaputrā yad uta traidhātakam.[14]

'O the sons of Jina, the three planes are only mind.'

The following may also be quoted in this connexion: Vk, 1: vijñaptimātram evaitad; LA, X. 77 : vijñaptimātraṃ tribhavam,

[11] Poussin has shown it in his *Le Buddisime d'après les sources brahmaniques* in *Le Muséon*, N. S. 1901, pp. 181-82; Ānandagiri and Vācaspati (*Bhamatī*) on BS, II. 2. 28; *Tātparyaṭīkā*, p 467; *Ślokavārttika* (ṭīkā), 290; *Nyāyakandalī*, p. 126; *Advaitabrahmasiddhi*, (Bib. Ind.) p 98; *Vivaraṇaprameyasaṃgraha*, p. 75. See also IHQ, Vol. IX, No. 4, 1933, pp. 979-80.

[12] For instance, MD with Śabara, I. 1.5; MŚV, *Nirālambavāda* and *Śūnyavāda*, pp. 217-345; BS with Ś, II. 2. 28.

[13] The Tibetan version runs:

lhan.cig.dmigs.pa.ṅes.paḥi.phyir |
sṅo.daṅ.de.blo.gshan.ma.yin |

See IHQ, IX, pp. 279 ff. and PVk², II. 388-391 :

sakṛtsaṁvedyamānasya niyamena dhiyā saha |
viṣayasya tato 'nyatvaṃ kenākāreṇa sidhyati ||
bhedaś ca bhrāntavijñānair dṛśyetendāv ivādvaye |
saṃvittiniyamo nāsti bhinnayor nīlapītayoḥ ||
nārtho 'saṃvedanaḥ kaścid anarthaṃ vāpi vedanam |
dṛṣṭaṃ saṃvedyamānaṃ tat tayor nāsti vivekitā ||
tasmād arthasya durvāraṃ jñānakālāvabhāsinaḥ |
jñānād avyatirekitvam* ||

[14] DS, p. 49; SS, p. 19; TA¹, p. 18. For further details see Lévi : *Matériaux pour l'étude du système Vijñaptimātra*, Paris, 1932, p. 43.

etc. And from this it follows that in reality there is no external object as the foolish imagine,[15] it being nothing but the transformation of the mind (*vijñānapariṇāma*) owing to *vāsanā*.[16]

In this kārikā *jñeya* 'object of knowledge' is to be taken in its ordinary sense and not in its particular significations, as in III.33, and IV.90.

We are now to discuss the second point, *i.e.*, the *dharmas* 'elements of existence' are *gaganopama*. From the absolute point of view (*paramārthataḥ*) the external things appear only in their imposed forms having no reality at all. They have not their intrinsic existence (*niḥsvabhāva*) and as such are void (*śūnya*) like the son of a barren woman. Hence they are *gaganopama*.[17] Śāntideva says in his BA, IX.155 :

sarvam ākāśasaṅkāśaṃ parigṛhṇantu madvidhāḥ ı

'Let those who are like me accept the doctrine that all is like the sky.'

Why is it like the sky? Prajñākaramati explains: because it is imposed and devoid of reality (*samāropitatattvaśūnyatvāt*). We read the following in ASP, p. 297 :

evam eva subhūte sarvadharmā ākāśagatikā ānāgatikā agatikā ākāśasamāḥ. yathākāśam anāgatam agatam akṛtam avikṛtam anabhisaṃskṛtam asthitam avyavasthitam anutpannam aniruddham evam eva subhūte sarvadharmā anāgatā agatā akṛtā avikṛtā

15 LA, p. 285:

bāhyo na vidyate hy artho yathā bālair vikalpyate |
vāsanair luḍitaṃ cittam arthābhāsaṃ pravartate ||

16 Tk, 1:

ātmadharmopacāro hi vividho yaḥ pravartate |
vijñānapariṇāmo'sau° ||

Sthiramati writes here in his bhāṣya: dharmāṇām ātmanaś ca vijñānapariṇāmād bahirabhāvāt.

17 BAP, p. 503 (with regard to *aṇu*) : ato 'bhiniṣkṛṣyamāṇo niḥsvabhāvatayā ākāśaṃ śūnyam eva: See pp. 504-505.

anabhisaṃskṛtā asthitā asaṃsthitā avyavasthitā anutpannā aniruddhā ākāśakalpatvād avikalpāḥ.

See BAP, p. 395, quoted above, and specially our text, IV. 93.

Or because the *dharmas* are beyond enumeration (*gaṇanāsamatikrānta*), they are *gaganopama*.[18]

Or, it may be that as *jñāna* is *asaṅga* and is thus like the sky, so are *asaṅga* the *dharmas*, and as such they are like the sky. See IV. 96. That the sky is *asaṅga* needs no explanation.

One of the grounds on which this theory is based is that the things are *niḥsvabhāva*, *i.e.*, without their *own* nature and condition or state of being (*svabhāva*). And that which has not its own state of being is nothing but the sky and void (*ākāśa*, *śūnya*).[19]

Or again, as in fact the things have naturally neither origination nor suppression, they are like the sky. See LA, X. 172:

aniruddhāḥ anutpannāḥ prakṛtyā gaganopamāḥ ı

Ś does not explain here as to how *jñāna* is *ākāśakalpa* and the *dharmas* are *gaganopama*. He would, however, explain the non-difference of *jñāna* and *jñeya* saying that *jñeya* refers to *ātman* (or strictly *ātmans*), and *jñāna* is not different from *ātman*.

18 ASP, pp. 278-279: sarvadharmā api subhūte 'cintyā atulyā aprameyā asaṃkhyeyā asamasamāḥ.' sarvadharmā api subhūte 'saṃkhyeyā gaṇanāsamatikrāntavāt. rūpam api subhūte 'samasamam evaṃ vedanā saṃjñā saṃskārā vijñānam api subhūte 'samasamam evaṃ sarvadharmā api subhūte samasamā ākāśasamatvāt subhūte sarvadharmāṇām.

BA, V. 12: durjanān gaganopamān on which BAP writes śatravo hi gaganasamatvād aparyantāḥ.

19 See BAP, p. 503: ato 'bhiniṣkṛṣyamāṇo niḥsvabhāvatayā ākāśaṃ śūnyam eva; pp. 504-505: tat ko 'tra kāyaḥ. tasya pratyavekṣamāṇasya bhavati—ākāśasamo 'yaṃ kāyaḥ.' sarvam etad ākāśam iti paśyati '

Now the word *dharma* used here in this kārikā and not ess than twenty-two times in this Book,[20] requires some explanation. It is very widely used in such cases as the present one throughout Buddhist literature in Sanskrit and also in Pali.[21] Figuratively it means a thing or object, a thing of which the senses or mind takes cognition and as such, it is synonym of such Sanskrit words as *artha* or *padārtha* or *viṣaya* or *prameya*. Literally it has among others the sense of nature, character, peculiar condition or essential quality, in Sanskrit *svabhāva* or *svalakṣaṇa*. It is derived from √*dhṛ* 'to hold, maintain, preserve, keep.' Because a thing in whatever form it may be maintains its own characteristics or essential quality (*svalakṣaṇa* or *svabhāva*), it is called *dharma*. So we read in AKB, p. 6: lakṣaṇadhāraṇād dharmaḥ (raṅ.gi.matshan. ñid.ḥdzin.paḥi,phyir.chos.te). See MV, pp. 304, 457. Buddhaghoṣa (AS, §94, p. 39) explains the term in the following words: (*i*) attano pana sabhāvaṃ dhārentīti dhammā, (*ii*) dhāriyanti vā paccayehi, (*iii*) dhāriyanti vā yathāsabhāvato'ti dhammā.[22] According to it *rasa*, *sparśa*, etc., are *dharmas*. Only these are there and not also *dharmins* 'those endowed with or having a *dharma*,' as the Buddhists hold unlike such non-Buddhist philosophers as Naiyāyikas and Vaiśeṣikas, according to whom earth, or jars, etc., are *dharmins*, while their qualities, *i.e.*, hardness (*kāṭhinya*), etc., are *dharmas*. In Buddhist philosophy it is only the quality of tangibility called 'hardness' (*kāṭhinya*, *sparśa*) that is regarded as existent, but

[20] IV. 1, 6, 8, 10, 21, 33, 41, 46, 53, 54, 58, 59, 81, 82, 91, 92, 93, 96, 98, 99. It is used also in II. 25 and III. 1, but evidently in a meaning different from that in Book IV.

[21] For instance, ASP, p. 39: sarvadharmā api devaputrā māyopamāḥ svapnopamāḥ; DP, 279 (Maggavagga, 7) sabbe dhammā anattā'ti.

[22] It is thus translated in Ex., p. 50: "Dharmas may be defined as those states which bear their own intrinsic natures, or which are borne by causes-in elation, or which are borne according to their own characteristics."

there is no entity excepting it that we call earth, or the element of earth. Ā r y a d e v a says in his CŚ, 309:

> kaṭhinā dṛśyate bhūmiḥ sā ca kāyena gṛhyate ।
> tena hi kevalaṃ sparśo bhūmir eṣe ti kathyate ॥ [23]

'It is seen that the earth is hard and that is perceived with one's body. Therefore it is said that the earth is only the quality of tangibility.'

Thus, as says S t c h e r b a t s k y in his *Central Conception of Buddhism*, p. 26, 'If we say "earth *has* odour, etc.," it is only an inadequate expression; we ought to say "earth is odour, etc.," since beside these sense-data there is absolutely nothing the name could be applied to."[24]

It is also to be borne in mind in this connexion that in the absolute truth there is nothing as *avayavin* 'one having portions' as in other systems. It is owing to this fact that expressions like the following are found in Buddhist works:

> nāstīha sattva ātmā vā dharmāstv ete sahetukāḥ | [25]

This theory of *dharma* seems to be exactly the same as that of the *tattva* of the Sāṅkhyas. The word *tattva* (*tat-tva*) literally

[23] This is a reconstructed verse from Tibetan which runs:

> sa . ni . brtan . shes . bya . bar . mthoṅ |
> de . yaṅ . lus . kyis . ḥdzin . par . ḥgyur |
> des . na . reg . pa . ḥbaḥ . shig . ḥdi |
> sa . ḥo . shes . ni . bya . bar . brjod ||

See V, 82; AK and AKV[1], I. 35 (p. 69): °pṛthivīdhātuḥ katamaḥ. khakkhaṭatvam iti vistaraḥ; MV, pp. 66-67: iha tu kāṭhinyādivyatirikta-pṛthivyādyasambhave sati na yukto viśeṣyaviśeṣaṇabhāvaḥ.° evaṃ pṛthivyādīnāṃ yady api kāṭhinyādivyatiriktaṃ vicāryamāṇaṃ lakṣyaṃ nāsti, lakṣyavyatirekeṇa ca lakṣaṇaṃ nirāśrayaṃ tathāpi saṃvṛtir eveti.° YB, 16[b]: khakkhaṭatvaṃ katamat, pṛthivī. This view is found also in the *Garbhopaniṣad*, 1: tatra yat kaṭhinaṃ sā pṛthivī.

[24] He quotes here the following from AKV,[2] IX p 717: pṛthvī gandhavatīty ukte rūpa-gandha-sparśebhyo nānyad darśayituṃ śakyate. Cf. *Soul Theory*, p. 742.

[25] Quoted in MV, p. 355 as a saying of the B h a g a v a t.

means 'thatness,' *i.e.*, 'the state of that (referring to a thing)' and hence it signifies 'nature (*svabhāva*)' or 'true nature.' Thus, in fact, *tattva* is a *guṇa*, yet each of the twenty-five categories in the system is considered as a *tattva* (*pañcaviṁśati tattva*), and not *tattvavat* 'having *tattva*.' When the three *guṇas*, *viz.*, *sattva*, *rajas*, and *tamas*, are in equal condition (*sāmyāvasthā*), they are collectively called *prakṛti*. It is itself a *tattva*, it *has* no *tattva*.[26] It consists in the three *guṇas*, it *has* no *guṇa*, though sometimes even in authoritative works it is loosely said that it *has* three *guṇas*. Thus it is a well-known fact that teachers belonging to other systems say that in Sāṃkhya there is no difference between a *guṇa* and a *guṇin* or *dravya*[27] (guṇadravyayos tādātmyam), or between a *dharma* and a *dharmin* (dharma-dharmiṇor abhedaḥ).[28]

Says Aśvaghoṣa (BCK, XII. 76):

> guṇino hi guṇānāṃ ca vyatireko na vidyate ।
> rūpoṣṇābhyāṃ virahito na hy agnir upalabhyate ॥

[26] See *Tattvayāthārthyadīpanī* included in the *Sāṃkhyasaṃgraha* (Chaukhamba Sanskrit Series), pp. 72-93: tattvānīti tāntrikī saṃjñā. tadarthaś cātmānātmavivekapratiyogyanuyoginas tattatpadārthāḥ. teṣāṃ bhāvaḥ tattatpadanimittāni puruṣatvaprakṛtitvādīni pañcaviṃśatijātayaḥ. dharmadharmyabhedād vyaktayo 'pi tattvānīty ucyate.

[27] Vasuvandhu gives (AK, IX. 290) the following definition of *dravya* rejecting that of the Vaiśeṣikas: vidyamānaṃ dravyam iti. Yaśomitra adds: yat svalakṣaṇato vidyamānaṃ tad dravyam. He does not accept the position that *smṛti*, *saṃskāra*, *icchā*, etc., are *guṇas* as held by Vaiśeṣikas (*Ibid*). See AK, III. 100[a-b]. But Vijñānabhikṣu who is undoubtedly much influenced by the Nyāya and Vaiśeṣika systems writes the following in his commentary on SS, I. 61: ayaṃ ca pañcaviṃśatiko gaṇo dravyarūpa eva, dharmadharmyabhedāt tu guṇakarmasāmānyādīnām atraivāntarbhāvaḥ. *Cf.* I.62: dharmadharmyabhedād dravyāṇām api tanmātratā smṛtā.

[28] See Vijñānabhikṣu on SS, II. 5 where the following is quoted:

> śaktiśaktimator bhedaṃ paśyanti paramārthataḥ |
> abhedaṃ cānupaśyanti yoginas tattvacintakāḥ ||

It may be noted in this connexion that Vasubandhu in his *Vijñānamātrasiddhi* applies the term *dharma* to the *tattvas* of the Sāṅkhyas (O. Rosenberg).[29]

It is not that in Brahmanical works the word *dharma* is not used in the above sense. For instance, see KU, I. 1. 21 : aṇur eṣa dharmaḥ.[30] Yāska (Nt, I. 20) writes *sākṣātkṛtadharmāṇaḥ*. Here the word *dharman* differs from *dharma* only in form and not also in sense, as the former, too, means *artha* or *padārtha* 'a thing.' Vācaspati explains in his *Tātparyaṭīkā* the word *sākṣātkṛtadharman* used by Vātsyāyana (NS, I. 1.7), saying sudṛḍhena pramāṇenāvadhāritā arthā yena sa sākṣātkṛtadharmā. Evidently he takes here *dharman* in the sense of *artha*. Vyāsa in his commentary on YS, II. 17, explains *dṛśya* by buddhisattvopārūḍhāḥ sarve dharmāḥ.

In our present Book here and in other places Ś takes *dharma* to mean *ātman*. But this seems to be forced. To imply *ātman* our author uses in every case *ātman* or *jīva*.[31] Why should he employ in this chapter *dharma* for it? Undoubtedly these two terms are well-known in their meanings. So there is no ground for giving preference to such a word as *dharma* in the sense of *ātman*. In all the twenty-two cases in the present Book *dharma* is easily construed in the sense of 'a thing,' literally 'an element of existence' as in Buddhist literature. But while in some of them Ś takes the word to mean *ātman*, in others he could not do so. In some cases he did not explain the word at all, and certainly the meaning *ātman* cannot be accepted

29 Stcherbatsky: *The Central Conception of Buddhism*, p. 27, n. 2.

30 The commentator, Ś, explains the word *dharma* here saying *ātmākhya dharma*. Undoubtedly *ātman* is a *dharma* as we have seen. But certainly it is not the actual meaning of the word though it may be implied with reference to the context. See also KU, II. 1. 14: *evaṃ dharmān pṛthak paśyan*.

31 See for *ātman* I. 12; II. 12, 17; III. 3, 4, 7, 8, 11, 13, 14; for *jīva* I. 16; III. 3, 4, 5, 6, 7, 11, 13, 14, 48; IV. 63, 68, 69, 70.

in them. For instance, in the text *sarve dharmā mṛṣā svapne* (IV. 33) the word *dharma* can in no way mean *ātman*. In two cases he explains it saying *hastyādīn bāhyadharmān* (IV. 41), and *bāhyadharmāḥ* (IV. 54). Once he writes *ātmāno 'nye ca dharmāḥ* (IV. 58). In one case (IV. 82), however, he gives the actual sense, *i.e.*, *vastu* 'thing.'[32]

It can further be shown from the words of the author himself that in meaning *dharma* and *bhāva* (=*vastu*=*padārtha*) are identical. See the following passages :

(*i*) ajātasyaiva bhāvasya (III. 20[a]) and ajātasyaiva dharmasya (IV. 6[a]).

(*ii*) ajāto hy amṛto bhāvaḥ (III. 20[c]) and ajāto hy amṛto dharmaḥ (IV. 6[c]).

(*iii*) svabhāvenāmṛto yasya bhāvaḥ (III. 22[c–d]) and svabhāvenāmṛto yasya dharmaḥ (IV. 7[c–d]).

It is to be noted that while *bhāva* is used only in the second and third Books[33] of the work, *dharma* in the above sense is used only in Book IV, and this is very significant indicating the Buddhist relationship of the subject dealt with in it.

There is one thing more. It is said in the kārikā that he to whom the author pays his homage perfectly understood the *dharmas*. Here if he is meant to be N ā r ā y a ṇ a one would naturally ask : What is the authority for it? Where is it found that he actually did so? This question demands a reply from those who hold that N ā r ā y a ṇ a is referred to here. Not only what we have seen above with regard to the first kārikā, but also the whole chapter, as can be shown, is in favour of the B u d d h a.

32 The text is: yasya kasya ca dharmasya, and Ś explains: yasya kasyacid vastunaḥ. This reading is in the MS *ca* of Anandashrama ed., the other readings add *dvaya-* before *vastunaḥ*.

33 Kārikās II. 1, 13, 16, 17, 19, 29, 33; and III. 20, 22.

2

In the second kārikā the author salutes the teacher of the *asparśayoga*:

> asparśayogo vai nāma sarvasattvasukho hitaḥ ।
> avivādo 'viruddhaś ca deśitas taṃ namāmy aham ॥

'I salute him (who has) taught the *asparśayoga* which conduces to happiness of all beings and is beneficial and free from dispute and opposition.'

I construe the kārikā taking *yena* 'by whom' as understood, thus differing a little from the commentator, Ś, who says that it is the *asparśayoga* that is saluted here.

In the kārikā *avivāda* refers to the fact that our theory is not contradicted by theories of other schools, and *aviruddha* implies that it involves no self-contradiction or is not against any other position held by us.

Now what is the *asparśayoga*, by whom and where has it been taught? The word does not occur in the Upaniṣads, though Ś says on III. 39, where also it is described, that it is well-known in the Upaniṣads (*prasiddham upaniṣatsu*). See also III. 37, 38. The following is found in KU, II. 3. 10:

> yadā pañcāvatiṣṭhante jñānāni manasā saha ।
> buddhiś ca na viceṣṭate tām āhuḥ paramāṃ gatim ॥

'When the five (instruments of) knowledge stand still together with the mind; and when the intellect does not move, that is called the highest state.'

Similar statements are met with in other Upaniṣads.[1] But though they in fact may point to what is called *asparśayoga*, as will presently be explained, it is not termed *asparśayoga*.

[1] For instance, BBU, 4-6; MU, VI. 34. See kārikā, III. 38.

The word *asparśayoga* literally means the yoga in which there is no contact, or the faculty of perception by touch. The author himself says (III. 37) it is a *samādhi* 'profound or abstract concentration,' it is very difficult to realize. It points to what is *asamprajñāta samādhi* (YS, I. 2, 18, 51 with the scholiast Vyāsa),[2] or *nirvikalpa samādhi* (PD, II. 28) of yogins. But nowhere in their systems, so far as my information goes, it is called *asparśayoga*.[3] Why is it that the word *asparśa* is used here?

I am inclined to think that it refers to the ninth or the last of the nine *dhyānas* or meditations called *anupūrvavihāra* (Pali *anupubbavihāra*) or the successive states of *dhyāna* which the Buddha taught and are found frequently in Buddhist texts.[4] They are as follows :

I. Four *rūpa dhyānas* or the meditations of which *rūpa* 'matter' is the object, *viz.*—

(*i*) *prathama dhyāna* or the first stage of meditation.

(*ii*) *dvitīya dhyāna* or the second stage of meditation.

(*iii*) *tṛtīya dhyāna* or the third stage of meditation.

(*iv*) *caturtha dhyāna* or the fourth stage of meditation.

II. The four *arūpa dhyānas* or the meditations of which the object is not matter, *viz.*—

(*i*) *ākāśānantyāyatana* (Pali *ākāsānañcāyatana*) or the place of infinity of space.

[2] Vyāsa explains (YS, I. 2) it: na tatra kiñcit saṃprajñāyata ity asaṃprajñātaḥ 'as nothing is known there it is called *asaṃprajñāta*.'

[3] *Cf. asparśasaṃvitprāpti* used in explaining *svarūpalābha* in the following line of the VV, p. 42: svarūpalābhaḥ samastakalpanottīrṇatvād akṛtaka-niravakāśa-niruttara-nistaraṅga-niravadhi-nirniketāsparśasaṃvitprāptir bhavati. This is kindly pointed out to me by Dr. S. N. Sen Gupta of the Lucknow University. The following occurs in the same work (p. 4) in the course of the explanation of *mahāśūnyatāpraveśa*: kulākulavikalpadośojjhito'vyapadeśya-mahānirāvaraṇa-niratyaya-vedyavedaka-niryukto varṇāvarṇanirvarṇottīrṇaḥ *sparśāsparśa*-prathāparivarjita upacārāt paramākāśādyabhidhānair abhidhīyate.

[4] AN, Vol. IV, pp. 410-448: nava yime bhikkhave anupubbavihārā°. nava yime bhikkhave anupubbavihārasamāpattio desissāmi, taṃ suṇātha.

(*ii*) *vijñānānantyāyatana* (Pali *viññāṇañcā°*) or the place of infinity of pure consciousness.

(*iii*) *ākiñcanāyatana* (Pali *ākiñcaññā°*) or the place of nothingness.

(*iv*) *naivasaṃjñā-nāsaṃjñāyatana* (Pali *nevasaññānāsaññā°*) or the place neither of consciousness nor of unconsciousness.

And the ninth is *saṃjñāveditanirodha* (Pali *saññāvedayita-nirodha*) or the cessation or complete suppression of consciousness and sensation.

As in the ninth or last stage of yoga or meditation not only sensation or consciousness, but also all the mental properties or mentals (*caitta* or *caitasika dharmas*), headed by *sparśa* (Pali *phassa*) 'contact,'[5] are restricted or suppressed with the *citta* or mind itself, it is called *asparśayoga*. It is to be noted that the word *sparśa* employed here implies also the other mentals of which it is the first. The cessation of *vedanā* is possible only when *sparśa* ceases, as is clearly shown in the SN, IV, p. 220 (XXXVI. 15.4): phassasamudayā vedanā-samudayo phassanirodhā vedanānirodho. It means that *sparśa* is the cause of *vedanā*, so when there is *sparśa* there is *vedanā*, and when there is no *sparśa* there is no *vedanā*.[6] The fact that in this state of *nirodha* (which is the same as *asamprajñāta* or *nirbīja* or *nirvikalpa samādhi*) the mind and its properties (*citta* and *caitta* or *caitasika*) completely cease to work is clearly described by Buddhaghoṣa in his VM, p. 552.[7]

It is said (III. 39) that *asparśayoga* is very difficult to realize. From this very fact the word *asparśayoga* may be explained

5 AAS, II. 2: phasso vedanā saññā catanā° cetasikā sabbacittasādhāraṇā nāma.

6 For its explanation see Sthiramati on Tk, p. 20, ll. 1, 2, 7, 9, 10; p 28, l. 18.

7 kā nirodhasamāpattīti. yā anupubbanirodhavasena cittacetasikānaṃ dhammānaṃ appavatti. See also SN, Vol. IV, p. 217 (=XXXVI. 11. 5): saññāvedayitanirodhaṃ samāpannassa saññā ca vedanā ca niruddhā honti.

quite in a different way. In Buddhist Sanskrit works there is frequent use of such words as *sparśavihāra* (MVt[1], 8349, 8351; Tk, p. 28, ll. 18), *sparśavihāratā* (MVt[1], 6288), and *asparśavihāra* (AAA, p. 326; Tk, p. 28, ll. 17, 19; p. 30, ll. 15, 20). Sthiramati explains the last word in his commentary on Tk, p. 28, l. 18, saying: sparśaḥ sukhaṃ tena sahito vihāraḥ sparśavihāraḥ, na sparśavihāro 'sparśavihāraḥ. He says that *sparśa* means *sukha* 'joy, content, ease, comfort'; *sparśavihāra* is a state with it; and *asparśavihāra* is its opposite. In Tibetan *sparśavihāra* is translated by bde.gnas.pa, literally the Sanskrit equivalent to which is *sukhasthiti* (or *sukhāvasthiti*) 'pleasant state.' In Pali *sparśavihāra* is *phāsuvihāra* in the same meaning.[8] In this light *asparśayoga* in sense is nothing but *asukhayoga* (*a-sukhayoga*) meaning thereby 'a yoga which is not one that can be attained with ease.' This explanation is fully supported by what we know of it in III. 39: It is very difficult to realize and yogins shrink from it seeing fear though in fact there is no fear.

We read in the present kārikā that this yoga conduces to happiness of all beings (*sarvasattvasukha*). This is found also in Buddhist works where it is said (SN, Vol. IV, p. 228=XXXIV. 19. 20)[9] that the highest bliss is felt in the *saññāvedayitanirodha* (or *sammāvedayita°* according to the Chinese version. *sammā*=*samyg*).

[8] It is, however, to be noted that, strictly speaking, Pali *phāsu* is not from Sanskrit *sparśa* the Pali form of which is *phassa*. In Northern Sanskrit Buddhist works Pali *phāsu* is wrongly translated into Sanskrit by *sparśa*. See the Pali Dictionary of Childers, p. 982. Sometimes in Buddhist Sanskrit *sukhasparśavihāra* is found for *phāsuvihāra*. It clearly indicates that the writers of the former did not think that mere *sparśavihāra* could imply the sense of *phāsuvihāra*.

[9] idhānanda bhikkhu sabbaso nevasaññānāsaññāyatanaṃ samatikkamma saññāvedayitanirodham upasampajja viharati. idaṃ kho ānanda etamhā sukhā aññaṃ sukhaṃ abhikkantataraṃ ca paṇītataraṃ ca. See also the next paragraph (21) for the reply to a question raised here. *Cf.* AN, Vol. IV, pp. 414-418

It may, however, be observed here that considering the use of the word *sparśa*, BG, II. 14, V. 27, and the explanations offered there by Ś and other commentators the interpretation as given in the present case as well as in III. 39 by Ś cannot be rejected.

It is to be noted here that attempt has been made above to interpret the word *asparśayoga* in different ways, but it seems that the best interpretation may be found in A s a ṅ g a 's *Yogācārabhūmi*. After what is written above a transcription[10] of that work has come to my hands and the following is quoted here from it :

[78*b*] kathaṃ nirodhaṃ samāpadyamānasya naivaṃ bhavati ahaṃ nirodhaṃ samāpadye vā vyuttiṣṭhe vā. samāpattikāle nirabhisaṃskāreṇa cittanirodhāt.°

kathaṃ nirodhād vyutthitas trīn sparśān spṛśati āniñjyam[11] ākiñcanyam ānimittaṃ. yad bhūyasā tasyāḥ samāpatter vyuttiṣṭhamānas trividhenālambanena vyuttiṣṭhate bhavālambanena viṣayālambanena nirodhālambanena ca. taiś ca vyuttiṣṭhamāno yathākramam eva trīn sparśān spṛśati. [79*a*] tatra bhavālambanena vyuttiṣṭhamānasya na bhavati cetasa iñjitatvam asmīty ayam asmīti bhaviṣyāmīti vistaraḥ. ata āniñyaṃ sparśaṃ spṛśatīty ucyate. viṣayālambanena vyuttiṣṭhamānasya na rāgakiñcanaṃ bhavati na dveṣakiñcanaṃ bhavati na mohakiñcanaṃ. tasmād ākiñcanyaṃ sparśaṃ spṛśatity ucyate. nirodhālambanena vyuttiṣṭhamānaḥ sarvanimittānām amanasikārād ānimittaṃ dhātum avalambate. tasmād ānimittaṃ sparśaṃ spṛśatīty ucyate.

(=XXXIV, 2-3) : kiṃ pan'et'ha *(i.e.,* in *nirvāṇa)* āvuso sāriputta sukhaṃ yad ettha n'atthi vedayitan'ti. etad eva khv ettha āvuso sukhaṃ yad ettha n'atthi vedayitaṃ.

10 This is made by R ā h u l a S ā ṅ k ṛ t y ā y a n a, and he has kindly given it to me. An edition of this work is undertaken by the present author for the Asutosh Sanskrit Series, Calcutta University.

11 For the variants of this word see AK, IV. 107 (where different authorities are quoted) ; MV, pp. 334-5 ; AKV², pp. 389 ff.

We know from it that in the stage of *nirodhasamāpatti* the *citta* or mind is completely suppressed, hence there is no experience whatsoever. But in the stage called *vyutthāna* 'rising up' one has three kinds of *sparśa* 'experience,' known as *āniñjya, ākiñcanya,* and *ānimitta.* The word *sparśa* in such cases means 'experience' or 'that which is experienced', √*spṛś* meaning here 'to experience.'[12]

Now, because in the yoga called *nirodhasamāpatti* there is no *sparśa* of anything, it is rightly named *asparśayoga.*

It is said (III. 39^{c-d}) of the *asparśayoga* that yogins or rather untrained ones shrink back from it, imagining fear where in reality there is no fear: *yogino bibhyati hy asmād abhaye bhayadarśinaḥ.* But what is the cause of their fear? Ś rightly says that the so-called yogins think that it will annihilate the very self.[13] Indeed, there is hardly any difference between a yogin in this state and a dead person, their respiration being completely stopped. So when the Blessed One entered that state, *i.e., saññāvedayitanirodha* before his *parinirvāṇa,* Ānanda took him to be dead. But the venerable Anuruddha said to him that that was not the case, the Blessed one only having entered the stage of the *dhyāna* called *saññāvedayitanirodha.* After a short time, however, He passed away.[14] It is therefore quite natural that an untrained yogin should be afraid of it, as of death.

Yet there is a real difference between death and *asparśayoga* or *saññāvedayitanirodha,* and Buddhaghoṣa has explained it in his VM, p. 558, quoting a passage from the *Suttapiṭaka.* It says that all the conditions in both of them are one and the same excepting this that in the latter the heat of the body is not

12 See KnU, IV-2: te hy enan nediṣṭhaṃ paspṛśuḥ. [te hy enat prathamo vidāñcakāra—this portion is grammatically defective and not in the *Jaiminīya Brāhmaṇa,* Chapter X which forms the KnU]; 3: sa hy enan nediṣṭhaṃ pasparśa; sa hy enat prathamo vidāñcakāra.

13 ātmanāśarūpam imaṃ yogaṃ manyamānā bhayaṃ kurvanti.

14 *Mahāparinibbānasutta,* VI. 8-9 (=DN, Vol. II, pp. 156-158).

lost, that life does not come to an end, and that the organs of sense are not destroyed, while in the former all these are annihilated.

We have seen in the present kārikā that this yoga is taught by the Buddha. It cannot be denied that up to the eighth of those successive states of *dhyāna* (*anupūrvavihāra*) already explained, *viz.*, 'neither-consciousness-nor-unconsciousness', there is nothing particularly Buddhist. For it is evident from Buddhist literature, both Pali and Sanskrit, that the Buddha's two teachers Ālāra Kālāma (Āḍāra Kālāpa) and Uddaka Rāmaputta (Rudraka Rāmaputra) knew the seventh and eighth of the *dhyānas*, respectively.[15] The Buddha was, however, not satisfied with what he had from his teachers, and he started thereupon to seek after a still higher state and succeeded in realizing it. It is this state which is called *saññāvedayitanirodha* or briefly *nirodha*.

There is one thing more which suggests that the *asparśayoga* was not originally taught in the Brahmanic system of yoga. It is said in the kārikā that this yoga is 'not disputed' (*avivāda*)[16] and 'not opposed' (*aviruddha*). It is implied, as said before, from these two words that in the acceptance of the *asparśayoga* by the Vedantists, among whom the author himself is included, there cannot be raised any dispute or opposition, for there is nothing to be opposed even from their own point of view.

Thus it is clear from what we have seen above that the real instructor of the *asparśayoga*, who is saluted here by the author, is no other than the Buddha.

Let us now follow what the author has to say in this Book (IV). The subject matter of it is *a-jāti* (=*an-utpatti*, *an-utpāda*) 'non-becoming' or 'non-origination,' or, in other words, the doctrine that there is nothing about which it can be said that it is produced.

15 MN, Vol. I, pp. 8-9 (*Ariyapariyesanasatta*, I. 3.6.); LV, Vol. I, pp. 238-239, 243-244; BCK, XII. 63, 83; Kern: *Manual of Buddhism*, 1896, p. 55.

16 See IV. 5.

There are two classes of teachers: one (*i.e.*, the followers of the systems of the Sāṅkhya and the Vedānta[1]) holding the doctrine of actual existence of an effect in its cause (*satkārya-vāda*), and the other (*i.e.*, the Naiyāyikas and the Vaiśeṣikas[2]) maintaining the theory of non-existence of an effect in its cause (*asatkāryavāda*). The author refers to these two views in the third kārikā which runs as follows:

3

bhūtasya jātim icchanti vādinaḥ kecid eva hi ı
abhūtasyāpare dhīrā vivadantaḥ parasparam ıı

'There are only certain disputants who maintain that *jāti* 'origination' is of a thing which is already existent, while there are others of firm resolve who hold that it is of a thing which is non-existent.[3] Thus they dispute with each other.'

1 See SK, IX; BS, II. 1. 14-18 with Ś; Ś on BU, I. 2. 2, (p. 20): kāryasya hi sato jāyamānasya kāraṇe saty utpattidarśanāt. Among the Buddhists the Vaibhāṣikas maintain *satkāryavāda*. See CŚ, IX. 15 and our text, IV, 11, note 1.

2 See NK, pp. 143 ff. Among the Buddhists Sautrāntikas and Yogācāras hold *asatkāryavāda*. CŚ, IX. 15.

3 The interpretation of the words *bhūta* and *abhūta* by Ś in the text here is quite different from that in III. 23, and it is very remarkable.

The Ācārya now proceeds to mention in the next kārikā the doctrine of the Buddhists who subscribe to neither of these two views asserting absolute 'non-becoming' (*ajāti*) of things:

4

bhūtaṃ na jāyate kiñcid abhūtaṃ naiva jāyate ı
vivadanto 'dvayā hy evam ajātiṃ khyāpayanti te ıı

'That which is already existent does not come into being, and that which is non-existent does not also come into being;

disputing thus the followers of the doctrine of *advaya* assert absolute non-becoming (*ajāti*).'

Before discussing the meaning of the kārikā it is to be noted that the reading that can reasonably be accepted in c is not *vivadanto dvayā* as in many editions, but *vivadanto'dvayā* with our MS. M[e], and some editions.[1] It is supported also by the commentary in those editions, as well as by the MS. *Ka* used in the Anandasram edition of 1900.

The word *advaya* in the kārikā is, in fact, identical in meaning with *Advayavādin*, which is well-known even to an ordinary reader of Sanskrit as one of the names for the Buddha.[2] Some of the commentators of Amk explain *advaya* in *advayavādin* as *advaita*.[3] But there is a marked difference between the two terms *advaitavāda* and *advayavāda*; while the former literally means the theory of non-difference, *i.e.*, the non-difference between, or identity of (according to the school of Ś) Jīva and Brahman, the latter means the theory of 'non-two', *i.e.*, neither of the two extreme views.

The two (*dvaya*) or the two extreme views are as follows: The Buddha does not hold that anything exists, nor does he hold that it does not exist. He rejects both of these two extreme views and propounds his view taking a middle path (*majjhimā patipadā* or *madhyamā pratipad*). So according to

1 Such as of Maheśacandra Pāla, Calcutta, Śaka 1806; Durgācaraṇa Sāṅkhyavedāntatīrtha, Calcutta, 1331, B.S.; and Gītā Press, Gorakhpur, 1993 V.S.

2 Amk, I. 1. 14; MVt[1], 23; DA, p. 95: buddhānaṃ bhagavatāṃ mahākāruṇikānām advayavādinām. In the *Index of words* to the last work, the word *advaitavādin* is wrongly written.

3 For instance, Bhānujidīkṣita: advayam advaitaṃ vadanty avaśyam; Kṣīrasvāmin: advayaṃ vijñānādvaitaṃ vadaty avaśyam.

Advayavādin, the exact Tibetan equivalent of which is gñis . su . med . pa . gsuṅ ba, and Chinese *pu-ěrh-yü*, both literally meaning 'one who says not two' is misunderstood in the *Sanskrit-Tibetan-English Vocabulary* (*Memoirs of the Asiatic Society of Bengal*, Vol. IV, 1913, p. 2, for the word can in no way mean 'not doubtful in his command' as it is explained there.

him nothing is existent, nor is anything non-existent; nothing comes into being (*anutpāda*), nor does anything disappear (*anirodha*); nothing is eternal (*aśāśvata*), nor has anything an end (*anuccheda*); nothing is identical (*eka*), nor anything differentiated (*aneka*); nothing moves hither (*anāgama*), and nothing moves thither (*anirgama*).[4]

This *advayavāda* is found throughout the Buddhist sacred literature both in Sanskrit and Pali.[5] That the reading in c of the kārikā must be with the word *advayāḥ* and not *dvayāḥ* will

[4] So says N ā g ā r j u n a, MV, p. 11:

> anirodham anutpādam anucchedam aśāśvatam |
> anekārtham anānārtham anāgamam anirgamam ||
> yaḥ pratītyasamutpādaṃ prapañcopaśamaṃ śivaṃ |
> deśayāmāsa sambuddhas taṃ vande vadatāṃ varaṃ ||

[5] astīti kāśyapa ayam eko'nto nāstīty ayaṃ dvitīyo'ntaḥ. yad anayor dvayor antayor madhyam iyam ucyate kāśyapa madhyamā pratipad dharmāṇāṃ bhūtapratyavekṣā. KP, §60 (p. 90). See MV, p. 270.

yad bhūyasā kātyāyanāyaṃ loko 'stitāṃ vābhiniviṣṭo nāstitāṃ ca tena na parimucyate. *Kātyāyanāvavāda* quoted in MV, p. 269.

So writes N ā g ā r j u n a:

> kātyāyanāvavāde cāsti[ti] nāstīti cobhayaṃ |
> pratiṣiddhaṃ bhagavatā bhāvābhāvavibhāvinā || MK, XV. 7.
> astitvaṃ ye tu paśyanti nāstitvaṃ cālpabuddhayaḥ |
> bhāvānāṃ te na paśyanti draṣṭavyopaśamaṃ śivaṃ || MK, V. 8.

sammādiṭṭhi sammādiṭṭhīti bhante vuccati. kittāvatā nu kho bhante sammādiṭṭhi hotīti. dvayanissito khv āyaṃ kaccāyana loko yebhuyyena atthitaṃ ceva na'tthitaṃ ca. SN, II, p. 17 (XII. 15). lokasamudayaṃ kho kaccāyana yathābhūtaṃ sammappaññāya passato yā loke na'tthitā sā na hoti. lokanirodhaṃ kho kaccāyana yathā- bhūtaṃ sammappaññāya passato yā loke atthitā sā na hoti° sabbaṃ atthīti kho kaccāyana ayam eko anto. sabbaṃ natthīti ayaṃ dutiyo anto, ete te kaccāyana ubho ante anupagamma majjhena tathāgato dhammaṃ deseti. SN, II, p. 17 (XII. 15).

nityam iti kāśyapa ayaṃ eko 'ntaḥ. anityam iti kāśyapa ayaṃ dvitīyo 'ntaḥ. yad etayor dvayor nityānityayor madhyaṃ tad arūpyanidarśanaṃ° | ātmeti kāśyapa ayam eko 'ntaḥ. nairātmyam iti dvitīyo 'ntaḥ. yad ātmanairātmyayor madhyaṃ tad.° saṃkleśa iti kāśyapa ayam eko 'ntaḥ vyavadānam ity ayaṃ kāśyapa dvitīyo 'ntaḥ. yo'syāntadvayasyānupagamo (Text *anugamaḥ* but see

further be perfectly clear to anyone when one considers that in the preceding kārikā two classes of teachers are referred to, who hold the theory of origination (*jātivāda*). According to one of them the origination is of the existent, while in accordance with the other, it is of the non-existent. These teachers are *dvaitins* 'advocates of dualism', *viz.*, the Sāṁkhyas, the Naiyāyikas and the Vaiśeṣikas. The teachers alluded to in the present kārikā are, however, quite of a different view. They do not discuss as to whether the origination is of the existent or of the non-existent, but assert that there is no origination at all (*ajātim khyāpayanti te*). Thus the teachers alluded to in kārikās 3 and 4 are different, though Ś takes them to be identical.

As is evident, the main subject of this chapter is the theory of non-origination (*ajātivāda*). In different systems of Indian philosophy it is held that things around us have their origination ; in other words, they are produced; they have their causes, they themselves being their effect. But it is the Buddhists who hold quite a different view emphatically denying the origination of anything in the world. Thus the first sentence of Nāgārjuna's MK begins with *anirodham*

Tib. version: khas. mi. len. ciṅ°) 'nudāhāro 'pravyāhāra iyam ucyate kaśyapa madhyamā pratipad dharmāṇāṃ bhūtapratyavekṣā. KP, pp. 86-88.

astīti nāstīti ubhe'pi antā
śuddhī aśuddhīti ime 'pi antā |
tasmād ubhe anta vivarjayitvā
madhye 'pi sthānaṃ na karoti paṇḍitaḥ ||
astīti nāstīti vivāda eṣa
śuddhī aśuddhīti ayaṃ vivādaḥ |
vivādaprāptyā na dukhaṃ praśāmyate
avivādaprāptyā ca dukhaṃ nirudhyate ||

SR, p. 30, quoted in MV, pp. 135, 270.

bhāvābhāvadarśanadvayaprasaṅgo yāvat tāvat saṃsāra ity avetya mumukṣubhir etaddarśanadvayanirāsena sadbhir madhyamā pratipad bhāvanīyā yathāvad iti. MV, p. 276. See the whole of chapter XV.

anutpādam[6] 'having neither origination nor suppression.' This *anutpāda* is thoroughly discussed and established in that work as in others. Let here be quoted only a few lines in translation from that book together with the commentary of Candrakīrtti (MK, I. 1 with MV, p. 12):

'Now...the Ācārya, thinking the facility in refuting *nirodha*, after *utpāda* is refuted, begins first with the refutation of the latter. *Utpāda* of a thing may be supposed by the opponents from a cause which may be either it itself, or something other than it, or both, or again, from one which is no cause at all. But in no way it can be justified. So he (the Ācārya) says:

"Nowhere and never are such things as are produced either from themselves, or from some other things, or from both, or from what is no cause at all." '[7].

This non-origination is asserted again and again in the same work and sometimes in identical words:

na svato jāyate bhāvaḥ parato naiva jāyate ।
na svataḥ parataś caiva jāyate jāyate kutaḥ ॥
MK, XXI. 13. See XXIII. 20.

'A thing does not come into being from itself, nor from other (=not-itself), nor from both, itself and other. How can it come into being?'

6 For the order of these two words see Candrakīrtti (MV, p. 12): atra ca nirodhasya pūrvaṃ pratiṣedha utpādanirodhayoḥ paurvāparyāvasthāyāḥ siddhyabhāvaṃ dyotayituṃ. vakṣyati hi (MK, XI. 3; MV, p. 221): pūrvaṃ jātir yadi bhavej jarāmaraṇam uttaram°. Our author, Gauḍapāda, too, has followed the same order in his widely quoted kārikā (III. 32): na nirodho na cotpattiḥ.°

7 idānīm° utpādapratiṣedhena nirodhapratiṣedhasaukaryaṃ manyamāna ācāryaḥ prathamam evotpādapratiṣedham ārabhate. utpādo hi paraiḥ kalpyamānaḥ svato vā parikalpyeta parata ubhayato 'hetuto vā parikalpyeta. sarvathā ca nopapadyata iti niścity āha:

na svato nāpi parato na dvābhyāṃ nāpy ahetutaḥ ।
utpannā jātu vidyante bhāvāḥ kvacana kecana॥
MK, I. 1; MV, p. 12.

Compare this with the following line from our kārikā, IV. 22 which speaks for itself:

svato vā parato vāpi na kiñcid vastu jāyate ।

'Nothing is produced either from itself or from other.'

For further details one may be referred to MK, I and XXIII with MV; CŚ, XV. See also our kārikā, IV. 22.

That there is no *jāti* or *utpāda* 'origination' is thus maintained also in a short line of the BA, IX. 106:

evaṃ ca sarvadharmāṇām utpattir nāvasīyate ।[8]

'Thus the origination of all things is not known.'

The first half of the present kārikā is undoubtedly based on such statement as the following of Nāgārjuna (MK, I. 6):

naivāsato naiva sataḥ pratyo'rthasya yujyate ।
asataḥ pratyayaḥ kasya sataś ca pratyayena kiṃ ॥[9]

For the wording in *b* of the kārikā (*abhūtaṃ naiva jāyate*) see CŚ, 373^d (XV. 23^d): *nābhūto nāma jāyate*. See here also Candrakīrtti on CŚ, 366 (XV. 16): *atrāha*: *jāto na jāyate ajāto 'pi na jāyate*.[10] It may be noted here that in this book, too, the doctrine of non-origination is fully discussed.

Ś explains the first half of the present kārikā as follows:

bhūtaṃ vidyamānaṃ vastu na jāyate vidyamānatvād eva°. tathā abhūtam avidyamānam avidyamānatvān naiva jāyate śaśaviṣāṇavat.

'The thing which is already existent does not (again) come into being owing to its very existence. And the thing that is

8 BAP runs here: evam eva yathoditanyāyena sarvadharmāṇāṃ sarvabhāvānām utpattir utpādo nāvasīyate na pratīyate. See the same work, pp. 355 ff.: na ca svaparobhayahetunibandhanam ahetunibandhanaṃ vā bhāvasya janmātipeśalam upapadyate. Here the subject is discussed to a great extent.

9 See MA, VI. 58; MV, pp. 82-83.

10 Reconstructed from the Tibetan version: ḥdir. smras. pa | skyes. pa. mi. skye. la. ma. skyes. pa. yaṅ. mi. skye. ste |

not existent does not come into being on account of its being non-existent, as, for instance, the horn of a hare.'[11]

G a u ḍ a p ā d a refers to the doctrine of *ajāti* in the present kārikā, and accepts it in the next which runs as follows:

5

khyāpyamānām ajātiṃ tair anumodāmahe vayam |
vivadāmo na taiḥ sārdham avivādaṃ nibodhata ||

'We express our approval of *ajāti* which they declare; we do not dispute with them, and listen how there cannot be any dispute.'

It is to be noted here that G a u ḍ a p ā d a is a Vedantist, and yet he accepts the doctrine of non-origination of the Advaya-vādins or Buddhists expressing his approval. He does not see any use disputing with them and invites apparently his Vedantist followers to listen to him as to why the view cannot be disputed.

Like the Sāṅkhyas, the Naiyāyikas, and the Vaiśeṣikas, etc., the Vedantists, are originally believers in the doctrine of origination, as is evident from the BS, I. 1. 2 (: janmādy asya yataḥ, 'From whom are the origination, etc. of this') which is based on such statements of the Upaniṣads as TU, III. 1. 1: yato vā imāni bhūtāni jātāni° tad Brahma, 'That is Brahman from whom these beings are originated.' The reality of this origination or creation is denied later on in the school of Ś in the absolute truth. This is due to the doctrine of G a u ḍ a p ā d a who invites here his followers to listen as to how

[11] B u d d h a p ā l i t a quoted in MV, p. 14: na svata utpadyante bhāvāḥ, tadutpādavaiyarthyād atiprasaṅgadoṣāc ca. na hi svātmanā vidyamānānāṃ padārthānāṃ punarutpāde prayojanam asti. atha sann api jāyeta na kadācin na jāyeta.

the non-origination doctrine of the Advayavādins can be approved.

Having thus introduced his readers to the subject he has to deal, the author now proceeds in the following kārikās to offer his arguments as to how the doctrine of *jāti* cannot be justified. He says:

6

ajātasyaiva dharmasya jātim icchanti vādinaḥ
ajāto hy amṛto dharmo martyatāṃ katham eṣyati ||[1]

'Disputants are of opinion that there is birth only of that thing (lit. 'element of existence') which is unborn. But how is it that the thing which is unborn and (consequently) immortal should become mortal?'[2]

It means that the teachers of both the classes referred to in kārikā 3 are agreed upon the point that birth is possible of what is unborn; for what is already born does not take birth again, and so it is useless to think of the birth of such a thing. Our author says that the birth of an unborn one cannot be justified, and he offers the following arguments: It is accepted on all hands that what has no birth (*ajāta*) has also no death (*amṛta*). Now when you say that birth is of an unborn one, you have necessarily to admit that it has death; and so it follows that you also admit the death of an immortal

[1] The kārikās 6, 7, and 8 of this Book are identical with the kārikās 20, 21 and 22 of the Book III respectively excepting only this that in kārikās III. 20 and 22 there is the word *bhāva*, while in IV. 6 and 8 the reading is *dharma*.

For the words *jāta* and *ajāta* see MK, XX. 12-14.

[2] According to Ś the second half of the kārikā ('But how is it that the thing which is unborn and immortal should become mortal') means, in fact, that how it should take birth in reality. He writes: svabhāvenāmṛto bhāvo martyatāṃ gacchati paramārthato jāyate. III. 22.

one. Now an unborn one is by its own nature immortal. And this death of the immortal one is utterly absurd.

The author continues in support of his above statement:

7

na bhavaty amṛtaṃ martyaṃ na martyam amṛtaṃ tathā ǀ
prakṛter anyathābhāvo na kathañcid bhaviṣyati ǁ[1]

'The immortal does not become mortal and a mortal one does not also become immortal; for the change of nature can in no way be possible.'

The second half of the kārikā is repeated in kārikā IV. 29, and seems to have mostly been taken here from Nāgārjuna's MK, XV. 8, which runs as follows:

> yady astitvaṃ prakṛtyā syān na bhaved asya nāstitā ǀ
> prakṛter anyathābhāvo na hi jātūpapadyate ǁ[2]

The author having shown here that nature does in no way change says in the next kārikā that if a thing which in its own nature is unborn (*ajāta*) and hence regarded as immortal (*amṛta*) comes into being (*jāyate*) and thus becomes mortal (*martya*), then owing to this very fact it cannot remain changeless. The point is that which is unborn or immortal by its own nature should remain always so. But if you say that the unborn takes

[1] See III. 21, and the note 1 on IV. 6.

[2] The following may also be quoted here from the same work:

> prakṛtau kasya cāsatyām anyathātvaṃ bhaviṣyati ǀ
> prakṛtau kasya ca satyām anyathātvaṃ bhaviṣyati ǁ XV. 9.
> kasya syād anyathābhāvaḥ svabhāvaś cen na vidyate ǀ
> kasya syādanyathābhāvaḥ svabhāvo yadi vidyate ǁ XIII. 4.
> kaḥ svabhāvaṃ prahāsyati ǀ XXIII. 24.
> svarūpasyānyathābhāvāsambhavāt.
>
> Candrakīrtti on CŚ, VIII. 4 (179).

birth, or the immortal becomes mortal, evidently it undergoes a change. But no change of nature is possible. The kārikā runs :

8

svabhāvenāmṛto yasya dharmo gacchati martyatām ।
kṛtakenāmṛtas tasya kathaṃ sthāsyati niścalaḥ ॥[1]

'How can he, accoding to whom a thing which is naturally immortal becomes mortal[2], maintain that an immortal thing, when it becomes artificial[3], will remain changeless?'

The following may here be quoted from N ā g ā r j u n a ' s MK, XV. 1-2 in which one should note the word *kṛtaka*:[4]

na sambhavaḥ svabhāvasya yuktaḥ pratyayahetubhiḥ ।
hetupratyayasambhūtaḥ svabhāvaḥ kṛtako bhavet ॥
svabhāvaḥ kṛtako nāma bhaviṣyati punaḥ kathaṃ ।
akṛtrimaḥ svabhāvo hi nirapekṣaḥ paratra ca ॥

1 See III. 22.

2 That is, takes birth. See note 2 on IV. 6.

3 The word *kṛtaka* in the kārikā (*a*) is to be explained taking it as noun, i.e., *kṛtakatva*, just as the word *anādi* in IV. 14 is evidently for *anāditva*. Ā n a n d a g i r i lends his support writing (III. 22) kṛtakeneti. kṛtakatvasya, yat kṛtakam tad anityam iti.° *Cf.* S ā y a ṇ a who explains *manasaspati* (TA, VII. 6) as °*patitva*.

4 It seems that our author had these kārikās of N ā g ā r j u n a in his mind while writing his own and so he has unconsciously written *kṛtaka* instead of *kṛtakatva* as is required.

In order to explain as to how nature (*prakṛti* or *svabhāva*) cannot change G a u ḍ a p ā d a proceeds to define it in the next kārikā:

9

sāṃsiddhikī svābhāvikī sahajāpy akṛtā ca yā |
prakṛtiḥ seti vijñeyā svabhāvaṃ na jahāti yā ||

'That is to be known nature (*prakṛti*) which is self-existent,[1] natural, innate, not artificial and one that does not give up its own being.'

As regards *svabhāva* C a n d r a k ī r t t i explains it following N ā g ā r j u n a in his MV, pp. 264-265, that it is nothing but always non-origination (*sarvadānutpāda eva*). He says that by *svabhāva* we are to understand that which is independent of other (*paranirapekṣa*) and as such not artificial (*akṛtrima*), and thus having no existence before it does not come into being (not *abhūtvā bhāvaḥ*). Therefore the *svabhāva* of fire is nothing but its non-origination (*anutpāda*), and not its heat, because it depends on its cause and conditions, and comes into being after having no existence at first[2].

1 The word *sāṃsiddhika* may also mean that which comes into being simultaneously (*saha-utpanna*) as illustrated by G a u ḍ a p ā d a and M ā ṭ h a r a (Chaukhamba Sanskrit Series, No. 296) in their commentaries on SK, XLIII of I ś v a r a k ṛ ṣ ṇ a: tatra sāṃsiddhikā yathā bhagavataḥ kapilasyādisarge utpadyamānasya catvāro bhāvāḥ sahotpannāḥ. The explanation of Ś is as follows: samyak siddhiḥ saṃsiddhis tatra bhavā sāṃsiddhikī. yathā yoginām aṇimādyaiśvaryaprāptiḥ prakṛtiḥ sā.'

2 MV, p. 265: sarvadānutpāda eva hy agnyādīnāṃ paranirapekṣatvād akṛtrimatvāt svabhāva ity ucyate,

Now having shown that there is no origination of anything the author proceeds to say in the next kārika that there is also neither decay nor passing away:

10

jarāmarananirmuktāḥ sarve dharmāḥ svabhāvataḥ I
jarāmaraṇam icchantaś cyavante tanmanīṣayā II

'All things are by nature free from 'old age' (decay) and 'death' (passing away), So the persons who believe in 'old age' and 'death' are reborn owing to their that very thought.'

That there can be neither *jarā* nor *maraṇa* is very elaborately established by Nāgārjuna in his MK, XI. 3 ff. from which we cull the following two couplets (3 and 4):

pūrvaṃ jātir yadi bhavej jarāmaraṇam uttaraṃ I
nirjarāmaraṇā jātir bhavej jāyeta cāmṛtaḥ II
paścāj jātir yadi bhavej jarāmaraṇam āditaḥ I
ahetukam ajātasya syāj jarāmaraṇaṃ kathaṃ II

For further details readers are referred to the original text of Nāgārjuna with MV.

The author attacks the doctrine of *jāti* from different points of view and refutes it in the following way referring first to the followers of the Sāṃkhya system who hold the theory of actual existence of an effect in its cause (*satkāryavāda*).[1]

11

kāranaṃ yasya vai kāryaṃ kāraṇaṃ tasya jāyate I
jāyamānaṃ katham ajaṃ bhinnaṃ nityaṃ kathaṃ ca tat II

'(It is to be admitted by him) according to whom the cause itself is the effect, that it is the cause that takes birth (*i.e.*, is

[1] See notes on IV. 3 and SK, IX.

produced). And in that case how is it that the thing which takes birth and is thus different (from the effect) can be regarded as unborn (*aja*) and how it can be permanent ?'[1]

In the Sāṅkhya system *prakṛti* or *pradhāna* is held to be the first or original cause (*mūla karaṇa*). It is 'unborn' (*aja*) and permanent (*nitya*). From it other things are gradually produced. This view is criticized in this and the following kārikās by our author.

[1] The point is that there must be some difference between that which is produced and that which is not produced (*jāyamāna* and *aja*).

Ś explains the word *bhinna* in a different way saying that it means 'rent asunder', 'divided into parts' or 'opened' (*vidīrṇa*, *sphuṭita*) implying thereby 'subject to some change.' And that which admits of any kind of change cannot be permanent.

The identity of cause and effect may be viewed from two different points, *viz*., the cause is not other than the effect (*kāryābhinnaṃ kāraṇam*), or the effect is not other than the cause (*kāraṇābhinnaṃ kāryam*). But in neither case can the Sāṁkhya system be defended, The object of the first viewpoint is shown in the present kārikā which says : If the cause is not different from the effect then it is to be admitted that it is the cause (and *not the effect*) that 'takes birth' (*jāyate*) and thus, if you accept it, the cause cannot be regarded as 'unborn' (*aja*), as you hold it to be.

Now, in order to avoid this difficulty one may follow the second point of view saying that the effect being not different from the cause the former is as *aja* as the latter ; and thus one cannot say that the cause is not *aja*. The author, however, says in the next kārikā that this argument, too, cannot be accepted :

12

kāraṇād yad[1] ananyatvam ataḥ kāryam ajaṃ yadi ।
jāyamānād dhi vai kāryāt kāraṇaṃ te kathaṃ dhruvam ॥

'If you hold that the effect is also 'unborn' (*aja*), for there is no difference of it from the cause (which is *aja*), then, how is it, in your opinion, that the cause is permanent when the effect is produced ?' [2]

[1] The reading should be here *yad* and not *yadi* as discussed elsewhere.

[2] Ś explains c saying that how it is that the cause being not different from the effect, that is, being produced, can be permanent: jāyamānād dhi vai kāryāt kāraṇam ananyan nityaṃ dhruvaṃ ca.

The author offers further grounds :

13

ajād vai jāyate yasya dṛṣṭāntas tasya nāsti vai ।
jātāc ca jāyamānasya na-vyavasthā prasajyate ॥

'There is no illustration (to give) for him who holds that a thing is produced from what is unborn[1]. (On the other hand, if it is maintained that) a thing is born from what is born, then there follows no finality, it leads to an endless series of causes (*anavasthā*).'

Here in the text in *d na* is to be taken with *vyavasthā* (as *na-vyavasthā* = *avyavasthā* = *anavasthā*) and not with *prasajyate*. Ś explains: na vyavasthā prasajyate anavasthānaṃ syād ity arthaḥ.

The second half of the kārikā means that if A is produced from B which you take as produced (*jāta*), by the very fact that it is produced it must have been produced

[1] That is, existing from all eternity.

from one C, and C, too, in the same way must have been produced from one D, and so on. Thus it is impossible to ascertain the ultimate cause of a thing.[2]

[2] Cf. Candrakīrtti (MV, p. 15): na ca vidyamānasya punar utpattau prayojanaṃ paśyāmaḥ, anavasthāṃ ca paśyāmaḥ; AKV (quoted in MV, p. 13): utpannasya punar utpattau kalpyamānāyām anavasthāprasaṅgaḥ; MA (quoted in MV, p. 13): jātasya janma punar eva ca naiva juktam; ŚS, p. 262 (from ASP): kiṃ punar āyuṣman subhūte utpanno dharma utpatsyata utānutpannaḥ. subhūtir āha. nāham āyuṣman sāriputra utpannasya dharmasyotpattim icchāmi na cānutpannasyeti. CŚ, 260:

> sambhavaḥ kriyate yasya prāk so'stīti na yujyate |
> sato yadi bhavej janma jātasyāpi bhaved bhavaḥ ||

In support of this *ajātivāda* the author offers further arguments :

14

> hetor ādiḥ phalaṃ yeṣām ādir hetuḥ phalasya ca |
> hetoḥ phalasya cānādiḥ kathaṃ tair upavarṇyate ||

'How can those who hold that the antecedent of a cause is its effect and the antecedent of an effect is its cause, describe that there is no beginning of the cause and the effect?'

In c *anādi* means 'absence of beginning' (*āder abhāvaḥ*). Ś explains it by *anāditva*. *Cf. kṛtaka* in IV. 8c.

Let us take here an example (IV. 20). As regards a seed (*bīja*) and its sprout (*aṅkura*) it is said that they have no beginning, for it cannot be ascertained as to whether the seed was first and then the sprout, or the sprout was first and then the seed, each of them being dependent on the other for their existence. Yet, they say that the antecedent of the sprout is the seed and that of the seed is sprout. This cannot be justified.

The point is further dealt with in the following kārikās :

15

hetor ādiḥ phalaṃ yeṣām ādir hetuḥ phalasya ca |
tathā janma bhavet teṣām putrāj janma pitur yathā ||

'To those who maintain that the antecedent of a cause is its effect and the antecedent of an effect is its cause, the production of a thing would be just after the manner of the birth of a father from the son.'

The point is that if it is held that the antecedent of a cause is its effect and *vice-versa*, then it would follow from it that as a cause produces its effect, so an effect, too, produces its cause ; and if one accepts it one would also accept that a son begets his father. But it is absurd.

Cf. Nāgārjuna in his ViV, 50 :

pitrā yady utpādyaḥ putro yadi tena caiva putreṇa |
utpādyaḥ sa yadi pitā vada tatrotpādayati kaḥ kam ||

Here in the second half *yadi*, though supported by the Tibetan text, seems to be redundant.

See NS, II. 1. 41, IV. 1. 39; BA, IX. 114 :

pitā cen na vinā putrāt kutaḥ putrasya sambhavaḥ |
putrābhāve pitā nāsti tathāsattvaṃ tayor dvayoḥ ||

As regards the relationship between *hetu* 'cause' and *phala* 'effect' see MK, XX, specially XX. 20 :

ekatve phalahetvoḥ syād aikyaṃ janakajanyayoḥ |
pṛthaktve phalahetoḥ syāt tulyo hetur ahetunā ||

MV writes here: na cānayor ekatvaṃ pitāputrayoś cakṣuś-cakṣurvijñānayor bījāṅkurayoś ca aikyaprasaṅgāt.

The next kārikā says that there must be an order (*krama*) of a cause and its effect as to whether the cause or the effect precedes, otherwise there cannot be any relationship between them, and consequently nothing can be produced:

16

sambhave hetuphalayor eṣitavyaḥ kramas tvayā |
yugapat sambhave yasmād asambandho viṣāṇavat ||

'As regards production (*sambhava*, i.e., *jāti*) you must determine an order of the cause and the effect; for, if they are simultaneous they cannot be related (to each other), as the horns (of an animal).'

This argument is found in Buddhist works as shown below. As regards the production of an effect by its cause only three orders are possible, and not more. For, it may be said that first there is the cause and then the effect (*pūrva-krama* 'prior order'); or it may may be said that first there is the effect and then the cause (*apara-krama* 'posterior order'); or, again, it may be said that the cause and the effect are simultaneous (*sahakrama* 'the order of simultaneity'). But it is clearly shown that none of them can be justified. Says Nāgārjuna, MK, XI. 2:

tasmān nātropapadyante pūrvāparasahakramāḥ | [1]

[1] Candrakīrtti introduces it (MV) saying: ata eva saṃsārābhāvāj jarāmaraṇādīnāṃ pūrvāparasahakramā api na santītyāha.

The following may be quoted here from MK, XI. 3-5:

pūrvaṃ jātir yadi bhavej jarāmaraṇam uttaraṃ |
nirjarāmaraṇā jātir bhavej jāyeta cāmṛtaḥ ||
paścāj jātir yadi bhavej jarāmaraṇam āditaḥ |
ahetukam ajātasya syāj jarāmaraṇaṃ kathaṃ ||
na jarāmaraṇenaiva jātiś ca saha yujyate |
mriyeta jāyamānaś ca syāc cāhetukatobhayoḥ ||

Op. cit. XI. 6 :

yatra na prabhavantyete pūrvāparasahakramāḥ |

For details the reader is referred to the whole of the chapters XI and XII.

In the kārikā under discussion Gauḍapāda referring to the *krama* of cause and effect refutes their simultaneity saying exactly what is said by Nāgārjuna (MK, XX. 7) and his commentator Candrakīrtti :

phalaṃ sahaiva sāmagryā yadi prādurbhavet punaḥ |
ekakālau prasajyete janako yaś ca jāyate ||

'Should an effect come into existence just with its cause in its entirety then that which produces and that which is produced become simultaneous.'

Here Candrakīrtti adds : na caikakālayoḥ savyetara-goviṣāṇayor janyajanakatvaṃ dṛṣṭaṃ vāmadakṣiṇakarayoś caraṇayor vā. 'But it is not seen that between two simultaneous things there is any such relation as between the producer (*janaka*) and the produced (*janya*), just like between the right and left hands or feet.' [2]

This order of cause and effect has again been referred to later on (IV. 19) by the word *kramakopa* 'incompatibility of order.' [3]

2 Sometimes the female breasts are cited as example in such cases.

3 See Candrakīrtti (MV, XI. 7-8) : tatra yadi pūrvaṃ kāraṇaṃ paścāt kāryaṃ syād akāryakaṃ kāraṇaṃ nirhetukaṃ syāt. atha pūrvaṃ kāryaṃ paścāt kāraṇam evam api kāraṇāt pūrvaṃ kāryaṃ nirhetukam eva syāt. atha yugapat kāryakāraṇe syātām evaṃ ubhayam apy a[hetu]kaṃ syāt.

Now, according to these three orders (*krama*) of cause and effect there may be three propositions respectively, *viz.*, (*i*) the cause produces its effect, (*ii*) the effect produces its cause; and (*iii*) the cause and its effect produce each other.[1] Of these three propositions the second[2] is taken up in the following kārikā :

17

phalād utpadyamānaḥ san na te hetuḥ prasidhyati |
aprasiddhaḥ kathaṃ hetuḥ phalam utpādayiṣyati ||[2]

'Your cause coming into being from the effect cannot come into existence ; how will, therefore, the cause that has not come into existence produce the effect ?'

The argument of our author seems to have been based on what Nāgārjuna has said (MK, X. 10):

yo 'pekṣya sidhyate bhāvas tam evāpekṣya sidhyati |
yadi yo 'pekṣitavyaḥ sa sidhyatāṃ kam apekṣya kaḥ ||

[1] See here Nāgārjuna with Candrakīrtti, MK, XX. 5-7, and specially the following line (MV, p. 395, ll. 5-6): yady evaṃ phalasya hetor utpattau doṣa evaṃ sati sahotpannaiva sāmagrī phalasya janikāstu tad yathā pradīpaprabhāyāḥ.

[2] It appears that a kārikā dealing with the first proposition is now lost between kārikās 16 and 17 For, as the second and third propositions are discussed (IV. 17, 18), one may naturally expect to have the discussion also of the first proposition, but it is not to be found. Can we think that the author himself has omitted it?

Candrakīrtti explains it thus (MV, p. 208) :

tatra yadi yo 'gnyākhyo bhāvo yam indhanākhyam bhāvam apekṣya sidhyati, indhanākhyaś ca bhāvo yo 'gninātmasiddhyartham apekṣitavyaḥ, sa yadi tam evāgnyākhyaṃ padārtham apekṣya sidhyati, kathyatām idānīṃ sidhyatāṃ kam apekṣya ka iti. yadā cāgnyabhāve satīndhanasya siddhir eva nāsti tadākāraṇasyendhanasyābhāvāt kutas taddhetuko 'gniḥ prasetsyati.

It says that if the fire is effected having regard to its fuel and the fuel is effected having regard to the fire, neither of them can be effected. See also the next kārikā (MK, X. 11) :

yo 'pekṣya sidhyate bhāvaḥ so 'siddho 'pekṣate kathaṃ |
athāpy apekṣate siddhas tv apekṣāsya na yujyate ||

Mark here the use of the root √*sidh* with or without the prefix *pra-* by Gauḍapāda, Nāgārjuna and Candrakīrtti.

This point is further discussed in the following kārikā :

18

yadi hetoḥ phalāt siddhiḥ phalasiddhiś ca hetutaḥ |
katarat pūrvam utpannaṃ yasya siddhir apekṣayā ||

'If the coming into being of the cause is from the effect and that of the effect is from the cause, which (of the two) has first come into being,—the coming into being of which is dependent?'

Read here the following quoted from Nāgārjuna's MK, X. 8 :

yadīndhanam apekṣyāgnir apekṣyāgniṃ yadīndhanaṃ |
katarat pūrvaniṣpannaṃ yadapekṣyāgnir indhanaṃ ||

MV (p. 207) runs here as follows :

asyendhanasyāyam agnir dāhakaḥ kartety evaṃ yadīndhanam apekṣyāgnir vyavasthāpyate, asyāgner idam indhanaṃ karmety-evam agnim apekṣya yadīndhanaṃ, tat katarad anayoḥ pūrva-niṣpannaṃ. kim indhanaṃ yad apekṣyāgniḥ syāt, utāgnir yam apekṣyendhanaṃ syāt.

Mark the wording of c in both the kārikās quoted above.[1]

[1] See Poussin: JRAS, 1913, p. 139

The author proceeds to show very clearly in the next kārikā as to how the Buddhas have explained the theory of *ajāti* 'non-origination' :

19

aśaktir aparijñānaṃ kramakopo 'tha vā punaḥ ।
evaṃ hi sarvathā buddhair ajātiḥ paridīpitā ॥

'As there is absence of capability, or complete ignorance, or, again, incompatibility of orders, the Buddhas elucidated (the theory of) absolute non-origination (*ajāti*)'.

Against the theory of *jāti* there are given three reasons in the present kārikā, *viz.*, (*i*) *aśakti* 'absence of capability', (*ii*) *aparijñāna* 'complete ignorance', and (*iii*) *kramakopa* 'incompatibility of orders'. Of these three the third, *i.e.*, *kramakopa* has already been discussed in kārikā 16.[1] But what do the other two terms *aśakti* and *aparijñāna* signify? The answer will be found in Buddhist works. In regard to *aśakti* it

[1] On this as well as on *aśakti* (*asāmarthya*) one may be referred to the *kṣaṇabhaṅga-vāda* in the Buddhist section of the SDS.

refers to IV. 3 where two classes of teachers are mentioned, one holding *satkāryavāda* and the other *asatkāryavāda*. It has already been shown (IV. 4) that the Buddhists subscribe to neither of these two views. Nāgārjuna says (MK, I. 6), as has once already been quoted :

> naivāsato naiva sataḥ pratyayo 'rthasya yujyate |
> asataḥ pratyayaḥ kasya sataś ca pratyayena kim ||

It says that one cannot be a cause of either an existent or a non-existent thing, for, how is it that there is a cause of a thing which is not in existence? And what is the use of a cause of that which is already existent?

The opponent may say here : Well, when we speak of the cause of a non-existent thing we thereby mean to say that the cause is of a *future* thing. Candrakīrtti replies (MV. on MK, I. 6) to it by quoting the following half of a verse in his MA (VI. 58) which is now available only in its Tibetan version edited by Poussin in BB (IX) :

> bhaviṣyatā ced vyavahāra iṣṭaḥ
> śaktiṃ vinā nāsti hi bhāvitāsya | [2]

It means that if you want to say that the cause is of a future thing, then owing to the want of energy that thing cannot come into being.

[2] In Tibetan

> gal. te. ḥbyuṅ. bar. ḥgyur. bas. besñad. ḥdod. na |
> nus. pa. med. par. ḥdi.yi. ḥbyuṅ. ḥgyur. med |

The other half of the verse in Tibetan runs :

> phan. tshun. don. la. brten. paḥi. grub. pa. ni |
> grub. min. ñid. ces. dam. pa. rnams. kyis. gsuṅs ||

It may be translated into Sanskrit as follows :

> parasparārthāśrayiṇī ca siddhiḥ |
> siddhir bhaven neti hi sadbhir uktam||

The point here is this that in the coming into being of anything there must be some *śakti* 'energy', otherwise everything is possible from everything, or nothing is possible from anything. But the existence of such a *śakti* cannot be established. For, as discussed by Candrakīrtti in his MA, VI. 57, it cannot be said that the *śakti* belongs to a thing that has come into being (*jāta*), or to one that has not yet come into being (*ajāta*).[3]

I think this *aśakti* is referred to here by Gauḍapāda in his present kārikā.

Now *aparijñāna* in the kārikā seems to me to be nothing but *pūrvāparāparijñāna* 'absolute ignorance of the first and last (points)' in kārikā IV.21. And this *pūrvāparāparijñāna* is in reality *pūrvāparakoṭi-aparijñāna*, that is, absolute ignorance of the first and last points, *i.e.*, the beginning and the end of the world as well as anything in it. To this theme a whole chapter (XI) is devoted in the MK, owing to which it is called *pūrvāparakoṭi-parīkṣā* 'the Examination of the First and the Last Points.' Let here be quoted the first kārikā of it (XI. 1):

> pūrvā prajñāyate koṭir nety uvāca mahāmuniḥ |
> saṃsāro 'navarāgro hi nāsyādir nāpi paścimaṃ ||

'The great sage said that the first point (of the world) is not known, for it is without the first and last points owing to the fact that it has neither the beginning nor the end.'

Candrakīrtti comments: koṭir bhāgo deśa iti paryāyāḥ. pūrvā koṭiḥ pūrvo deśa ity arthaḥ. yadi hi saṃsāro nāma kaścit

[3] skyes. la. nus. pa. srid. pa. yod. ma. yin |
ma. skyes. ṅo. bo. laḥaṅ nus. yod. min. ni |

The Sanskrit rendering in prose may be: jāte śaktir na sambhavati, ajātasvabhāve' pi śaktir nāsti.

syāt niyataṃ tasya pūrvam api syāt paścimam api ghaṭādīnām iva. uktaṃ ca bhagavatā anavarāgro hi bhikṣavo jātijarāmaraṇasaṃsāra iti.[4] tasmān nāsti saṃsāraḥ pūrvāparakoṭyanupalambhād alātacakravad iti sthitaṃ.

It is to be noted here that *pūrvāparakoṭyaparijñāna* (or °*koṭyanupalambha*) is not only of the world, but also of everything. So says Nāgārjuna (MK. XI. 8):

pūrvā na vidyate koṭiḥ saṃsārasya na kevalaṃ |
sarveṣām api bhāvānāṃ pūrvā koṭir na vidyate||

' It is not only of the world, but also of every thing that there is no existence of the first point.'

Nāgārjuna proceeds to say (MK, XI. 2) :

naivāgraṃ nāvaraṃ yasya tasya madhyaṃ kuto bhavet |

' How is it that that which has no beginning nor the end should have the middle? '

And the very thing is said also by our author (II, 6, IV. 31) :

ādāv ante ca yan nāsti vartamāne 'pi tat tathā |[5]

' That which is not in the beginning, nor in the end, is so[6] also in the present.'

See IV, 31

[4] See DA, p. 197, l. 5; SN, Vol. II, pp. 178, 193, Vol. III, pp. 149, 151, MP, II. 3. 2 (pp. 50-51); KV, I. 1. 159.

[5] ādāvante ca yan nāsti madhye 'pi tat tathā.

Nayopadeśa, 14.

jassa n'atthi purā pacchā majjhaṃ tassa kuo siyā.

ĀS, 4.4.1.3.

It is not also in the middle, as says Ś (tan madhye 'pi nāstīti).

It has been shown before that causation (*hetuphalabhāva*) in cases of origination is not possible. But one may meet the objection offering the example of seed and sprout (*bīja* and *aṅkura*). For it is evident that a sprout comes into being from a seed and a seed from a sprout. There is an endless series of it, yet the fact cannot be denied. Thus by dint of the example causation is established. The author, however, says that the example does not establish any causation, though it may appear to do so, according to you. Therefore until it is established to the satisfaction of both the parties this example cannot be cited. Thus he says :

20

bījāṅkurākhyo dṛṣṭāntaḥ sadā sādhyasamo hi naḥ ı
na ca sādhyasamo hetuḥ siddhau sādhyasya yujyate ॥

'To us the illustration of a seed and its sprout is always like a thing that is yet to be proved (*sādhyasama*). And a reason (*hetu*) which is like one that is yet to be proved (*sādhyasama*) cannot be used for establishing a thing in question'.

Nāgārjuna has discussed (MK, X) the point thoroughly taking the example of fire and fuel (*agni-indhana*) and has arrived at the conclusion that there cannot be any causation (*hetuphalabhāva*) of anything. Let us cite here only the following few lines from this work :

yad indhanaṃ sa ced agnir ekatvaṃ kartṛkarmaṇoḥ |
anyaś ced indhanād agnir indhanād apy ṛte bhavet ||

nityapradīpta eva syād apradīpanahetukaḥ |
punar ārambhavaiyarthyam evaṃ cāk?makaḥ sati|| X. 1-2.

ągnīndhanābhyāṃ vyākhyāta ātmopādānayoḥ kramaḥ |
sarvo niravaśeṣeṇa sārdhaṃ ghaṭapaṭādibhiḥ || X. 15.

Candrakīrtti says on CS, IX.8 : tasmād evaṃ hetuphalabhāvavyavasthābhāvād dvayam api (*hetu* and *phala*) svarūpeṇa na sidhyati.[1]

sādhyasama hetu is one of the fallacies of a reason (*hetvābhāsa*). It is an assertion identical with the point to be proved, *petitio principii*. See NS, I. 2. 4, 8; V. 1. 4.

The word *hetu* has been used here in the kārika in the sense of *dṛṣṭānta*, as says S.

1 The Sanskrit text has not yet been discovered hence it is reconstructed (see my edition) from the Tibetan version which runs: deḥi. phyir. de. ltar. na. rgyu. daṅ. ḥbras. bu. dṅos. po. rnam. par. gnas. pa. med. paḥi. phyir. gñi. ga. raṅ. gi. ṅo. bos. grub. pas. yod. pa. ma. yin. no || See also the kārikā and MA, p. 150.

The opponent says referring to kārika IV. 19 :

21

pūrvāparāparijñānam ajāteḥ paridīpakam |
jāyamānād dhi vai dharmāt kathaṃ pūrvaṃ na gṛhyate ||

'The absolute ignorance of the first and the last (points of a thing) is elucidator of non-origination; but how is it that the first (point) is not known (of a thing) which actually comes into being ?

The word *pūrvāparāparijñāna* has already (IV. 19) been explained.

To the question raised above the author gives his reply in the following kārikā actually in the words of Nāgārjuna and his followers :

22

svato vā parato vāpi na kiñcid vastu jāyate ।
sad asat sadasad vāpi na kiñcid vastu jāyate ॥

'Nothing is produced either from itself or from other than itself, nor is anything produced which is existent, non-existent, or both existent and non-existent '[1]

The author wants to say here that should there be a thing that originates (*jāyate*) one may say that it has its first point (*pūrva koṭi*), *i.e.*, the state of its becoming or being produced, but in reality there is nothing of the kind. For the first half of the kārikā see Nāgārjuna:

na svato jāyate bhāvaḥ parato naiva jāyate |
na svataḥ parataś caiva jāyate jāyate kutaḥ ||[2]

MK, XXI. 13, see also XXIII. 20.

'A thing comes into being neither from itself, nor from another, nor from both, itself and another; and that being the case, how can it come into being at all ?'

na svato nāpi parato na dvābhyāṃ nāpyahetutaḥ |
utpannā jātu vidyante bhāvāḥ kvacana kecana||

Op. cit, I. 1.

'There are nowhere and never such things as are produced either from themselves or from others, or from both, or from one that is no cause at all.'

1 Here the point 'not existent-and-non-existent (*na sad-asad*)' may also be added. See IV. 83.

2 Quoted in BAP, p. 339, and SS. p. 18.

For the second half of the kārikā the reader is referred to the following line of Nāgārjuna (MK, I.7):

na san nāsan na sadasan dharmo nirvartate yadā |
kathaṃ nirvartako hetur evaṃ sati hi yujyate ||[3]

'When nothing existent, non-existent, or both existent and non-existent, comes into being, how is it reasonable to say that a cause brings about a thing?'

[3] See:

na san nāsan na sadasan na cāpyanubhayātmakam |
catuṣkoṭivinimuktaṃ tattvaṃ mādhyamikā viduḥ||

This couplet is attributed to Sarahapāda in SS, p. 15 and found in a book *Jñānasārasamuccaya*, 28. The original Sanskrit of this work is not yet found, but there is a Tibetan version (Tanjur, Mdo, Tsh; Cordir. III, p. 29). Here the authorship of the original book is attributed to Āryadeva. In Tibetan it is called Ye. śes. sñiṅ. po. kun. las. btus. pa. The present kārikā is quoted in BAP, p. 359, and many other books both Buddhist and non-Buddhist. In this connection see IV. 83-84, and atas tattvaṃ sadasadubhayānubhayātmaka-catuṣkoṭivinirmuktaṃ śūnyam eva in SDS (Buddhism section). Bib. Ind., 1858, p. 14.

The next kārikā is a reply to those who maintain the theory of origination (*jātivāda*) on the ground of the rule of cause and effect (*hetuphalavyavasthā*) saying that both of them are without a beginning and as such cannot come into existence :

23

hetur na jāyate 'nādiḥ phalaṃ vāpi svabhāvataḥ |
ādir na vidyate yasya tasya jātir na vidyate ||[1]

[1] All the MSS. utilized for the Anandasram editions as well as those (not less than sixteen) collected from different provinces and examined by myself including different extant editions read *'nādeḥ* for *nādiḥ* in *a* and *hy ādir* for *jātir* in *d*. With these original readings the kārikā hardly gives any appreciable sense. What does the second half with that reading (ādir na vidyate yasya tasya hy ādir na vidyate) mean? With the reading *jātir* for *hyādir* suggested by me the sense is quite clear and it is in one way supported by the explanation given by the commentator, Ś, who has twisted the text with the reading *hy ādiḥ* saying:

'A cause as well as an effect having no beginning does not naturally come into being, for that which has no beginning has no origination.'

Compare BC, IX. 123 :

hetor ādir na ced asti phalasyādiḥ kuto bhavet |

'Should there be no beginning of a cause how could an effect have a beginning ?'

yasmād ādiḥ kāraṇaṃ na vidyate yasya loke tasya ādiḥ pūrvoktā jātir na vidyate. The reason for suggesting *'nādiḥ* for *'nādeḥ* is this that by doing so the meaning becomes quite clear and only as such is supported by the second half of the kārikā.

24

Now, a few words are necessary to introduce the words *prajñapti* and *saṃkleśa* in the next kārikā. We say 'It is a tree', and by saying so we affirm the existence of the tree. We know thereby that in reality there is a thing which is called 'tree.' But some thinkers including a class of Buddhists would utterly deny the existence of such a thing. According to them there is nothing that can be called a tree. That which is known to us as a tree is nothing but a mere understanding (*saṃkhyā*), a designation (*saṃjñā*); it is only making known to others (*prajñapti*), that is, the practical denomination, simply a common use (*vyavahāra*), it is merely a name (*nāman*) and nothing else. And it is only on account of its having the branches, the leaves etc., that it comes under the generally understood term of 'tree.' Similarly there is nothing in fact like a branch, a leaf, and so on, it being merely a current term, an enumeration, a designation, an expression or a distinctive mark of discourse.[1]

[1] DS, § 1308 (see *Buddhist Psychology*, pp. 340-341): katame dhammā paññatti. yā tesaṃ tesaṃ dhammānaṃ sankhā samaññā paññatti voharo nāmaṃ nāmakammaṃ nāmadheyaṃ nirutti vyañjanaṃ abhilāpo. Compare here the theory against that of what is known as *Avayavivāda*, BA with BAP, IX. 79 seq. and ASP, p. 97. There is also a small separate treatise entitled *Avayavi-*

The true literal significance of the word *prajñapti*, 'practical denomination', is 'making known' (*bhāvasādhana*); or 'that by which a thing is made known' (*karaṇasādhana*), *i.e.*, name or term. Or, again, it may mean what is made known (*karmasādhana*).[2] In the present case the word is used in either of the first two senses.

On the use of the word *prajñapti* in Buddhist works Kumārila's observation (TV, I. 3. 12, p. 234) is interesting: śākyādigrantheṣu punar yadapi kiñcit sādhuśabdābhiprāyeṇāvinaṣṭabuddhyā prayuktaṃ tatrāpi prajñapti-vijñapti-paśyatā-tiṣṭhatādiprāyaprayogāt kiñcid evāviplutaṃ labhyate. kim uta yāni prasiddhāpabhraṣṭadeśabhāṣābhyo 'py apabhraṣṭatarāṇi bhikkhave ityevamādīni. See here its Ṭīkā *Nyāyasudhā*.

As regards *saṃkleśa* it has also a special sense in Buddhist works. It is well-known in Buddhist literature along with its opposite term *vyavadāna*. They mean 'impurity and purification' respectively. See BA with BAP, IX. 28. By impurity the mind (*citta*) becomes impure and by purification it becomes pure. This *saṃkleśa* is threefold: (1) *kleśa* 'passion' (*i.e.*, *rāga*, *dveṣa* and *moha*), that can be avoided by right view (*darśana*) and meditation (*bhāvanā*); (2) *karman* 'act,' bad (*akuśala*), and good-impure (*kuśalāsrava*); and (3) *janman* 'birth' (or *phala* 'fruit', recompense that projects the existence). See Vis, pp. 214 ff. Let the following be quoted here from Tk, p. 28 :

tatra kleśakarmajanmātmakas trividhaḥ saṃkleśaḥ.

nirākaraṇa by Paṇḍita Aśoka in the *Six Buddhist Nyāya Tracts*, Bib. Ind., pp. 78 ff. The well-known 'Chariot Simile' in the *Milindapañha*, pp. 27 ff. (II. 1. 1) may also be referred to here. The *Avayavivāda* is established among others in the following works of Brahmanic authority: NS, II. 1. 33 ff., PB with NK on VSt., pp. 41 ff.

[2] ASh, § 107 paññatti pana paññāpiyattā (Skt. *prajñāpyatvāt*) paññatti. paññāpanato (Skt. *prajñāpanataḥ*) vā paññattīti ca duvidhā hoti. Thus the first is *karmasādhana* and the second *bhāvasādhana*,

The following occurs in MSBT, pp. 34-35 :

[kleśa eva śaṃkleśa iti kleśa] saṃkleśaḥ. evaṃ karma-[saṃkleśo] janmasaṃkleśaḥ. kleśo hi pravartamānaḥ svaparātmanor vyābādhakatvāt saṃkleśaḥ. yathoktaṃ sūtre[3] rakto hi rāgaparīta ātmavyābādhāyāpi cetayate paravyābādhāyāpi cetayata ubhayavyābādhāyāpi cetayate. evaṃ dveṣamohayor api jñātavyam iti. karma janma ca saṃkleśapravartanād api saṃkleśaḥ.

3 This is, as pointed out by S. Yamaguchi, from AN, III. 54.

Now, the opponent having his hold on the meaning of the word *prajñapti* as well as *saṃkleśa* well-known among, and accepted by, Vijñānavādins, who maintain that there is, in fact, only *vijñāna* and the external word has no reality at all, proceeds to refute their views, the purpose thereof being that if the existence of external things is once established one will have to accept their *jāti*, too.

The kārikā runs thus:

prajñapteḥ sanimittatvam anyathā dvayanāśataḥ |
saṃkleśasyopalabdheś ca paratantrāstitā matā ||

'The practical denomination (*prajñapti*) has its (objective) cause (nimitta),[1] for otherwise there is the disappearance of the two; (owing to this fact) as well as the experience of

1 For *nimitta* see IV. 25, 27, 75, 77, 78; LA, pp. 225-226: tatra nimittaṃ punar mahāmate jac cakṣurvijñānasyābhāsām āgacchati rūpasaṃjñakam, evaṃ śrotraghrāṇajihvākāyamanovijñānānāṃ śabdagandharasaspraṣṭavyadharmasaṃjñakam, etaṃ nimittam iti vadāmi; p. 228: tatra mahāmate nimittaṃ yat saṃsthānākṛtiviśeṣākārarūpādilakṣaṇaṃ dṛśyate tan nimittam.

impurities (*saṃkleśa-upalabdhi*) (their) existence is regarded as dependent (*paratantra*).[2]'

It says that it must be admitted that *praññapti* must have its *nimitta* ; *i.e.*, the objective cause ; for otherwise there will be no notion of the (*dvaya*)[3], *i.e.*, *grāhya* and *grāhaka* 'the percipient and the perceptible,' in other words, the subject and the object,—a fact that cannot be denied. And, again, owing to *saṃkleśa-upalabdhi* it is also to be admitted that there must be some things (for example, as the Buddhists would say, *śkandhas, dhātus, āyatanas*) that are the causes of these *saṃkleśas*. Thus the things to which the *prajñapti* and the *saṃkleśa-upalabdhi* owe their existence are external and have their origination (*jāti*).

The argument advanced here has two parts: first, owing to the existence of *prajñapti* the existence of its cause, too, is to be admitted; and second, as there is the experience of *saṃkleśas* there must be also their cause. Both the parts of the argument are taken from Buddhist works. As regards the first let us quote here a few lines from the LA, p. 104 :

punar aparaṃ mahāmatir āha. nanu bhagavann abhilāpasadbhāvāt santi sarvabhāvāḥ. yadi punar bhagavan bhāvā na syur abhilāpo na pravartate, pravartate ca. tasmād abhilāpasadbhāvād bhagavan santi sarvabhāvāḥ. bhagavān āha. asatām api mahāmate bhāvānām abhilāpaḥ kriyate yad uta śaśaviṣāṇakūrmaromabandhyāputrādīnāṃ loke dṛṣṭo[4] 'bhilāpaḥ. te ca mahāmate na bhāvā nābhāvā abhilapyante ca. tad yad avocas tvaṃ mahāmate abhilāpasadbhāvāt santi sarvabhāvā iti sa hi vādaḥ prahīṇaḥ.

[2] For the word *paratantra* see IV. 24, 73, 74.

[3] For *dvaya* see II. 14; III. 29, 30; IV. 24, 61, 72, 75, 79, 87.

[4] The printed text reads '*dṛṣṭo* which is evidently wrong.

"M a h ā m a t i says again : 'Is it not, O Blessed One, that all beings exist, for they all have their expressions (*abhilāpa*). If, O Blessed One, there exist no beings there cannot be their expressions. Therefore, all beings exist on account of their expressions.' Says the Blessed One : 'There are, O M a h ā m a t i, expressions also for those which are non-existent, for example, the horn of a hare, the hair of a tortoise, the son of a barren woman, and so on. These are O M a h ā m a t i, neither beings, nor non-beings, yet they are expressed. Therefore, O M a h ā m a t i, the theory, as you say, that owing to expressions all beings exist, is lost.' "[5]

The following couplet from the same work (LA. p. 105) supplies the gist of the above :

> ākāśaṃ śaśaśṛṅgaṃ ca bandhyāyāḥ putra eva ca |
> asanto hy abhilapyante tathā bhāveṣu kalpanā ||

It is quoted in MV, p. 528, where occurs the following :

tatrāpi bhāvakalpanāpratiṣedhamātraṃ nābhāvakalpanā bhāvatvāsiddher eveti vijñeyaṃ. bandhyāputra iti śabdamātram evaitat. nāsyārtha upalabhyate yasyārthasya bhāvatvam abhāvatvaṃ vā syād iti kuto 'nupalabhyamānasvabhāvasya bhāvābhāvakalpanā yokṣyate.

The following is taken also from LA, p. 319 (X. 430):

> asatsu sarvadharmeṣu prajñaptiḥ kriyate mayā |
> abhilāpo vyavahāraś ca bālānāṃ tattvavarjitaḥ ||

It is to be noted that *abhilāpa* and *prajñapti* are synonymous with each other. See DSṇ, § 1308, quoted above, p. 129.

[5] See III. 37 : sarvābhilāpavigataḥ.

Now, as regards the second part we should like to quote a few lines also from a Buddhist work. Candrakīrtti introduces the sixth chapter of the MK thus (MV, p. 137) :

atrāha. vidyata eva skandhā[yatana]dhātavaḥ. kutaḥ tadāśrayasaṃkleśopalabdheḥ. iha yan nāsti na tadā[śraya]saṃkleśopalabdhir asti bandhyāduhitur iva bandhyāsūnoḥ. santi ca rāgādayaḥ kleśāḥ saṃkleśanibandhanaṃ.

'Here (the opponent) says: "Verily there are the *skandhas*,[6] *āyatanas*,[7] and *dhātus*[8]. Why? Because there is experience of *saṃkleśas* arising from them ; and because, on the other hand, there is no experience of *saṃkleśas* arising from that which has no existence, as of a barren woman's daughter from a barren woman's son." ' And there are attachment and other passions, the cause of *saṃkleśa*.

With regard to *prajñāpti* the following may also be quoted in this connexion :

prajñaptir nāmamātreyaṃ[9] lakṣmaṇena na vidyate |
LA, X. 23 (p. 267).

prajñaptimātraṃ tribhavaṃ nāsti vastu svabhāvataḥ |
prajñaptiṃ vastubhāvena kalpayiṣyanti tārkikāḥ||
Op. cit, X. 86 (p. 275).

Now the author proceeds to give his reply to the above *prima facie* case :

6 Five: rūpa, vedanā, saṃjñā, saṃskāra, and vijñāna.

7 Twelve: six organs of sense and their objects, *viz.*, six internal: eye, ear, nose, tongue, body, and mind; and six external: form, sound, odour, taste, contact and ideas.

8 Eighteen: six organs of sense, their six objects, and six kinds of consciousness arising from them.

9 Calcutta ed. has *prajñaptināmamātredam.*

25

prajñapteḥ sanimittatvam iṣyate yuktidarśanāt I
nimittasyānimittatvam iṣyate bhūtadarśanāt II

'Seeing the reason (advanccd above) one wants (to say) that the *prajñapti* has its *nimitta* ; but seeing the reality (we) want (to say) that the *nimitta* is no *nimitta* at all.'

The opponent says, as we have seen, *prajñapti* must have its objective cause, but the argument drawn from the real nature of things points to the conclusion that what is called by him a *nimitta* (cause) is in reality no *nimitta* at all. The reason hereof is advanced in the following kārikā :

26

cittaṃ na saṃspṛśatyarthaṃ nārthābhāsaṃ tathaiva ca I
abhūto hi yataś cārtho nārthābhāsas tataḥ pṛthak II

'The mind does not touch (*i.e.* relate itself to) an object nor does its appearance (*arthābhāsa*), for the object is unreal and its appearance is not different from it.'

The mind has no contact with its object owing to the absence of the object itself. For in this theory (of the Vijñānavādins) there is nothing but the mind (*citta*). Now it goes without saying that the mind having no contact with its object has in fact no contact also with its appearance (*arthābhāsa*). The second half of the kārikā offers the reason hereof. It means that the object is unreal and it being so its appearance which depends on it is also unreal ; and thus both of them being unreal the latter is in this respect not different from the former. This being the case the mind can in no way be related either to its object or its appearance. Therefore it cannot be said, as done in the first half of the preceding kārikā, that *prajñapti* has its *nimitta*. One must remember here that according to the Vijñānavādins there is no reality of external things. Let us read here the following from the MVBT, p. 10:

[°athavā cittacaitasikā rūpato dravyataś ca santīti yeṣāṃ dṛṣṭis teṣāṃ pratiṣedhārtham uktam] abhūtaparikalpo['stīti]. [tasmād] asti dravyataḥ. nāsti rūpaṃ tadvyatiriktaṃ. [nāsti] dravyata iti. kiṃ kāraṇaṃ. yasmād dvayaṃ tatra na vidyate. na hy abhūtaparikalpaḥ kasyacid grāhako nāpi kenacid gṛhyate. kiṃ tarhi. grāhyagrāhakatva [rahitaṃ vastumātraṃ. tathā hi vijñānād bahir na rūpādi gṛhyate svapnādivat vijñānaṃ hi rūpādyā]bhāsam utpadyate. tasmān nirabalambanam eva svapnādāv ivānyatrāpi svabījaparipākād arthābhāsaṃ vijñānam utpadyata ity eva jñeyaṃ, grāhyā[bhāve grāhako na bhavatīti grāhyābhāve grāhakābhāvo na yujyate. ato rūpam abhūtaparikalpān na pṛthagbhūtaṃ].

The opponent may argue here: Well, according to you there are no external things. But you cannot deny that there is an appearance of things round us. It may be a false one in your opinion. Yet, it must have some cause. What is it? It is nothing but the contact of the mind with an object. Thus even for a false notion or impression (*viparyāsa*) the existence of an object must be postulated.

The author rejoins that it is quite true that even false impressions are possible only when there is a contact of the mind with an object, but when that contact itself is never and in no way possible there is no possibility also of them. How to explain, then, the false impressions? He would reply that it is the nature of the mind itself that even in the absence of any object it transforms into various objects under the influence of *vāsanās*. For it is the seed of all (*sarvabīja*) having possessed the power of producing everything. Says Sthiramati (Tk, p. 36, l. 7 on kārikā 17: *sarvabījaṃ hi vijñānam*):

tatra sarvadharmotpādanaśaktyanugamāt sarvabījam.

LA, X. 49 (p. 271) :

cittaṃ vicitraṃ bījākhyaṃ khyāyate cittagocaram |
khyātau kalpenti utpattiṃ bālāḥ kalpadvaye ratāḥ||

Proceeds our author :

27

nimittaṃ na sadā cittaṃ saṃspṛśaty adhvasu triṣu |
animitto viparyāsaḥ kathaṃ tasya bhaviṣyati ||

'Never in the three divisions of time (*i.e.*, the past, the present, and the future) the mind touches any cause (object), how is it then that a false impression would arise without any cause thereof ?'

See IV. 41, 77, 78; LA, X. 123 :

viparyāsasya vastutvād yad yad evopalabhyate |
niḥsvabhāvaṃ bhavet tad dhi sarvathāpi na vidyate||

That in the above kārikās (25-27) the doctrine of the Vijñānavādins is supported by our author is clearly admitted by Ś in the following words introducing the next kārikā (28) :

prajñapteḥ sanimittatvam ityādy etadantaṃ vijñānavādino bauddhasya vacanaṃ bāhyārthavādipakṣapratiṣedhaparam ācāryeṇānumoditam.

Now the Ācārya draws his conclusion from what is said above in this connexion :

28

tasmān na jāyate cittaṃ cittadṛśyaṃ na jāyate |
tasya paśyanti ye jātiṃ khe vai paśyanti te padam ||

'Hence neither the mind (*citta*), nor that which is cognizable by it (*cittadṛśya*) is originated. Those who see its (*i.e.*, of the *citta* and *cittadṛśya*) origination see the (foot-) mark (of birds) in the sky.'

'Hence (*tasmāt*)' refers to the reason advanced above in 26 and 27: because there is no contact of the mind with any object. The belief in the origination of things is as absurd as the seeing of foot-marks of birds flying in the sky.

For this simile compare DP, 93 (=TG, 92):

> ākāse va sakuntānaṃ padaṃ tassa durannayaṃ |

This simile in our kārikā can be better explained by what Buddhaghoṣa has said in his DPA on the above line:

padaṃ tassa durannayan'ti yathā ākāse gacchantānaṃ sakuntānaṃ imassiṃ ṭhāne pādehi akkamitvā gatā idaṃ ṭhānaṃ udarena pahāritvā gatā idaṃ sīsena idaṃ pakkhehīti na sakkā ñātuṃ evam eva...

It says with reference to an Arhat that as in the case of birds flying in the sky it cannot be ascertained that they have gone away stepping on this spot with the legs and striking this spot with the wings, just so...

A similar verse is quoted by Ś in IV. 91. It runs:

> śakunānām ivākāśe gatir naivopalabhyate |

Cf. DP, 92:

> ākāśe'va sakuntānaṃ gati tesaṃ durannayā |

The following is quoted by Ś in his commentary on MU, III. 2. 6:

> śakunīnāmivākāśe jale vāricarasya ca |
> padaṃ yathā na dṛṣyeta tathā jñānavatāṃ gatiḥ ||

On such texts is based the following observation of Ś in his commentary on the BU, IV. 4. 6 (p. 637) :

ta utsahante khe' pi śākunaṃ padaṃ draṣṭum.

For further details see IV. 91.

As regards the main proposition here the following lines from *Āryaratnacūḍaparipṛcchā* (quoted in BAP, IX. 18, p. 392; MV, p. 62; ŚS, p. 235) deserve to be cited :

sa cittaṃ parigaveṣamāṇo nādhyātmaṃ cittaṃ samanupaśyati na bahirdhā cittaṃ samanuśyati.° sa cittamasamanupaśyan cittadhārāṃ paryeṣate kutaś cittasyotpattir iti. tasyevaṃ bhavati. ālambane sati cittam utpadyate. tat kim anyad ālambanam anyac cittaṃ. tadā dvicittatā bhaviṣyati. atha yadevālambanaṃ tad eva cittaṃ. tat kathaṃ cittena cittaṃ samanupaśyati. na ca cittaṃ cittaṃ samanupaśyati. tad yathāpi nāma tayaivāsidhārayā saivāsidhārā na śakyate chettuṃ. na tenaivāṅgulyagreṇa tad evāṅgulyagraṃ śākyate spraṣṭuṃ. evam eva na tenaiva cittena tad eva cittaṃ śakyaṃ draṣṭuṃ.°

And the following is from KP, 149 (§102)[1] :

cittaṃ hi kāśyapa parigaveṣyamāṇaṃ na labhyate. yan na labhyate tan nopalabhyate. tan nātītāṃ. nānāgataṃ, na pratyutpannaṃ. yan nātītaṃ nānāgataṃ na pratyutpannaṃ tat tryadhvasamatikrāntam. yat tryadhvasamatikrāntaṃ tan naivāsti naiva nāsti. yan naivāsti na nāsti tad ajātaṃ. yad ajātaṃ tasya nāsti svabhāvaḥ. yasya nāsti svabhāvaḥ tasya nāsty utpādaḥ. yasya nāsty utpādaḥ tasya nāsti nirodhaḥ.° [2]

[1] See MV, p. 45 (KP = *Ratnakūṭasūtra*): ŚS, p. 233; BAP, IX. 106 (p. 338).

[2] On *citta* see the work, pp. 142-150.

Having shown that the *citta* does not originate the Ācārya comes to his main thesis, the theory of *ajāti* 'non-origination.' Says he :

29

ajātaṃ jāyate yasmād ajātiḥ prakṛtis tataḥ ǀ
prakṛter anyathābhāvo na kathañcid bhaviṣyati ǁ

'As it is one unborn (*ajāta*) that is born (*jāta*), non-birth (*ajāti*) is its very essence (*prakṛti*). And there can be in no way any change of essence.'

For *a* see jāta eva na jāyate, BU, III. 9, 25 ; and *ante* ajātasyaiva dharmasya jātim icchanti vādinaḥ, III. 20, IV. 6 ; and note on IV. 13.

If a man is born it must be said that before his birth he was unborn, and this state of being unborn before the birth is his essence. Now, if it is accepted, and it must be accepted, as his essence, there cannot be his birth which is a change, for essence can in no way change, as essence and change are two contradictory terms. Similarly before a *citta* is produced it must be considered as unproduced, and that being its essence which can never change it cannot be produced at all. This law holds good wherever there is the question of *jāti*.

For the wording of the second half of the kārikā which is found also in III. 21 see MK. XV. 8 :

prakṛter anyathābhāvo nahi jātūpapadyate.

On this point one may be referred to also :

kasya syād anyathābhāvaḥ svabhāvo yadi vidyate ǁ
tasyaiva nānyathābhāvo nāpy anyasyaiva yujyate ǀ
yuvā na jīryate yasmād yasmāj jīrṇo na jīryate ǁ

Op. cit., XIII. 4, 5.

In the next kārikā the author says that an advocate of the theory of *jāti* cannot account for his two propositions : first, *saṃsāra* 'continued existence'[1] is without a beginning,[2] but has an end ; and the second, liberation is with a beginning, but has no end. He says :

30

anāder antavattvaṃ ca saṃsārasya na setsyati |
anantatā cādimato mokṣasya na bhaviṣyati ||

'It would not be established that *saṃsāra* is without a beginning, but has an end ; nor would it be possible that liberation which has a beginning has no end.'

An advocate of the theory of origination has to admit that *saṃsāra* has its origination; and if it is so, it must have a beginning. And that being so, the tenet that *saṃsāra* has no beginning cannot be maintained. Similarly according to him liberation also has its origination, and as such it must be with a beginning, and consequently must have an end, and in that case one cannot say that it has no end.

The point discussed in the next few kārikās is this that it is only when there is the existence of *saṃsāra* that there arises the question as to whether it has or has not a beginning

[1] khandhānaṃ paṭipāṭī ca dhatu-āyatānāna ca |
abbhocchinnaṃ vattamānaṃ saṃsāro ti pavuccati ||

[2] That *saṁsāra* is *anādi* is admitted on all hands. As for Buddhists see MK, XI. 1 with its vṛtti :

pūrvā prajñāyate koṭir nety uvāca mahāmuniḥ |
saṃsāro 'navarāgro hi nāsyādir nāpi paścimaṃ ||

or an end; but in fact it has no existence at all. Says the Ācārya:

31

ādāv ante ca yan nāsti vartamāne'pi tat tathā ।
vitathaiḥ sadṛśāḥ santo 'vitathā iva lakṣitāḥ ॥ [1]

'That which is not at the beginning, nor at the end, is not also in the present, (*i.e.*, in the middle [2]); [3] being like the unreal things still appear as not unreal.'

Compare here what N ā g ā r j u n a says in his MK, XI. 2:

naivāgraṃ nāvaraṃ yasya madhyaṃ tasya kuto bhavet.

'How should that which has neither the anterior point, nor the posterior one, have the middle?'

C a n d r a k ī r t t i comments:

agram ity ādiḥ pūrvaṃ prathamam ucyate. avaram ity avasānaṃ vyavaccheda ucyate. yasya saṃsārasya ādir antaś ca pratiṣiddhaḥ tasya madhyaṃ kuto bhaviṣyati. tataś ca saṃjñāmātrakam eva viparyāsaparavaśamānasānāṃ saṃsāra ādimadhyāvasānavirahitatvād ākāśavad alātacakravad iti bhāvaḥ.

The following may also be quoted here:

yassa n'atthi purā pacchā
majjhaṃ tassa kuo siyā ॥ ĀS, I. 4. 4. 3.

ādāv ante ca yan nāsti
madhye'pi ca na tat tathā । *Nayopadeśa*, 14.

[1] See II. 6.

[2] yad ādāv ante ca nāsti vastu mṛgatṛṣṇikādi tan madhye'pi nāstīti niścitaṃ loke. Ś on II. 6.

[3] *Cf.* adāv eva hi yan nāsti kāraṇāsambhavāt svayam ।
vartamāne'pi tan nāsti nāśaḥ syāt tatra kīdṛśaḥ ॥ YV. III. 11. 13.

na yat purastād uta yan na paścān
madhye ca tan na vyapadeśamātram |
bhūtaṃ prasiddhaṃ ca pareṇa yad yat
tad eva tat syād iti me manīṣā ||

BP, XI. 28. 21.

That *saṃsāra* has neither a beginning nor an end is fully discussed in MK with MV, XI.

Now, there are two kinds of things, one kind experienced in dream (*svapna*), and the other in wakefulness (*jāgrat*); and it has been thoroughly established in Book II (Vaitathya Prakaraṇa) that there is no difference between the states of dream and wakefulness, and so the things experienced in the latter are as false as those in the former. The author here puts forth the same argument in the same language with a view to show that the thing which is as false as that in one's dream cannot come into being in reality, and so the *jātivāda* cannot stand. He says:

32

saprayojanatā teṣāṃ svapne'pi pratipadyate |
tasmād ādyantavattvena mithyaiva khalu te smṛtāḥ ||

'That the things have some purpose in dream also is known; hence owing to their beginning and end, indeed, they are regarded as false.'

One may object to the falsity of the phenomena of waking experience on the ground that they really serve some purpose; as for instance, water, when it is drunk, quenches one's thirst, while the phenomena in dream are not such. To this the author replies in the above kārikā. His point is this that the phenomena of dream are linked with one another by some purpose no less than those of waking experience. In dream also one drinks water to quench one's thirst. So the phenomena like those in dream having a beginning and an end have no reality at all; for that which has a beginning and an end cannot be real, as the mirage.

This kārikā is identical with II. 7. See the note on it for a different reading.

It is said that the things seen in the waking state are false, because, as regards nature, they have no difference from those seen in dreams which are evidently false. But why the latter are so the author says in the next few kārikās as in II. 1-10:

33

sarve dharmā mṛṣā svapne kāyasyāntar[1] nidarśanāt |
saṃvṛte[2] 'smin pradeśe vai bhūtānāṃ darśanaṃ kutaḥ ||

'All things in dream are false as they are seen within the body; for how can objects be seen in this confined space (of the body)?'

[1] For *a* see II. 1[c].

[2] II. 1[d], 4[d]

34

na yuktaṃ darśanaṃ gatvā kālasyāniyamād[1] gatau |
pratibuddhaś ca vai sarvas tasmin deśe na vidyate ||[2]

'(In dream) the seeing (of a thing at a distance) having gone (up to it) is not reasonable; for there is no fixed rule of time for the act of going (there), and no persons being awake exist in the place (where they dream themselves to be).'

[1] *Cf.* adīrghatvāc ca kālasya, II. 2[a].

[2] Identical with II. 2[c—d].

35

mitrādyaiḥ saha saṃmantrya prabuddho[1] na prapadyate ।
gṛhītaṃ cāpi yat kiñcit pratibuddho na paśyati ॥

'When awake, he does not find his friends and others with whom he had deliberated, nor does he see all that which he had (then in dream) grasped.'

[1] With a large number of MSS. I read this for *sambuddha* in printed editions.

36

svapne cāvastukaḥ kāyaḥ pṛthag anyasya darśanāt ।
yathā kāyas tathā sarvaṃ cittadṛśyam avastukam ॥

'In dream the (active) body is unreal, for (quite) a different body is seen (in the place where one dreams); and as the body so all the things which are cognizable by the mind are unreal.'

37

grahaṇāj jāgaritavat taddhetuḥ svapna iṣyate ।
taddhetutvāc ca tasyaiva saj jāgaritam iṣyate ॥

'The experience (of dream) being like (that of) wakefulness, it (wakefulness) is considered to be the cause of dream; and that being so it is (also) considered that wakefulness is real only to him (*i.e.*, the dreamer).'

It is a fact that cause and its effect must be of the same nature. Accordingly wakefulness and dream being the cause and the effect respectively must be of the same nature. So if a dream is false wakefulness is also false. And as a dream appears to be real only to the dreamer, so wakefulness, too, is real only to an ordinary unenlightened man.[1]

[1] I think the logical order of the following four kārikās, *viz.*, 38-41 should be as follows: 39, 41, 38 and 40. For the kārikās 39 and 41 with 32-37 form the same subject of discussion, *i.e.*, the equality of the states of dream and wakefulness, while the kārikās 38 and 40 are meant for showing the impossibility of origination directly. The traditional order is shown in the present edition by the figures in parenthesis.

38 (39)

asaj jāgarite dṛṣṭvā svapne paśyati tanmayaḥ |
asat svapne 'pi dṛṣṭvā ca pratibuddho na paśyati || [1]

'In the waking state one sees an unreal thing and being absorbed in it sees it (also) in a dream. And in a dream, too, one sees an unreal thing, but does not see it when one awakes.'

To see the unreal is common to both the states, dream and wakefulness; the only difference between them is, however as stated in the kārikā itself.

[1] yathaiva kāmān supinānti seviya
pratibuddhasetuḥ(?) puruṣo na paśyati | SR, IX, p. 29.

39 (41)

viparyāsād yathā jāgrad acintyān bhūtavat spṛśet [1] |
tathā svapne viparyāsād dharmāṃs tatraiva paśyati ||

[1] For the use of √spṛś in such cases see IV. 27.

'As in the waking state[2] through mistake one may see unthinkable things[3] as real, so in dream it is owing to mistake that one sees things only in that (state).'

[2] The word *jāgrad* is taken here in the locative sense. See III. 29 together with Ś's commentary thereon and on IV. 40 (41): '*jāgraj jāgarite. Cf.* IV. 65 and BU, IV. 3. 14 with the comm. *jāgraj jāgaritadeśe.* See also IV. 61, note 3.

[3] Such as *rajju-sarpa* '*string serpent*,' etc.—Ś.

Having established above that a thing which are as false as that in a dream cannot come into being the author shows his conclusion of the *ajātivāda* by some other arguments:

40 (38)

utpādasyāprasiddhatvād ajaṃ sarvam udāhṛtam I
na ca bhūtād abhūtasya saṃbhavo 'sti kathañcana II

'As origination is not established all are said to be without origination. There is in no way origination of the non-existent from the existent.'

The origination of the non-existent, such as the horns of a hare, etc., is in no way seen.—Ś.

In the next kārikā the author says with regard to causation referred to just now that it itself is not reasonable:

41 (40)

nāsty asaddhetukam asat sad asaddhetukaṃ tathā I
sac ca saddhetukaṃ nāsti saddhetukam asat kutaḥ II

'There is no non-existent arising from the non-existent, nor is there any existent arising from the non-existent; again there is no existent arising from the existent and where is the non-existent arising from the existent?'

Here are four points :

(*i*) An unreal thing cannot have an unreal cause,
(*ii*) nor can a real thing have an unreal cause; again,
(*iii*) a real thing cannot have a real cause,
(*iv*) nor can an unreal thing have a real cause.

Let us read here the following from MK, XXI. 12:

(*iii*) na bhāvāj jāyate bhāvo
(*ii*) bhāvo 'bhāvān na jāyate ।
(*i*) [nābhāvāj jāyate 'bhāvo
(*iv*) 'bhāvo bhāvān na jāyate ॥][1]

This is fully explained in MV. See the following from MK:

sadbhūtaḥ kārakaḥ karma sadbhūtaṃ na karoty ayam ।
kārako nāpy asadbhūtaḥ karmāsadbhūtam īhate ॥ VIII. 1.

satā ca kriyate nāsan nāsatā kriyate ca sat ।
kartrā sarve prasajyante doṣās tatra ta eva hi ॥ VIII. 8.

nāsadbhūto 'pi sadbhūtaṃ sadasadbhūtam eva vā ।
karoti kārakaḥ karma pūrvoktair eva hetubhiḥ ॥ VIII. 10.

[1] These last two lines of the kārikā missing in Sanskrit are rightly reconstructed by Poussin from the Tibetan which runs as follows:

dṅos. med. dṅos. med mi. skye. ste |
dṅos. med. dṅos. las. mi. skyeḥo ||

This kārikā is identical with CŚ, 364 (XV. 14) of Āryadeva.

Having thus refuted the *jātivāda* and established thereby the *ajātivāda* of the Buddhists the author goes on to reconcile some statements made by the Buddhas themselves, which appear to be irreconcilable with the *ajātivāda* doctrine.

These statements, some of which are quoted in the foot-note,[1] are in support of *jāti*. Besides, the Buddhas are found to have instructed their followers on causation, as their well-known *pratītyasamutpāda* 'dependent origination' itself shows very clearly.[2] It must, therefore, be admitted that the Buddhas have not denied *jāti* altogether. The Ācarya takes up the point and gives his reply in the following two kārikās, the first of which runs thus :

42

upalambhāt samācārād astivastutvavādinām |
jātis tu deśitā buddhair ajātes trasatāṃ sadā ||

'But *jāti* is taught by the Buddhas for those who from their perception and common practice hold that things exist (in reality) and are afraid of (the doctrine of) *ajāti*.'

These people who are intent upon the reality of things around them are of a lower order and are consequently frightened when they hear of the doctrine of *ajāti* and *nairātmya* (absence of *ātman*, i.e., *svabhāva* 'nature') as taught by the Buddhas.[3] The Buddhas are, however,

1 PSP, p. 9: buddhā bhagavanta utpannāḥ, p. 79: pañcendriyāṇi utpatsyante, p. 91: arhantaḥ samyak saṃbuddhā loka utpatsyante; SN, IV, p. 14: yo bhikkhave cakkhussa uppādo ṭhiti abhinibbatti pātubhāvo; MV, p. 145: uktaṃ hi bhagavatā trīṇīmāni bhikṣavaḥ saṃskṛtasya saṃskṛtalakṣaṇāni. saṃskṛtasya bhikṣava utpādo'pi prajñāyate vyayo'pi sthityanyathātvam apīti. na ca avidyamānasya kharaviṣāṇasyeva jātyādilakṣaṇam asti. See also AN, I, p. 162.

2 SN, IV, p. 33: cakkhuñ ca paticca rūpe ca uppajjati cakkhuviññāṇaṃ.

3 advitīyaṃ śivadvāraṃ kudṛṣṭīnāṃ bhayaṅkaram |
viṣayaḥ sarvabuddhānām iti nairātmyam ucyate ||
asya dharmasya nāmno'pi bhayam utpadyate 'sataḥ
balavān nāma ko dṛṣṭaḥ parasya na bhayaṅkaraḥ ||

CŚ, 288-289.

On the word *nairātmya* Candrakīrtti writes here: tatrātmā nāma yo 'parāyattasvarūpaḥ svabhāvaḥ [tadabhāvo nairātmyam]. Tibetan: de. med. pa. ni. bdag. med. paho.

very kind-hearted and so in order to lead them easily and gradually to the truth (*tattvāvatāra*)[4] followed the disposition of their minds and preached to them of *jāti*, though in fact there is nothing of the kind. The author himself says elsewhere (III. 15) that the creation described differently in the Upaniṣads with illustrations of earth, iron, sparks of fire and such other things is meant only as a means devised for making one 'descend to', *i.e.*, realize, truth (*upāyaḥ so'vatārāya*). This act is called *avatāraṇasandhi* 'intention of making one descend' of the Buddha.[5] It has found its expression in Buddhist works from which some passages are quoted here in the foot-note.[6]

4 See MV, p. 340.

5 MS, XII. 16-17: tatrāvatāraṇābhisandhiḥ śrāvakeṣu draṣṭavyaḥ, śāsanāvatāraṇārtham anuttrāsāya rūpādyastitvadeśanāt. The word *sandhi* is here in the sense of *abhisandhi*.

6 lokāvatāraṇārthaṃ ca bhāvā nāthena deśitāḥ |
trāso nārabhyate 'dṛṣṭe dṛṣṭe 'paiti sa sarvaśaḥ |
niyamenaiva kiñcijjñe tena trāso vidhīyate || CŚ, 283.

Candrakīrtti on CŚ, 183:

tattvāvatārasopānabhūtatvāt pravṛttyupadeśo'pi kartavyaḥ.
lokāvatāropāyatvāt sadasadādideśanānām.

Op. cit., 196.

dharmadhātor asambhedād yānabhedo 'sti na prabho |
yānatritayam ākhyātaṃ tvayā sattvāvatārataḥ ||

NSt, 21.

nānavadhārya yathārthaṃ śūnyatāṃ kaścic chaktaḥ saṁsāre saṅgam avadhūya nirvāṇaspṛhām utpādayitum. sa ca śūnyatārtho jagatām atīvottrāsakaratvād apriyāvedananipuṇapuruṣeṇa rājñaḥ priyabhāryāmaraṇakramāvedana-saumanasyotpādanavat kayāpi yuktyā viduṣāvatāryaḥ.

CŚ,[a] p. 514.

astitvanāstyadṛṣṭipatitānāṃ teṣām uttrāsaḥ syād iti uttrāsyamānā mahāmate dūre bhavanti mahāyānāt. LA, p. 167.

etāni kāśyapa pañca bhikṣuśatāni dṛṣṭiprаskandhānīmāṃ gambhīrāṃ dharmadeśanāṃ nāvataranti nāvagāhante nādhimucyanta uttrasyanti saṃtrasyanti santrāsam āpadyante. KP (=*Ratnakūṭa*) in MV, pp. 337-338.

As regards the different modes of teaching of the Buddhas he following couplet may be quoted :

> deśanā lokanāthānāṃ sattvāśayavaśānugā |
> bhidyate bahudhā loka upāyair bahubhiḥ kila||[7]

'The teachings of the Lords of the worlds (*i.e.*, the Buddhas) following the disposition of the people differ in the world in many ways according to the diversity of methods.'[8]

That was their 'skilfulness in method (*upāyakauśalya)* by which all discrepancies in their teachings are explained.

tatra tathāgato mahākāruṇiko lokatrāsapadaparihārārthaṃ vyavahāravaśād uktavān utpadyante nirudhyante ca na cātra kasyacid dharmasyotpādo na nirodha iti. BAP, p. 589.

evam ukte bhagavān āyuṣmantaṃ śāriputram etad avocat. alaṃ śāriputra etenārthena bhāṣitena. tat kasya hetoḥ. uttrasiṣyati śāriputrāyaṃ sadevako loko 'sminn arthe vyākriyamāṇe. SP, II, p. 36.

āha. yad etad uktaṃ bhagavatā saṃskṛtā dharmā utpadyante nirudhyante cety asya tathāgatabhāṣitasya ko 'bhiprāyaḥ. āha. utpādanirodhābhiniviṣṭaḥ kulaputra lokasaṃniveśaḥ. tatra tathāgato mahākāruṇiko lokasyottrāsapadaparihārārthaṃ vyavahāravaśād uktavān utpadyante nirudhyante ca. na cātra kasyacid dharmasyotpādo na nirodha iti. ŚS, p. 263.

See also MN, I. 136-137; SR, pp. 70-71.

7 *Bodhicittavivarana* (Tib. version) 97-98. It is quoted in the Buddhist section of SSD. See *The Basic Conception of Buddhism*, pp. 27ff. Sometimes there is in *d* of the kārika *punaḥ* for *kila*.

8 See

> kṛtvā dharmeṣv avasthānaṃ tattvaṃ deśemi yoginām |
> tattvaṃ pratyātmagatikaṃ kḷpyakalpena varjitaṃ ||
> deśemi jinaputrāṇaṃ neyaṃ bālāna deśanāḥ |
> vicitrā'hi yathā māyā dṛśyate na ca vidyate |
> deśanāpi tathā citrā deśyate vyabhicāriṇī ||
> deśanā hi yad anyasya tad anyasyāpy adeśanā |
> āture āture yadvad bhiṣag dravyaṃ prayacchati ||
>
> LA. pp. 48-49.

See also *Op. cit*, X. 611-613 (pp. 340-341); SP, pp. 44 ff.; SS, pp. 14-15; MV, pp. 359-360, 369-372.

Now, when there is in fact no *jāti* it is certainly no good to teach it and consequently some evil would result from such teaching. The author, however, says that in reality there would arise no evil, or if it actually does, it would be very small which can easily be overcome (by following the path of the truth):

43

ajātes trasatāṃ teṣām upalambhād viyanti ye |
jātidoṣā na setsyanti doṣo'py alpo bhaviṣyati ||

'Those who (being instructed of *ajāti*) go asunder owing to the perception (of things) and are afraid of (thinking) *ajāti*, are not affected with the evils resulting from (the perception of) *jāti*; (or if there be any evil) the evil will be a small one.'

The reality of a thing cannot be proved on the evidence of mere perception and common practice. For an elephant called up by illusion (*māyāhastin*) cannot exist in fact though we all may see it moving or carrying men. Thus the author says that it is only on account of perception and common practice that it is said of a thing that it exists, but in reality it does not:

44

upalambhāt samācārān māyāhastī yathocyate |
upalambhāt samācārād asti vastu tathocyate ||

'As an elephant called up by illusion is said to exist owing to perception and common practice, so on the same grounds it is said of a thing that it exists.'[1]

[1] For *māyāhastin* see LA, X, 126:
māyāhastī yathā citraṃ patrāṇi kanakā yathā |
tathā dṛśyaṃ nṛṇāṃ khyāti citte ajñānavāsite ||

TSN, 27-28 :

mayākṛtaṃ mantravaśāt khyāti hastyātmanā yathā |
ākāramātraṃ tatrāsti hastī nāsti tu sarvathā ||
svabhāvaḥ kalpito hastī paratantras tadākṛtiḥ |
yas tatra hastyabhāvo 'sau pariniṣpanna iṣyate |

In the next kārikā the author says, as a Vijñānavādin can say, that there is only *vijñāna* (=*citta*) 'mind', and nothing else, yet it appears variously :

45

jātyābhāsaṃ calābhāsaṃ vastvābhāsaṃ tathaiva ca |
ajācalam avastutvaṃ vijñānaṃ śāntam advayam ||

' There is only *vijñāna* without the two (*advaya*),[1] which is quiescent (free from all sorts of disturbances), it has no origin (*aja* 'unborn'),[2] it does not move (*acala*), nor is it an object (*avastutva*),[3] yet it appears to have an origin (*jātyābhāsa*), it appears to admit movements (*calābhāsa*), and it also appears to be an object.

It is to be noted here that *vijñāna*,[4] *citta* and *manas* are synonyms. See LA. X. 459 :

cittaṃ vikalpo vijñaptir mano vijñanam eva ca |
ālayas tribhavaś ceṣṭā ete cittasya paryayāḥ ||

[1] The word *dvaya* refers to *grāhya* and *grāhaka* ' the percipient and the perceptible' respectively.

[2] But truly speaking according to the Buddhist theory it cannot be described even as *aja* See IV. 74.

[3] Literally, one that has no quality of an object.

[4] Here in the kārikā under discussion the word *vijñāna* does not refer to Ātman or Brahman of the Vedāntist. The following kārikā (46) using *citta* which alludes to *vijñāna* in the present kārikā clearly bears it out. Ś takes here *vijñāna* as *vijñapti*, but in the next kārikā (IV. 46) he interprets it in the sense of *ātman* (: evam eva yathoktaṃ vijñānaṃ jātyādirahitam advayam ātmatattvaṃ vijānantaḥ).

Ak. II. 34:

cittaṃ mano'tha vijñānam ekārtham.

Cf. SN, II. 94.

What follows from this discussion is shown in the next kārikā :

46

evam na jāyate cittam[1] evaṃ dharmā ajāḥ smṛtāḥ |
evam eva vijānanto na patanti viparyaye ||[2]

'Thus the mind is not originated, and thus the objects[3] are declared to be without origination. Those who know it in this way do not fall into error.'

[1] *Cf.* YV, III. 13-15 : evaṃ na jāyate kiñcit.

[2] See IV, 58.

[3] Ś takes here the word to imply *ātmans*, but in IV. 54 to mean external things (*bāhyadharmāḥ*) ; and in IV. 58 he writes *ātmāno 'nye ca dharmāḥ*.

This truth is profusely illustrated in the next kārikās (47-52) by the simile of a fire-brand (*alāta*). The author says, that as the different appearances of a fire-brand in motion, such as a circle or a straight line, do not come into existence from a thing other than itself, nor do they go out to a place other than itself when it is at rest, and at the same time they do not enter into itself, even so when the mind vibrates its appearances in the form of different objects they do not come into being from any thing other than itself, and when it does not vibrate they do not go out anywhere, nor do they enter into it:

47

ṛjuvakrādikābhāsam alātaṃ spanditaṃ[1] yathā |
grahaṇagrāhakābhāsaṃ vijñānaṃ spanditaṃ tathā[2] ||

'As a fire-brand being moved appears to be straight, or crooked, and so on, even so the mind when it moves appears as the perceiver (*i.e.*, subject) and the perceptible (*i.e.*, object).'

1 Comparing and considering all the readings in kārikās 47-51 in connection with the use of *vijñāna* and the derivatives of the root *spand* I think in the present kārikā one may incline to read *alātaṃ spanditaṃ* and not *alataspanditaṃ*, a compound word, though the former is not supported by any MS consulted by me. In either case the import of the karika is the same.

2 Cf. *cittaspanditam* (with the variant *cittaṃ spandati vai sarvam*) in IV. 72, with *vijñānaṃ spanditam* (or *vijñānaspanditaṃ*) in *d* of the present kārikā.

48

aspandamānam ālātam anābhāsam ajaṃ yathā |
aspandamānaṃ vijñānam anābhāsam ajaṃ tathā ||

'As a fire-brand when it does not move has no appearance (of its being straight, crooked, etc.), and is (thus) 'unborn', even so when the mind does not move it has no appearance (of any subject or object), and is (thus) 'unborn.'

For *anābhāsa* in the text cf. *arūpaka*, III. 36.

In the text *ālāta* supported by many MSS, is, according to lexicons, another form of *alāta*.

49

alāte spandamāne vai nābhāsā anyatobhuvaḥ ।
na tato 'nyatra nispandān nālātaṃ praviśanti te ॥

'The appearances in a moving fire-brand are not produced from anything other than it, and when it is at rest they are not in a place other than it (the fire-brand), nor do they enter into it.'

50

na nirgatā alātāt te dravyatvābhāvayogataḥ ।[1]
vijñāne 'pi tathaiva syur ābhāsasyāviśeṣataḥ ॥

'They (*i.e.*, the appearances) do not go out from the fire-brand, for they have no qualities of a substance (*dravya*), and with reference to the mind, too, they must be the same, for there is no difference in appearances.'

It is a substance, *dravya*, that can move from one place to another, but appearances are not substances, and hence they cannot move. The second half of the kārikā says that as an appearance there is no difference whatsoever in the two cases, that is, the case of a fire-brand and that of the mind.

1 See IV. 52^{a-b}.

51

vijñāne spandamāne vai nābhāsā anyatobhuvaḥ ।
na tato 'nyatra vijñānān na vijñānaṃ viśanti te ॥

'When the mind vibrates the appearances are not produced from anything other than it and when it is at rest they are not in a place other than it (the mind), nor do they enter into the mind.'

52

na nirgatās te vijñānād dravyatvābhāvayogataḥ I [1]
kāryakāraṇatābhāvād yato 'cintyāḥ sadaiva te II

'They do not go out from the mind, for they have no qualities of a substance, and as there is no state of cause and effect they are always unthinkable.'

All this is Buddhistic, and so are also arguments and the words as the following quotations will show :

sa mahārāja tāvān abdhātur utpadyamāno na kutaścid āgacchati° niruddhyamāno na kvacid gacchati.

Pitāputrasamāgamasūtra quoted in ŚS, pp. 247.

evam eva kulaputra teṣāṃ tathāgatānāṃ kāyapariniṣpattir na kutaścid daśa diśi lokād āgatā nāpi kvacid daśa diśi loke gacchati.° tad yathāpi nāma kulaputra vīṇāyāḥ śabda utpadyamāno na kutaścid āgacchati nirudhyamāno 'pi na kvacid gacchati na kvacit saṃkrāmati.°

ASP, pp. 515-516.

anyato nāpi cāyātaṃ na tiṣṭhati na gacchati |
māyātaḥ ko viśeṣo 'sya yan mūḍhaiḥ satyataḥ kṛtam ||
māyayā nirmitaṃ yacca hetubhir yac ca nirmitaṃ |
āyāti tat kutaḥ kutra yāti ceti nirūpyatām ||

BA, IX. 143-144.

Cf. āgacchaty anyato nāgnir indhane 'gnir na vidyate |

MK. X. 13.

atha paṇḍitu kaś ci mārgate
kuta 'yam āgatu kutra yāti vā |
vidiśo diśa sarvi mārgato
nāgatir nāsya gatiś ca labhyati ||

quoted in MV, p. 216; BAP, p. 533; ŚS, p. 240.

1 See IV. 50^{b-d}

utpannasyāgatir nāsti niruddhasya gatis tathā |
evaṃ sati kathaṃ naiva bhavo māyopamo bhavet ||[2]
CŚ, 360.

[2] This is reconstructed by the present author from the Tibetan text which runs:

skyes. pa. la. ni. ḥoṅ. ba. daṅ |
de. bzin. ḥgags. la. ḥgro. ba. med |
de. ltar. yin. na. ci. lta. bur |
srid. pa. sgyu. ma. ḥdra. ma. yin ||

It is shown (IV. 14-18, 52) that there is no causation (*hetuphalābhāva* or *kāryakāraṇatābhāva*). This is further explained in the following kārikā :

53

dravyaṃ dravyasya hetuḥ syād anyad anyasya caiva hi |
dravyatvam anyabhāvo vā dharmāṇāṃ nopapadyate ||

'A substance can be a cause of another substance ; and a thing can be the cause of a different thing only; but it is unreasonable to hold that things can have substantiality or mutual difference.'

A substance must have three qualities, (i) origination (*utpāda*), (ii) change (*vyaya*), and (iii) continuance (*sthiti*). But in fact there is no such thing called substance, as the Buddhists hold. See MK with MV, VII ; AN, I. 152. Again, it is well-known that from one thing a different thing is produced, and not the same thing from the same thing ; for instance, from a seed there is the sprout. Thus there is a difference between a cause and its effect. But in reality this difference, too, cannot be maintained. See MK, X.1 and 15 :

yad indhanaṃ sa ced agnir ekatvaṃ kartṛkarmaṇoḥ |
anyaś ced indhanād agnir indhanād apy ṛte bhavet ||
agnīndhanābhyāṃ vyākhyāta ātmopādānayoḥ kramaḥ |
sarvo niravaśeṣeṇa sārdhaṃ ghaṭapaṭādibhiḥ ||

The author arrives at the conclusion :

54

evaṃ na cittajā dharmāś cittaṃ vāpi na dharmajam I
evaṃ hetuphalājātiṃ praviśanti manīṣiṇaḥ II

'Thus the things are not produced from the mind (*citta*= *vijñāna*), nor the mind from the things. And thus the wise enter into (the doctrine of) the non-origination of cause and effect.'

Cf. IV. 46.

55

yāvad dhetuphalāveśas tāvad dhetuphalodbhavaḥ I
kṣīṇe hetuphalāveśe nāsti hetuphalodbhavaḥ II

'As long as there is a strong adherence to cause and effect there is the origination of cause and effect, but when the strong adherence to cause and effect is lost there is no existence of cause and effect.'

Here and in the next kārikā (56) the word *āveśa* in the text is the same as *abhiniveśa* (IV. 75, 79) 'strong adherence.' These are synonyms (to which *graha* and *grāha*, may be added). The latter is frequently used in Buddhist works in which it is clearly shown that not only cause and effect but everything round us owes its existence to one's stong adherence to it. The following may be cited here :

tad yathāpi nāma mahārāja puruṣaḥ suptaḥ svapnāntare piśācena paritāpyamāno bhītaḥ sammoham āpadyate. sa śayita-vibuddhas taṃ piśācaṃ taṃ ca moham anusmaret. tat kiṃ manyase mahārāja saṃvidyate svapne piśācaḥ saṃmoho vā.

yāvad evam eva mahārāja bālo 'śrutavān pṛthagjanaś cakṣuṣā rūpāṇi dṛṣṭvā upekṣāsthānīyāny abhiniviśate 'bhiniviṣṭaḥ san muhyati mūḍho mohajaṃ karmābhisaṃskaroti.

ŚS, p. 254.

bālo mañjuśrīr aśrutavān pṛthagjano 'tyantaparinirvṛtān sarvadharmān aprajānāna ātmānaṃ paraṃ copalabhate, upalabhy [ābhiniviśate abhiniviṣṭaḥ san rajyate duṣyate muhyate. sa rakto duṣṭamūḍhaḥ san] trividhaṃ karmābhisaṃskaroti.

MV, p. 296.

yas tu bhāvasvarūpam adhyāropya tadvigamāvigamata etā dṛṣṭīr utpādyābhiniviśate. tasyām abhiniveśo nirvāṇapuragāminaṃ panthānaṃ viruṇaddhi, sāṃsārikeṣu ca duḥkheṣu niyojayatīti vijñeyaṃ.

Op. cit., p. 537.

56

yāvad dhetuphalāveśaḥ saṃsāras tāvad āyataḥ |
kṣīṇe hetuphalāveśe saṃsāro nopapadyate ||

'As long as there is a strong adherence to cause and effect the world is extended, but when that strong adherence to cause and effect is lost the world is not possible.'

Thus having propounded to some extent the *vijñānavāda* our author proceeds incidentally to show also with the Buddhists that neither of the two theories, *śāśvatavāda* 'the theory that everything is eternal' and *ucchedavāda* 'the theory that every thing has annihilation'[1] can be maintained :

[1] These two views are specially with regard to soul and world. See, for nstance, DN, I. 13, 39; MK XXVII.

57

samvṛtyā [1] jāyate sarvaṃ śāśvataṃ tena nāsti vai |
svabhāvena [2] hy ajaṃ sarvam ucchedas tena nāsti vai ||

'In the practical truth (*saṃvṛti*) everything comes into being; hence there is nothing eternal. (On the other hand), everything is naturally without origination; hence there is no annihilation.'

It says that in the practical truth we say that a thing comes into being. In that case we cannot hold, so far as the practical truth is concerned, that there is any eternal thing. For that which has origination cannot be eternal, as an earthen jar. Again, as we have seen above, nothing has naturally any origination, and one that has no origination can have no annihilation also.

It is a fact that a sprout comes out only if there is a seed and not otherwise. Now the sprout is neither identical with, nor different from the seed. When there is a sprout the seed is not completely destroyed, nor is it absolutely in the same state as before. Hence it can be said that there is neither eternality nor annihilation.[3]

1 See IV. 73.

2 All MSS. and editions examined by me read *sadbhāvena* for *svabhāvena* in c, yet I think the latter to be the actual reading. Everywhere in similar cases the author employs *svabhāva* (III. 22, IV. 8, 10, 23, 81) and not *sadbhāva*. In the same sense he uses also the word *prakṛti* (III. 21, IV. 9, 29, 91, 92, 93, 94). If one accepts the reading *sadbhāvena* the meaning will be, according to Ś, 'in transcendental truth' (*paramārthasadbhāvena-pāramārthikasattayā*). That the reading is *svabhāvena* is supported also by IV. 29 in which we read *ajātiḥ prakṛtiḥ*.

3 bījasya sato yathāṅkuro na ca yo bīja sa caiva aṅkuro |
na ca anyu tato na caiva tad evam anuccheda-aśāśvatadharmatā ||
mudrāt pratimudra dṛśyate mudrasaṃkrānti na copalabhyate |
na ca tatra na caiva sānyato evaṃ saṃskāra 'nucchedaśāśvatāḥ ||
LV, 210.

Some of the teachers hold either of these two theories, the *śāśvatavāda* 'the theory of eternality,' and *ucchedavāda* 'the theory of annihilation.' But in the teachings of the Buddhas who maintain the Middle Path (*madhyamā pratipad*), there is no room for any one of them. So his doctrine is said to be free from both the theories (*anuccheda aśāśvata*).[4] This view of the Buddhists is too well-known to require here any particular treatment.

The Buddhists also proclaim that there are two truths (*satya*) which they call *saṃvṛti satya* 'practical or empirical truth' and *paramārtha satya* 'absolute or supreme or transcendental truth,' corresponding to *vyavahāranaya* and *paramārthanaya* of the Jainas, and *vyāvaharika satya* and *pāramārthika satya* of Ś respectively.[5]

śūnyatā ca na cocchedaḥ saṃsāraś ca na śāśvataṃ |
karmaṇo vipraṇāśaś ca dharmo buddhena deśitaḥ || MK, XVII. 20.

yasmāt pravartate bhāvas tenocchedo na jāyate |
yasmān nivartate bhāvas tena nityo na jāyate || CŚ, X. 25.

utpādabhaṅgarahito lokaḥ khapuṣpasannibhaḥ |
sadasan nopalabdho 'yaṃ prajñayā kṛpayā ca te ||
śāśvatocchedavarjaś ca lokaḥ svapnasamaḥ sadā | LV, X. 1-2.

4 anekārtham anānārtham anucchedam aśāśvataṃ |
etat tal lokanāthānāṃ buddhānāṃ śāsanāmṛtaṃ || MK, XVIII. 11.

For the *ucchedavāda* and *śāśvatavāda* in Brahmaṇical literature see Vyāsa on YS, II. 15, and MB, XII. 222 :

ucchedaniṣṭhā nehāsti bhāvaniṣṭhā na vidyate | 6
evaṃ sati ka ucchedaḥ śāśvato vā kathaṃ bhavet | 5

5 dve satye samupāśritya buddhānāṃ dharmadeśanā |
lokasaṃvṛtisatyaṃ ca satyaṃ ca paramārthataḥ ||
ye 'nayor na vijānanti vibhāgaṃ satyayor dvayoḥ |
te tattvaṃ na vijānanti gambhīraṃ buddhaśāsane ||
vyavahāram anāśritya paramārtho na deśyate |
paramārtham anāgamya nirvāṇaṃ nādhigamyate || MK, XXIV. 8-10.
duve saccāni akkhāsi saṃbuddho vadataṃ varo |
sammutiṃ paramatthaṃ ca tatiyaṃ nūpalabbhati ||

quoted by Buddhaghoṣa in the *Aṭṭhakathā* on KV, p. 30; *Sumangalavilāsinī* (DN: *Poṭṭhapādasutta*), p. 251.

It may be observed here that these two truths are not specified in the Upaniṣads and I am inclined to think that Ś has accepted them in his system from the Buddhists through G a u d a p ā d a.

satya ime duvi lokavidūnāṃ diṣṭa svayaṃ aśruṇitva pareṣāṃ |
saṃvṛti yā ca tathā paramārtho satyu na sidhyati kiṃ ca tṛtīyu ||
Pitāputrasamāgama quoted in BAP, pp. 361-362.

saṃvṛtiḥ paramārthaś ca satyadvayam idaṃ matam | BA, IX. 2.

On the explanation of *saṃvṛti* see BAP, pp. 352 ff : saṃvriyata āvriyate yathābhūtaparijñānam svabhāvāvaraṇād āvṛtaprakāśanāc cānayeti saṃvṛtiḥ. avidyā moho viparyās iti paryāyāḥ. MV, pp. 492-3: samantād varanaṃ saṃvṛtiḥ. ajñānaṃ hi samantāt sarvapadārthatattvācchādanāt saṃvṛtir ity ucyate.* atha vā saṃvṛtiḥ saṃketo lokavyavahāra ityarthaḥ. sa cābhidhānābhidheyajñānajñeyādilakṣaṇaḥ. loke saṃvṛtir lokasaṃvṛtiḥ. See MA, VI. 28:

mohaḥ svabhāvāvaraṇād dhi saṃvṛtiḥ
satyaṃ tayā khyāti yad eva kṛtrimaṃ |
jagāda tat saṃvṛtisatyam ity asu
muniḥ padārthaṃ kṛtakaṃ ca saṃvṛtiṃ ||
quoted in BAP, p. 353.

58

dharmā ya iti jāyante saṃvṛtyā te na tattvataḥ |[1]
janma māyopamaṃ teṣāṃ sā ca māyā na vidyate ||

'The things which are said as generated are so in the empirical truth and not in fact. Their generation is like illusion, and that illusion, too, does not exist.'

The phrase 'generation is like illusion' may be explained saying that generation is *like* illusion, but itself is *not* illusion. The true sense is, however, not so. It says that generation is

1 See III. 27.

identical with illusion, there being no difference whatsoever between them (*advayam advaidhīkāram*).[2]

As regards the non-existence of illusion see

yāvat pratyayasāmagrī tāvan māyāpi vartate |
BC, IX. 10.

See also 27, 28.

[2] See ASP, pp. 39-40 : kiṃ punar ārya subhūte māyopamās te sattvā na te māyā. subhūtiḥ° avocat. māyopamās te° sattvā iti māyā ca sattvāś cādvayam etad advaidhīkāram iti.

According to this Mādhyamika theory even the Buddha and *nirvāṇa*, and, if there is anything higher than *nirvāṇa*, that, too, are illusion, *i.e.*, those things and illusion are one and the same thing.

59

yathā māyāmayād bījāj jāyate tanmayo 'ṅkuraḥ |
nāsau nityo na cocchedī tadvad dharmeṣu yojanā ||

'From an illusive seed comes forth an illusive sprout, and that (sprout) is neither eternal nor is attended with destruction. The same applies to all things.'

Cf. yathā hi kṛtakād bījāj jāyate tanmayo 'ṅkuraḥ |
CŚ, X. 28.[1]

[1] This is the reconstructed text from the Tibetan which runs:
ji. ltar. sa. bon byas. pa. las |
myu. gu. byas. pa. skye. ḥgyur. ba ||

60

nājeṣu sarvadharmeṣu śāśvatāśāśvatābhidhā |
yatra varṇā na vartante vivekas tatra nocyate ||

'When all things are without generation, there is no room for the appellations 'eternal' and 'non-eternal'; for where words fail discrimination cannot be expressed.'

The following may be cited here :

yasmāt pravartate bhāvas tenocchedo na jāyate |
yasmān nivartate bhāvas tena nityo na jāyate||

CŚ, XI. 25.

Now the Ācārya takes up again the *vijñānavāda* of the Buddhists showing that there is nothing but the *citta* which is the same as *vijñāna* or *manas* 'mind' that is transformed into the external world. And in doing so he shows that there is no difference whatsoever between the experiences in the waking state and those in dream, as has already been shown (II. 1-10) :

61

yathā svapne dvayābhāsaṃ cittaṃ calati māyayā |
tathā jāgrad dvayābhāsaṃ cittaṃ calati māyayā ||[1]

'As owing to illusion the mind in dream moves with the appearance of the two (*i.e.*, the subject and the object, or, in other words, the percipient and the perceived)[2], even so owing to illusion the mind in waking condition[3] moves with the appearance of the two.'

1 This as well as the next kārikā is the same as III. 29 and 30 respectively with a few variants.

2 See IV. 72: grāhyagrāhakavad dvayam; IV. 75; Ś on III. 29, 30: grāhyagrāhakarūpeṇa dvayābhāsam. In Buddhist works in such cases the word *dvaya* is frequently used in the same meaning. For instance, advayārthena paśyati, MS, XIV. 32; dvayagrāhavisaṃyuktaṃ grāhyagrāhagrāhakagrāhavisaṃyogāt, advayārthenāti agrāhyagrāhakārthena, *Ibid*, p. 94. See II. 14; III. 29, 30; IV. 62, 72, 75, 87.

3 The word *jāgrad* is to be taken here in the locative case. See IV. 39, note and 62.[4]

62

advayaṃ ca dvayābhāsaṃ cittaṃ svapne na saṃśayaḥ |
advayaṃ ca dvayābhāsaṃ cittaṃ jāgran na saṃśayaḥ ||

'There is no doubt that in dream the mind which is without the two has the appearance of the two, even so there is no doubt that in the waking state the mind which is without the two has the appearance of the two.'[1]

See III. 30.

[1] See IV. 61, notes.

63, 64

svapnadṛk pracaran svapne dikṣu vai daśasu sthitān |
aṇḍajān svedajān vāpi jīvān paśyati yān sadā ||

svapnadṛkcittadṛśyās te na vidyante tataḥ pṛthak |
tathā taddṛśyam[1] evedaṃ svapnadṛkcittam iṣyate ||[2]

'The animals, oviparous or engendered by heat and moisture, which a dreamer moving in dream sees at any time in any of the ten directions, are visible (only) to the mind of the dreamer, and do not exist apart from it (*i.e.*, mind); and this which is visible only to it (*i.e.*, the mind) is to be accepted (*lit.* wished) as the mind of the dreamer.

[1] See IV. 77.

[2] See IV. 65, 66.

65, 66

carañ jāgarite jāgrad dikṣu vai daśasu sthitān |
aṇḍajān svedajān vāpi jīvān paśyati yān sadā ||

jāgraccittekṣaṇīyās te na vidyante tataḥ pṛthak |
tathā taddṛśyam evedaṃ jāgrataś cittam iṣyate ||[1]

'The animals, oviparous or engendered by heat and moisture, which a waking one moving about in the state of wakefulness sees at any time in any of the ten directions, are visible (only) by the mind of the waking one and do not exist apart from it (*i.e.*, the mind of the waking one); and this which is visible only to it (*i.e.*, the mind of the waking one) is to be accepted as the mind of the waking one.'

In these four kārikās (IV. 63-66) it is said that whatever one sees in the waking state is nothing but one's *citta* 'mind', just as the things in one's dream. This view has repeatedly been expressed among others in LA, and specially in its Chapter X where the Buddha is reported to have said again and again that all the phenomena are *citta* (X. 483, 484, 692) : cittamātraṃ vadāmy aham 'I say (all this is) only *citta*.'[2]

The word *cittadṛśya* here (IV. 64) and elsewhere (IV. 28, 36, 77) of which the equivalent is *cittekṣaṇīya* (IV. 66) is found in frequent use in LA, pp. 56 (four times), 79, 84 (twice), 93, 94, 186 (twice), 338 (twice), etc.

[1] See IV. 63, 64.

[2] See also X. 101 :

svacittābhiniveśena cittaṃ vai sampravartate |
bahirdhā nāsti vai dṛśyam ato vai cittamātrakam ||

67

ubhe hy anyonyadṛśye te kiṃ tad astīti cocyate |
lakṣaṇāśūnyam ubhayaṃ tanmatenaiva gṛhyate ||

'You say that the cognition of both of them is dependent on each other, but you do not say what remains then. Both of them have no characteristics, yet they are cognized owing to their (previous) thought.'

In the text *ubha* and *ubhaya* refer to 'mind' (*citta*) and *jīvas* or objects in general referred to in the preceding kārikās. Their cognition depends on each other; for no object is perceived without the thought of the object, nor is the thought of an object possible without the existence of the object.[1] So they are interdependent in this respect. Owing to this interdependence neither of them is established as a real thing, and as such they have no characteristics and yet they are cognized owing to our previously existing thoughts of them.

The following may be quoted on this point :

atītaṃ subhūte cittaṃ nopalabhyate. anāgataṃ cittaṃ nopalabhyate. pratyutpannaṃ cittaṃ nopalabhyate. VC, 39.

uktaṃ ca lokanāthena cittaṃ cittaṃ na paśyati |
na cchinatti yathātmānam asidhārā tathā manaḥ ||

BA, IX. 17-18.

sa cittaṃ gaveṣayamāṇo nādhyātmaṃ cittaṃ samanupaśyati na bahirdhā cittaṃ samanupaśyati na skandheṣu cittaṃ samanupaśyati. na dhātuṣu cittaṃ samanupaśyati. nāyataneṣu cittaṃ samanupaśyati. sa cittam asamanupaśyaṃś cittadhārāṃ paryeṣate kutaś cittasyotpattir iti. ālambane sati cittam utpadyate. tat kim anyat cittam anyad ālambanam. atha yad

[1] Ś writes : na hi ghaṭamatiṃ pratyākhyāya ghaṭo gṛhyate nāpi ghaṭaṃ pratyākhyāya ghaṭamatiḥ. tanmatenaiva taccittatayaiva.

evālambanaṃ tad eva cittaṃ. yadi tāvad anyad ālambanaṃ anyac cittam tad dvicittatā bhaviṣyati. atha yad evālaṃbanaṃ tad eva cittaṃ, tat kathaṃ cittaṃ cittaṃ paśyati. na hi cittaṃ cittaṃ samanupaśyati. tad yathā no tayevāsidhārayā saivāsidhārā śakyate chettum. na tenaivāṅgulyagreṇa tad evāṅgulyagraṃ spraṣṭuṃ śakyate. evam eva tenaiva cittena tad eva cittaṃ draṣṭum iti vistaraḥ.

Āryaratnacūḍasūtra quoted in BAP, pp. 392-393 ; MV, pp. 62-63 ; ŚS, p. 235.

For *lakṣaṇāśūnya* which is the same as *lakṣaṇa*° in meaning see the following :

yad dhi cittaṃ mahāmate na nityaṃ nānityaṃ na kāryaṃ na kāraṇaṃ na saṃskṛtaṃ nāsaṃskṛtaṃ° na lakṣyaṃ na lakṣaṇaṃ° tad vāṅmātraṃ° tad anutpannaṃ yad anutpannaṃ tad aniruddhaṃ° ākāśasamam°. tatredam ucyate

pramāṇendriyanirmuktaṃ na kāryaṃ nāpi kāraṇam |
buddhiboddhavyarahitaṃ lakṣyalakṣaṇavarjitam ||

LA, pp. 189-190.

tasmān na vidyate lakṣyaṃ lakṣaṇaṃ naiva vidyate |
lakṣyalakṣaṇanirmukto bhāvo 'pi naiva vidyate ||

MK, V. 5.

upāyadeśanā mahyaṃ nāhaṃ deśemi lakṣaṇaṃ |
bālā gṛhṇanti bhāvena lakṣaṇaṃ lakṣyam eva ca ||

LA, X. 21.

lakṣyalakṣaṇavarjitam.

Op. cit., X-224.

68-70

yathā svapnamayo jīvo jāyate mriyate 'pi ca |
tathā jīvā amī sarve bhavanti na bhavanti ca ||

yathā māyāmayo jīvo jāyate mriyate 'pi ca |
tathā jīvā amī sarve bhavanti na bhavanti ca ||

yathā nirmitako jīvo jāyate mriyate 'pi ca |
tathā jīvā amī sarve bhavanti na bhavanti ca ||

'As a creature formed of dream, or made of illusion or supernatural power (*nirmitaka*[1]) takes birth and dies, even so all those creatures exist and do not exist.'

The word *nirmita* or *nirmitaka* in the above sense is frequently used mainly in Buddhist works. Among many others the following may be quoted here :

nirmitopamāḥ pratibimbopamāḥ sarvadharmāḥ jñātavyāḥ. SR, p. 27.

acintiyān nirmita nirminotyā-
deśeti dharmaṃ bahu prāṇakoṭinaṃ |

Ibid., p. 23.

yathā nirmitakaṃ śāstā nirmimītardhisampadā |
nirmito nirmimītānyaṃ sa ca nirmitakaḥ punaḥ ||[2]
tathā nirmitakākāraḥ kartā yat karma tat kṛtaṃ |
tad yathā nirmitenānyo nirmito nirmitas tathā ||

MK, XVII. 31-32.

ekasmiṃ bhāṣamānasmiṃ sabbe bhāsanti nimmitā |
ekasmiṃ tuṇhīm āsīne sabbe tuṇhī bhavanti ca ||

DN, II. 212.

[1] Ś. says nirmitako mantrauṣadhyādibhir abhiniṣpāditaḥ 'created by incantation, herbs, etc.'

[2] *Cf. Śūnyatāsaptati* as quoted by Poussin in a note on MV, p. 330.

The following is the Sanskrit version :

ekasya bhāṣamāṇasya sarve bhāṣanti nirmitāḥ |
ekasya tūṣṇīmbhūtasya sarve tūṣṇīṃ bhavanti ca ||

Quoted as in *Āgama* in MV, p. 331; DA, p. 166; AKV,[1] p. 27.

See *Āryaratnakūṭasūtra* quoted in MV, pp. 336 ff.; *Āryagaganagañjasūtra* quoted in ŚS, p. 270 ; BA, V. 57. *Cf.* the *nimāṇakāya* of a Buddha. Poussin : *The Three Bodies of a Buddha*, JRAS, 1906, (Oct.) ; JA, 1913, pp. 581 ff ; ERE, Vol. 9, pp. 852-853.

The use of such words as *nirmāṇa*, *nirmāṇakāya*, and *nirmāṇacitta* occurs also in the Yoga system (YS, IV. 4, 5 with *scholiasts*).

The use of the word *nirmāṇa* in almost the same sense can, however, be traced back to Upaniṣadic texts :

sa yatra prasvapity asya lokasya sarvāvato mātrām upādāya svayaṃ vihatya svayaṃ nirmāya° prasvapiti. BU, IV. 3, 9.

ya eṣa supteṣu jāgarti kāmaṃ kāmaṃ puruṣo nirmimāṇaḥ | KU, V. 8.

It appears, however, that it is the Buddhists who first used the word in that definite sense.

Now having thus established his thesis the author asserts his conclusion in the following kārikā, which is already found once more (III. 48) :

71

na kaścij jāyate jīvaḥ[1] sambhavo 'sya na vidyate |
etat tad uttamaṃ satyaṃ[2] yatra kiñcin na jāyate ||

[1] *Cf.* SR quoted in MV, p. 109 : na hi kaści jāyati na ca mriyate.

[2] For the wording *cf.* etat tu paramaṃ satyaṃ, MV, p. 120.

'No Jīva of any kind takes birth, nor is there any possibility of it. It is that highest truth in which nothing originates.'

See III. 48.

Now it is affirmed in the next kārikā that the world consisting of the subject and the object has no reality at all, it being the creation of the movement of mind which in fact has no object at all, and as such it is held to be always free from any sort of attachment or relationship to an object (*asaṅga*) :

72

cittaspanditam evedaṃ grāhyagrāhakavad dvayam |
cittaṃ nirviṣayaṃ nityam asaṅgaṃ tena kīrttitam ||

'This duality which consists of the subject and the object (lit. the perceiver and the perceptible) is only the vibration of the *citta* 'mind'. *citta* has no object, therefore it is said to be always *asaṅga* 'having no attachment (or relation to an object).'

See IV. 79 (*niḥsaṅga*). *Cf.* *anābhāsa* (=*nirābhāsa*), III. 46; IV. 48.

As regards *asaṅga* see LA, p. 157 : asaṅgalakṣaṇaṃ jñānaṃ viṣayavaicitryasaṅgalakṣaṇaṃ vijñānam°, asaṅgasvabhāvalakṣaṇaṃ jñānaṃ°, aprāptilakṣaṇaṃ jñānam.

The following lines also from the LA may be cited here :

cittamātram idaṃ sarvaṃ dvidhā cittaṃ pravartate |
grāhyagrāhakabhāvena ātmātmīyaṃ na vidyate ||
brahmādisthāna(?)paryantaṃ cittamātraṃ vadāmy ahaṃ |
cittamātravinirmuktaṃ brahmādir nopalabhyate ||

III. 121-122.

cittamātraṃ na dṛśyo'sti dvidhā cittaṃ hi dṛśyate |
grāhyagrāhakabhāvena śāśvatocchedavarjitaṃ ||

III. 65.

grāhyagrāhakabhāvena cittaṃ namati dehināṃ |
dṛṣyasya lakṣaṇaṃ nāsti yathā bālair vikalpyate ||

X. 58.

taraṅgā hy udadher yadvat pavanapratyeritāḥ |
nṛtyamānāḥ pravartante vyucchedaś ca na vidyate ||

ālayaughas tathā nityaṃ viṣayapavaneritaḥ |
citrais taraṅgavijñānair nṛtyamānaḥ pravartate ||

II. 99, 100 ; X. 56, 57.

Cf. (*i*) spandāspandasvabhāvaṃ hi cinmātram iha vidyate |
khe vāta iva tat spandāt sollāsaṃ śāntam anyathā ||

cittvaṃ (?) cittaṃ bhāvitaṃ sat spanda ity ucyate budhaiḥ |
dṛśyatvābhāvitaṃ caitad aspandanam iti smṛtam ||

spandāt sphurati citsargo niḥspandād brahma śāśvatam |
jīvakāraṇakarmādyā citspandasyābhidhā smṛtā ||

YV, III. 67. 6-8.

(*ii*) svabhāvād vyatiriktaṃ tu na cittasyāsti cetanam |
spandād ṛte yathā vāyor antaḥ kiṃ nāma cetyate ||

Op. cit., III. 66. 16.

Having shown that the duality consisting of the subject and the object is the creation of mind the author says in the next kārikā that its existence is only in empirical (*saṃvṛti*) and not in absolute (*paramārtha*) truth. For a thing which is dependent (*paratantra*) for its existence may exist in empirical and not in absolute truth:

73

yo 'sti kalpitasaṃvṛtyā paramārthena nāsty asau |
paratantro[1] 'bhisaṃvṛtyā syān nāsti paramārthataḥ ||

'Whatever exists in empirical truth (*saṃvṛti*) which is imagined (*kalpita*) does not exist in absolute truth (*paramārtha*), for one that is dependent (*paratantra*, for its existence or origination) may exist (only) in empirical truth which is the cause (of existence or origination), and not in absolute truth.'

For the first half of the kārikā see IV. 57*a* and 58*a-b*.

1 Here the actual reading in all the editions and MSS. examined is *paratantrābhi°* and not *paratantro'bhi°* as given above. The reading in c of the next kārikā (74), too, is *paratantrābhi°* in all of them excepting the MS. *k* of the Anandashram edition and the edition of Maheśacandra Pāla, both of which read here *paratantro'bhi°*. As the sense requires and is supported by Buddhist works, as we shall presently see, the genuine reading here in the kārikā (73) must be *paratantro'bhi°* (See the discussion in the body). Here *abhisaṃvṛti* in this kārikā (73) in meaning is, as appears to me, nothing but *abhiniṣpatti saṃvṛti* in kārikā 74. Now *abhiniṣpatti saṃvṛti* means *saṃvṛti* which is the cause of existence, or appearance of things (*abhiniṣpadyate 'nayā*). One should therefore read *paratantro'bhi°* in 73 in accordance with the reading in 74. Otherwise the kārikās cannot properly be explained. One can hardly ollow Ś who explains *paratantrābhisaṃvṛtyā* as *paraśāstravyavahāreṇa* and *paratantrābhiniṣpatyā* as *paraśāstrasiddhim apekṣya* in 73 and 74 respectively. Whether one can read *hi* for *'bhi* in *c* of the presant kārikā may also be considered.

It follows from what is said above that a thing is to be regarded as having no origination (*aja*). Our author, however, says that this assertion can be made only so far as the empirical truth is concerned, but in absolute truth even this is not possible, for a dependent thing comes into being only in empirical truth :

74

ajaḥ kalpitasaṃvṛtyā paramārthena nāpyajaḥ |
paratantro'bhiniṣpattyā saṃvṛtyā jāyate tu saḥ ||

'One (held) to be unborn (*aja*) is so in empirical truth which is imagined, but in absolute truth it is even not unborn; for that which is dependent comes into being in empirical truth, the cause of appearance.'

The words *saṃvṛti* and *paratantra* in kārikās 73 and 74 are very important and require some explanation. The first of them has, however, already been discussed above (IV. 56, 57) to some extent and the following may be added thereto. In the Mādhyamika system as in the school of Vedānta *saṃvṛti satya* is called also *vyavahāra* or *vyāvahārika* ('practical') *satya*. The two kinds of truth, *saṃvṛti*, or *vyavahāra* or *vyāvahārika* and *paramārtha* are regarded in Buddhism as the means (*upāya*) and the end (*upeya*) respectively.[1]

[1] MA, VI. 80 quoted in BAP, p. 372 :

upāyabhūtaṃ vyavahārasatyam upeyabhūtaṃ paramārthasatyam |

See also MK, XXIV. 20 :

vyavahāram anāśritya paramārtho na deśyate |
paramārtham anāgamya nirvāṇaṃ nādhigamyate ||

In Pali Buddhism *saṃvṛti satya* is *sammuti sacca* (Skt. *sammati satya*) 'truth by general consent'. Poussin writes (JA, 1903, Tome II, p. 302) : "vèrite conferme à l'assentiment universel mais erronè" ('truth conformed to universal assent but erroneous'). The literal meaning of the word *saṃvṛti* is that by which (the true nature of a thing) is 'covered' (*svabhāvā-*

varaṇāt) and it is regarded as truth because it brings to light what is covered (*āvṛtaprakāśanāt*). See IV. 57, and BAP on IX. 2 (p. 352). The following may be quoted here from MA, VI. 23 as cited in BAP, p. 361 :

samyagmṛṣādarśanalabdhabhāvaṃ
rūpadvayaṃ bibhrati sarvabhāvāḥ |
samyagdṛśāṃ yo viṣayaḥ sa tattvaṃ
mṛṣādṛśāṃ saṃvṛtisatyam uktaṃ ||

Now as regards *paratantra* 'dependent' it has a special significance as evident from Buddhist sources. In Buddhism there are three characteristics (*lakṣaṇa*) or natures (*svabhāva*) of a thing, *viz.*, (*i*) *parikalpita* 'imagined', (*ii*) *paratantra* 'dependent', and (*iii*) *pariniṣpanna* 'perfect'.[1] Sometimes they are briefly called (*i*) *kalpita*, (*ii*) *tantra*, and (*iii*) *niṣpanna* respectively.[2] Any object, for instance, an elephant, according to Mādhyamikas or Yogācāras is *śūnya* or merely a creation of mind, yet we know it as a particular object. This characteristic of it is an imagined one (*parikalpita*). Now the notion or imagination of the object depends for its being on its cause (or cause and conditions, *hetu-pratyaya*), and so the characteristic is called *paratantra* (=*pratītyasamutpanna*). That the object is in fact always devoid of the imagined characteristics referred to above is *pariniṣpanna*. It is so also because there

[1] MVt[1], LXXXVII; Tk, 39; TSN, 1 :

kalpitaḥ paratantraś ca pariniṣpanna eva ca |
trayaḥ svabhāvā dhīrāṇāṃ gambhīrajñeyam iṣyate ||

MVST, I. 6 :

kalpitaḥ paratantraś ca pariniṣpanna eva ca |

[2] LA, X. 374 :

buddhyā vivecyamānaṃ hi na tantraṃ nāpi kalpitaṃ |
niṣpanno nāsti vai bhāvaḥ kathaṃ buddhyā prakalpyate ||

is perfect invariation or because it is free from any change.[3] They are called 'nature' (*svabhāva*) owing to such practice of the people though in fact they do not exist.[4] V a s u b a n d h u gives here an example in his TSN, 27, 28: Suppose one creates an elephant by dint of one's spell. There the elephant appears, but there is only the form of the elephant, and in no way the elephant itself. Here the elephant is *parikalpita*; the form of the elephant is *paratantra*, and the absence of the elephant is *parinispanna*.[5]

Of these three *lakṣaṇas* or *svabhāvas*[6] the first, *parikalpita*, may roughly be compared in the system of the Advaita Vedānta of Ś

[3] Tk, 40: avikāraparinispattyā sa parinispannaḥ ; MVBT, p. 19 : tasyāsaṃskṛtatvān nirvikāratvena parinispannatvāt.

[4] Writes S t h i r a m a t i in MVBT, p. 19: sa punar dravyato 'sann api vyavahārato 'stīti svabhāva ucyate.

[5] māyākṛtaṃ mantravaśāt khyāti hastyātmanā yathā |
ākāramātraṃ tatrāsti hastī nāstī tu sarvathā ||
svabhāvaḥ kalpito hastī paratantras tadākṛtiḥ |
yas tatra hastyabhāvo 'sau parinispanna iṣyate ||

Cf. MSA, XI. 19 :

tadākṛtiś ca tatrāsti tadbhāvaś ca na vidyate |

[6] For easy reference the following may be quoted here:

Tk. p. 39:

yena yena vikalpena yad yad vastu vikalpyate |
parikalpita evāsau svabhāvo na sa vidyate || 20

(This is based on LA, p. 163: yat punar uktaṃ bhagavatā yena yena vikalpena ye ye bhāvā vikalpyante na hi sa teṣāṃ svabhāvo bhavati parikalpita evāsau°.)

S t h i r a m a t i: ādhyātmikabāhyavikalpyavastubhedena vikalpānām ānantyaṃ pradarśayann āha y e n a y e n a v i k a l p e n e t i. y a d y a d v a s t u v i k a l p y a t e.° ādhyātmikaṃ bāhyaṃ vāntaśo yāvad buddhadharmā api. p a r i k a l p i t a e v ā s a u s v a b h ā v a ity atra kāraṇam āha n a s a v i d y a t a iti yad vastu vikalpaviṣayas tad yasmāt sattvābhāvān na vidyate tasmād tad vastu parikalpitasvabhāvam eva na hetupratyayapratibaddhasvabhāvam.° parikalpitānantaraṃ paratantrasvabhāvo vaktavya ity ata āha

paratantrasvabhāvas tu vikalpaḥ pratyayodbhavaḥ |

with *prātibhāsika satya* 'the truth that exists only in appearance'; as for example, mirage, or the appearance of a snake on a piece of string; *paratantra* with *vyāvahārika satya* 'the practical truth' (this is called by the Buddhists *sāṁvṛta* 'pertaining to *saṃvṛti*', or *vyavahāra satya*), the phenomena in the waking state are its examples; and *pariniṣpanna* with *pāramārthika satya* 'supreme or transcendental truth', e.g., Brahman of the Vedāntins.[7]

S t h i r a m a t i : atra vikalpa iti paratantrasvabhāvam āha. p r a t y o d b h a v a ity anenāpi paratantrābhidhānapravṛttinimittam āha.° parair hetupratyayais tantryata utpādyata iti paratantra ity arthaḥ. (As the sense requires the order of the last four words is slightly changed. See MVBT, p. 19: grāhyaṃ grāhakaṃ ca svabhāvaśūnyatvād abhūtam apy astīti parikalpyata iti parikalpita ity ucyate. sa punar dravyato 'sann api vyavahārato 'stīti svabhāva ucyate. paratantraḥ paravaśo hetupratyayapratibaddhajanmakatvāt. p. 20: parair hetupratyayais tantryate janyate na tu svayaṃ bhavatīti paratantraḥ.) svato'nyahetupratyayapratibaddhātmalābha ity uktaṃ bhavati. uktaḥ paratantraḥ. pariniṣpannaḥ katham ity ata āha

niṣpannas tasya pūrveṇa sadā rahitatā tu yā || 21

(MVBT, p. 19:

kalpitena svabhāvena tasya yātyantaśūnyatā |
svabhāvaḥ pariniṣpanno 'vikalpajñānagocaraḥ ||

V a s u b a n d h u says on the point, *Op. cit.*, p. 20: grāhyagrāhakābhāvaḥ pariniṣpannaḥ. In TSN, 3 *sadā rahitatā* of Tk. 21, and *atyantaśūnyatā* of MVBT referred to above are expressed by *sadā 'vidyamānatā*.)

S t h i r a m a t i : avikārapariniṣpattyā sa pariniṣpannaḥ. t a s y e t i paratantrasya p ū r v e ṇ e t i parikalpitena. tasmin vikalpe grāhyagrāhakabhāvaḥ parikalpitaḥ. tathā hi. tasmin vikalpe grāhyagrāhakatvam avidyamānam eva parikalpyata iti parikalpitam ucyate. tena grāhyagrāhakeṇa paratantrasya s a d ā sarvakālam atyanta r a h i t a t ā yā sā pariniṣpannasvabhāvaḥ.

According to Buddhists *nirodha*, *nirvāṇa*, and *ākāśa* are the examples of *pariniṣpanna*.

[7] For a detailed discussion and bibliography and sources, ancient and modern, see ViS, pp. 514-561; TSN; LA, pp. 126, 127, 169, 170, 176, etc.; MSA, VI. 1, XI. 13, 38-41, XIX. 51, 78, 79; SNS, VI.

It is to be noted that *saṃvṛti* consists in *parikalpita* and *paratantra svabhāvas* and *paramārtha* in *parinispanna*. Thus it is rightly said in the kārikā 73 that *paratantra* can exist only in practical truth (*saṃvṛti*) and not in any way in absolute truth. This is fully explained by P r a j ñ ā k a r a m a t i (in his BAP, pp. 354-355) saying that whatever comes into existence (*jāyate*) does so being dependent on the entirety of the cause and conditions (*hetupratyayasāmagrī*), and that which is thus dependent for its existence has no existence in reality, like a shadow on a looking glass. Let the following be quoted here :

api tu hetupratyayasāmagrīṃ pratītya māyāvad utpadyate. tadvaikalyato nirudhyate ca. hetupratyayasāmagrīṃ pratītya jātasya parāyattātmalābhasya pratibimbasyeva kutaḥ satsvabhāvatā. na ca kasyacid padārthasya paramārthato hetupratyayasāmagrītaḥ samutpattiḥ sambhavati.

Let us quote also the following few lines :

māyayā nirmitaṃ yac ca hetubhir yac ca nirmitam |
āyāti tat kutaḥ kutra yāti ceti nirūpyatām ||
yad anyasannidhānena dṛṣṭaṃ na tadabhāvataḥ |
pratibimbasame tasmin kṛtrime satyatā kutaḥ ||

BA. IX. 144, 145.

yaḥ pratyayair jāyati sa hy ajāto
na tasya utpādu sabhāvato'sti |
yaḥ pratyayādhinu sa śūnya ukto
yaḥ śūnyatāṃ janati so 'pramattaḥ

Anvavataptahradāpasaṃkramaṇasūtra
quoted in BAP, *loc. cit.* and MV, p. 239.

The subject under discussion is that nothing originates (etat tad uttamaṃ satyaṃ yatra kiñcin na jāyate, III. 48, IV. 71). It has been shown in establishing it that the notion of origination is only in empirical reality and not in absolute reality in which we cannot assert the existence of even a thing that is without origination. The author now says in the next kārikā that the notion of origination is due to a strong adherence (*abhiniveśa*) to the unreal (*abhūta*) referring hereby to the two (*dvaya*), *i.e.*, the percipient and the perceptible (*grāhya* and (*grāhaka*) :

75

abhūtābhiniveśo 'sti dvayaṃ tatra na vidyate |
dvayābhāvaṃ sa buddhvaiva nirnimitto na jāyate ||

'There is a strong adherence to what has not been (*abhūta*[1]), for the two[2] are not there. Just when he understands the non-existence of the two it goes beyond the range of its cause and does not come into being.'[3]

The cause of origination is *abhūtābhiniveśa*. When one clearly understands the true nature of the two which have no existence at all that *abhiniveśa* goes away and consequently the notion of origination does not arise.

Ś explains the word *he* (*saḥ*) in the original (c) in the following way : dvayābhāvaṃ buddhvā nirnimitto nivṛttamithyādvayābhiniveśo yaḥ sa na jāyate—'He who having understood the absence of the two is beyond the cause and (thus) whose strong adherence to the two which are false has turned back, is not born.'

This explanation does not appear to be proper when one reads the karikā under discussion with the kārikā IV. 79, where the same phrase (dvayābhāvaṃ sa buddhvaiva, 75) occurs once more with a slight variation (*vastvabhāvaṃ* for *dvayābhāvaṃ*), there being no difference of meaning (*vastvabhāva*=*dvayābhāva* —Ś). Let the kārikā be quoted here :

abhūtābhiniveśād dhi sadṛśe tat pravartate |
vastvabhāvaṃ sa buddhvaiva niḥsaṅgaṃ vinivartate ||

[1] That is, 'unreal,' referring to the two (*dvaya*) that follows.

[2] The percipient and the perceptible (*grāhya-grāhaka*), see IV. 72.

[3] See IV. 79.

How is it to be explained? The meaning is simple and clear. It says that it is only owing to one's persistent belief in unreality that it (*citta* 'mind') goes onward to a similar object (*i.e.*, the mind relates itself to an unreal object), but as soon as one understands the absence of a thing it becomes free from contact and turns back.

But here is a difficulty regarding grammar. In accordance with Pāṇini, III. 4. 21, the agent (*kartṛ*) of both the verbs *buddhvā* and *vinivartate* in the second half of the kārikā must be the same; but the fact is not so, for the agent of the former is *saḥ*, while that of the latter is *tat* in the first half.

This anomaly is however found in writings even of such great poets as Kālidāsa. He writes in his *Raghuvaṃśa*, I. 77:

matprasūtim anārādhya prajeti tvāṃ śaśāpa sā |[4]

In defence of Pāṇini, or in other words, to meet the difficulty arising from his rule later grammarians say that such words as *sthita* and the like are to be understood in such cases, so that there may be the same agent of the verbs used.[5]

The use of the gerund in the Vedic language in this respect is not so strict as in the classical Sanskrit that follows Pāṇini. See the following sentences in which the verbs have different agents: striyaṃ dṛṣṭāya kitavaṃ tatāpa 'having seen

[4] Mallinātha attempts to explain it away taking *anārādhya* in the causative sense (*asevayitvā*). Similar instances are many:

(*i*) yaj jñātvā neha bhūyo 'nyaj jñātavyam avaśiṣyate || BG, VII. 2.

(*ii*) tac ca saṃsmṛtya saṃsmṛtya rūpam atyadbhutaṃ hareḥ |
vismayo me mahān rājan hṛṣyāmi ca muhurmuhuḥ || BG, XVIII 77.

(*iii*) mṛtaṃ dṛṣṭvā duḥkhaṃ bhavati, (*iv*) priyaṃ dṛṣṭvā sukhaṃ syāt, sukham utpadyate, etc.

[5] See *Saṃkṣiptasāra* with Vṛtti and Ṭīkā ed., Śyāmācaraṇa Kaviratna, Calcutta, 1318, B.S., Kṛdantapāda, 407; *Mugdhabodha*, ed., Subalacandra Mitra, Calcutta, 1316, B.S., Sūtra, 1116; *Kalāpavyākaraṇa* with commentaries ed. Gurunātha Vidyānidhi Bhaṭṭācāryya, Calcutta, 1835 Śaka, Kṛdvṛtti, Sūtra 433.

a woman (it) pains a gambler' (RV, X. 34. 11). Similar uses are found also in the Brāhmaṇas. The following is from the *Śatapatha Brāhmaṇa* : te paśava oṣadhīr jagdhvā apaḥ pītvā tata eṣa rasaḥ saṃ bhavati 'the beasts having eaten the plants and drunk water—then the vital sap arises.'

Following this the line under discussion (IV. 79) would be explained by a grammarian thus : sa (yadā) vastvabhāvaṃ buddhvaiva (bhavati tadā) tan niḥsaṅgaṃ vinivartate,—'just when he understands the absence of things it (mind) turns back being free from relation'. Now in the kārikā (79) the word *sa(ḥ)* must refer to one (understood) whose *abhūtābhiniveśa* is stated.

In the same way, I think, the kārikā 75, too, should be explained : It is the *abhūtābhiniveśa* itself and not the person whose *abhūtābhiniveśa* is alluded to, that does not arise (*jāyate*).[6]

Naturally one has a persistent belief in the *abhūta* or unreal things, *i.e.*, the percipient and the perceptible which have, in fact, no existence at all. So when one clearly understands their non-existence there is no room for that persistent belief to come into being.

Now, as regards *abhūtābhiniveśa* compare *abhūtaparikalpa* of the Buddhists. We read the following in the LA, pp. 149-150 :

abhūtaparikalpa 'bhūtaparikalpa iti bhagavann ucyate. katamasyaitad bhagavan dharmasyādhivacanaṃ yad utābhūtaparikalpa iti kiṃ vā prativikalpayann abhūtaparikalpo bhavati. bhagavān āha sādhu sādhu mahāmate° nṛṇāṃ grāhyagrāhakābhiniveśābhiniviṣṭānāṃ ca° bāhyavicitrārthopalambhābhiniveśāc cittacaittakalāpo vikalpasaṃśabditaḥ pravartamānaḥ pravartata ātmātmīyābhiniveśāt.

[6] Or one may take here *nirnimitto na jāyate* with reference to *yo 'sti kalpita*° (IV. 73) and it may be explained saying that which is or originates in the empirical truth does not do so when one has no notion of the two (*grāhya* and *grāhaka*), there being no cause (*nirnimitta*) for origination.

The *abhūtābhiniveśa* in our work (IV. 75, 79) is, in fact, *abhūta-parikalpa* of the Yogācāras. See the following line in the *Madhyāntavibhaṅga* (I. 2^{a-b}) of M a i t r e y a n ā t h a:

abhūtaparikalpo 'sti dvayaṃ tatra na vidyate | [7]

From this it is perfectly clear that the first half of our kārikā under discussion is in reality taken from M a i t r e y a n ā t h a.

The word *nimitta* in *nirnimitta* 'devoid of *nimitta*' has a special sense in Buddhist literature. There is a very common phrase: na nimittagrāhī bhavati, Pali °ggāhī hoti, DSṇ, §§ 1345-6. It means that when a *nimitta* 'specific appearance'[8] of a thing is grasped in the way such as a male, a female, pleasant, etc., a man is entangled in various worldly troubles, and so it is advised that he should not be a *nimittagrāhin* 'grasper of *nimittas*.' As the specific appearances are the causes of attachment, aversion, and delusion (*rāga*, *dveṣa*, and *moha*) they are called *nimittas*.[9] See AS, p. 400.

This special meaning seems not to have been intended in the present case. We may take the word here as well as in IV. 77 and 78 in the sense of 'objective cause' which is expressed by the word *artha* in IV. 24.

Having said as to how that persistent belief disappears, the author proceeds to discuss in the following kārikās how the non-origination (*anutpatti*) of mind is effected which is to be realized:

[7] MVBT, pp. 9 ff. On *b* of the kārikā S t h i r a m a t i writes: svātmany avidyamānena grāhyagrāhakākāreṇa prakhyāte [na vyaktaṃ bhrāntirūpatvaṃ].

[8] AKV as quoted in DS, p 41: nimittaṃ vastuno 'vasthāviśeṣo nīlatvādiḥ; Tr., p. 21, l. 3: nimittaṃ tad- (referring to *viṣaya*) viśeṣo nīlapītādyālambana-vyavasthākaraṇaṃ. See AS, pp. 291, 308.

[9] AS, p. 400: itthipurisanimittaṃ vā subhanimittādikaṃ vā kilesavatthubhūtaṃ nimittaṃ.

76

yadā na labhate hetūn uttamādhamamadhyamān |
tadā na jāyate cittaṃ hetvabhāve phalaṃ kutaḥ ||

'When the mind does not have any cause, superior, inferior, or middle, it does not originate; for how is there the effect in the absence of the cause?'

Here *hetu* is nothing but *nimitta* in the preceding kārikā. See IV. 77-78.

77

animittasya cittasya yānutpattiḥ samādvayā |
ajātasyaiva sarvasya cittadṛśyaṃ hi tad yataḥ ||

This kārikā seems to have been handed down defectively. For, evidently in the first half the sentence is not complete, as the conjunctive pronoun *yad* (in feminine *yā*) requires the pronoun *tad* in feminine (in any case-ending), but it is not to be found in either of the two halves. Nor is there the antecedent of *tad* in the second half which clearly shows to have supported something stated before. But what is it? The explanation of Ś appears to be far-fetched and far from satisfactory, nor has he explained the word *tad* which has altogether been overlooked. It seems to me, therefore, that the above two lines are taken by mistake from two different kārikās of which the other two lines are lost. I leave the present kārikā, as it is before us, untranslated, as it does not give any complete sense, so far as I can understand. The first half may, however, be explained thus:

The non-origination (*anutpatti*) of the causeless (*animitta*)[1] mind (*citta*) is the same (*samā*, *i.e.*, unconditioned—always in the same condition) and free from the two (*advaya*, *i.e.*,

[1] See IV. 75.

free from the notion of the *grāhya* 'receptible', and the *grāhaka* 'recipient').

See kārikā IV. 80. For the word *sama* or *sāmya* see III. 2, 38; IV. 80, 93, 95, 100 with the author's explanation; and MuU, III. 1. 3. *cf*. BG, V. 19: nirdoṣaṃ hi samaṃ brahma. See MV, pp. 374-75: mañjuśrīr āha. paramārthataḥ sarvadharmānutpāda-samatayā parmārthataḥ sarvadharmātyantājātisamatayā paramārthataḥ samāḥ sarvadharmāḥ.

For *cittadṛśya* in the second half see III. 31, IV. 28, 36.

78

buddhvā 'nimittatāṃ satyaṃ hetuṃ pṛthag anāpnuvat[1] ।
vītaśokaṃ tadā 'kāmam abhayaṃ padam aśnute ॥

'When one understands its[2] true state of causelessness[3] it (*citta*) does not have any other cause,[4] and as such reaches then a position[5] which is free from sorrow, desire, and fear.'

I read with MS. D^2 *anāpnuvat* for *anāpnuvan* in editions and other MSS., construing it with *citta* referred to in the preceding kārikā (77). It is to be noted that it is *citta* that is referred to in kārikās IV. 76-80. In kārikā 79 the pronoun *tad* refers to *citta*, as says Ś, too, expressly. One may naturally expect to have its mention or reference also in the present kārikā. To introduce a person who reaches the position is rather abrupt. It is also to be considered that it is *citta* and not the person that is concerned with the cause or causes (IV. 76).

In this case the grammatical difficulty is to be removed as in IV. 75.

1 See the Variants.

2 That is, of the *citta* 'mind.' See IV. 25, 26, 27, 75, 77.

3 That is, the state of being without the objective cause.

4 See IV. 76.

5 *pada*=*sthiti*, IV. 80.

Accepting the reading *anāpnuvan* the kārikā may be translated thus :

'Having understood the true state of the causelessness and having no other cause one reaches then a position free from sorrow, desire and fear.'

79

abhūtābhiniveśād dhi sadṛśe tat pravartate |
vastvabhāvaṃ sa buddhvaiva niḥsaṅgaṃ vinivartate ||

'Owing to a persistent belief in what is non-existent it goes onwards to a similar object, but as soon as one understands the absence of a thing it turns back being free from relativity.'

The word *sadṛśa* means what is thought to be similar to one in which one has strong or persistent belief. *niḥsaṅga* means one beyond the reach of any connection with the object.

For c one is referred to IV. 75. See III. 45; IV. 72, 75, 96, 99.

80

nivṛttasyāpravṛttasya niścalā hi tadā sthitiḥ |
viṣayaḥ sa hi buddhānāṃ tat sāmyam ajam advayam ||

'At that time when (the *citta*) has turned back from and does not go (again) onwards to (its object), its position is firm (*i.e.*, unwavering in the least). That is the field of activity of the Buddhas,[1] and that is the same,[2] unborn, and free from the two.'[3]

1 *Cf.* III. 34: pracāraḥ sa tu vijñeyaḥ.

2 See III. 2, 38. See also Vch, p. 41: api tu khalu punaḥ subhūte samaḥ sa dharmo na tatra kaścid viṣamaḥ. tenocyate 'nuttarasamyaksambodhiḥ. nirātmatvena niḥsattvatvena nirjīvatvena niṣpudgalatvena samā sānuttarā samyaksambodhih.

3 The perceptible and the percipient (*grāhya* and *grāhaka*).

In c *viṣaya* may be taken in the sense of the object of knowledge.

See III. 46 and IV. 77 from which it will be evident that this state is the *summum bonum* of both the Buddhists and the Vedāntists, which they call *nirodha* or *nirvāṇa* and *brahman* respectively. The Vedāntist commentator, Ś, writes here very clearly that this state of mind is *brahman* :

cittasya niścalā calanavarjitā brahmasvarūpaiva tadā sthitir yaiṣā brahmasvarūpā sthitiś cittasyādvayavijñānaikarasaghana-lakṣaṇā.

And again on IV. 77 he says :

animittasya cittasyeti yā mokṣākhyānutpattiḥ.[4]

That this state of *citta* is the field of activity of the Buddhas is clearly said in Buddhist works :

> cittamātraṃ nirābhāsaṃ vihāro buddhabhūmi ca |
> etad dhi bhāṣitaṃ buddhair bhāṣante bhāṣayanti ca ||
>
> LA, X. 105.

> arthābhāse ca vijñāne jñānaṃ tathatāgocaram |
> parāvṛttaṃ nirābhāsaṃ āryāṇāṃ gocaro hy asau ||
>
> *Op. Cit.*, X. 148.

This state is the same as what we know from such lines as the following from Buddhist works : vijñaptimātratāyāṃ cittam avasthitaṃ bhavati. Tk., p. 43.

For the wording of c (viṣayaḥ sa hi buddhānāṃ) see CŚ, p. 497 : viṣayaḥ sa hi buddhānāṃ ; Vk, p. 6 : yo buddhānāṃ viṣayaḥ ; p. 11 : buddhagocaraḥ ; SŚP, p. 120, *5*a* : yatpramāṇo buddhaviṣayaḥ ; MSA, XX-XXI. 26 : buddhānāṃ viṣayād api ; LA, III. 80 : āryāṇāṃ gocaro yathā.

[4] See cittaṃ pravartate cittaṃ cittam eva vimucyate |
cittaṃ hi jāyate nānyac cittam eva nirudhyate || *Op. Cit.*, X. 145.

This state of mind to which the Buddhas aspire is further described in the following kārikā :

81

ajam anidram asvapnaṃ prabhātaṃ bhavati svayam |
sakṛd vibhāti hy evaiṣa dharmo dhātuḥ svabhāvataḥ ||

See III. 36.

'It shines forth itself having no origination, nor sleep, nor dream. Indeed, this object (*dharma*), the fundamental element (*dhātu*), is naturally illumined once for all.'

The word *dharma* in the second half of the kārikā may be taken in its general sense, an element of existence, an object, thing. But considering the views of the Yogācāras, and specially what Vasubandhu and his commentator Sthiramati have said in describing this state of mind[1] it is to be taken in the sense of a special kind of *dharma*, *i.e.*, *āśrayaparāvṛtti* 'revolution or change of the recipient (*i.e.*, *ālayavijñāna* which is the seed of all, *sarvabījaka*).'[2]

A few words are here required with regard to the reading *dharmo dhātuḥ svabhāvataḥ*. This reading is found in some of

[1] See Tk, pp. 43-44: yadaivaṃ vijñaptimātratāyāṃ cittam avasthitaṃ bhavati tadā kathaṃ vyapadiśyata ity āha :

acitto 'nupalambho 'sau jñānaṃ lokottaraṃ ca tat |
āśrayasya parāvṛttir dvidhā dauṣṭhulyahānitaḥ || 29
sa evānāsravo dhātur anityaḥ kuśalo dhruvaḥ |
sukho vimuktikāyo 'sau dharmākhyo 'yaṃ mahāmuneḥ || 30

[2] For *parāvṛtti* in *āśrayaparāvṛtti* we have sometimes *parivṛtti* or *parivartana* (Tib. gnas. gyur. pa, or gnas. yoṅs. gyur. pa, or gshan. du. gyur. pa. See Tib. translation of Tk, Tanjur, Mdo, Śi, Fol. 190*a*). For *āśrayaparāvṛtti* see among others Tk, *loc. cit.*; MSA, XIX. 54; LA, p. 338; DB, App. p. 27, pp. 190ff. : tasya tathā paribhāvitaṃ tal laukikaṃ pariśuddhaṃ dhyānaṃ āpāyikakleśapakṣyaṃ duṣṭhulyam āśrayād apakarṣati. acireṇa tasya prahānād āśrayo'sya bodhisattvasya parivartate pāpakasyāpāyikasya karmaṇo 'tyantam akaraṇatāyai apāyāgamanatāyai ca. For its different explanation see ViS, pp. 609-612.

the MSS. of the Anandashram edition and in some others, too, examined by me, while others read *dharmo dhātusva*°. Ś accepts the latter and Ā n a n d a g i r i supports it sayin dhātusvabhāvata ity ekam padaṃ gṛhītvā vyācaṣṭe. This implies that the reading *dhātuḥ sva*° was also known to him. But neither of them seems to be very satisfactory and this leads the present writer to amend the reading as *dharmadhātuḥ svabhāvataḥ*. The reading *dharmo dhātuḥ* appears to be due to the unfamiliarity of the commentators with the significance of the word *dharmadhātu* which is quite appropriate here. Let us therefore explain the kārikā in this light.

In accordance with this reading the second half may be translated thus :

'Indeed the essence of reality (*dharmadhātu*)[3] is naturally illumined once for all.'

See I. 14, 16; III. 36, 37. For *c* see ChU, VIII. 4. 1-2 which is the same. See also NUU, 9; MkU, 2-23.

We take the next three kārikās together. The kārikā 82 is incomplete and as such should be construed with 83.

[3] The word *dharmadhātu* may be translated by 'the essence of reality.' It is devoid of the characteristics of subject and object (*viyukto grāhyagrāhakalakṣaṇena*) or undifferentiated into subject and object (*grāhyagrāhakarahita*). It is a synonym for *paramārtha* or *paramārthatattva*, MVt, § XCIX. 8; Tk, p. 41, l. 26; BAP, p. 354: parama uttamo 'rthaḥ. akṛtrimaṃ vasturūpaṃ yadadhigamāt sarvāvṛtivāsanānusandhikleśaprahāṇaṃ bhavati. sarvadharmāṇāṃ niḥsvabhāvatā śūnyatā tathatā bhūtakoṭiḥ dharmadhātur ityādiparyāyāḥ. Again, p. 421: bodhir buddhatvam ekānekasvabhāvaviviktam anutpannāniruddham anucchedam aśāśvataṃ sarvaprapañcavinirmuktam ākāśapratisamaṃ dharmakāyākhyaṃ paramārthatattvam ucyate. etad eva ca prajñāpāramitāśūnyatā-tathatā-bhūtakoṭi-dharmadhātvādiśabdena saṃvṛtim upādāyābhidhīyate

Writes M a i t r e y a n ā t h a (MVBT,[1] p. 41):

tathatā bhūtakoṭiś cānimittaḥ pa[ramārthakaḥ] |
dharmadhātuś ca paryāyāḥ śūnyatāyāḥ samāsataḥ ||
ananyathāviparyāsatannirodhāryagocaraiḥ |
hetutvāc cāryadharmāṇāṃ paryāyārtho yathākramam || I. 15-16.

As regards *dharmadhātu* V a s u b a n d h u says here (pp. 41-42): āryadharmahetutvād dharmadhātuḥ. āryadharmāṇāṃ tadālambanaprabhavatvād. hetvartho hy atra dhātvarthaḥ (see Tk, p. 44, ll. 20, 21). On the last words

82

sukham āvriyate nityaṃ duḥkhaṃ vivriyate sadā ।
yasya kasya ca dharmasya graheṇa bhagavān asau ॥

83

asti nāsty asti nāstīti nāsti nāstīti vā punaḥ ।
calasthirobhayābhāvair āvṛṇoty eva bāliśaḥ ॥

84

koṭyaś catasra etās tu grahair yāsāṃ sadāvṛtaḥ ।
bhagavān ābhir aspṛṣṭo yena dṛṣṭaḥ sa sarvadṛk ॥

'It is the adherence to (an idea of) a thing—whatsoever it may be,[1] by which bliss is constantly covered and misery is unfolded. The glorious one (*dharmadhātu*)—

(*i*) is, (*ii*) is not, (*iii*) is and is not (*i.e.*, both), or (*iv*) neither is nor is not (*i.e.*, not both)—with these (notions) the childish obscure it (respectively[2] in accordance with their own ideas of its being) (*i*) steady,[3] (*ii*) unsteady, (*iii*) both,[4] and (*iv*) the absence (of both).[5]

Sthiramati comments: svalakṣaṇopādāyarūpadhāraṇo 'py ayaṃ dhātuśabdo vartata ity āha hetvartho°. The word *dhātu* also means one that supports its own particularity (*svalakṣaṇa*) and the secondary qualities of matter (*upādāya* or *bhautika rūpa*), including evidently, as observes Stcherbatsky (MVD, p. 050) also the primary qualities of matter (*mahābhūta*). *Dharmadhātu* also means the mental state considered as element (*dhātu*) owing to its ultimate reality. See Pali Text Society's Dictionary, s.v. *dhamma*; *Compendium of Philosophy*, pp. 254-255.

1 This adherence is mainly four-fold as shown in the next kārikā.

2 In explaining *calasthira*° in c of 83 *sthira* is to be taken first as required by the sense (*arthakrama*) even discarding the order of reading (*pāṭhakrama*).

3 That is, permanent.

4 That is, steady and unsteady.

5 That is, neither steady nor unsteady.

These are the four points by the adherence to which the glorious one is always covered, but (in fact) it is not touched by them. One who realizes it is omniscient.'

In *nāsti nāstīti vā* in c of kārikā 83 take the first *na* with both *asti* and *nāsti*, as *na asti* and *na nāsti*.

These four points are maintained by four classes of disputants according to their ideas of the Absolute, as it is permanent, not permanent, both, or not both. But some of the Buddhists (Vijñānavādins and Mādhyamikas) do not subscribe to any one of these views, their point is quite free from all of them, while in the Vedānta the first point is avowedly held ; *e.g.*, KU, VI. 12 and 13 :

> astīti bruvato 'nyatra kathaṃ tad upalabhyate |
> astīty evopalabdhavyaḥ |

TU, II. 6. 1:

> asti brahmeti ced veda santam enaṃ tato viduḥ |

MU, IV. 4:

> asti brahmeti brahmavidyāvid abravīt.

As regards the position of the Buddhists it is also very clear :

> na san nāsan na sadasan na cāpy anubhayātmakaṃ |
> catuṣkoṭivinirmuktaṃ tattvaṃ mādhyamikā viduḥ ||
>
> S a r a h a in SS, fol. 17.[6]
>
> kāraṇaiḥ pratyayaiś cāpi yeṣāṃ lokaḥ pravartate |
> cātuṣkoṭikayā yuktā na te mannayakovidāḥ || LA, III. 20.

punar aparaṃ mahāmate bālapṛthagjanā anādikālaprapañca-dauṣṭhulyasvaprativikalpanā nāṭake nṛtyantaḥ svasiddhāntanaya-deśanāyām akuśalāḥ svacittadṛśyabāhyabhāvalakṣaṇābhiniviṣṭā

[6] See *Muśeon*, 1903, IV, p. 389. This kārikā is widely quoted : JS, 28; SDS, *Bauddhadarśana* ; SSS, III. 7 (with the reading *na cobhābhyāṃ vilakṣaṇaṃ* in c); catuṣkoṭivinirmuktaṃ śūnyaṃ tattvam iti sthitam—*Ibid*, 9; BAP, p. 359; SāS, I. 44 (V i j ñ ā n a b h i k ṣ u); *Cf.* BJS, II. 27 (=DN I, 27).

upāyadeśanāpāṭham abhiniviśante na svasiddhāntanayaṃ cātuṣkoṭikanayaviśuddhaṃ pratịvibhāvayanti. LA, p. 171.

yac ca mahāmate na kāryaṃ na kāraṇaṃ tan na san nāsad yac ca na san nāsat tac cātuṣkoṭikabāhyam. cātuṣkoṭikaṃ ca mahāmate lokavyavahāraḥ. *Op. cit*, p. 188.[7]

Cf. punar aparaṃ mahāmate catuṣṭayavinirmuktā tathāgatānāṃ dharmadeśanā yad utaikatvānyatvobhayānubhayavivarjitā nāstyastisamāropāpavādavinirmuktā satyapratītyasamutpādanirodhamārgavimokṣapravṛttipūrvakā mahāmate tathāgatānāṃ dharmadeśanā. *Op. cit.*, p. 96.

It is to be noted here that according to Ś the word *bhagavat* 'the glorious one' in 82*d* and 84*c* refers to *ātman*. On the following grounds, however, I think, it is the *dharmadhātu* in 81*c*, which is alluded to.

The subject matter here in kārikās 80-84 is the unwavering or the firm state of the mind which has turned back from and does not go onwards again to its object—the state which is *dharmadhātu* and to which aspire the Buddhas. This is further dealt with in the following two kārikās (85-86). There is, therefore, no room for *ātman* to which the word *bhagavat* may refer.

An objection may be raised here that the word *bhagavat* is used with reference to a conscious or sentient being, and as such it cannot refer to *dharmadhātu* which is nothing but the *niścalā sthiti* of the mind. One can, however, meet it in the following way. Such common phrases as *bhagavatī śrutiḥ*, *bhagavān vedaḥ*, *bhagavatī bhavitavyatā*, etc., will show that the word under discussion is employed also to non-sentient

[7] Sometimes instead of the four points (*catuṣkoṭi*) referred to there are only first three excluding the last. See MK, I. 7, VII. 20; CŚ, XVI. 25; LA, p. 156. Sometimes only the first two are mentioned. See my paper, *Catuṣkoṭi*, in the *Jhā Commemoration Volume*, 1937, pp. 85 ff. where similar passages are quoted from Vedantic texts.

beings. It is found that anything, irrespective of its being sentient or otherwise, that is powerful or commands respect, regard, faith, confidence, or reverence may be referred to by *bhagavat*.

It is also to be taken into consideration that this *dharmadhātu* is in fact Brahman of the Vedāntists as shown in the clearest possible words by the author himself in III. 46 which we have already discussed. Again, the *dharmadhātu* is the same as what we understand by the word *prajñāpāramitā*.[7] And it is very well-known that *prajñāpāramitā* is reverently mentioned with the epithet *bhagavatī*. Besides, this *dharmadhātu* which is the same as *prajñāpāramitā* is nothing but *advaya jñāna*, *i.e.*, the *jñāna* which is free from the subject and the object, and this is identified with *Tathāgata* as is evident from the following couplet from the PAS of Diṅnāga as quoted by Haribhadra in his AAA, p. 28.[8]

> prajñāpāramitā jñānam advayaṃ sa tathāgataḥ |
> sādhyā tādarthyayogena tācchabdyaṃ granthamārgayoḥ ||

The first half of this kārikā is based on such old texts as the following :

> cittamātrāvatāreṇa prajñā tāthāgatī matā | LA, III. 43.

See *Ibid.*, pp. 187-190 ending with yat sarvaprapañcātītaṃ sa tathāgataḥ. See also pp. 191 ff.[9]

[7] See BAP, p. 421 : etad eva ca prajñāpāramitā-śūnyatā-tathatā° ādiśabdena° abhidhīyate. This passage is quoted once more. See IV. 81, note 3, p. 189.

[8] See E. Obermiller: DPP, pp. 7, 45 ; SS, p. 14.

[9] Let us quote here another passage which is very significant, though a little lengthy, from the same work, *i.e.*, LA, pp. 191-193 :

na hi mahāmate abhāvas tathāgatagato° kintu mahāmate manomayadharmakāyasya tathāgatasyaitad adhivacanaṃ yatra (yat?) sarvatīrthakaraśrāvakapratyekabuddhasaptabhūmipratiṣṭhitānām aviṣayaḥ. so(yo?) 'nutpādas tathāgatasyaitan mahāmate paryāyavacanam. tad yathā mahāmate indraḥ śakraḥ purandaraḥ hastaḥ karaḥ pāṇis tanur dehaṃ śarīraṃ pṛthivī bhūmir vasundharā kham ākāśaṃ gaganam ity evamādyānāṃ bhāvānām ekaikasya bhāvasya bahavaḥ tathatākāreṇa tathāgataṃ paśyāmy avikalpākāreṇānupalambhayogena. evam anutpādākāreṇa tathāgataṃ paśyāmi, yāvad abhāvākāreṇa tathāgataṃ paśyāmi.° SŚP, p. 119.

For *Tathāgata* see also MK, XXII.

No objection can therefore be raised here with regard to the use of the word *bhagavat*.

paryāyavācakāḥ śabdā bhavanti vikalpitā na caiṣāṃ nāmabahutvād bhāvabahutvaṃ vikalpyate na ca svabhāvo na bhavati, evaṃ mahāmate aham api sahāyāṃ lokadhātau tribhir nāmāsaṃkhyeyaśatasahasrair bālānāṃ śravaṇāvabhāsam āgacchāmi taiś cābhilapanti māṃ na ca prajānanti tathāgatasyaite nāmaparyāyā iti. tatra kecin mahāmate tathāgatam iti māṃ prajānanti. kecit svayambhuvam iti nāyakaṃ vināyakaṃ pariṇāyakaṃ buddham ṛṣiṃ vṛṣabhaṃ brahmaṇaṃ (v l. brāhmaṇaṃ, brahmāṇam?) viṣṇum īśvaraṃ pradhānaṃ kapilaṃ bhūtāntam ariṣṭaṃ neminaṃ (ariṣṭaneminam?) somaṃ bhāskaraṃ rāmaṃ vyāsaṃ śukaṃ indraṃ baliṃ varuṇam iti caike saṃjānanti. apare 'nirodhānutpādaṃ śūnyatāṃ tathatāṃ bhūtatāṃ bhūtakoṭiṃ dharmadhātuṃ nirvāṇaṃ nityaṃ samatāṃ advayam anirodham animittaṃ pratyayaṃ buddhahetūpadeśaṃ vimokṣaṃ mārgasatyāni sarvajñaṃ jinaṃ manomayam iti caike saṃjānanti. evamādibhir mahāmate° māṃ janāḥ saṃjānanta udakacandra ivāpraviṣṭanirgatam. na ca bālā avabudhyante dvayāntapatitayā santatyā.

It is said in the preceding kārikā that one, who realizes that truth, becomes omniscient. The present kārikā tells us that omniscience being realized, there is nothing that can be desired, for every desire is fulfilled thereby :

85

prāpya sarvajñatāṃ kṛtsnāṃ brāhmaṇyaṃ padam advayam |
anāpannādimadhyāntaṃ kim ataḥ param īhate ||

'Having realized the full omniscience and (thereby) that state which is befitting a Brāhmaṇa,[1] and free from the

[1] In Buddhist literature a Brāhmaṇa is held in as much respect as a Śramaṇa, and this is evident from the well-known phrase *śramaṇa-brāhmaṇa* which is so frequently used. See DP, XXVI. Sometimes a true Brāhmaṇa is regarded as, or identified with a Buddha :

two,[2] and has no beginning, middle and end, what may one desire beyond it?'

It is to be noted that the final aim is described here to be the realization of omniscience (*sarvajñatā, cf. sarvākārajñatā* or *bodhi*) which can be asserted more preferably from the Buddhist point of view than from the Vedāntist.

usabhaṃ pavaraṃ vīraṃ mahesiṃ vijitāvinaṃ |
anejaṃ nahātakaṃ buddhaṃ tam ahaṃ brūmi brāhmaṇaṃ ||
Op. cit., XXVI. 40.

It may be noted that according to Buddhists a Brāhmaṇa is so called because he is *vāhitapāpa* 'one whose sin is removed' (*Op. cit.*, XXVI. 6). This is, however, far-fetched. The following may be quoted here:

ye ca vāhitapāpatvād brāhmaṇāḥ pāramārthikāḥ |
abhyastāmalanairātmyās te muner eva śāsane ||
ihaiva śramaṇas tena caturdhā parikīrttyate |
śūnyāḥ parapravādā hi śramaṇair brāhmaṇais tathā || TS, 3589, 3590.

Kamalaśīla writes on it in his *Pañjikā*: ata eva bhagavatoktam ihaiva śramaṇaḥ ihaiva brāhmaṇaḥ śūnyāḥ parapravādāḥ śramaṇair brāhmaṇair iti.

[2] The subject and the object.

The following kārikā says that this realization of omniscience is the object of *vinaya* 'discipline' and real *śama* 'quiescence' and *dama* 'introversion' of the senses.

86

viprāṇāṃ vinayo hy eṣa śamaḥ prākṛta ucyate |
damaḥ prakṛtidāntatvād evaṃ vidvāñ śamaṃ vrajet ||

'This is, indeed, the discipline of the wise, and is said to be the natural quiescence, and the introversion (of the senses) owing to (their) being naturally introverted. Knowing thus one should become quiescent.'

The reality set forth in the preceding kārikās (IV. 80-86) is further described in the next three kārikās showing that that is the *lokottara* 'supra-mundane' knowledge through the realization of which one becomes omniscient :

87, 88

savastu sopalambhaṃ ca dvayaṃ laukikam iṣyate |
avastu sopalambhaṃ ca śuddhaṃ laukikam iṣyate ||

avastv anupalambhaṃ ca lokottaram iti smṛtam |
jñānaṃ jñeyaṃ ca vijñeyaṃ sadā buddhaiḥ prakīrttitam ||

'That which consists of the two, the object and (its) perception, is regarded as mundane ; one without the object, but with the perception is regarded as pure mundane ; while one without the object and the perception is said to be supra-mundane.—This is to be understood to be the knowledge and the knowable[1] as is always declared by the Buddhas.'

In our ordinary experience when one perceives a jar there are both the object, the jar, and its perception. This knowledge is called *laukika* 'mundane', *i.e.*, belonging to or occurring in ordinary life. When one, however, in a higher grade of wisdom, with the clear knowledge of unreality or the imagined or imposed form of the jar, perceives it, that knowledge is with perception, but not with the object. This is called 'pure mundane', *i.e.*, it belongs to ordinary life and is covered (*āvṛta*) ; it is pure,—'pure' because it is not so obscure as the mundane, its obscurity having been removed to a great extent. Finally when the reality is perfectly realized, when the mind rests on itself being completely suppressed (*niruddha*) there is neither the jar, nor the perception, and as such this knowledge is regarded as *lokottara* 'supra-mundane,' surpassing the ordinary life.

Of these three kinds of *jñāna*, *viz*., (*i*) *laukika*, (*ii*) *śuddha laukika*, and (*iii*) *lokottara*, the first is well-known to all and

[1] We have already (IV. 1) seen that there is no difference between *jñāna* and *jñeya*. Or it may mean that whatever we may know by the terms *jñāna* and *jñeya* is only the three things mentioned in the kārikās.

is met with in every system ; and the last two are to be found in Yogācāra texts. For instance, MVT[1], p. 19 :

paratantrasvabhāvo hi śuddhalaukikagocaraḥ |

Tk, p. 40 : nirvikalpalokottarajñānadṛśye pariniṣpanne svabhāve adṛṣṭe apratividdhe asākṣātkṛte tatpṛṣṭhalabdhaśuddhalaukikajñānagamyatvāt paratantro 'nyena jñānena na gṛhyate. na punar lokottarajñānapṛṣṭhalabdhenāpi jñānena na dṛśyate.

In LA, p. 156, these *jñānas* are found as (*i*) *laukika*, (*ii*) *lokottara*, and (*iii*) *lokottaratama* respectively. The difference is only in nomenclature and as such is not important. The LA, p. 157, describes them very clearly in the following words which deserve here to be considered carefully :

(*i*) tatra laukikaṃ jñānaṃ sadasatpakṣābhiniviṣṭānāṃ sarvatīrthakarabālapṛthagjanānāṃ ca.

(*ii*) tatra lokottaraṃ jñānaṃ sarvaśrāvakapratyekabuddhānāṃ svasāmānyalakṣaṇapatitāśayābhiniviṣṭānāṃ.

(*iii*) tatra lokottaratamaṃ jñānaṃ buddhabodhisattvānāṃ nirābhāsadharmapravicayād anirodhānutpādadarśanāt sadasatpakṣavigataṃ tathāgatabhūminairātmyādhigamāt pravartate.[2]

This reality with which we are concerned here is described by V a s u b a n d h u in his Tk, verse 29 in the following words which may be quoted here :

acitto 'nupalambho 'sau jñānaṃ lokottaraṃ ca tat |

S t h i r a m a t i comments :

tad anena ślokadvayena darśanamārgam ārabhyottaraviśeṣagatyā phalasampattir udbhāvitā vijñaptimātrapraviṣṭayoginaḥ. tatra grāhakacittābhāvād grāhyārthānupalambhāc ca acitto

[2] Generally in Buddhist works things are divided into two categories, (*i*) *laukika*, and (*ii*) *lokottara* (see MV, p. 501) ; as for instance, all mental states are *laukika* excepting only nine, *viz*., four paths (*maggas*), four fruits (*maggaphalas*), and one uncompounded element (*asaṃkhatadhātu*), *i.e.*, *nibbāna*, —these are *lokottara*. DSṇ, § 1093, 1094.

'nupalambho 'sau. aparicitatvāt[3] loke samudācārābhāvāt nirvikalpatvāc ca lokād uttīrṇam iti jñānaṃ lokottaraṃ ca tat.

So far as goes my information, such division of *jñāna* or *jñeya* is not to be found in Upaniṣads.

Ś explains the above three kinds of *jñāna* as the conditions of (*i*) waking, (*ii*) dream, and (*iii*) sleep respectively (*jāgrat*, *svapna*, *suṣupti*).

3 The printed text reads *anucitatvāt*, but it does not give any appropriate sense. We should, therefore, read here *aparicitatvāt* with the Tibetan version which has *ḥdris.par.ma.byas.pa.*

89

jñāne ca trividhe jñeye krameṇa vidite svayam |
sarvajñatā hi sarvatra bhavatīha mahādhiyaḥ ||

'The threefold knowledge and knowable being gradually understood everywhere spontaneously evolves here the state of omniscience of a man of high intellect.'[1]

That the *jñāna* is *trividha* 'threefold' is just now seen in the preceding two kārikās. According to its function, too, it is *trividha*. We read in the LA, p. 157 :

tatra trividhaṃ jñānaṃ svasāmānyalakṣaṇāvadhārakaṃ cotpādavyayāvadhāraṇakaṃ cānutpādānirodhāvadhārakaṃ ca.[2]

The omniscience (*sarvajñatā*) referred to is Buddhahood (*buddhatva*).[3]

1 The word *mahādhī* is nothing but *dhīmat* which is a name for a Bodhisattva. See MSA, XIX. 73; MVt,[1] 627.

2 As regards the nature of *jñāna* the following may be cited from LA, p. 157: asaṅgalakṣaṇaṃ jñānam.° asaṅgasvabhāvalakṣaṇaṃ jñānam.° aprāptilakṣaṇaṃ jñānaṃ svapratyātmāryajñānagatigocaram apraveśānirgamatvād udakacandravaj jale.

3 See BAP, pp. 447-8; ASP, pp. 42-3. *Buddhatva* = *sarvajñatva* consisting in (*i*) *sarvākārajñatā*, (*ii*) *mārgajñatā*, and (*iii*) *vastujñāna*.

Ś explains *sarvajñatā* as sarvaś cāsau jñaś ceti sarvajñaḥ. tasya bhāvaḥ sarvajñatā.

In the next kārikā the author tells his followers to understand certain things:

90

heyajñeyāpyapākyāni vijñeyāny agrayānataḥ[1] |
teṣām anyatra vijñeyād upalambhas triṣu smṛtaḥ ||

'That which is to be abandoned, that which is to be known, that which is to be attained, and that which is to be matured are to be understood from the *Agrayāna*. It is said that among them there is perception of the three, but not of that which is to be known.'

The *Agrayāna* in the text is nothing but the Mahāyāna, as is evident from a number of Buddhist works in which the word occurs as a synonym for Mahāyāna.[2]

Now, what are we to understand by *heya*, etc.? As regards *heya* and *jñeya*, if we follow here A s a ṅ g a, they are *paratantra* and *parikalpita svabhāvas* (see IV. 74-75) respectively.[3] *Āpya* (=*prāpya*) 'attainable' implies *dharma*

1 All the editions and MSS examined have °*yāṇa* instead of °*yāna* as expected.

2 MSA, p. 53: piṭakatrayaṃ sūtravinayābhidharmāḥ. tad eva trayaṃ hīnayānāgrayānabhedena dvayaṃ bhavati. See SP, III. 1, V. 61; MSA, p. 83; SRS (R a j e n d r a l a l M i t r a's *Buddhist Manuscripts from Nepal*), p. 229; LV, p. 408; VCh., pp. 30, 33. Sometimes it is also called *Śreṣṭhayāna*, Vch., p. 30.

3 Let us quote here the following from the MSA. XI. 13 (p. 58): where *heya* and *jñeya* are explained:

tattvaṃ yat satataṃ dvayena rahitaṃ bhrāntes ca saṃniśrayaḥ
śakyaṃ naiva ca sarvathābhilapituṃ yac cāprapañcātmakam |
jñeyaṃ heyam atho viśodhyam amalaṃ yac ca prakṛtyāmalaṃ
yasyākāśasuvarṇavārisadṛśī kleśād viśuddhir matā ||

dhātu or *dharmadhātu* already alluded to (IV. 81),[4] which is *parinișpanna*, and *pākya* 'to be matured' refers to the act of maturing by discipline for the attainment of the Absolute. The last is not only for others, but also for one's own self.[5]

The second half of the kārikā says that among these four things only three, *i.e.*, *heya*, *āpya*, and *pākya*, can be perceived, but not the *jñeya* or *vijñeya*. For it is *parikalpita* 'imagined,' and a thing which is only imagined owing to its very nature cannot be perceived, just like mirage, as it

satataṃ dvayena rahitaṃ tattvaṃ parikalpitaḥ svabhāvo grāhyagrāhakalakṣaṇenātyantam asattvāt. bhrānteḥ saṃniśrayaḥ paratantras tena tatparikalpanāt. anabhilāpyam aprapañcātmakaṃ ca parinișpannaḥ svabhāvaḥ. tatra prathamaṃ tattvaṃ parijñeyaṃ dvitīyaṃ praheyaṃ tṛtīyaṃ viśodhyaṃ cāgantukamalād viśuddhaṃ ca prakṛtyā. yasya prakṛtyā viśuddhasyākāśasuvarṇavārisadṛśī kleśād viśuddhiḥ. na hy ākāśādīni prakṛtyā aśuddhāni. na cāgantukamalāpagamād eṣāṃ viśuddhir neṣyate.

4 MSA, XIX. 56 : prāpyaṃ dharmadhātuḥ.

5 MSA, XX-XXI 42 : sattvaparipākacaryā dvayor eva paripācanārthaṃ. paripācanaṃ hy atra vinayanam; XVII. 3, 22, 36; XIX. 56; DA, p. 125; BBh, p. 22. As regards the maturation of one's own self (*ātmaparipāka*) the following may be quoted from MSA, VIII. 1 :

rucih prasādaḥ praśamo 'nukampanā kṣamātha medhā prabalatvam eva ca |
ahāryatāṅgaiḥ samupetatā bhṛśaṃ jinātmaje tat paripākalakṣaṇam ||

rucir mahāyānadeśanādharme. prasādas taddeśike. praśamaḥ kleśānām. anukampā sattveṣu. medhā grahaṇadhāraṇapratibedheṣu. prabalatvam adhigame. ahāryatā mārapravādibhiḥ. prāhāṇikāṅgaiḥ samanvāgatatvam. bhṛśam iti rucyādīnāṃ adhimātratvaṃ darśayati. eṣa samāsena navaprakāra ātmaparipāko veditavyaḥ.

See also, VIII. 11 :

iti navavidhavastupācitātmā paraparipācanayogyatām upetaḥ |
śubhamayasatatapravardhitātmā bhavati sadā jagato 'grabandhubhūtaḥ ||

KP, § 31 : tad yathā kāśyapa tejodhātuḥ sarvasasyāni paripācayati evam eva kāśyapa bodhisattvasya prajñā sarvasattvānāṃ sarvaśukladharmān paripācayati.° See also the stanza which follows it.

In BBh, a whole chapter named *Paripākapaṭala* (VI) is devoted to it giving particulars.

Cf. *lokapakti* 'maturation of the world' in the ŚB, XI. 5. 7. 1.

has no existence, it is merely an imagination, simply a word, only a name; it is not perceived, and hence there is no perception.[6]

[6] It may be noted that sometimes five *jñeyas* are found (BAP, p. 447 : jñeyaṃ pañcavidham), as says Sthiramati in MVT[1], p. 6, *viz*, (*i*) the worlds (*lokadhātu*), (*ii*) the living beings (*sattva*), (*iii*) the elements of existence (*dharma*), (*iv*) the discipline (*vinaya*), and (*v*) the means (*upāya*). These seem to have no connexion herewith.

In the next few kārikās the author gives some leading thoughts of the Agrayāna alluded to above:

91

prakṛtyākāśavaj jñeyāḥ sarve dharmā anādayaḥ ।
vidyate na hi nānātvaṃ teṣāṃ kvacana kiñcana ॥

'All the elements of existence are without beginning, and by nature they are to be known like the sky. Verily they have nowhere any variety.'

For the first half of the kārikā see IV. 1, where we have already seen that things are just like the sky as said in such texts as the ASP, p. 297 : yathākāśam° already quoted there.

For the second half where it is said that there is no variety of things see the well-known Upaniṣadic texts : neha nānāsti kiñcana, BU, IV. 4. 19 ; KU, IV. 11 ; KtU, III. 8 ; NS, IV. 1. 34 ff (with Vātsyāyana). See also our own text, II. 34, IV. 94, 100.

92

ādibuddhāḥ[1] prakṛtyaiva[2] sarve dharmāḥ suniścitāḥ ।
yasyaivaṃ bhavati kṣāntiḥ so 'mṛtatvāya kalpate ॥

[1] See *ādau buddhāḥ*, IV. 98; *cf*. *ādiśānta*, IV. 93, Tib. gzod.ma.nas.shi.ba, from this one is to take *ādi-* here for *āditaḥ* meaning 'from the outset.'

[2] See IV. 93.

'By the very nature all elements of existence are well ascertained as originally knowledge. One who has such acquiescence is fit for immortality.'

The word *buddha* in *ādibuddha* means here *bodha* 'knowledge,'[3] *i.e.*, *advaya jñāna* which is called Tathāgata as we have already seen (IV. 82-84). See also SŚP, p. 124 :

tathāgataṃ bhadanta śāradvatīputra paryeṣitukāmenātmā paryeṣitavyaḥ. ātmeti bhadanta śāradvatīputra buddhasyaitad adhivacanam.

All phenomena are only in their imposed or imagined forms, they being *buddha*, or *bodha* or *jñāna*.

Cf. here the well-known phrase in later Vedāntic works[4]: *nityaśuddhabuddhamuktasatyasvabhāva* for Brahman.

As regards the meaning of the word *kṣānti*[5] a few words are required here. Generally, *kṣānti* means 'patience.' In Buddhism there are different *kṣāntis* of which the following three are often mentioned : (*i*) *duḥkhādhivāsanākṣānti* 'patience accepting miseries,' (*ii*) *dharmanidhyāna*° 'patience by meditating upon the elements of existence,' and (*iii*) *parāpakāramarṣaṇa*° 'patience bearing injuries done by others.'[6]

Besides, in Buddhism it has other meanings. In explaining *kṣānti* (Pali *khanti*) in AN, I. 94, the commentary, *Manorathapūraṇī*, writes: *khamatīti adhivāsanakhanti*. It says that *khanti* means *adhivāsana* 'acquiescence,' 'consent,' or 'acceptance.' Again, we read in the AN, III. 118 :

imesaṃ āvuso tiṇṇaṃ puggalānaṃ katamo te puggalo khamati abhikkantataro ca paṇītataro ca.

3 Ś explains : ādibuddhāḥ nityabodhasvarūpāḥ.

4 Such as VeS, pp. 38-39 (§ 28).

5 Ś : bodhakartavyatānirapekṣatā.

6 As described in BA and BAP, VI (pp. 172 ff); ŚS, IX (pp. 179 ff). *Cf.* DS, CVII.

The commentary explains *khamati* saying *khamatīti ruccati.* Accordingly the passage quoted above may be translated thus :

'Which of these three persons is, O friend, agreeable to you as the most excellent and exalted?'

Here evidently *kṣānti* is *ruci* 'pleasure', 'liking.' This is quite clear also from a passage of the SNt, 897,[7] where the commentator in his MNs explains *khanti* (*kṣānti*) in the text by *pema* (*preman*) 'fondness, predilection,' *chanda* 'desire,' and *rāga* 'lust,' which are in fact, the same as *ruci*.[8]

Again, in Buddhist texts (CN, p. 164, see Vbh, p. 245) *kṣānti* is described as synonymous with the following words : (*i*) *dṛṣṭi* (Pali *diṭṭhi*) 'view,' 'belief,' 'theory,' (*ii*) *ruci* 'pleasure,' 'liking,' (*iii*) *labdhi* (Pali *laddhi*) 'view,' 'belief,' 'theory'; (*iv*) *adhyāśaya* (Pali *ajjhāsaya*) 'intention,' 'thought,' and (*v*) *abhiprāya* (Pali *adhippāya*) 'intention,' 'opinion.' It is therefore quite clear from the above that *kṣānti* sometimes means *dṛṣṭi* 'view'.[9] And so far as I can understand in the present case it is used in this sense.

See SP, p. 136 ; MSA, XI. 52; SRS, VII ; DS, p. 63 ; Poussin : MV, pp. 362ff., and AK, VI, pp. 165 ff., as well as the works quoted herein ; St. LA, p. 396.

[7] yā kāc'imā sammutiyo puthujjā sabbā 'va etā na upeti vidvā |
anūpayo so upayaṃ kim eyya diṭṭhe sute khantim akubbamāno ||

[8] See SN, IV. 348 : bhūtapubbaṃ bhante cattvāro satthāro nānādiṭṭhikā nānākhantikā nānārucikā ; MN, I. 487, II. 43. See also the *Sumaṅgalavilāsinī* on DN, II. 213 : khantīti tattha katamā khanti. yā khamanatā adhivāsanatā acaṇḍikkaṃ anasuropo attamanatā cittassāti evaṃ vuttā adhivāsanakhanti.

[9] It may be noted that in Sanskrit, too, √*kṣam* is not always used in the sense of 'to be patient,' or 'to endure,' etc. *Cf.* UC, I. 14 : tan no yad uktam aśivaṃ na hi tat kṣamaṃ te. Here *kṣama* has nothing to do with 'patience' or 'forbearance,' etc. In Pali (DhA, I. 40) √*khama* is said to mean 'to be fit,' 'to seem good,' specially in such cases as *yathā te khameyya* 'as may seem good to you.'

It is well-known in *Prajñāpāramitāsūtras* and the works based thereon that all elements of existence are devoid of the characteristics of their own (*niḥsvabhāva*), they neither originate (*anutpanna*), nor disappear (*aniruddha*), and as such they are quiescent from the outset (*ādiśānta=prakṛtiśānta*), and by the very nature they are merged in *nirvāṇa* (*prakṛtinirvṛta*). This point is mainly described in the following kārikā :

93

ādiśāntā[1] hy anutpannāḥ prakṛtyaiva sunirvṛtāḥ ।
sarve dharmāḥ samābhinnā ajaṃ sāmyaṃ[2] viśāradam[3] ।

'All elements of existence are quiescent from the outset, non-originated, and by the very nature perfectly merged in *nirvāṇa* ; they are all equal and not different. (The absolute) is unborn, equal and fearless.'

Let us quote here the following from MSA, XI. 51 :

niḥsvabhāvatayā siddhā uttarottaraniśrayāt |
anutpannāniruddhādiśāntaprakṛtinirvṛtāḥ || [4]

Here follows the commentary :

niḥsvabhāvatayānutpādādayaḥ. yo hi niḥsvabhāvaḥ so 'nutpanno yo 'nutpannaḥ so 'niruddho yo 'niruddhaḥ sa ādiśānto ya ādiśāntaḥ sa prakṛtinirvṛtaḥ.

1 Tib. gzod.ma.nas.shi.ba, lit. *āditaḥ śāntaḥ*.

2 See III. 2, 38; IV. 77, 80, 95, 100.

3 See the note on *vaiśāradya* in the next kārikā. *Cf. nirbhaya* in I. 25, III. 35; and *abhaya* in IV. 78, and Upaniṣads, ChU, I. 4. 4, 5; IV. 15. 1. etc.

4 This is as reconstructed by Lévi according to the Chinese version. The original Sanskrit is lost. The scribe has, however, given here a corrupted kārikā and it is as follows :

niḥsvabhāvatayā siddhā uttarottaraniḥśrayāḥ ।
anutpādo 'niruddhaś cādiśāntiḥ parinirvṛtiḥ ॥

See MSA., Tome II (French Translation), p. 122.

'Owing to the absence of nature there are no origination, etc. That which is devoid of nature is not originated; that which is not originated is not suppressed (destroyed); that which is not suppressed is quiescent from the outset; and that which is quiescent from the outset is naturally merged in perfect nirvāṇa.'

In the text *śānti* (connected with *ādiśānta*) and *nirvṛti* or *nirvāṇa* (connected with *sunirvṛta=parinirvṛta*) are actually nothing but *apravṛtti* meaning 'not coming forth,' 'not arising,' 'not originating.' Elements of existence are *ādiśānta* and *su-* (*=pari-*) *nirvṛta*; it implies that originally they do not originate, and so to speak, they are in *śānti* and *nirvāṇa*. For the above explanation of the two words see MV, p. 529: yā'pravṛttis tan nirvāṇam iti vyavasthāpyate; p. 538: ya upaśamo 'pravṛttis tan nirvāṇam.

Poussin observes (ERE, Vol. 9, p. 851): "From an absolute point of view (*paramārthatas*) there is no difference (*nānābhāva*)[5] among things and the characters of things. Things are void (*śūnya*) like the daughter of a barren woman; characters are void like the beauty of this unreal daughter. Things are void, because there is no real origination of things—if no origination, no destruction, an eternal non-existence. There is no difference between existence (*saṃsāra*) and *nirvāṇa*. Not being produced (*anutpanna*), not being destroyed, things are from the beginning quiescent (*ādiśānta*), they are really, naturally (*prakṛtyā*) in *nirvāṇa* (*parinirvṛta*)."

For the wording and thought of the first half of the kārikā the following passages, besides MSA, XI. 51 already cited (p. 204), may be quoted:

(*i*) ādiśāntā hy anutpannāḥ prakṛtyaiva ca nirvṛtāḥ |
dharmās te vivṛtā nātha dharmacakrapravartane ||[6]

[5] See our text: vidyate nahi nānātvaṃ teṣāṃ kvacana kiñcana, IV. 91, and also II. 34; III. 24; IV. 93-94.

[6] Quoted in MV, p. 225, and SuS, p. 20 from *Āryaratnameghasūtra*. See Poussin: JRAS, 1910, pp 138-39; Sylvain Lévi: MSA, Tome II (French tr.), p. 122.

(*ii*) ataḥ sattvāḥ prakṛtyā parinirvṛtāḥ | BA, IX. 104.

(*iii*) tasmāt sarvadharmā anutpannāniruddhasvabhāvatayā ādiśāntāḥ prakṛtinirvṛtāḥ. BAP, p. 589.

(*iv*) paramārthasatyataḥ prakṛtinirvāṇatayādiśāntatvāt. prakṛtinirvṛtatvāt sarvadharmāṇām iti.

Ibid, p. 385.

(*v*) ādipraśāntā imi sarvadharmāḥ | SP, II. 68.

The next kārikā is in support of what is said in the preceding one :

94

vaiśāradyaṃ tu vai nāsti bhede vicaratāṁ sadā |
bhedanimnāḥ pṛthagvādās tasmāt te kṛpaṇāḥ smṛtāḥ ||

'But verily those who always move following difference have no intrepidity. Those who maintain that a thing is diverse[1] (*pṛthak*=*nānā*) are prone to difference, and are, therefore, regarded as pitiable.'

The word *viśārada* in IV. 93 of which the noun, *vaiśāradya*, is used here requires some explanation. According to Ś they mean 'pure' (*viśuddha*) and 'purity' (*viśuddhi*) respectively. It is supported by Bhojarāja saying in his vṛtti on YS, I. 47 that *vaiśāradya* means 'clearness' (*nairmalya*). This exposition is based on that of Vyāsa on the same YS.[2] The idea behind it may be explained in another way.[3]

[1] See IV. 91 and note 5 on IV. 93.

[2] aśuddhyāvaraṇamalāpetasya prakāśātmano buddhisattvasya rajastamobhyām anabhibhūtaḥ svacchaḥ sthitipravāho vaiśāradyam. Wood translates it thus: 'When freed from obstruction by impurity the *sattva* of thinking substance, the essence of which is light, has a pellucid steady flow not overwhelmed by *rajas* and *tamas*.'

[3] As in India the season *śarad* 'autumn' is particularly clear, anything in that season (*śārada* 'autumnal'), such as the moon or water, is also clear. Thus *śārada* with the prefix *vi-* which here simply emphasizes the idea might have gradually been employed in the sense of 'clear,' its noun *vaiśāradya* meaning 'clearness'.

The word *viśārada* is, however, of doubtful derivation.[4] The prefix *vi-* only intensifies the meaning of *śārada* one of the meanings of which is 'mature,' *i.e.*, 'rich in years' (*śarad* 'a year'), 'old.' Accordingly the secondary meaning with the prefix *vi-* is *pravīṇa* 'clever.' As boldness (*pragalbhatā*) generally depends on one's maturity *viśārada* also means 'bold' (*pragalbha*).

In both Sanskrit and Pali the word *śārada* (Pali *sārada*) means *apratibha* or *apragalbha* 'timid,' 'not bold,'[5] and *viśārada* (Pali *visārada*) is used to mean 'scholar' (*paṇḍita*) and 'bold' (*pragalbha*).[6]

In Buddhist writings *vaiśāradya* (Pali *vesārajja*) is explained as opposite to **śāradya* (Pali *sārajja*)[7] which means 'timidity.' That *vaiśāradya* is 'intrepidity' (*nirbhayatā*) is very clearly said in AKV², p. 646.[8] In Buddhism *vaiśāradya* is four-fold, *viz.*, the *vaiśāradya* regarding (*i*) the highest knowledge of all things (*sarvadharmābhisambodhivaiśāradya*), (*ii*) the knowledge of destroying all the human passions (*sarvāsravakṣayajñana°*), (*iii*) rightly describing the impediments (*antarāyikadharmānanyathātvaniścitavyākaraṇa°*), and (*iv*) the rightness of the way leading to salvation (*nairyāṇikapratipattathātva°*).[9]

[4] It is read in the group of *dṛḍhādi* (Pāṇini, V. 1. 123), and Vardhamāna explains it in his GM, p. 221, taking it in the sense of *pravīṇa* 'skilful,' 'clever' : śāradaśabdaḥ pratyagravācī. yathā rajjuśāradam udakam, dṛṣacchāradāḥ saktavaḥ. sadyo hi rajjvoddhṛtam udakaṃ pratyagram anupahataṃ rajjuśāradam ucyate. sadyaś ca dṛṣadā piṣṭāḥ saktavo dṛṣacchāradāḥ. śārada(tva)m pratyagratvam abhinavatvam. tad vigatam asya viśāradaḥ pravīṇaḥ. pravīṇo lakṣaṇayā.° He himself is, however, not satisfied with it and goes on to say : athavā vyutpattiśūnyaḥ pravīṇavācī viśāradaśabdaḥ.

[5] See AmK, III. 3. 95 : dvau tu śāradau | pratyagrāpratibhau vidvatsupragalbhau viśāradau || AP, 984 : sārado saradubbhūte appagabbhe mato tisu.

[6] AP, 228, 959 : vutto visārado tīsu suppagabbhe ca paṇḍite ||

[7] vesārajjānīti ettha sārajjapatipakkho vesārajjaṃ. MP on AN, II. 8 ff.

[8] nirbhayatā hi vaiśāradyam. The Tib. term for *vaiśāradya* is *mi.ḥjigs.pa* which means *nirbhaya* or *nirbhayatā*.

[9] MVt², 8. In the same work (28) there is a different kind of *vaiśāradya* which is also four-fold. Again, the following four-fold *vaiśāradya* is enumerated

By modern scholars *vaiśāradya* is variously explained or translated. Childers says (*Dictionary*, p. 564) it is 'confidence or fearlessness,' evidently taking *viśārada* to mean 'bold' (*pragalbha*). Lévi explains it as 'assurance' (MSA, French tr., p. 319). Kern in his Eng. translation of SP[1] (SBE, Vol. XXI), p. 246, interprets (referring to Burnouf: *Lotus*, p. 396; S. Hardy: *Eastern Monachism*, p. 291) it as 'absence of hesitation.' But to be consistent with the explanations offered by Vyāsa and Bhojarāja, Kern's exposition of the word in his *Histoire du Bouddhisme dans l'Inde* (French translation by G. Huet in the *Annales du Musée Guimet*, Tome X), Tome I, p. 283, deserves to be consulted in this connection.

in the MVu, Vol. II, p. 261 : (*i*) *kāya*°, (*ii*) *vācā*°, (*iii*) *citta*° and (*iv*) *pṛthu*°. The last term is not clear, and Senart supposes (p. 545) that it is *pṛthag*°. Still it is to be ascertained.

In Śīlāṅka's ṭīkā on SKr, XIV. 17, *viśārada* (Pkt. *visāraya*) is explained as *pratipādaka*.

95

aje sāmye tu ye kecid bhaviṣyanti suniścitāḥ |
te hi loke mahājñānās tac ca loko na gāhate ||

'But only those who are quite certain about the *aja* 'unborn' and *sāmya* 'same'[1] are possessed of great wisdom. The people, however, do not penetrate into it.'[2]

[1] For *aja* and *sāmya* see IV. 77, 80, 93, 100.

[2] It refers to *aja* and *sāmya* in the text. Ś explains *tat* taking it to signify the *vartman* 'way' of the sages which an ordinary man cannot grasp. Here Ś quotes the following from the MB(?) :

sarvabhūtātmabhūtasya sarvabhūtahitasya ca |
devā api mārge muhyanty apadasya padaiṣiṇaḥ |
śakunīnām ivākāśe gatir naivopalabhyate ||

The first two lines with some variations in *c* are quoted also by Sāyaṇa in his commentary on the TA, VIII. 2 (p. 547). For *śakunīnām*° see Ś on BU, p 637 : ta utsahante khe 'pi śākunaṃ padaṃ draṣṭum; DP, 92-93 (with Aṭṭhakathā) : ākāse 'va sakuntānāṃ gati tesaṃ durannayā; Again, antarīkṣi śakunasya

Until and unless the knowledge becomes completely free from any relation to its object the highest cannot be attained. Therefore the knowledge must be *asaṅga*, *i.e.*, detached from its objects. This state of its detachment is described in the following two kārikās (96, 97), the first of which runs :

vā padam, quoted from *Āryaratnākarasūtra* in MV, 90; tad yathāpi nāmākāśe śakunipadam, SŚP, p. 137; yathāntarikṣe śakuneḥ padaṃ budhair, vaktuṃ na śakyam na ca darśanopagam, quoted by Poussin in his French tr. of MA, p. 12 in *Le Muséon*, 1907, p. 261.

96

ajeṣv ajam asaṃkrāntaṃ dharmeṣu jñānam iṣyate ।
yato na kramate jñānam asaṅgaṃ tena kīrtitam ॥

'It is accepted[1] that knowledge which is unborn does not go (*i.e.*, relate itself) to the elements of existence, which are (also) unborn. As the knowledge does not go (to the elements of existence) it is declared to be free from attachment (*asaṅga*, *i.e.*, free from any relation to its object).'

See IV. 72, 79 (*niḥsaṅga*), 97, 99 ; *cf. agraha*, III. 32. See also IV. 72 :

cittaṃ nirviṣayaṃ nityam asaṅgaṃ tena kīrtitam ।

See IV. 1, note 5 where passages are quoted to show that *jñāna* is *asaṅga*.

[1] Lit. desired (*iṣyate*).

97

aṇumātre'pi vaidharmye jāyamāne 'vipaścitaḥ ।
asaṅgatā sadā nāsti kim utāvaraṇacyutiḥ ॥

'If there be even the least difference (of elements of existence[1] in the mind) of an unwise man, there is no state of

[1] It is to be remembered that all elements of existence are in fact non-different : sarve dharmāḥ samābhinnāḥ (IV. 93), as we have already seen.

(its) being always free from attachment (*asaṅgatā*), not to speak of the disappearance of the covering.'

The state of being always *asaṅga* of *jñāna* or *citta* is referred to in the preceding kārikā (96).

As regards *āvaraṇa* 'covering' or 'obstruction', it is two-fold, (*i*) *kleśa-āvaraṇa* and (*ii*) *jñeya-āvaraṇa*[2]. *kleśa* literally means that which troubles one by the strokes of various kinds of misery, as Vācaspati Miśra would explain it (YS, I. 24). Accordingly, as sinful desires, vices, or passions are for misery they are termed *kleśa*. For the same reason it also means 'impurity', 'stain'. Sometimes the word stands for 'lust' or 'sensuality' (*rāga*), 'aversion' (*dveṣa*), and 'bewilderment' (*moha*). There are also ten *kleśas*, *lobha*, *dveṣa*, *moha*, *māna*, etc. (DSn, §1548).[3] For further details see *Pali-English Dictionary*, PTS, s.v. *kilesa*, and MV, p. 361. *Kleśa-āvaraṇa* thus means the *āvaraṇa* 'covering' or 'obstruction' in the form of *kleśas*. Until and unless they are destroyed (*kleśaprahāṇa*) the truth is not manifested, nor can one attain to the highest bliss.[4] *Kleśas* are regarded as the mother of all miseries. Similarly *jñeya* is also an *āvaraṇa*. The word *jñeya* means 'knowable,' *i.e.*, the *dharmas* 'elements of existence' which are not substantial and thus they have no reality. Yet one perceives them (*jñeyopalabdhi*). And as long as one continues to do so one is far from the goal. Thus *jñeya* is regarded as an *āvaraṇa*,[5]

[2] DS, CXV; MSA, IX. 3, 12, XX-XXI, 44; BA, IX. 55.

[3] In YS, II. 3, 5-9, there are five kinds of *kleśa*, viz., *avidyā*, *asmitā*, *rāga*, *dveṣa*, and *abhiniveśa*.

[4] See MV, p. 538 : kleśānām apravṛttyā vā prapañcopaśamaḥ.

[5] BAP, pp. 447 : kleśā evāvṛtiḥ. jñeyaṃ cāvṛtir āvaraṇam. °jñeyam eva samāropitarūpatvād āvṛtiḥ. Sometimes *jñeyāvaraṇa* is explained as jñeye āvaraṇam (Tk, p 15 : jñeyāvaraṇam api sarvasmin jñeye jñanapratibandhabhūtam akliṣṭam ajñānam), 'the obstacle regarding the knowable,' (*i.e.*, the reality or the things in their true nature). See TSP, pp. 869-890. Sometimes (AN, III. 436; AK, IV. p. 201) there are three *āvaraṇas*, (*i*) *kleśāvaraṇa*, (*ii*) *karmāvaraṇa* (5 *ānantaryas* and 10 *akuśala karmapathas*), and (*iii*) *vipākāvaraṇa* (8 *akṣaṇas*).

and it must be removed (*jñeyānupalabdhi*) for the realization of *nirvāṇa*. *Jñeyāvaraṇa* disappears by one's realizing the unreality of the elements of existence as separate entities (*dharma-nairātmya*), while *kleśāvaraṇa* goes away by the realization of the unreality of the individual ego (*pudgalanairātmya*).[6] Or both the *āvaraṇas* can be removed by the meditation on *śūnyatā* (BA, IX. 55).

[6] LA, VII, p. 241: jñeyāvaraṇaṃ punar mahāmate dharmanairātmya-darśanaviśeṣād viśudhyate. kleśāvaraṇaṃ tu pudgalanairātmyadarśanābhyāsa-pūrvakaṃ prahīyate. See Sthiramati on Tk, p. 15.

The removal of *āvaraṇa* is referred to in the preceding kārikā, but in the next kārikā it is said that, in fact, there is no *āvaraṇa* at all:

98

alabdhāvaraṇāḥ sarve dharmāḥ prakṛtinirmalāḥ |
ādau buddhās tathā muktā budhyanta iti nāyakāḥ ||

All the elements of existence have always been without any covering and unsullied in their nature. From the beginning they are knowledge as well as in *nirvāṇa* (*mukta*)—this the Buddhas understand.'

For *ādau buddhāḥ* see IV. 92,93. Because the elements of existence do not originate they are said as *mukta, i.e.*, in *śānti* or *nirvāṇa*. On this see IV. 93, p. 205.

For *prakṛtinirmala* see IV. 91; MV, p. 539:

avāca 'nakṣarāḥ sarva śūnyāḥ śāntādinirmalāḥ |
ya evaṃ jānati dharmān kumāro buddha socyate ||

MV, p. 444: prakṛtiprabhāsvarāḥ sarvadharmāḥ; LA, X. 750, 753, 754: prakṛtiprabhāsvaraṃ cittam; ASP, p. 47: ādi-śuddhatvād ādipariśuddhatvāt sattvasya; CVP, 28:

ādiśuddham anutpannaṃ niḥsvabhāvam anāvilam |
jagad bhāvena sampaśyan na baddho na ca mucyate ||[1]

In the kārikā the word *nāyaka* is a name for the Buddha, MVt[1], §1. 20; AP, 4. 725; BA, II. 31, 66; ŚS, p. 5, l. 8.

[1] See Poussin, JRAS, 1910, p. 139.

Let us remember here that at the very beginning of the present Chapter (IV. 1) the author has told us, that in the opinion of 'the greatest of men' (*dvipadāṃ vara*), *i.e.* the Buddha, *jñāna* and *jñeya* are identical. He has also repeatedly shown above[1] and specially in IV. 96, that *jñāna* is *asaṅga* as it does not relate itself to the *dharmas* or objects which have no reality. The author refers now to this fact and concludes showing the supreme truth that according to the Buddha there is in reality neither the *jñāna* nor the *jñeya* or *dharmas* as he has said neither of them :

99

kramate na hi buddhasya jñānaṃ dharmeṣu tāyinaḥ I
sarvadharmās tathā jñānaṃ naitad buddhena bhāṣitam II

'According to the Buddha who instructs the way known to him (*tāyin*),[2] *jñāna* does not approach the *dharmas* (*i.e.*, it does not relate itself to the objects).[3] But all *dharmas* as well as *jñāna*—this has not been said by the Buddha.'

[1] See IV. 72, 79, 96. *Cf.* III. 32.

[2] The word *tāyin* is thus interpreted in BAP, p. 75 : *tāyinām iti.* svādhigatamārgadeśakānām. yad uktam *tāyaḥ svadṛṣṭamārgoktiḥ* (PV, 2 145). See my paper, *Pramāṇavārttika* of *Dharmakīrtti*, IHQ, Vol. XIII, 1937. This explanation is partly followed by U d a y a n ā c ā r y a in his *Tātparyaṭīkā-pariśuddhi*, Bib. Ind., p. 8 in explaining *tāyin* in V ā c a s p a t i M i ś r a 's *Tātparyaṭīkā*, 2 (akṣapādāya tāyine) : tāyī tattvādhyavasāyasaṃrakṣaṇakṣama-sampradāyapravartakaḥ. P r a j ñ ā k a r a m a t i in his BAP, p. 75, offers another explanation : athavā tāyaḥ santānārthaḥ. āsaṃsāram apratiṣṭhita-nirvāṇatayā avasthāyinām. This word is widely used both in Buddhist (LV, p. 421; BA, III. 2; SP[1], pp. 25, 57, 67, etc.,) and Jaina (YŚ, Vol. I, pp. 1, 47; DV, p. 115) works and is misunderstood. Sometimes it is read as *trāyin* 'protector,' and *tāpin* (as in the present case, see Variants . The word *tāyin* as a name for Buddha is translated into Tibetan by *sky.b.pa* (MVt[1], § 1. 15) which suggests its Sanskrit equivalent *trāyin* 'a protector.' See JRAS, 1910, p. 140; JPTS, 1891-1893, p. 53; JA, 1912, p. 243; *Proceedings and Transactions of the Second Oriental Conference*, Calcutta, 1922, pp. 450-1.

[3] See IV. 96.

What is the significance of the second half of the kārikā : 'all *dharmas* as well as *jñāna*—this has not been said by the Buddha?' Let us quote here a few passages showing that the Buddha has never said a word.

(*i*) Nāgārjuna in his MK, XX. 25 :

sarvopalambhopaśamaḥ prapañcopaśamaḥ śivaḥ |
na kvacit kasyacit kaścid dharmo buddhena deśitaḥ ||

(*ii*) *Tathāgataguhyasūtra* quoted in MV on the above :

yāṃ ca rātriṃ tathāgato 'nuttarāṃ samyaksambodhim abhisambuddho yāṃ ca rātrim upādāya parinirvāsyati atrāntare tathāgatena ekam apy akṣaraṃ nodāhṛtaṃ na vyāhṛtaṃ nāpi pravyāharati nāpi pravyāhariṣyati.

(*iii*) LA, pp. 142-3 :

yāṃ ca rātriṃ tathāgato 'bhisambuddho yāṃ ca rātriṃ parinirvāsyati atrāntare ekam apy akṣaraṃ tathāgatena nodāhṛtaṃ na pravyāhariṣyati. avacanaṃ buddhavacanam.

(*iv*) Nāgārjuna in his NSt, 17 :

nodāhṛtaṃ tvayā kiñcid ekam apy akṣaraṃ vibho |
kṛtsnaś ca vaineyajano dharmavarṣeṇa tarpitaḥ ||

(*v*) Bhagavat quoted in MV, p. 264 and BAP, p. 365 (with a slight variation) :

anakṣarasya dharmasya śrutiḥ kā deśanā ca kā |
śrūyate deśyate cāpi samāropād anakṣaraḥ[4] ||

(*vi*) LA, p. 137 :

na me yānaṃ mahāyānaṃ na ghoṣo na ca akṣarāḥ[4] |

(*vii*) LA, p. 48 :

(*a*) tattvaṃ hy akṣaravarjitam ; p. 194 :

(*b*) nirakṣaratvād dharmasya.

(*viii*) VCh, pp. 24 :

(*a*) tat kiṃ manyase subhūte asti sa kaścid dharmo yas tathāgatena deśitaḥ. evam ukta āyuṣmān subhūtir bhagavantam evam avocat. yathāhaṃ bhagavan bhagavato bhāṣitasyārtham

[4] *Cf*. IV. 60 : yatra varṇā na vartante.

ājānāmi nāsti sa kaścid dharmo yas tathāgatenānuttarā samyak sambodhir ity abhisambuddhaḥ nāsti dharmo yas tathāgatena deśitaḥ.

(*b*) p. 29 : tat kiṃ manyase subhūte api nv asti sa kaścid dharmo yas tathāgatena bhāṣitaḥ. subhūtir āha. no hīdaṃ bhagavan nāsti sa kaścid dharmo yas tathāgatena bhāṣitaḥ.

ix) LA, p. 144 :

yasyāṃ ca rātryāṃ dhigamo yasyāṃ ca parinirvṛtaḥ |
etasminn antare nāsti mayā kiṃcit prakāśitam ||

(*x*) MV, p. 539 :

avāca 'nakṣarāḥ sarva śūnyāḥ.° [5]

Let us now make an attempt to understand the significance of such passages as cited above saying that the Buddha said nothing.

This statement is on two grounds, (*i*) *pratyātmadharmatā*, *i.e.*, the nature of (the highest truth) which is realized in one's own self, and (*ii*) *paurāṇasthitidharmatā*, *i.e.*, the nature of the elements of existence that remains from the past. This requires some explanation. As regards the first it is held that the transcendental truth (*paramārtha*) springs up only as an inward conviction (*pratyātmavedya*), it cannot be attained through instruction from another (*aparapratyaya* = *paropadeśāgamya*), for it cannot be expressed by any speech or word. So we are told that for the noble the transcendental truth is silence.[6] This is well-known also in the Vedānta.[7] Candrakīrtti writes (MV, p. 493) :

sarva evāyam abhidhānābhidheyajñānajñeyādivyavahāro'śeṣo lokasaṃvṛtisatyam ity ucyate. na hi paramārthata eva tat sambhavati. kutas tatra paramārthe vācāṃ pravṛttiḥ kuto vā jñānasya. sa hi paramārtho 'parapratyayaḥ śāntaḥ pratyātmavedya āryāṇāṃ sarvaprapañcātītaḥ. sa nopadiśyate na cāpi jñāyate.

5 See IV. 98 where the kārikā is entirely quoted.

6 MV, p. 56 : paramārtho hy āryāṇāṃ tūṣṇīmbhāvaḥ.

7 TU, II. 4. 1 : yato vāco nivartante aprāpya manasā saha; KU, II. 3; BS, III. 2. 17; *The Basic Conception of Buddhism*, pp. 19 ff.

Thus the Buddha did not say anything in fact, yet the people according to their own dispositions think that he did so. We read therefore in a text, *Tathāgataguhyasūtra*, quoted in MV, p. 539, just after the passage (*ii*) cited above :

atha ca yathābhimuktāḥ sarvasattvā nānādhātvāśayās tāṃ vividhāṃ tathāgatavācaṃ niścarantīṃ saṃjānanti. teṣām evaṃ pṛthak pṛthag bhavati. ayaṃ bhagavān asmabhyam imaṃ dharmaṃ deśayati. vayaṃ ca tathāgatasya dharmadeśanāṃ śṛṇumaḥ. tatra tathāgato na kalpayati na vikalpayati sarvakalpavikalpajālavāsanāprapañcavigato hi śāntamate tathāgata iti vistaraḥ.°

Continues MV :

yadi tarhy evaṃ [na] kvacit kasyaci[t kaści]d dharmo buddhena deśitas tat katham ima ete vicitrāḥ pravacanavyavahārā jñāyante. ucyate. avidyānidrānugatānāṃ dehināṃ svapnāyamānānām iva svavikalpābhyudaya eṣaḥ ayaṃ bhagavān sakalatribhuvanasurāsuranaranātha imaṃ asmabhyaṃ deśayatīti.

The following may also be quoted here from the LA, p. 194 :

na ca mahāmate tathāgatā akṣarapatitaṃ dharmaṃ deśayanti.° punar mahāmate yo.'kṣarapatitaṃ dharmaṃ deśayati sa pralapati. nirakṣaratvād dharmasya. ata etasmāt kāraṇān mahāmate uktaṃ deśanāpāṭhe mayānyaiś ca buddhabodhisattvair yathaikam apy akṣaraṃ tathāgatā nodāharanti na vyāharantīti. tat kasya hetor yad utānakṣaratvād dharmāṇām. na ca nārthopasaṃhitam udāharanti. udāharanty eva vikalpam upādāyānupadāyān mahāmate sarvadharmāṇāṃ śāsanalopaḥ syāt.°

And the conclusion arrived at here is that one should rest on the sense and not on letters, for one who rests on letters not only ruins oneself, but also cannot make others understand :

arthapratisaraṇena[8] mahāmate bodhisattvena mahāsattvena bhavitavyaṃ na vyañjanapratisaraṇena. vyañjanānusārī mahāmate kulaputro vā kuladuhitā vā svātmānaṃ ca nāśayati parārthaṃś ca nāvabodhayati. *Op. cit.*, pp. 194-195.

8 In Buddhist Sanskrit texts we have often °*śaraṇa* for °*saraṇa* in such cases

The second ground is this : The Buddha has said nothing, because what he is reported to have said was from the past. Nothing depends on the birth or absence of birth of the Tathāgatas, the true nature of elements of existence remains always the same. This is meant by the statement that the speech of the Buddha is no speech (*avacanaṃ buddhavacanam*). Taking both the grounds together the LA, pp. 143-144, says :

yad idam uktaṃ bhagavatā yāṃ ca rātriṃ tathāgato 'bhisambuddho yāṃ ca rātriṃ parinirvāsyati atrāntara ekam apy akṣaraṃ tathāgatena nodāhṛtaṃ na pravyāhariṣyati avacanaṃ buddhavacanam iti. kim idaṃ sandhāyoktaṃ.° bhagavān āha. dharmadvayaṃ mahāmate sandhāya mayaitad uktaṃ. katamad dharmadvayaṃ. yaduta pratyātmadharmatāṃ ca paurāṇasthitidharmatāṃ ca.° utpādād vā tathāgatānām anutpādād vā tathāgatānāṃ sthitaivaiṣāṃ dharmāṇāṃ dharmatā dharmasthititā dharmaniyāmatā paurāṇanagaramahāpathavan mahāmate.° tad yathā mahāmate kaścid eva puruṣo 'ṭavyāṃ paryaṭan paurāṇaṃ nagaram anupaśyed avikalapathapraveśaṃ. sa taṃ nagaram anupraviśet tatra praviśya pratiniviśya nagaraṃ nagarakriyāsukham anubhavet. tat kiṃ manyase mahāmate api nu tena puruṣeṇa sa panthā utpādito yena pathā taṃ nagaram anupraviṣṭo nagaravaicitryaṃ ca. āha. no bhagavan. bhagavān āha. evam eva mahāmate yan mayā taiś ca tathāgatair adhigataṃ sthitaivaiṣā dharmatā dharmasthititā dharmaniyāmatā tathatā bhūtatā satyatā. ata etasmāt kāraṇān mahāmate mayedam uktam yāṃ ca rātriṃ tathāgato 'bhisambuddho yām ca rātriṃ parinirvāsyati atrāntara ekam apy akṣaraṃ tathāgatena nodāhṛtaṃ nodāhariṣyati.

The following may also be quoted here from the VCh, p. 243 just after the passage (*viii*) cited above :

tat kasya hetoḥ. yo 'sau tathāgatena dharmo 'bhisambuddho deśito vā agrāhyaḥ so 'nabhilāpyaḥ. na sa dharmo nādharmaḥ. tat kasya hetoḥ. asaṃskṛtaprabhāvitā hy āryapudgalāḥ.

It is thus quite reasonable that the author should declare at the end of his discussion the transcendental truth of *jñāna* and *jñeya* or *dharma* which he begins the chapter with and discusses it throughout.

In the last kārikā of his work the author pays his homage to the highest truth to be realized, *i.e.*, *nirvāṇa* of the Buddhists, and Brahman of the Vedāntins ;

100

durdarśam atigambhīram ajaṃ sāmyaṃ viśāradam I[1]
buddhvā padam anānātvaṃ namaskurmo yathābalam II

iti gauḍapādīya āgamaśāstre 'lātaśāntyākhyaṃ caturthaṃ prakaraṇaṃ samāptam.

'Having understood that state which is difficult to be seen, very deep, unborn,[2] equal,[3] fearless,[4] and free from variety,[5] we salute it according to our power.

Here ends, in the *Āgamaśāstra* of G a u ḍ a p ā d a,

Book Four called the Cessation of the Fire-brand.'

The word *pada* 'state' in Buddhist literature is used also to mean *nirvāṇa*.[6] But though it cannot be taken as a peculiarity in that literature, for the word is employed in the similar sense, *i.e.*, *mokṣa* or *Brahman* also in Brāhmaṇical works,[7] one is inclined to take it in the sense of *nirvāṇa* considering all that is discussed in this chapter. The two epithets *durdarśa* and *atigambhīra* strengthen the view. In Buddhist literature

[1] See IV. 93*d* which is the same as *b* of the present kārikā.

[2] I. 16; III. 1, 19, 26, 33, 43, 47; IV. 11, 12, 13, 38, 46, 48, 57 60, 74, 80, 93, 95, 96.

[3] III. 2, 38; IV. 77, 80, 93, 95.

[4] IV. 93. *Cf. abhaya*, IV. 78; *nirbhaya*, III. 35.

[5] III. 13; IV. 91; BU, IV, 4. 19; KU, IV. 10-11.

[6] AP, 819 : padaṃ ṭhāne parittāṇe nibbānamhi ca kāraṇe.

[7] For instance, KU, II. 15, III. 7-9

sudurdṛśa (Pali *sududdasa*) is given as a synonym for *nirvāṇa* (AP, 7) and the words *durdṛśa* (Pali *duddasa*) 'difficult to be seen' and *gambhīra* 'deep' are frequently used in connection with it.[8]

The word *bala* 'power' in *yathābala* refers to the well-known five-fold *bala* in Buddhism, *viz.*, (1) *śraddhā-bala*, (2) *vīrya*°, (3) *smṛti*°, (4) *samādhi*°, and (5) *prajñā*°, or the power of faith, energy, recollection, contemplation, and wisdom respectively.[9] By using the word it is implied that *nirvāṇa* is realized by the exercise of the five-fold power referred to.

In the colophon for *alāta* 'fire-brand' see IV. 47-50. The use of the word *alātaśānti* 'cessation of the fire-brand' is very significant and appropriate indicating the quintessence of what is discussed herein.

Poussin has traced (JRAS, 1910, p. 135) the simile of the firebrand (*alātacakra*) in the MU,[10] VI. 24.[11] But this simile can in no way be connected with the name of the present chapter, *alātaśānti*. For the use of the simile in that Up, is

8 See nirvāṇarūpo dharmo gambhīro durdṛśaś ca, LV, pp. 509, 513, 515; gambhīraṃ durdarśaṃ sūkṣmaṃ dharmacakram, *Ibid*, pp. 422, 436 (gambhīro durdṛśo mama); ASP, p. 341: gambhīram iti subhūte śūnyatāyā etad adhivacanam° virāgasya nirodhasya nirvāṇasya vigamasyaitad adhivacanaṃ yad uta gambhīram iti; MVg, I. 5. 2. 8: ayaṃ dhammo gambhīro duddaso. *Cf.* KU, II. 12 where *durdarśa* is used as an adjective of the *deva* referring, according to the Commentators, to *ātman*.

9 AN, III. 12; DN, II. 120; etc., DS, XLVIII. These five are well-known also in the system of Yoga (YS, I. 20), though these are not described here as *bala*. According to scholiasts *śraddhā* implies the clearness (*samprasāda*, *prasāda*) of the mind. Vasubandhu (AK, VIII. 9) is of the same opinion. See *ibid*. also II. 25.

10 *Maitrāyaṇa Brāhmaṇa Up.* is another name for it. But it does not show any Vedic traces. From its language, style, and contents it appears that it belongs to a considerably later period.

11 It runs: alātacakram iva sphurantam ādityavarṇam ūrjasvantaṃ brahma tamasaḥ paryapaśyat. Cowell (Bibl. Ind.) translates it: "he beholds Brahman flashing like the circle of a whirling torch, in colour like the sun, full of vigour."

not for showing any unreality of Brahman but simply for indicating his splendour. On the other hand, here in our work, as well as in Buddhist works, frequently, and in every case, so far as goes my information, it is used as one of the numerous symbols of unreality.[12] The following may be quoted here from CŚ, 325 :

alātacakranirmāṇasvapnamāyāmbucandrakaiḥ |
dhūmikāntaḥpratiśrutkāmarīcyabhraiḥ samo bhavaḥ ||

Poussin observes (JRAS, 1910, p. 136) that the title of the fourth Chapter, *alātaśānti*, cannot be said so far to be Buddhist, as the phrase *alātaśānti* has not been traced in Buddhist books. We cannot however, think so. For, it may equally be said that it is not traced in any Brāhmaṇic work older than the ĀŚ.[13] Now, it may not be traced in Buddhist works, but the word *alāta* as a symbol of unreality according to the Buddhists, of which their works are full,[14] is very well-known. Gauḍapāda himself has used it as such in his ĀŚ not less than four times (IV. 47-50). He has shown taking the stand of a Buddhist, the unreality of the visible world comparing it with *alāta*, and finding out the cause of its appearance and showing thereby as to how it ceases. And if it is so, we cannot say that the title of the chapter is not Buddhist.

12 Such as *marumarīcikā*, *gandharvanagara*, *khapuṣpa*. See MVt[1], 139. 21.
13 A similar phrase, *mṛgatṛṣṇājalabhrāntiśānti*, occurs in YV, III. 6. 2.
14 See among others LA, pp. 9, 96, etc.

FINIS.

APPENDIXES

I

MĀṆḌŪKYA UPANIṢAD

A

Text

1

om ity etad akṣaram idaṃ sarvaṃ tasyopavyākhyānaṃ[1] bhūtaṃ bhavad[2] bhaviṣyad[3] iti sarvam oṅkāra eva. yac cānyat trikālātītaṃ tad apy oṅkāra eva.

2

sarvaṃ hy etad[4] brahmāyam ātmā brahma so'yam ātmā catuṣpād.

3

jāgaritasthāno bahiṣprajñaḥ saptāṅgo ekonaviṃśatimukhaḥ sthūlabhug vaiśvānaraḥ prathamaḥ pādaḥ.

4

svapnasthāno 'ntaḥprajñaḥ saptāṅga ekonaviṃśatimukhaḥ praviviktabhuk taijaso[5] dvitīyaḥ pādaḥ.

1 ChāU, I. 1. 1 : om ity akṣaram* tasyopavyākhyānam ; *cf.* TU, I. 8. 1 : om itīdaṃ sarvam.

2 A[4] omits it.

3 *Cf.* BU, III. 8. 3, IV. 6. 7 : yad bhūtaṃ ca bhavac ca bhaviṣyac ca.

4 For *hy etad* A[4] *tad.*

5 A[2] adds *hiraṇyagarbho* after it.

5

yatra supto[6] *na kañcana kāmaṃ kāmayate na kañcana svapnam paśyati*[7] tat suṣuptam. suṣuptasthāna ekībhūtaḥ[8] prajñānaghana evā[9]nandamayo hy ānandabhuk cetomukhaḥ prājñas- tṛtīyaḥ pādaḥ.

6

eṣa sarveśvara[10] *eṣa sarvajña*[11] eṣo *'ntaryāmy*[12] eṣa *yoniḥ* sarvasya[13] *prabhavāpyayau*[14] hi bhūtānām.

7

nāntaḥprajñaṃ na bahiṣprajñaṃ nobhayataḥprajñaṃ na prajñānaghanaṃ na prajñaṃ nāprajñam adṛṣṭam avyavahāryam agrāhyam alakṣaṇam acintyam avyapadeśyam ekātmapratyaya-sāraṃ[15] prapañcopaśamaṃ śāntaṃ śivam advaitaṃ caturthaṃ manyante. sa ātmā sa vijñeyaḥ.

6 A[4] *suṣupto* for *supto*, adds *tu* before *kañcana*, and omits *eva* after *°ghana*.

7 BU, IV. 3. 19.

8 *Cf. ekībhavati*, PU, IV. 2; BU, IV. 4. 2.

9 BU, IV. 5. 13 : ātmānantaro 'bāhyaḥ kṛtsnaḥ prajñānaghana eva.

10 BU, IV. 4. 22 : sa vā eṣa mahān aja ātmā yo 'yaṃ vijñānamayaḥ prāṇeṣu ya eṣo 'ntarhṛdaya ākāśas tasmiñ chete° eṣa sarveśvaraḥ°.

11 MuU, I. 1. 9 : yaḥ sarvajñaḥ; PU, IV. 10 : sa sarvajñaḥ.

12 BU, III. 7. 3 : eṣa ta ātmāntaryāmī.

13 *Cf. bhūtayoni*, MuU, I. 1. 6 : yad bhūtayoniṃ paripaśyanti dhīrāḥ.

14 A[2] *prabhāvā°*, D[2] prabhavo° for *prabhavā°*. KU, II. 2. 11.

15 A[1] reads *nāntaḥprajñaṃ na bahiṣprajñam* after *nāprajñam*, and has *na prajñaṃ nāprajñaṃ na ghanaṃ na ghanaprajñaṃ na prajñānaghanam* for *na prajñāna° nāprajñam*. A[4] omits *na prajñānaghanam*. After *alakṣaṇam* A[1] *anigamano* (? *aliṅgam*) adding to it *bahiḥprajñaṃ* (Ś reads in his commentary : alakṣaṇam aliṅgam ananumeyam ityarthaḥ) *nāntaḥprajñam* and reading *cintyaṃ* for *acintyam*. D[1] and D[2] add *aliṅgam* before *acintyam*. A[4] *ekāntam* for *ekātma-°*, T' and V* *aikātmyapra°* for *ekātmapra°*.

8

so 'yam ātmā 'dhyakṣaram oṅkāro 'dhimātraṃ pādā mātrā mātrāś ca pādā akāra ukāro makāra[16] iti.

9

jāgaritasthāno vaiśvānaro 'kāraḥ[17] prathamā mātrāpter[18] ādimattvād vāpnoti ha vai sarvān kāmān ādiśca bhavati ya evaṃ veda.

10

svapnasthānas taijasa ukāro dvitīyā mātrotkarṣād ubhayatvād votkarṣatiha vai jñānasantatiṃ samānaś ca bhavati nāsyābrahmavit kule bhavati ya evaṃ veda.

11

suṣuptasthānaḥ prājño makāras tṛtīyā mātrā miter apīter vā minoti ha vā idaṃ sarvam apītiś ca bhavati ya evaṃ veda.

12

amātraś caturtho 'vyavahāryaḥ prapañcopaśamaḥ śivo 'dvaita evam oṅkāra ātmaiva. saṃviśaty *ātmanātmānaṃ*[19] ya evaṃ veda.

iti māṇḍūkyopaniṣat samāptā.

---

16 A² A³ IO °*raś ceti* for °ra iti.

17 A¹ omits '*kāraḥ*.

18 A¹ *prāpter*(?), IO *āptor* for *āpter*.

19 VS, XXXII. 11 : ātmanātmānam abhi saṃ viveśa. A² adds *paśyati* after °*tmānaṃ*. K¹ Ch M' repeat *ya evaṃ veda* which follows.

B

Translation

1

Om, this syllable is all this. Its further explanation is: the past, the present, the future—all this is verily *om*. And whatever else that is beyond the three times, that, too, is verily *Om*.

2

Verily all this is Brahman; this self (*ātman*) is Brahman. This same self has four fourths.

3

The first fourth is the V a i ś v ā n a r a 'common-to-all-men,' *i.e.*, universal, (active) in the waking state, cognitive outwardly, having seven limbs[1] and nineteen mouths[2] enjoying the gross.

[1] According to Ś who follows here ChāU, V. 18. 2, these seven limbs are described thus: The very bright one (*sutejas*), *i.e.*, the heaven is the head. One with various forms (*viśvarūpa*), *i.e.*, the sun is the eye. That which has various paths, *i.e.*, the wind is the breath. The extended space (*bahula*) is the body. Wealth (*i.e.*, water) is the bladder. And the earth is the feet. Here in the ChāU the number is more than seven.

[2] *I.e.*, the means for experience of objects. According to Ś these are the following: The five organs of sense (*buddhīndriya*), the five organs of action (*karmendriya*), the five vital breaths (*prāṇa*), the mind (*manas*), the intellect (*buddhi*), egoism (*ahaṅkāra*), and thinking (*citta*). For an explanation of the last four one may be referred to the following:

mano buddhir ahaṅkāraś cittaṃ karaṇam āntaram |
saṃśayo niścayo garvaḥ smaraṇaṃ viṣayā ime ||

These are regarded as 'mouths,' because these are the instruments with which one experiences the objects.

4

The second fourth is the T a i j a s a 'brilliant,' (active) in the dreaming state, cognitive inwardly, having seven limbs and nineteen mouths, enjoying the subtle.

5

That is deep sleep in which one asleep desires no desire whatsoever, nor does he see any dream.

The third fourth is P r ā j ñ a 'wise.' He is in the sphere of deep sleep, and just unified, a cognition-mass, consisting of bliss and enjoying bliss having the mind as mouth.

6

This is the lord of all, this is the knower of all, this is the controller of all. This is the source of all, for this is the origin and end of beings.

7

Not inwardly cognitive, not outwardly cognitive, not bothwise cognitive, not a cognition-mass, not cognitive, not non-cognitive, not seen, not to be dealt with, not graspable, having no distinctive marks, not thinkable, not to be defined, the essence of the consciousness of the oneness of the self, the cessation of the expression,[3] quiescent, blissful, without a second—(such) they think is the fourth. He is the self. He is to be realized.

8

The same self is *om* from the point of view of a syllable, and from the point of view of its measure, the fourths are measures and the measures are fourths, and they are A, U and M.

[3] Or, the expansion of the universe, as explained generally.

9

V a i ś v ā n a r a 'common-to-all-men' who is (active in) the waking state is the first measure, A, on account of its obtaining[4] (*āpti*), or on account of its being the first. Verily, indeed, he obtains all desires and becomes first, who knows thus.

10

T a i j a s a 'brilliant' who is (active in) the sleeping state is the second measure, U, on account of exaltation or intermediateness.

Verily, indeed, he exalts the continuity of knowledge, becomes equal,[5] and none who does not know Brahman is born in the family of him who knows thus.

11

P r ā j ñ a 'wise' who is (active in) the state of deep sleep is the third measure, M, on account of measuring and immerging.

Verily, indeed, he measures all this and becomes (its) immerging—he who knows thus.

12

The fourth is without any measure, with which there can be no dealing, it is cessation of expression, blissful, without the second. Thus *om* is the self, indeed. Enters he with his self into the self—he who knows thus.

Here ends the Upaniṣad called M ā ṇ ḍ ū k y a.

---

4 Or, pervading.

5 See the note in H u m e ' s translation.

II

VARIANTS

Book I

1. *a.* All excepting A^4 *bahiḥprajño* for *bahiṣprajño*. *d.* A^4 PU^1 PU^2 *smṛtaḥ*, N Th *mataḥ* for *sthitaḥ*.

2. *a.* A^2 *dakṣiṇāgni°*, V^g *dakṣiṇekṣi°* for *dakṣiṇākṣi°*; D^2 *°mukho* for *mukhe*. *b.* T^e *°ś ca* for *°s tu*. *c* and *d* are omitted in A^2.

3. *a* and *b* excepting *praviviktabhuk* are omitted in A^2. *d.* A^2 adds *tan* before *nibodhata*.

4. *b.* A^2 *ca* for *tu* which is omitted in A^4. *c.* A^1 A^2 K^3 IO *ānandaṃ* for *ānandaś*; V^g A^4 *tu* for *ca*; IO *prājñaḥ* for *prājñaṃ*. *d.* A^3 *trividhā* for *tridhā*; A^2 *tṛptaṃ* for *tṛptiṃ*; A^1 A^2 A^4 K^3 *vijānata*, KN *vijānatha* for *nibodhata*.

5. *a.* A^1 *dhāmastu* for *dhāmasu*. *b.* K^3 *yas tu* for *yaś ca*. *c.* D^3 V^n *vastu* for *yas tu*.

6. *a.* K^3 *°bhūtānāṃ* for *bhāvānāṃ*. *b.* D^1 D^2 *°ity eva niścayaḥ* for *°iti viniścayaḥ*; D^3 *sa niścayaḥ* for *viniścayaḥ*. *c.* D^1 *sarve* for *sarvaṃ*; D^1 D^2 *prāṇā*, A^1 *prāṇāṃ°* for *prāṇa°*; A^1 *°ś cetostana*, D^3 PU^2 *°ś ceto'ṃsūn* for *°ś ceto'ṃśūn*.

7. *a.* A^4 D^2 *vibhūti pra°*, A^3 *vibhūtiḥ pra°* for *vibhūtiṃ pra°*; KN, *prabhavaṃ* for *prasavaṃ*; K^4 *pravadanty anye* for *prasavaṃ tv anye*. *c.* A^e *°sarūpeti* for *°svarūpeti*. *d.* V^g *vikalpyate*, IO *vikalpitāḥ* for *vikalpitā*.

8. *b.* A^2 omits *vi* of *viniścitāḥ*; V^g *sṛṣṭir vi°* for *sṛṣṭau vi°*. *c.* K^3 adds *bhūtiṃ* before *bhūtānāṃ*. *d.* A^1 *matyante*, K^1 *mānte* for *manyante*.

9. At the end of the kārikā IO adds the first two ślokas of Ś's commentary, *viz.*, *prajñānāṃśu°* and *yo viśvātmā.°*

10. *a.* A^1 *nivṛttiḥ*, T^e *nivṛtte* for *nivṛtteḥ*. *c.* A^e °*bhūtānāṃ* for °*bhāvānāṃ*. IO omits the kārikā here, but reads it just after kārikā 12.

11. *a.* A^1 A^2 A^3 D^2 °*buddhau* for °*baddhau*. *d.* A^e M^e V^g D^3 V^n A^4 K^3 *dvau tau*, PU^2 and the MSS A B C D F of NSi (pp. 194, 246) *dvau tu*, A^1 A^2 D^1 *dvaita*, PU^1 *dvaitaṃ*, K^3 PU^2 *dvau tu* for *dve tu*, while for this line K^3 reads *dvau turye na tu sidhyataḥ*.

12. *a.* V^g *parai°* for *parāṃ°*. *b.* V^g *vānṛ°* for *cānṛ°*, PU^1 *cāpi nānṛtam* for *nāpi cānṛtam*. *d.* K^3 A^e A^1 A^2 A^3 D^1 D^3 V^n *turyaṃ tat* (*cf.* Ś), KN *turīyaṃ* for *turīyaḥ*.

13. *d.* K^3 *tu* for *ca*.

14. *c.* *svapnaṃ tu* for *ca svapnaṃ*.

15. *a.* D^2 PU^1 *grahṇataḥ* for *gṛhṇataḥ*. *c.* A^1 *'nayoḥ* for *tayoḥ*.

16. *b.* A^1 *sa bu°*, A^2 *svabu°* for *prabu°*. *c.* D^1 *asuptam* for *asvapnam*. *c* and *d.* A^4 *advaitam asvapnaṃ* for *asvapnam advaitaṃ*.

17. *a* and *b.* A^4 *vidyate vivartate* for *vidyeta nivarteta*. *c.* A^4 *sarvam* for *dvaitam*.

18. *a.* K^3 *na nivarteta* for *vinivarteta*; K^1 omits it. *b.* K^1 *vikalpito* for *kalpito*.

19. *a.* A^4 °*syādivi°* for °*syātvavi°*.

20. *a.* All excepting A^e V^n V^g *vijñāne* for *vijñāna*. *b.* A^1 A^2 A^4 *sphuṭaḥ* for *sphuṭam*. *c.* A^2 *saprati°* for *samprati°*. *d.* A^1 °*vidhim* for °*vidham*.

21. *b.* D^2 PU^2 *mānaṃ sā°* for *mānasā°*. *c.* A^2 *saprati°* for *samprati°*. *d.* A^1 *laye sā°*, D^2 *layaḥ sā°* for *layasā°*.

22. *a.* All excepting PU^1 *yat* for *yaḥ* supported by Ś. *b.* D^1 IO PU^2 *veti*, K^3 *ceti* for *vetti*; A^4 *tadvataḥ*, K^3 *niścitam*, PU^1 *niścittaḥ* for *niścitaḥ*. *c.* M^e *sampū°* for *sa pū°*. *d.* M^e °*caiṣa* for °*caiva*.

23. *a.* D^2 *nayati* for *nayate*. *d.* M and KN *'gatiḥ* for *gatiḥ*.

24. *a.* A^4 *oṅkāro* for *oṅkāram*.

25. *a.* *praṇavo* for *praṇave*.

26. *a.* For this K[1] *praṇavo brahmaparaḥ brahma.* *b.* A[1] A[2] A[3] D[1] D[2] M[e] V[g] V[n] *paraḥ* for *paraṃ*; IO *paraḥ smṛtaḥ* for *paraṃ smṛtaḥ*.

27. *d.* A[2] °*taraḥ* for °*taram*.

28. *a.* A[4] omits *hi* before *īśvaram*. *b.* A[1] A[4] Gh Ch J N V[g] *hṛdaye sthitam* for *hṛdi saṃsthitam*.

29. *b.* A[4] *smṛtaḥ* for *śivaḥ*.

Colophon :

A[4] māṇḍūkyopaniṣat samāptā.

D[1] D[2] māṇḍūkyopaniṣadvyākhyāne gauḍapādabhagavataḥ kṛtau oṅkāranirṇayaḥ prathamaṃ prakaraṇam.

IO iti māṇḍūkyopaniṣat samāptā.

K[1] iti māṇḍūkyopaniṣadgauḍapādavyākhyāne oṅkārākhya-prathamaṃ prakaraṇaṃ samāptam.

K[3] iti māṇḍūkyopaniṣat samāptam (*sic*). hare kṛṣṇa hare kṛṣṇa°.

PU[1] prathamaṃ prakaraṇam.

PU[2] iti śrīgovindapūjyapādaśiṣyasya paramahaṃsaparivrājakā-cāryasya śaṅkarabhagavataḥ kṛtāv āgamaśāstravivaraṇe prathama-prakaraṇe māṇḍūkyavyākhyānaṃ samāptam.

V[g] māṇḍūkyopaniṣat samāptā.

V[n] iti māṇḍūkyākhyaṃ prathamaṃ prakaraṇam.

Book II

1. *a.* A[2] °*bhūtānāṃ* for °*bhāvānāṃ*. *c.* A[1] A[2] Conc. *bhedānām* for *bhāvānāṃ*.

2. *b.* V[g] D[e] *dehān* for *deśān*. *c.* V[g] *prabuddhaś* for *pratibuddhaś*.

3. Before this kārikā B[2] reads here the kārikā 4 once more.

4. *b.* A[3] A[e] B[2] IO K[1] M[e] PU[2] *tasmāt* for *tathā*. *d.* All *saṃvṛtatvena* for *saṃvṛtatvaṃ na*; A[3] *vidyate* for *bhidyate*.

5. *a.* A[2] omits *svapna*°; A[e] A[3] B[2] D[1] D[2] IO PU[2] V[g] V[n] °*ritasthāne* for °*rite sthāne*.

7. *b.* PU[2] *svapno* for *svapne*; V[g] ca *prati*°, all others *viprati*° for *'pi prati*.°

8. *a.* A^2 A^3 B^2 apūrvasthānidharmo, A^1 B^1 D^1 D^2 M^e PU^1 PU^2 V^g V^n *apūrvaṃ* sthanidharmo for *apūrvāḥ sthānidharmāḥ*. *c.* V^n *matvā* for *gantvā*. *d.* K^1 V^n *yadaive*° for *yathaive*.°

9. *a.* A^1 °*vṛttāv ayaṃ tv anta*°, A^2 °*vattāv artheṣv ānt*°, B^1 J Jh V^n °*vṛttāv apy anta*°, Gh C °*vṛttāpy anta*°, IO °*vṛttāv apy anta*° for °*vṛttāv api tv anta*°; K^1 °*svanta*° for °*tv anta*°. *b.* V^g *kalitaṃ* for *kalpitaṃ*; B^1 D^1 D^2 Gh J Jh K^1 *asat*, A^2 IO *tad asat*, A^1 *tad idam asat* for *tv asat*. *c.* A^1 A^2 B^1 C D^1 D^2 IO Jh K^1 N PU^2 V^n °*ś cetasā* for °*ś ceto*°, A^1 A^2 B^1 IO add *hi* and C J Jh N add *ca* after *gṛhītam*. *d.* V^n *vaitathyam ubhayor api* omitting *dṛṣṭam*, A^1 K^1 *sadasator vaitathyam* omitting *dṛṣṭam*, B^1 C D^1 D^2 IO J Jh N *sadasator vaitathyaṃ dṛṣṭam*, A^2 *sadasator vaitathyaṃ yuktam*.

10. *a.* A^2 D^1 D^2 *anta*°, V^n *hy anta*° for *tv anta*°. *b.* B^1 D^1 D^2 Gh J Jh K^1 V^n *asat*, A^1 A^2 *tad idam asat* for *tv asat*. *c.* A^1 A^2 B^1 D^1 D^2 Gh J Jh K^1 PU^1 PV^2 V^n °*ś cetasā* for °*ś ceto*°, A^1 A^2 B^1 IO add *hi*, the last one *omitting sat*, C J Jh N add *ca* omitting *sad*, A^1 A^2 B^1 Gh J Jh add *hi* after *gṛhītaṃ*. *d.* A^1 A^2 *sadasator vaitathyaṃ dṛṣṭam*, B^1 D^1 D^2 Gh J Jh V^n *sadasator vaitathyaṃ yuktam*, K^1 *satyadator vaitathyam* for *yuktaṃ vaitathyam etayoḥ*. IO and P omit the kārikā entirely.

11. *a-b.* A^2 adds *tad* after *vaitathyaṃ*, V^n *bhedānāṃ vaitathyaṃ* for *vaitathyaṃ bhedānām*. *c.* V^n *ekatān* for *ka etān*.

12. *a.* P *ātmani* as a different reading for *ātmānam*. *b.* K M^e *ātmadehaḥ* for *ātmā devaḥ*. *c.* V^g *bhogān* for *bhedān*.

13. *b.* All except P *vyavasthitān* for *'vyavasthitān*. *c.* A^1 A^2 B^1 IO °*ś cittaṃ* for °*ś citta*, B^2 first °*ś cittaṃ* then the *anusvāra* is struck off.

14. *a.* B^1 °*lāś ca* for °*lā hi*, K^1 *yetas* for *ye'ntas*. *b.* D^2 *ya* for *ye*.

15. *d.* A^2 *viśeṣā mānyahetukaḥ* (evidently for *viśeṣo nānyahetukaḥ*) for *viśeṣas tv indriyāntare*. After that reading the MS reads *asti tv indriyāntare*.

18. *d.* A^1 A^2 B^1 D^1 D^2 PU^1 *ātmāvi*° for *ātmavi*°.

19. *a.* A^e A^2 B^1 M^e V^n °*ś ca* for °*s tu*. *b.* D^2 *kalpitā* for

kalpitaḥ. *d*. A[1] A[2] B[1] B[2] IO K[1] PU[1] *saṃmo°*. V[g] *yan mo°* for *'yaṃ mo°* supported by Ś.

20. *a*. A[e] A[3] B[2] D[1] K[1] IO PU[1] PU[2] V[n] *prāṇa* for *prāṇā*. *b*. D[2] *bhūtā iti* for *bhūtānīti*. *c*. B[1] *guṇa* for *guṇā*. *d*. K[1] *tadvivaḥ* for *tadvidaḥ*.

21. *b*. A[1] *viṣayā i bhūtānīti ca*, A[2] *bhūviṣayāti ca* for *viṣayā iti*; PU[1] adds *ca* after *iti*. *c-d*. A[2] *vedā iti vedavido yajñā°* (*i.e.*, *a* and *b* of the next kārikā) for *lokā iti lokavido*.

22. *a-b*. A[2] *lokā iti lokavido devā iti ca tadvidaḥ* for the whole line. M[e] adds *ca* after *iti* in *a*. *c*. A[2] omits *ca*. *d*. M[e] V[g] *°jya* for *°jyam*. K[1] omits c and *d*.

23. *d*. V[g] *amūrta* for *'mūrta* omitting *ca* after *iti*.

24. *a*. IO *kālā* for *kāla*. *c*. V[g] *pata iti vāta°* for *vādā iti vāda°*. *d*. B[1] V[n] *bhuvanāni ca* for *bhuvanānīti*.

25. *a*. V[g] *ca tadvido*, Gh C Ch *mana°* for *mano°*.

27. *a*. D[1] D[2] *lokāloka°*, IO *lokāl loka°* for *lokā lloka°*. *b*. IO adds *ca* after *iti*. *c*. D[1] D[2] *°napuṃsakapuṃliṅgāḥ* for *°puṃnapuṃsakaṃ laiṅgāḥ*; PU[1] *liṅgāt*, PU[2] *liṅgā* for *laiṅgāḥ*. *d*. D[1] D[2] *parasparam* for *parāparam*; B[1] *atho°* for *athā°*.

28. *d*. A[e] M[e] V[n] *sarve* for *sarvaṃ*; V[n] *tehe tu saṃyatāḥ* for *ceha tu sarvadā*.

29. *a*. K[1] *yad* for *yaṃ*. *b*. *tad* for *taṃ*; A[2] *san* for *sa*. *c*. A[1] *vāvaṃ vipra bhū* for *cāvati sa bhū°*; *vāvati* for *cāvati*.

30. *d*. V[g] *°yed yo vi°* for *°yet so 'vi°*.

32. Before this kārikā A[1] B[1] and V[n] read :

tamaḥ svapnanibhaṃ dṛṣṭaṃ varṣabudbudasaṃnibham |
nāśaprāyaṃ sukhāddhīnaṃ nāśottaram abhāvajam ||

(*a*. C *nabhasy abhra°* for *tamaḥ svapna°*; A[e] *śvabhra°* for *svapna°*. *d*. A[e] B[1] *abhāvagam*, V[n] *abhāvataḥ* for *abhāvajam*). It is quoted by Ś in his commentary on the preceding kārikā as from the *Vyāsasmṛti*. P takes it as one of the verses included in the text and comments upon it.

b. V[g] *baddho* and *sādhyakaḥ* for *bandho* and *sādhakaḥ* respectively.

33. *c*. A^1 *atha dva°*, A^2 *artha dva°* for *apy adva°*. *d*. A^2 *yasmā°* for *tasmā°*, *śivaḥ* for *śivā*.

34. *a*. A^2 *nātmābhāvena*, all others *nātmabhāvena* for *nānyabhāvena*; J *nābhedaṃ* for *nānedaṃ*. *c*. A^2 *pṛthaktvāt pṛthak ki°*, A^3 *pṛthaktvāt pṛthaktvaṃ ca*, D^1 *pṛthan nāpṛthat ki°*, D^2 *pṛthaktvāpṛthak ki°* for *pṛthaṅ nāpṛthak ki°*.

36. *b*. B^2 *yojayot* for *yojayet*.

37. *a*. PU^1 *niḥstutir* for *nistutir*, A^2 *°stuto* for *°skāro*.

38. *a*. K^1 *mātattva°* for *tattva°*.

Colophon :

B^1 iti śrīgovindabhagavatpūjyapādaśiṣyasya paramahaṃsaparivrājakācāryasya śrīśaṅkarabhagavatpādasya kṛtāv āgamaśāstravivaraṇe dvitīyaṃ prakaraṇaṃ vaitathyākhyaṃ samāptaṃ.

K^1 iti śrīmāṇḍūkyopaniṣadgauḍapādavyākhyāne vetadhāsa (*sic*) dvitīyaṃ prakaraṇaṃ samāptam.

PU^2 iti śrīgovindabhagavatpūjyapādaśiṣyasya paramahaṃsaparivrājakācāryasya śrīśaṅkarabhagavataḥ kṛtāv āgamaśāstravivaraṇe dvitīyaṃ prakaraṇaṃ vaitathyākhyaṃ samāptam.

V^g °āgamaśāstre vaitathyākhyaṃ dvitīyaṃ prakaraṇaṃ samāptam.

V^n °vaitathyākhyaṃ dvitīyaṃ prakaraṇam.

Book III

1. *a*. A^1 *upāsāśri°* for *upāsanāśri°*. *b*. A^1 A^2 A^3 Gh N J *jñāte* for *jāte*.

2. *b*. D^2 *°sajāti* for *°m ajāti*; A^1 A^2 IO *yathā* for *gataṃ*. *c*. A^1 A^2 *tathā* for *yathā*.

In D^1 the leaf containing kārikās 2-7 is missing.

3. *c*. K^1 *ghaṭārvahavac ca* for *ghaṭādivac ca*. *d*. *°tāv evan ni°* for *°tāv etan ni°*.

4. *b*. V^g *°kāśoda°* for *°kāśāda°*. *c* and *d* are omitted in V^g. *d*. M^e *jīva* for *jīvā*.

6. *a*. For it K^1 *nūparāgasamasmāc ca*; V^n *°s tu* for *°ś ca*.

7. *c*. V^g *naivanmanaḥ* for *naivātmanaḥ*. *d*. V^g *°rāvayau* for *°rāvayavau*. *c* and *d* are omitted in V^n.

8. *b*. A^1 *gagamąnaṃ* for *gaganaṃ*; A^2 *malino* for *malinaṃ*.

9. c. All *sthitau* for *sthitaḥ* in V^g. *c-d*. V^g Jh °*rīreṣu hy ākā*°, A^1 V^n °*rīreṣv ākā*° (but on margin °*rīreṣu ākā*°) for °*rīreṣu ākā*°. *d*. A^2 °*vicakṣaṇaḥ* for °*vilakṣaṇaḥ*.

10. *b*. A^1 A^2 B^1 (on margin *visa*°) IO *vivarjitāḥ* for *visarjitāḥ*; V^g *ātmā*° for *ātma*° and °*rjitaḥ* for °*rjitāḥ*. *d*. A^1 *bhidyate* for *vidyate*.

11. *d*. A^2 *svayaṃ yā*, A^e B^1 B^2 IO PU^1 PU^2 V^g *khaṃ yathā for sa-yathā*; A^1 A^2 *kham samprakīrti*°, D^1 D^2 V^n *khaṃ prakāśi*° for *samprakāśi*°.

12. *d*. IO °*kāśapra*° for °*kāśaḥ pra*°; V^g *prakāśaṃ* for *prakāśitaḥ*.

13. *a*. A^2 °*tmāno* for °*tmano*°, A^1 *ajanyatvam* for *ananyatvam*. c. A^3 IO *bhidyate* for *nindyate*. *d*. A^3 B^2 C D^1 D^2 M^e *eva* for *evaṃ*.

14. c. Ch. *gauṇatvaṃ* for *gauṇaṃ tan*. *d*. A^1 A^2 B^1 B^2 D^1 D^2 IO JN PU^1 PU^2 V^g V^n *hi na* for *na hi*.

15. *a*. A^1 A^2 °*liṅgais tu* for *liṅgādyaiḥ*. *b*. A^2 *voditā* for *coditā*.

17. *a*. A^2 *susi*° for *svasi*°; A^3 *sumiddhāvadāvasthāstu* for *a*.

18. *b*. *sad* for *tad*. c. IO *ubhayatā* for *ubhayathā*.

19. c. °*māno* for °*māne*.

21. *b*. *yathā* for *tathā*. See IV. 7^b.

22. *d*. A^2 *sthāsya viniścitam* for *sthāsyati niścalaḥ*.

23. *a*. K^2 *bhūto 'bhuta*° for *bhūtato 'bhuta*°.

24. *a*. A^1 A^2 *cāśrīyāt* for *cāmnāyād*.

25. c. A^1 A^2 *kas tv enaṃ* for *ko nv enaṃ*.

26. c and *d* are omitted in A^2. The examination of K^2 shows that the order of the kārikās Nos. 25, 26 and 27 is actually the same as in other MSS, but owing to a mistake of the scribe in copying the commentary that order has been changed, they being copied as Nos. 25, 27 and 26 respectively.

27. *a* and *b* are omitted in A^2.

28. c. A^1 C D^1 D^2 P V^n °*suto* for °*putro*.

31. *a*. A^1 A^2 °*mukha*° for °*dṛśya*°; B^1 *ṣarvaṃ* for *dvaitaṃ*. c. A^2 *manasā* for *manaso*; B^2 *unmanī*° for *amanī*°.

32. *c.* A^{2} *amanaskaṃ* for *amanastāṃ*. *d.* D^{2} *grāhyabhā°* for *grāhyābhā°*.

33. *b.* A^{1} A^{2} *jñeyaṃ bhi°* for *jñeyābhi°*; *pracakṣyate* for *pracakṣate*.

34. *c.* A^{1} *pravāraḥ* for *pracāraḥ*.

35. *a.* Ch *suṣuptau* for *suṣupte*. *b.* V^{g} *suṣuptasya ni°* for *suṣupte tan ni°*; A^{1} A^{2} *na ni°* for *tan ni°*.

36. *c-d.* K^{1} *sarvajñopacāraḥ* for *sarvajñaṃ nopacāraḥ*.

37. *a.* A^{1} A^{2} *°bhimānavimataḥ*, IO V^{n} *°bhilāṣavigataḥ* for *°bhilāpavigataḥ*. *b.* V^{g} *°mujjhitaḥ* for *°mutthitaḥ*. *d.* A^{1} *'bhavaḥ* for *'bhayaḥ*.

38. *b.* B^{2} *citā* for *cintā*. *c-d.* A^{1} *jñāyam ajñātiḥ*, A^{2} *jñāyanajñātiḥ* for *jñānam ajāti*.

39. *a.* IO V^{g} *°yogo nāmāyaṃ*, A^{1} A^{2} *°yogī nāmāyaṁ*, PD *°yogo nāmaiṣaḥ* for *°yogo vai nāma*. *d.* A^{1} *bhayadarśataḥ*, A^{2} *tattvadarśinaḥ* for *bhayadarśinaḥ*.

40. *a.* A^{1} IO *nigraho yat tad*, A^{2} *nigraho yat tam* for *nigrahāyattam*.

43. *b.* A^{1} A^{2} *°bhogaṃ* for *bhogān*.

44. *b.* PU^{1} *samayet* for *śamayet*. *d.* B^{2} *samam prāptaṃ*, all others *samaprāptaṃ* for *śamaprāptaṃ* (=*°t śama°*) in VeS, § 33 and supported by *Vidvanmanorañjanī*; C *vicālayet* for *cālayet*.

45. *a.* VeS with *Subodhinī* and *Vidvanmanorañjanī*, loc. cit., *rasaṃ* for *sukhaṃ*. *c.* A^{1} A^{2} *niścitāṃ ci°*, IO *niścitaṃ ci°*, B^{2} *niścaraṃś ci°* for *niścarac ci°*.

46. *b.* A^{1} A^{2} PU^{1} *manaḥ* for *punaḥ*. *c.* A^{1} *aniṅgita°*, A^{2} *anaṅgita°*, B^{1} D^{2} *aliṅgana°* for *aniṅgana°*. *d.* K M^{e} *tathā* for *tadā*.

47. *d.* A^{1} A^{2} *sa sarvajñaḥ parīkṣite* for *sarvajñaṃ paricakṣate*.

48. *b.* B^{1} *sambhāvo* for *sadbhāvo*.

Colophon :

B^{1} PU^{2} iti śrīgovindabhagavatpūjyapādaśiṣyasya paramahaṃsaparivrājakācāryasya śaṅkarabhagavataḥ kṛtāv āgamaśāstravivaraṇe advaitākhyaṃ tṛtīyaṃ prakaraṇaṃ samāptam.

PU^1 iti śrīgauḍapādācāryaviracitam advaitākhyaṃ tṛtīyaṃ prakaraṇam.

V^g āgamaśāstre advaitākhyaṃ tṛtīyaṃ prakaraṇaṃ samāptam.

V^n gauḍapādīye advaitanirṇayo nāma tṛtīyaṃ prakaraṇam.

Book IV

1. c. A^1 *saṃvṛddha°*, A^2 *sambhinna°* for *sambuddha°*. *d.* PU^2 *°ntaraṃ* for *varam*.

2. *d.* V^g *darśata°* for *deśita°*.

3. *a.* V^g *jāta°* for *jāti°*. *b.* B^1 first *sarva* then corrected to *kecid* as in the text.

4. *a.* All excepting D^e GP M^e *dvayā* for *'dvayāḥ*. *d.* A^{1}A^2 *na jātim*, V^g *°ajātaṃ* for *ajātiṃ*.

6. *d.* A^2 *martya nu* for *martyatām*; A^{1}A^2 *iṣyati* for *eṣyati*.

7. *a.* D^1 *martye* for *martyaṃ*. *b.* D^{1}D^2 *mṛtyu°* for *martya°*; A^{1}A^2 Jh V^g *yathā* for *tathā*. See III. 21^b.

9. *a.* A^1 *nisvābhāvikī* for *svābhāvikī*. *b.* IO *kṛtā*, B^1 B^2 K^1 GP Me V^g *akṛtā*, A^1 A^2 *amṛtā*, Jh *kṛtakā*, C *°py ākṛtā* for *°py akṛtā*; Jh *yathā* for *ca yā*. *c.* A^1 *°ś ceti*, A^2 *sveti*, A^3 *°s seti* for *seti*. K^1 reads only *d* omitting other lines altogether.

10. *b.* A^1 A^2 *sarva°* for *sarve*. *d.* A^1 A^2 *tanmayā api* for *tanmanīṣayā*.

It is to be noted that in D^1 kārikās from 10 to 53 are wanting.

11. *d.* B^1 *nityaṃ bhinnaṃ* for *bhinnaṃ nityaṃ*; A^1 A^2 *yat* for *tat*.

12. *a.* A^1 A^3 A^e B^1 B^2 M^e D^2 V^n *yady ananyatvam*, A^2 *yayam ananyatvam*, V^g *yad anyatvam* for *yad ananyatvam*. As the word *yadi* occurs in *b* here in *a* one should read *yad* as actually found in V^g though it reads in *b tava* for *yadi*.

13. *c-d.* A^2 *°mānas tasya vyavathā* for *°mānasya na-vyavasthā*. *d.* V^g *prajāyate*, PU^1 PU^2 *prasajjate* for *prasajyate*.

14. *a.* A^2 *°di samaṃ* for *°dīḥ phalaṃ*. IO omits the kārikā.

15. *b.* V^g *ādihetuḥ* for *ādir hetuḥ*; A^1 A^2 IO *phalaṃ ca yat* for *phalasya ca*. *d.* A^1 *putra°* for *putrāj°*.

16. *b.* V^g °*eṣitaḥ*, B^1 K^1 °*iṣitavyaḥ* for °*eṣitavyaḥ*. *d.* A^2 *viṣayāvat* for *viṣāṇavat*.

17. *a.* B^2 *phalātanupa*° for *phalād utpa*°. *b.* A^1 A^2 *to* for *te*.

18. *b.* A^1 *hetuḥ*, A^2 *hetuṣu* for *hetutaḥ*; C Jh *phalāsiddhiḥ* for *phalasiddhiḥ*. *c.* A^1 A^2 *paraṃ tat* for *katarat*.

B^2 gives the number of the kārikā as 16 instead of 18 and henceforth the scribe counts the following kārikās accordingly, *i.e.*, 17, 18, etc.

19. *a.* A^2 *atrokti*° for *aśakti*°; A^1 A^2 °*pavijñānaṃ* for °*parijñānam*. *d.* A^1 A^2 °*jāti* for °*jātiḥ*; A^1 °*vāpitā* for °*dīpitā*.

20. *b.* A^1 A^2 °*tamo* for °*samo*; A^e A^1 A^2 A^3 B^1 B^2 D^1 IO PU^1 PU^2 V^g V^n *saḥ* for *naḥ* in C D^2. *c.* A^e A^3 B^1 B^2 IO PU^1 PU^2 V^g V^n *hi* for *ca* in A^1 A^2 supported by Ś.

21. *a.* Gh °*parapari*° for °*parāpari*°. *b.* V^g °*dīpikam* for *dīpakam*.

22. *a.* IO omits *vā* after *svato*.

23. *b.* A^e A^1 A^2 A^3 B^1 B^2 D^1 IO M^e PU^1 PU^2 *cāpi* for *vāpi*. *d.* PU^1 on the margin *jātir* for *hy ādir*.

24. *d.* A^1 A^2 *parataṃ nāsti nāma tā* (the former °*tāḥ* for °*tā*) for the line; V^n °*matāṃ* for *matā*.

25. *a.* A^1 A^2 *prajñapte* for *prajñapteḥ*. *b.* A^1 *bhukti*° for *yukti*°; A^2 °*anyathā dvayanāśataḥ* for *b*; K^1 *bhūta*° for *yukti*°. *c* and *d* are omitted in K^1.

26. *a.* V^g °*arthān* for °*artham*. *b.* A^2 *nābhāsaṃ*, V^g *arthābhāsas ta*° for *nārthābhāsaṃ ta*°. *d.* A^2 IO °*bhāsaṃ* for °*bhāsas*; A^1 *tata*, C *tathā* for *tataḥ*.

27. *a.* A^3 *sahā* for *sadā*. *b.* *pañcasu* for °*ty adhvasu*. *c.* A^1 *viparyātsaḥ* for *viparyāsaḥ*.

28. *b.* *cittaṃ* for *citta*°. *c.* A^1 *jāti*, A^2 *yānti* for *jātiṃ*. *d.* V^g *te* for *khe* and *khe* for *te*.

29. *a.* A^2 *tasmād* for *yasmād*. *b.* A^1 A^2 D^2 *tathā* for *tataḥ*. *c.* A^2 '*nyathā* for °*r anyathā*.

30. *c.* A^1 *anantabhāvādimato*, A^2 *anantatā vādimate*, C D^2 *anantatā ādimato* for *anantatā cādimato*.

31. *c-d.* A^2 *santyevi*°, A^3 D^2 *santo vi*° (in the latter between *santo* and *vi*° there is an *avagraha* mark above the line and it seems to have been struck off) for *santo 'vi*°; A^2 D^2 *lakṣitā* for *lakṣitāḥ*.

32. *b.* All excepting D^2 *vipratipadyate* for *'pi pratipadyate*. See II. 7.

33. *a.* All *sarve dha*° for *sarvadha*° in A^1; PU^2 *mṛṣāḥ* for *mṛṣā*. *b.* A^2 V^g *kāryasyā*° for *kāyasyā*°. *c.* B^1 B^2 M^e V^n *saṃvṛtte* for *saṃvṛte*.

34. *a.* A^2 *jñātvā* for *gatvā*. *b.* A^2 *kālālaisyā*° for *kālasyā*°. *d.* IO *darśe* for *deśe*.

35. *b.* A^e A^3 B^1 B^2 K^1 M^e *sambuddho* for *prabuddho*. *c.* A^2 D^2 *vāpi* for *cāpi*.

36. *b.* D^2 °*s tadarśanāt* for °*sya darśanāt*.

37. *c.* A^e B^1 B^2 PU^1 V^g °*tvāt tu* for °*tvāc ca*. *d.* A^1 A^2 D^2 *sajāga*° for *saj jāga*°.

38(39). *b.* A^1 *tanmayā* for *tanmayaḥ*. *c.* A^1 A^2 *dṛṣṭāc ca* for *dṛṣṭvā ca*.

39(41). *b.* A^2 °*cintyāt* for °*cintyān*. *c.* Gh *yathā* for *tathā*; A^1 A^2 *viparyāsaṃ* for *viparyāsāt*. *d.* A^1 A^2 *tatra ca* for *tatraiva*.

41(40). *c.* B^2 *sa* for *sac*.

42. *a.* A^2 *upālambhāt* for *upalambhāt*. *d.* A^1 A^2 °*ś ca satāṃ*, B^1 °*s trasyatāṃ* for °*s trasatāṃ*.

43. *a.* A^1 °*s tv asatyaṃ*, A^2 °*s tu satāṃ*, D^2 *susatāṃ*, B^1 °*s trasyatāṃ* for °*s trasatāṃ*. *b.* A^1 D^2 *te* for *ye*; V^g first *te* then corrected to *ye*.

45. *a.* A^1 A^2 *vastvabhāsaṃ* for *vastvābhāsaṃ*. *d.* A^1 *śāntim*, B^2 *sāntam* for *śāntam*; D^2 *avyayam*, V^n *sadvayam* for *advayam*.

46. *a-b.* B^2 *cittacintaṃ* for *cittam evaṃ*. *c.* V^n °*m ajānanto*, PU^2 *jānanto*, C *vijñāto na* for *vijānanto*. *d.* A^1 *tapati*, A^2 A^3 *tapanti* for *patanti*.

47. *d.* All excepting B^1 C Jh PU^1 *vijñanaspa*° for *vijñānaṃ spa*

48. *a.* A^e A^3 D^1 IO M^e PU^1 PU^2 *alātam* for *alātam*. In A^1 *a* and *b* are omitted. *c.* A^1 °*māna vi*° for °*mānaṃ vi*°.

A^2 reads *c-d* as *a-b*, and *a-b* as *c-d* with the following variants : *c.* °*māna vi*° for °*mānaṃ vi*°, and °*prajaṃ* for °*m ajaṃ*. V^g is damaged here.

49. *b.* D^2 B^2 *nābhāsa* for *nābhāsā*; A^1 A^2 A^3 Kh Gh J N °*ś cānyato* for *anyato*. *c-d.* A^1 *nispandāṃ nā*°, A^2 *nispandā na*, Gh *nispandan nā*° for *nispandān nā*°.

50. *a-b.* B^2 °*nirgatālātā dra*° for *nirgatā alātāt te dra*°. *c-d.* A^1 °*vāsya nābhāsasthāvi*° for °*va syur ābhāsasyāvi*°.

51. *c.* A^1 A^2 A^3 *nispandaṃ na* for *nispandān na*.

52. *a.* K Jh °*rgatā vijñā*° for °*rgatās te vijñā*°; K Jh M^e V^g °*tā vijñānāt te*, B^1 °*tā vijñānas te*, B^2 °*tā vijñānā te*, PU^1 °*t te vijñānāt* for °*tās te vijñānād*. *b.* A^1 A^2 A^3 *dravyatvaṃ bhā*° for *dravyatvābhā*°. *c-d.* A^1 °*yogādānovittāḥ*, A^2 *yogād ato cittāḥ* for °*bhāvād yato 'cintyāḥ* ; A^3 *cintyā* for *'cintyāḥ* ; A^1 A^2 *hi* for *te*.

53. *c.* A^2 °*m anyathābhā*° for °*m anyabhā*°.

54. *b.* A^2 B^2 D^1 V^g *cāpi* for *vāpi*; A^3 *dharmajāḥ* for *dharmajam*. *c.* A^2 °*jātiḥ* for °*jātiṃ*.

55. *a.* V^n *yād dhetu*°, PU^1 *yāva hetu*° for *yāvad dhetu*°. *c.* D^1 D^2 °*hetuḥ* for *hetu*°.

56. *d.* A^e A^3 B^1 B^2 D^1 D^2 M^e PU^1 V^g V^n *saṃsāraṃ na prapadyate*, A^2 *saṃsāran nopapadyate* for *saṃsāro nopapadyate* in A^1 and IO.

57. *a.* A^1 A^2 *svapnaṃ* for *sarvaṃ*. *b.* A^e B^1 B^2 M^e PU^1 PU^2 *nāsti tena vai* for *tena nāsti vai*. *c.* All *sadbhāvena* for *svabhāvena*. *d.* A^2 *nāsmi* for *nāsti*.

58. *b.* All excepting V^n *jāyante* for *saṃvṛtyā* supported by Ś.

59. *a.* A^2 °*yā jātā*° for °*yād bījā*°. *c.* A^1 A^2 *na sa* for *nāsau* ; A^1 *bocche*° for *cocche*°.

60. *a.* A^1 *nādyeṣu*, A^2 *nājyeṣu* for *nājeṣu*. *b.* A^1 *śāśvatā nāsti dhīyate*, A^2 *śāśvatāśāśvato'bhidhā* for this line. *c.* V^g °*nyamūdyante vartante* for *na vartante*.

62. *a.* V^g *tu* for *ca*. *b.* A^1 A^2 B^1 D^1 D^2 *manaḥ* for *cittaṃ*. *c.* V^g *tu* for *ca*. *d.* A^1 *jāgraṃ na*, A^2 *jāgreṇa* for *jāgran na*.

63. *a.* A^1 A^2 *pracalan*, C *kvācaran* for *pracaran*. *b.* A^1 *disam utthitān*, A^2 *diśamurcchitān* for *daśasu sthitān*. *c.* A^1 *añjanān* for *aṇḍajān* ; B^2 *svapne* for *vāpi*.

64. *a.* D^1 *svapne* for *svapna°*; A^1 A^2 *°kiṃ na*, A^3 D^1 *°kitta°* for *°citta°*. *b.* A^1 A^2 *bhidyante* for *vidyante*. *c.* A^2 *na dṛśya°* for *taddṛśya°*, A^1 *°m etedaṃ* for *°m evedaṃ*. *d.* A^1 *kiṃ ta°*, A^2 *kaṃ ta°*, A^3 D^1 *kitta°* for *citta°*; K^1 *jāgrataś ci°* for *svapnadṛk ci°*.

65. *a.* A^1 A^2 *varaṃ* for *carañ*. *a-b.* V^n *tasmā dikṣu* corrected to *tac ca tyakṣu* for *jāgrad dikṣu*. *b.* A^2 *dasmutthitān* for *daśasu sthitān*. *c.* D^1 *cāpi* for *vāpi*.

66. *a.* D^1 ^{c}*kṣiṇīyās°*, V^n *°kṣaṇīyāṃ°* for *°kṣaṇīyās°*. *b.* A^1 *bhidyante*, A^2 *bhidyanti* for *vidyate*. *c.* A^1 *dṛśyam idaṃ vedam* for *tad dṛśyam evedam*. *d.* B^1 *jāgrac* for *jāgrataś*.

67. *c.* C *°dṛśyeta* for *°dṛśye te*. *b.* A^1 A^2 A^3 B^1 B^2 C Ch D^1 D^2 G IO K M^e PU^1 PU^2 V^g *ca* for *na*. After this kārikā D^2 adds :

> pramāṇaśūnyam ubhayaṃ cittaṃ caittaṃ dvayaṃ yataḥ |
> tanmatenaiva tac cittaṃ tayaiva ca tad gṛhyate ||

There are different readings for which see Ś's commentary (A^e) from which it is taken. Here *d* is defective of metre.

68. *d.* Kh Gh N Jh *na bhavanti* for *bhavanti na*.

69. A^1 A^2 omit it. In A^3 it is not in the body but on the margin by a second hand. *b.* K^1 *mriyate jāyate* for *jāyate mriyate*. *d.* Kh Gh N J *na bhavanti* for *bhavanti na*.

70. A^2 V^n omit the kārikā. *a.* A^1 K^1 V^g *nimittako*, B^1 B^2 *nirmittako* for *nirmitako*. *b.* A^e D^1 D^2 M^e *vā* for *ca*.

71. *c.* A^2 *ya etad u°* for *etat tad u°*; A^2 V^n *sarvaṃ*, K^1 *patraṃ* for *satyaṃ*.

72. *a.* For this A^1 A^2 *cittaṃ spandati me sarvaṃ*. *b.* D^1 D^2 *grāhyaṃ grā°* for *grāhyagrā°*.

73. *c.* All *paratantrābhi°* for ***paratantro*** *'bhi°*. *d.* For this V^n *paramārthena nāsty asau*. Then again it has c and *d*.

74. *a.* A^1 °*saṃvṛttāḥ* for °*saṃvṛtyā*. *b.* A^2 °*rtho na* for °*rthena*. c. A^e A^1 A^2 A^3 B^1 B^2 D^1 D^2 V^g V^n *paratantrā*° for *paratantro'*° in K M^e.

75. *c.* V^g *dvayābhāsaṃ* for *dvayābhāvam*. *d.* A^1 A^2 *tannimitto* for *nirnimitto*.

76. *a.* PU^1 *labhyate* for *labhate*. *c.* A^2 *taṃ* for *tadā*. *d. hetubhāve* for *hetvabhāve*.

77. *c.* A^2 *pūrvasya* for *sarvasya*.

78. *a.* A^2 *satyaṃ* for *satyām*. *b.* For this A^2 *hetunyapyagate bruban* ; V^g *hetu - thag*°, IO *hetuprathag* for *hetuṃ pṛthag*° ; V^n °*nāpnuyāt*, others °*nāpnuvan* for *nāpnuvat* in D^2. c. All excepting A^2 V^g *tathā* for *tadā* ; A^e M^e *kāmam* for *'kāmam*.

79. *a.* A^1 °*niveśyādbhiḥ*, IO °*niveśyāddhiḥ* for °*niveśad dhi*. c. A^1 *yaṣ tva*°, A^2 *yat tva*°, B^1 *vastvā*°, V^n *dvayā*° for *vastva*° ; all excepting A^1 and A^2 *sa buddhvaiva*, A^1 *subuddhyaiva*, A^2 *subudhyeva* for *sa buddhvaiva* ; A^1 adds *ca* after *buddhvaiva*. *d.* A^1 *na niva*°, A^2 *hi niva*°, V^n *ca niva*° for *viniva*°.

80. *b.* Gh *niścalaṃ* for *niścalā*. *c.* A^3 D^1 V^g *sā* for *sa* ; A^1 A^2 V^n *tu* for *hi*. *d.* K M^e *svāmya*° for *sāmya*° ; V^n °*jadvayam* for °*jam advayam*.

81. *a.* A^2 *unnidram* for *anidram*. *b.* A^1 A^2 *prabhāvam* for *prabhātam*. *c.* A^2 *vibhānto* for *vibhāto*. *d.* A^e B^1 V^g *dharmo dhātusva*°, Gh *dharmo dhātuṃ sva*° for *dharmo dhātuḥ sva*°.

82. *a.* A^1 A^2 *āśrayate* for *āvriyate*. *b.* A^2 *va vriyate*, B^2 *vriyate*, D^2 *vā vriyate* for *vivriyate* ; A^1 *tadā* for *sadā*. *c-d.* For this A^1 A^2 IO *yasya dharmasya grahaṇaṃ bhagavān api so 'śnute*.

83. *b.* V^g *vai* for *vā*. *c.* A^1 A^2 °*bhāsair* for °*bhāvair*.

84. *a.* A^3 *catasro* for *catasra* ; A^1 A^2 °*ś ca*, B^1 °*su* for °*s tu* ; C °*ś ca tatparāyā*° for °*ś catasra etā*°. *b.* A^3 *gṛhai*° for *grahai*° ; C °*s tāsāṃ* for °*r yāsāṃ*.

85. *a.* D^2 *kṛsnakṛtāṃ* (corrected by a second hand to *sarvajñatāṃ*) *sarvāṃ* for *sarvajñatāṃ kṛtsnāṃ*. *b.* A^1 *agrayam*, D^1 D^2 *avyayam* for *advayam*. *c.* A^1 *annā*° for *anā*°.

87. *a.* A^1 *avastu*, A^2 *suvastu* for *savastu*. *c* and *d* are omitted in K^1.

88. *a.* V^n °*palaṁ* for °*palambhaṃ*.

89. *a.* B^1 *dvividhe* for *trividhe*. *b.* D^1 *vịndate*, D^2 *vidate* for *vidite*.

90. *a.* A^1 A^2 °*jñeyasya vākyāni*, IO °*jñeyāpavākyāni* for °*jñeyāpyapākyāni*. *d.* D^2 °*lambho*° for °*lambha*°.

91. *a.* A^1 A^2 A^3 °*vijñeyāḥ* for °*vaj jñeyāḥ*. *a-b.* Ch reads *sarve* before *jñeyāḥ*. *b.* All *sarve dharmā* excepting A^1 V^g which read *sarvadharmā*. *c.* V^g *ca* for *hi*.

92. *b.* All *sarve dharmāḥ* excepting V^g which reads *sarvadharmāḥ*.

93. *b.* A^2 *prakṛtau va* for *prakṛtyaiva*; A^2 J *sunirmitāḥ*, V^g *suniścitāḥ* for *sunirvṛtāḥ*. *c.* A^2 V^g *sarvadha*° for *sarve dha*°. *d.* A^1 A^2 *śyāmaṃ* for *sāmyam*; A^2 °*radām* for °*radam*. For *d* B^2 *prakṛtyaiva sunirvṛtāḥ* repeating c and *d* as in the text.

94. *c.* A^1 *vedabhinnāḥ*, A^2 *vedābhinnāḥ*, V^n *bhedaniṣṭhā* for *bhedanimnāḥ*.

95. *a.* A^1 A^2 *ajaṃ* for *aje*; A^1 *sāmyaṃ* for *sāmye*. *b.* A^1 A^2 *vipaścitam*, IO *viniścitaiḥ* for *suniścitāḥ*.

96. *a.* A^1 *ajetyojam*, M^e *aje 'py ajam* for *ajeṣv ajam*; D^2 *ajaṃ krāntaṃ* for *asaṃkrāntaṃ*. D^1 and D^2 add here *sarvabhūtātmabhūtasya sarvabhūtahitasya ca* which is found in Ś's commentary on the preceding kārikā.

97. *a.* IO *vaidharme* for *vaidharmye*. *d* A^2 *udāharaṇe* for *utāvaraṇa*°; D^1 °*varaṇā*° for °*varaṇa*°.

98. *c.* A^1 *budhās*, A^2 *buddhas* for *buddhās*; A^1 *yuktā*, A^2 *yukta* for *muktā*. *d.* A^2 *budhyanti*, IO *budhyante* for *budhyanta*.

99. *a.* A^1 *budhasya* for *buddhasya*. *b.* A^1 *no manaḥ*, A^2 first *bodhinaḥ* then corrected to *vyāpinaḥ*, D^1 D^2 K^1 M^e PU^1 *tāpinaḥ*, A^e *tāpi(yi)naḥ* for *tāyinaḥ*. *c.* All excepting A^1 A^2 *sarve dha*° for *sarvadha*°. *d.* A^1 *budhena* for *buddhena*.

100. *a.* V^n *durdaśam* for *durdarśam*. *b.* A^1 *śyāmaṃ* for *sāmyaṃ*; A^2 °*radām* for °*radam*. *d.* A^1 *manaḥ kurmo*, A^3 *manaskurmo*, A^2 D^2 V^n *namaḥ kurmo* for *namaskurmo*.

Colophon :

A^1 A^2 ity upadeśagranthe 'lātaśāntyākhyaṃ prakaraṇaṃ samāptam.

A^3 adds to the above only *caturthaṃ* after *prakaraṇaṃ*.

B^1 B^2 iti śrī govindabhagavatpūjyapādaśiṣyaśaṅkarabhagavataḥ kṛtāv āgamaśāstravivaraṇe alātaśāntākhyaṃ caturthaṃ prakaraṇaṃ samāptam (B^2 sampūrṇam).

D^1 D^2 iti śrīgauḍapādabhagavataḥ kṛtau āgamagranthe upadeśagranthe vedāntamūle gauḍapādīyaṃ caturthaṃ prakaraṇam.

IO ity alātākhyaṃ caturthaṃ prakaraṇam upaniṣat samāptam (*sic*). śiva śiva ... (17 times).

K^1 iti māṇḍūkyopaniṣadgauḍapādavyākhyāne.

PU^1 iti śrīmadgauḍapādācāryakṛtau māṇḍūkyavārttike alātaśāntyākhyaṃ caturthaṃ prakaraṇaṃ samāptam. prakaraṇacatuṣṭayātmakaṃ śāstraṃ sampūrṇam.

PU^2 iti śrīgovindabhagavatpūjyapādaśiṣyasya śrīśaṅkarabhagavataḥ kṛtāv āgamaśāstravivaraṇe alātaśāntyākhyaṃ caturthaṃ prakaraṇaṃ samāptam.

V^g iti śrīgauḍapāda-āgamaśāstre alātaśāntyākhyaṃ caturthaprakaraṇaṃ samāptam.

V^n iti śrīgauḍapādīye upadeśagranthe alātaśāntyākhyacaturthaprakaraṇam.

III

INDEX OF THE KĀRIKĀS

IV

INDEX OF THE PASSAGES OF THE MĀṆḌŪKYA UPANIṢAD

V

INDEX OF IMPORTANT WORDS IN THE KĀRIKĀS

VI

INDEX OF TEACHERS AND WORKS QUOTED OR REFERRED TO IN THE KĀRIKĀS

N.B.—*Words with a hyphen indicate that they are not actually used, but reconstructed from the contexts. Buddhist works may be taken with discretion.*

VII

INDEX OF WORDS IN THE KĀRIKĀS USED IN PARTICULAR SENSES ORIGINALLY OR MAINLY IN BUDDHIST WORKS[1]

---

[1] See the Annotation. It is to be noted that all the words excepting only two or three are in Book IV.

VIII

INDEX OF TIBETAN VERSES

IX

INDEX OF TEACHERS, SCHOLARS AND PLACES, ETC.

N.B.—*Teachers mentioned in Appendix VI are not included here.*

X

INDEX OF WORKS

N.B.—*Abbreviated names are given here in full*

34—1201B.

XI

INDEX OF SUBJECTS

P.=Pali, S.=Sanskrit

ADDENDA ET CORRIGENDA

INTRODUCTION

P. xlix, note 2. Certainly this reason *dṛśyatva* is not in our text, but in Śaṅkara's own commentary (II. 4: dṛśyatvād iti hetuḥ). It may be noted here in this connexion that in the later Vedāntic works *dṛśyatva* is one of the main *hetus* for inferring that the outward world is false (*Advaitasiddhi*, Advaitamañjarī ed., p. 2: vimataṃ mithyā dṛśyatvād).

P. lxxxix. As regards the commentary on the NUTU, I am thankful to Sachindra Nath Ghose of Benares for his kindly sending me a transcription of it made by himself in Bengali characters from a MS in the library called *Mālatīsāradāsadana* of Ray Govinchandji in Benares. It is not complete and runs up to *pratyagekarasaḥ* of the original text in the ninth and the last section. Yet, it contains a separate loose page in which the last portion of the commentary is copied. Here in some of the colophons it is called *Vivaraṇa*, while in others *Vivṛti*. According to the present MS this commentary is by Gauḍapāda as is quite clear from the colophons, some reading Śrīgauḍapādīya° and others °śrīśukayogīndraśiṣyaśrīgauḍapādācāryakṛti°. It begins thus:

śrīgaṇeśāya namaḥ. śrīnṛsiṃhāya namaḥ.

nirastasakalānarthaparamānandarūpiṇe |
nṛsiṃhāya namaskurmaḥ sarvadhīvṛttisākṣiṇe || 1

yatpādābjarajoleśasamparkāt sahasā sakṛt |
sarvasaṃsārahīno 'haṃ tān nato 'smi gurūn sadā || 2
tāpanīyarahasyārthavivṛti[r] leśato mayā |
kriyate 'lpadhiyāṃ tasmāt kṣantavyaṃ kṣatam
uttamaiḥ || 3

iha pūrvasmin granthe nṛsiṃhākārabrahmaviṣayā nirupādhikabrahmavidyāphalādhigatā. tathā hy uktaṃ vārttikakṛdbhiḥ

nṛsiṃhabrahmavidyaiṣā vyākṛtā jñānasiddhaye |

And it ends thus :

tāpanīyarahasyārthadīpikā timirāpahā |
gurvanugrahalabdhaiṣā satām astu sukhāptaye ||
saccidānandapūrṇ[āya] pratyagekarasātmane |
tejase mahate bhūyān namaḥ puṃsiṃharūpiṇe ||
yasya saṃsmṛtimātreṇa taranti bhavasāgaram |
taṃ nato 'smi guruṃ bhaktyā dhiyā vācā ca
karmaṇā ||

iti śrīmatparamahaṃsaparivrājakācāryaśrīmacchukamunīndraśiṣya-śrīmadgauḍapādamuniviracite uttaratāpanīyavivaraṇe navamaḥ khaṇḍaḥ. śubham astu. śrīlakṣmīnṛsiṃho rakṣatu mām. nṛsiṃhārpaṇam astu.

tāraṇe vatsare māsi śrāvaṇe 'sitapakṣage |
pañcamīrevatīyukte tithau kumbheśapattane ||
nṛsiṃhatāpanīyākhyaṭīkāṃ gauḍābhidhāṃ satīm |
vyāseśvaro 'likhat svast[y]ai
nṛsiṃhas tena nuṣṭha(tuṣya?)tām ||

It is interesting to note that the following passage from this *Vivaraṇa* (pp. 25-26) is identical with that in

Ś a ṅ k a r a ' s commentary on the MāU, 11, excepting a few unimportant variations as noted in the foot-notes :

mīyate iva hi viśvataijasau prājñena pralayotpattyoḥ praveśanirgamābhyāṃ prastheneva yavāḥ. tathoṅkāra-samāptau punaḥ punaḥ[1] prayoge ca praviśya nirgatāv[2] ivākārokārau makāre 'ntye 'kṣare ekībhūtāv ivākārokārau. tathā suṣupte prājñe viśvataijasau°.[3] minoti jāgradādi-yāthātmyaṃ jānātīty arthaḥ.[4] apītiś ca jagatkāraṇātmā ca[5] bhavati.

P. cxxxv. Regarding the identity of *citta* and Brahman, see YV, III. 64. 31 ; 65. 3 ; 66. 14 ; 96. 56, 66, 73; IV. 35. 20-23, 54. 20. From these verses we can gather that *jīva*, *cit*, *ātman*, *brahman*, *śūnya*, *nairātmya*, etc., are the different expressions of *citta*. From the same authority (III. 122. 35) we also know that such names are made by the authors of *śāstras* in order to supply some terms required by them :

śāstrasaṃvyavahārārthaṃ tasyāsya vitatākṛteḥ |
cidbrahmātmeti nāmāni kalpitāni kṛtātmabhiḥ ||

P. cxxxvi, note 8. For *manaḥkṣaya* there is *manaḥ-parikṣaya* in YV, III. 116. 13. It has also *manonāśa* (III. 95. 35-36) and *manaḥpraśamana* (III. 122. 27).

1 Ś omits it.
2 Ś nirgacchata.
3 For suṣupte °taijasau° Ś has viśvataijasau suṣuptakāle prājñe.
4 Ś minoti ha vā idaṃ sarvaṃ jagad.
5 Ś omits it.

BOOK I

5. It is quoted in ŚV, p. 27.

6. On the creation from Prāṇa see KtU, III. 3 and BS, I. 1. 23, 28. Here in the kārikā we have an Idealistic view (Vijñānavāda).

9. For *āptakāma* see BU, IV. 4. 6. For *bhogārthaṃ sṛṣṭiḥ* see Śrīdharasvāmin on BP, III. 7. 4: avidyopādher jīvasya bhogārtham īśvaraḥ sṛṣṭyādi karoti.

10. See BU, IV. 2. 4; 4. 22; 5. 15.

12. The word *sarvadṛś* in sense is the same as *sarvajña* 'omniscient' (III. 36). His omniscience is, according to Śaṅkara (BS, I. 1. 4), on account of his capacity for all knowledge (sarvajñānaśaktimattvenaiva sarvajñatvam abhyupagantavyam), or owing to the fact that he is never dissociated from his intelligence, *i.e.*, all-embracing knowledge (*Op. cit.*, I. 3. 42: sarvajñatvalakṣaṇayā prajñayā niyatam aviyogāt).

On this kārikā as well as on I. 15 see *Upadeśasāhasrī*, XVIII. 26.

13. In this and the following kārikās *nidrā* in sense is, in fact, *suṣupta*. Here *nidrā* is said to be *bīja* 'seed', *i.e.*, origin, because *nidrā* being non-realization of truth is the cause of both dream and waking. See *Upadeśasāhasrī*, XVIII. 26 as quoted in NSi, IV. 43:

suṣuptākhyaṃ tamo 'jñānaṃ bījaṃ svapnaprabodhayoḥ |
ātmabodhāgnidagdhaṃ syād bījaṃ dagdhaṃ yathābhavam ||

This explanation of *bīja* slightly differs from the one given before on p. 6.

14. See I. 16; III. 35. 36; IV. 81. In the fourth state, Turya, there is no *nidrā* nor *svapna*. In such cases

while *nidrā* means the *laya* or *mūḍha* 'infatuated' state of the mind, *svapna* indicates the state called *vikṣepa* 'distraction'. This state of Turya is the state of Brahman.

15. For *b* of the kārikā *cf.* YS, I. 10: abhāva-pratyayālambanā vṛttir nidrā. This kārikā is quoted in NSi, IV. 42.

16. This kārikā is quoted in MnU, I. 13, with the reading *ajanmanidram* for *ajam anidram* in *c*.

17. The following is quoted as from Gauḍapāda in Śaṅkara's *Viṣṇusahasranāma-bhāṣya*, Mysore ed., p. 18:

yad yad dvaitaṃ prapañcasya tan nivartyaṃ hi cetasā |
manovṛttimayaṃ dvaitam advaitaṃ paramārthataḥ ||

19. The Praṇava-upāsana referred to here is well-known in Upaniṣads, older and later alike (ChU, I. 1. 1, 4. 1; PU, V. 1-2; TU, I. 8. 1; MuU, II. 2. 6; MU, IV. 4. 37). Here a few words are necessary for the real significance of *upāsana* (sometimes *upāsanā*), which is enjoined (yuñjīta praṇave cetaḥ, I. 25) and described to some extent here by our author. The word *upāsana* is derived, as well-known to all, from *upa-√ās* literally 'to seat near at hand (in order to honour or wait upon),' and figuratively 'to do homage, worship, be devoted to', etc. But in such Upaniṣadic texts as mano brahmety upāsīta (ChU, III. 18. 1), or, sa yo nāma brahmety upāste (*Op. cit.*, VII. 1. 5), it has some special meaning. The first sentence quoted above does not mean 'One should *worship* the mind as Brahman,' nor do we understand from the second sentence 'He who *worships* the name as Brahman.' In both of the cases *upa-√ās*

or *upāsana* gives the sense of meditation (*dhyāna*). It is in the words of Ś a ṅ k a r a a continuous flow of one and the same idea having an *ālambana* 'support' recommended by the scripture, unmixed with other ideas. (BS, IV. 1. 7 : upāsanaṃ nāma samānapratyayapravāha-karaṇam. See ChU, I. 1. 1 and our text, p. 48). The best *ālambana* for the *upāsana* of Brahman, as in the present case, is Om. We read in the KU, I. 2. 17 :

etad ālambanaṃ śreṣṭham etad ālambanaṃ param |
etad ālambanaṃ jñātvā brahmaloke mahīyate||

The meditation of Om as Brahman, just as the meditation of an image (*pratimā*) as Viṣṇu 'the all-pervading one', is the means for the realization of Brahman. It is to be noted, according to Ś a ṅ k a r a's school, that while *Brahmajñāna* leads one immediately and directly to *mokṣa*, *Brahma-upāsana* does not do so, it helps one in gradually attaining to it and to prosperity. Ś a ṅ k a r a says, it effects the purity of the mind and making the truth clear thereby helps us in acquiring the knowledge of Brahman. Besides, there being an *ālambana* 'support' it is easy to make an *upāsana*.

It is to be further noted that there are two kinds of *upāsana*, that involving the contemplation of the Self (*ahaṃgrahopāsana*), and that which is symbolical or concerned with external symbols (*pratīkopāsana*). In the former, the Self, the Paramātman, is contemplated in his conditioned form (*saguṇa*) with the idea that 'I am he'. For instance, we read in the TA, VII. 6 :

sa ya eṣo 'ntarhṛdaya ākāśaḥ, tasmin ayaṃ puruṣo manomayo 'mṛto hiraṇmayaḥ.

'It is that space within the heart. Here is the Person, formed of thought, undying and golden'.

Here the person (*i.e.*, Paramātman) within the space of the heart with those qualities is to be meditated with the thought that 'I am the Person'.

But where a worldly or external thing which is other than Brahman is contemplated being regarded as a higher god or Brahman himself that contemplation or *upāsana* is symbolical (*pratīkopāsana*). For instance, in the case of the text, mano brahmety upāsīta (quoted above), the mind is to be contemplated as Brahman. So here is another instance of *pratīkopāsana*. For details see BS, III. 3 and IV. 1.

Now with regard to our own case, Om is to be meditated as the Self, and so we have also here an instance of *pratīkopāsana*. The three measures (*mātrās*) of Om are to be meditated as Viśva, Taijasa and Prājña respectively. And that Om which has no measure (*amātra*), *i.e.*, the measures of which are not considered separately, and which is thus immeasurable (*amātra*), or which, in other words, is with unlimited measure (*anantamātra*) is to be meditated as Turya.

It is said that in an *upāsana* one thing is to be viewed as another thing; for instance, here the first measure of Om, *a*, is to be regarded as Viśva. It amounts to saying that these two things are identical. But how can this identity be possible? The answer is this that such identity is by no means actual, but owing to some common quality (*sāmānyadharma*) of the two the identity of which is intended. This is a well-known practice among us. We say of a brave lad that he is a lion (*siṃho māṇavakaḥ*), though in fact he is not so. It is only on account of the common quality, bravery, of the lad and a lion that we identify them employing the phrase. Simply following this method of expression our teacher has shown some common qualities of the Puruṣa and Om (I. 19 ff.) owing to which their identity has been made possible. Let us remember here the following line of Yāska in his Nt, VII. 24: bahubhaktivādīni brāhmaṇāni bhavanti. It means that the Brāhmaṇas have a great deal of *bhaktivāda*. But what is *bhaktivāda*? Durgācārya says in explaining the above line of Yāska: bhaktir nāma guṇakalpanā. tena kenacid guṇena brāhmaṇaṃ sarvaṃ sarvathā varṇayati. tatra tattvam anveṣyam. It says that *bhakti* means assumption or consideration of a quality by which a Brāhmaṇa describes all things in all kinds of way. But the truth must be investigated there.

I. 20. Evidently the meaning 'subsequence' of the word *utkarṣa* as given in the translation (p. 10) is far-fetched. The explanation as offered in the *Vivaraṇa* attributed to Gauḍapāda on the NUTU, 2 (see pp. 291 ff.) seems to be better. Besides 'excellence', the word *utkarṣa* means 'attracting' or 'pulling upwards'. Taking this last sense the *Vivaraṇa* says that among the three components, *a*, *u* and *m* of Praṇava *a* is guttural and *u* is labial. So while *a* is pronounced from the lower part (throat) of the mouth, *u* is done from the upper one (lips). Such being the case, in pronunciation *u* is, as it were, pulled upwards,

Or it may be that *u* is higher than *a*, because the former is manifested on the lips filling completely or stepping beyond the throat, and because it is manifested with an effort more than that required for the latter. Let the passage be quoted here as it is in the transcription (p. 25) :

akārād utkarṣa ūrdhvam ākṛṣṭa iva hy ukāra[ḥ] praṇave dṛśyate. taijasaś ca viśvata[ḥ]. svapnādiṣu akārata utkṛṣṭaḥ. uttamo vā ukāraḥ vyāptyatiśayād balātiśayāc ca. akārasthānaṃ kaṇṭhaṃ vyāpya atikram[y?]a oṣṭhasthāne hi tasyābhivyaktiḥ. tenākārādhikavyāptimattvenokta ukāraḥ virāja iva hiraṇyagarbhaḥ. balātiśayatvaṃ ca kharaprayatnavyaṅgyatvāt praṇavasthokārasya mandaprayatnavyaṅgyam akāram apekṣya.

The *utkarṣa* 'excellence' of Taijasa in this respect in relation to Viśva is this that the former is nearer by one step than the latter to Turīya.

26. See MU, VI. 5; PU, V. 2 : etad vai satyakāma paraṃ cāparaṃ ca brahma yad oṃkāraḥ.

28. Note 1. Add *ŚU, III. 13* ; *IV. 17.*
Note 2. Read *21* for *22*.

BOOK II

1. The phrase, āhur manīṣiṇaḥ, is often used not only in our text (II.5, IV. 54), but also in an Upaniṣad (KU, III.4) itself and the BG (XVIII.3).

4. It may be noted that *saṃvṛtatva* is referred to by Ś in his commentary on BS, III. 2. 3.

5. Cf. MnU, I. 8-11 :

antar asminn ime lokā antar viśvam idaṃ jagat |
bahirvan māyayā bhāti darpaṇe pratibimbitam ||
svapne svāntargataṃ viśvaṃ yathā pṛthag avekṣyate |
tathaiva jāgratkāle 'pi prapañco 'yaṃ vivicyatām ||
svapne svasattaivārthānāṃ sattā nānyeti niścitā |
ko jāgrati viśeṣo'sti jaḍānām āśunāśinām ||
svapne prakāśo bhāvānāṃ svaprakāśān na hītaraḥ |
jāgraṭy api tathaiveti niścinvanti vipaścitaḥ ||

For *prasiddha* see Ś on BS, I.1.22.

7. P. 20, l. 1. Read '*That* for '*that*.

9-10. Cf. MnU, I. 7-8.

21. P. 31, l. 17. For *6.3*, *8.3* read 6—8.

24. P. 34, l. 16. Read *jyoti*° or *yoti*°

32. P. 41, l. 1. Read *kārikā* for *kāṅkā*.

34. For *anyabhāva* see IV. 53.

A piece of crystal which is naturally white becomes red in contact with a red flower, yet, it cannot be said that it is red either in its own nature (*svabhāva*) or in the nature of other (*anyabhāva*). It is true that under the circumstances it looks red, yet it is actually not so, it only appears to be so, for its innate whiteness does in no way change. See Śaṅkara on BS, III. 2. 11 : na hi svacchaḥ san sphaṭiko 'laktakādyupādhiyogād asvaccho bhavati, bhramamātratvād abhiniveśasya, upādhīnāṃ cāvidyāpratyupasthāpitatvāt.

35. P. 43, l. 5. Read *NPTU*, *NUTU* and *RUTU* for *NPU*, *NUU* and *ṚUU* respectively, and √*paj-pañj* for √*pajpañj* in l. 10.

For the *Prapañcavilayavāda* showing the relationship between the *karma-* and *jñāna-kāṇḍas* in connexion with *niyoga* one may be referred to Hiriyanna : *Journal of Oriental Research*, 1927, pp. 109 ff, and the original authorities cited therein.

36. The *smṛti* quoted here is *Vasiṣṭhasmṛti* or *Vasiṣṭha-dharmaśāstra*. Ś quotes here also the following couplet which is not traced :

yaṃ na santaṃ na cāsantaṃ nāśrutaṃ na bahuśrutam |
na suvṛttaṃ na durvṛttaṃ veda kaścit sa brāhmaṇaḥ ||

38. For the stanza, śūnyam ādhyātmikaṃ° see AK, IX. 250. For *paśya* the reading is also *paśyan*.

BOOK III

1. The *upāsanā* mentioned here may refer also to *Praṇava-upāsana* in I. 19 ff. See III. 16. For the true significance of *upāsana* or *upāsanā* see pp. 295 ff., and modify the Annotation here in accordance with it.

3. See MnU, III. 9 :

ghaṭākāśo mahākāśo ghaṭopādhikṛto yathā |
dehopādhikṛto bhedo jīvātmaparamātmanoḥ ||

and III. 25-26 :

dehendriyamanobuddhiprāṇāhaṃkārasaṃhatam ||
ātmasaṅkalanād ajñair ātmatvaṃ pratipādyate |
vahnidhīḥ kāṣṭhalohādau vahnisaṃkalanād iva ||

According to Brahmadatta, one of the Samuccayavādin Vedantist, Brahman has both origination (*utpatti*) and disappearance (*laya*). See *Proceed-*

ings and Transactions of the Fourth Oriental Congress, pp. 188-89 ; *Śrībhāṣya*, I.4.2 ; *Mahānārāyaṇopaniṣad*, I.4 ; ViP, VI.40.39.

4. Cf. BP, XII, 5.5 :

ghaṭe bhinne ghaṭākāśa ākāśaḥ syād yathā purā |
evaṃ dehe mṛte jīvo brahma sampadyate punah ||

6. P. 52, l. 26. Read *11* for *12*.

11. This kārikā supports Śaṅkara's second interpretation (idaṃ tv iha vaktavyam°) refuting that of the Vṛttikāra in the *Ānandamayādhikaraṇa* of the BS, I. 1. 12-19. On this see MnU, III. 27-31 also :

deham annamayaṃ kośam āviśyātmā prakāśate |
sthūlo bālaḥ kṛśaḥ kṛṣṇo varṇāśramavikalpavān ||
prāṇakośe 'pi jīvāmi kṣudhito 'smi pipāsitaḥ |
saṃśito niścito manya iti kośe manomaye ||
vijñānamayakośastho vijānāmīti tiṣṭhati |
ānandamayakoṣākhye tv ahaṅkāre purākṛtaiḥ ||
puṇyair upāsanābhiś ca sukhito 'smīti modate |
evaṃ kañcukitaḥ kośaiḥ kañcukair iva pañcabhiḥ ||
paricchinna ivābhāti vyāpto 'pi parameśvaraḥ |

12. Cf. ChU, I. 9. 1, VIII. 14. 1 ; BS, I. 1. 22, 3. 41.

14. See RV, I. 164. 20 ; ŚU, IV. 6-7 ; MuU, III. 1. 1-3.

15. P. 58, l. 18. Omit *IV.2.14*.

16. P. 59, l. 14. Omit *etc*.

17. See IV. 5.

23. Gauḍapāda says here that between the

two statements in the scripture that which is with a reason is acceptable. Cf. Ś on BS, II. 1. 4:

yathā ca śrutīnāṃ parasparavirodhe saty ekavaśenetarā nīyante evaṃ pramāṇavirodhe 'pi tadvaśenaiva śrutir nīyeta. dṛṣṭasāmyena cādṛṣṭam arthaṃ samarthayantī yuktir anubhavasya saṃnikṛṣyate, viprakṛṣyate tu śrutir aitihyamātreṇa svārthābhidhānāt.

On reasoning (*tarka*) see Ś on BS, II. 1. 11. With regard to *yukti* we may remember here what is said in YV, II. 18. 2-4 about the two *śāstras*, *ārṣa* 'derived from *ṛṣis*' and *pauruṣa* 'derived from men'. The author says that a *śāstra*, though it is a *pauruṣa*, deserves to be accepted, if it is reasonable. One must follow reason. A speech, if reasonable, must be accepted even from a child, but that which is not reasonable should be rejected like a piece of straw though it might be uttered even by Brahman, the creator. That man is certainly not wise who rejecting the beautiful water of the Ganges flowing before him drinks from a well thinking only that it belongs to his father:

api pauruṣam ādeyaṃ śāstraṃ ced yuktibodhakam |
anyat tv ārṣam api tyājyaṃ bhāvyaṃ nyāyaikasevinā ||
yuktiyuktam upādeyaṃ vacanaṃ bālakād api |
anyat tṛṇam iva tyājyam apy uktaṃ padmayoninā |
yo 'smattātasya kūpo 'yam iti kaupaṃ pibaty apaḥ |
tyaktvā gāṅgaṃ purasthaṃ taṃ ko na śāsty atigarhitam ||

27[b]. Read *yujyate* for *jujyate*.

29, P. 66. l. 19. Add *the* after *with*,

30. Here is the Tibetan version:

gñis. min. yid. ni. rmi. lam na |
gñis. su. snaṅ. ste. the. tshom med |
de. bshin. gñid. kyis. ma. log. tshe |
gñ's. m'n. gñis. snaṅ. the. tshom. med ||

P. 67, l. 5. Read *the two* for *a second.*

31. For *manodṛśyam* see *cittadṛśyam*, IV. 28, 36, 77.

P. 67, l. 13. Read *perceptible* for *perceived.*

2. P. 68, l. 2. Read *ViS* for *Vis.* and add *38* after III.

35 Note 1. Add *44, 46* after *42.*

36. Note 3. Add *cf. sarvadṛś*, I. 12 ; IV. 84.

P. 70, l. 6. Read *TAk* for TA.

39. Read *vai nāma* for *nāmaiṣa.*

46. P. 80, l. 24. Read *buddha*° for *baddha*°.

P. 81, l. 13. Ś shows here the Buddhist views. On the next line read *549* for *587*.

BOOK IV

1. P. 86, last line. Read *TA'* for *TA*'.

P. 89, l. 6. Add *a* after *is*, and *sva* before *lakṣaṇa*° on l. 14.

P. 91, ll. 29, 32.° Read *SāS* for *SS.*

P. 92, note 30. On the word *dharma* quoted from KU see Glasenapp: *Buddhism* in *Kaṭhopaniṣad* in the *New Indian Antiquary*, Vol. I, No. 2, pp. 138 ff., and Stcherbatsky, *Op. cit.*, p. 68 ff; SMV, pp. 136-7, See also MV p. 355: nāstīha sattva ātmā vā dharmās tv ete sahetukāḥ.

2. The word *asparśayoga* is found at least once in a Buddhist work. See *Bauddha Gāna O Dohā*, Sāhityapariṣad Granthāvalī 55, 1323 B.S., p. 19. Here the Sanskrit ṭīkā which is not edited critically and full of mistakes reads referring to a yoga *aspṛśayogotvāt* for which the Tibetan version (Tanjur, Narthang, Rgyud, Tsi, 175ᵃ. 4) has mi. reg. pahi. sbyor. baḥi. phyir. te clearly suggesting its Sanskrit equivalent *asparśayogāt*. The only notable difference between the two versions, Sanskrit and Tibetan, is this that while the former has *aspṛśa* the suggested reading in the latter is *asparśa*. But considering the uncritical way in which the edition of the Sanskrit text is prepared and the well-known occurrence of the word *sparśa* it naturally occurs to one's mind that the reading *aspṛśa* for *asparśa* is a misprint or a mistake of the scribe of the MS used for that edition. Another difference is the use of *-tva* in the Sanskrit text, which is not to be found in the Tibetan one. According to the former the latter should have been written sbyor. baḥi. ñid. kyi for sbyor. baḥi. But it is often found in Tibetan versions of Sanskrit texts that *ñid* for *-tva-* (or *eva*) is not used even when it is necessary; on the contrary, it is employed when it is not required at all.

4. P. 102, l. 6. For *our MS. Me and some* read *Me and some other.*

11. P. 113, l. 5. Read *kāraṇa* for *karaṇa*.

12. Note 1. Here 'elsewhere' refers to *Variants*, p. 237.

20. P. 125, last line. Read *cākramakaḥ*.

23. Note 1. PU actually has *jātir* in the margin for *hyādir* in *d*. Read here *edition* for *editions*.

P. 130, l. 31. Read *AS* for *ASh*.

24. P. 132, note 3. Add *62* after *61* and omit *79*.

28. P. 138, l. 26. Read *MuU* for *MU*.

30. Note 1. The couplet is from VM, Simon Hewavitarane Bequest ed. p. 407 with the variant khandhānaṃ ca paṭipāṭi in *a* as in Bhāratīya Vidyā Series ed., Part I, p. 282.

31. The first half of the kārikā is identical with that of YV, IV. 45. 45.

33[a]. In such cases (*viz*., IV. 10, 91-93) one may be inclined to read with some of the MSS (*i.e.*, A[1],A[2], V) *sarvadharmāḥ* for *sarve dharmāḥ* agreeing with Buddhist works.

38. Note 1. In *b* read *pratibuddhavantaḥ* as in *Gilgit Manuscripts*, Vol. II, p. 100.

42. P. 150, note 5. Read *MSA* for *MS*.

51[c]. Read *nispandāt* for *vijñānāt*.

58. For the first half see IV, 57[a]. For *d* see LA, pp. 28-49 : vicitrā hi yathā māyā dṛśyate na ca vidyate. See our text, p. 151, note 8. Read *BA* for *BC* on p. 164, l. 5, and *kṛtako* for *tanmayo* on l. 19.

60[c]. See IV. 99.

71. Note 2. It is a speech of B h a g a v a t .

72[a]. See LA, II. 151-152 : vijñānabījaṃ spandate[0].

74. P. 177, l. 16. Read *nāsti* for *nāstī-*

81[c]. Read *vibhāto* for *vibhāti*.

P. 188, Note 2. For the meaning of the word *parāvṛtti* see P. C. B a g c h i : *Studies in the Tantras*, Calcutta University, 1939, pp. 87 ff.

83[a-b]. Read °*asti-nāstīti nāsti-nāstīti*° for °*asti nāstīti nāsti nāstīti*°.

84[d]. For *sarvadṛś* cf. *sarvajña* (I. 12, III. 36) and *sarvajñatā* (IV. 85. 89).

On this see E. Obermiller (*The Doctrine of Prajñāpāramitā*, etc., p. 44): "When the Bodhisattva° has attained the highest of the Unimpeded Paths in the Path of Concentrated Contemplation, he is considered to have terminated his course of training in the path. This last moment of Concentrated trance called the 'thunderbolt-like' (*vajropama samādhi*) is characterized by the removal of the most subtle forms of defilement and of ignorance. It is simultaneous with the final momentary Illumination (*ekakṣaṇa-abhisambodha*), and the culmination of the Bodhisattva's intuition of the absolute. All the factors for the attainment of the Omniscience of the Buddha are now brought to accomplishment. Owing to this, the representation of the Absolute appears in its full light ; the differentiation to subject and object ceases to exist, the accidental obscurations which had hitherto separated the Germ of the Absolute in the living being now completely vanish, and the Germ now coalesces with the Unique Ultimate Essence which is personified as the Cosmical body (*dharmakāya*) of the Buddha".[1]

1 "At the second moment we have the last Path of Deliverance (*vimukti-mārga*). At that time the double representation (*i.e.*, of subject and object) disappears, and the object of Concentration (in its true aspect) becomes one with the knowledge cognizing it like one particle of water uniting with another (chu-la chu bshag-pa-ltar = *jale jalanikṣepavat*). In the aspect of this intuition all the things cognizable in their varieties become directly perceived like a myrobalan (*āmalaka*) fruit on the palm of the hand (*karatalāmalakavat*)."

"The special Omniscience which is peculiar only to the Buddha (*sarva-ākāra-jñātā*) is the knowledge of all the aspects of existence as being devoid of an independent separate reality and as not being liable to origination from the standpoint of the Absolute". *Op. cit.*, p. 64.

See Vācaspatimiśra's *Nyāyakaṇikā* (Reprint from the *Pandit*), pp. 110, 147, 205.

90. See MSA, XIX, 56: pañcavidhaṃ hi vastu bodhisattvānām aprameyam. paripācyaṃ vastu sattvadhātur aviśeṣeṇa. viśodhyaṃ lokadhātur bhājanalokasaṃgṛhītaḥ. prapyaṃ dharmadhātuḥ. paripācanayogyaṃ vineyadhātuḥ. samyagdeśanāvastu vineyopāyadhātuḥ.

94. P. 206, note 2. Read *Woods* for *Wood*.

P. 207, l. 13. The word *śāradya* actually occurs in Sanskrit as in *pariṣacchāradya*. It means *saṅkoca* 'shrinking'. In Tibetan for it we have *bskumps. pa* from *skum. pa* 'to contract.' See MV, p. 46; ŚS, p. 296.

99. P. 212, note 2, l. 31. Read *skyob. pa* for *skyb. pa*.

100. For *durdarśa* see KU, I. 2. 12.

For *alāta* see MV, p. 219: pūrvāparakoṭyanupalambhād [alāta]cakravat (mgal. meḥi. hkhor. lo. bshin. no); p. 221: ādimadhyāvasānavirahitatvād alātacakravat.